God, Humanity and the Cosmos

God, Humanity and the Cosmos

A Textbook in Science and Religion

CHRISTOPHER SOUTHGATE
CELIA DEANE-DRUMMOND
PAUL D. MURRAY
MICHAEL ROBERT NEGUS
LAWRENCE OSBORN
MICHAEL POOLE
JACQUI STEWART
FRASER WATTS

TRINITY PRESS INTERNATIONAL
HARRISBURG, PENNSYLVANIA

Published in Great Britain by T&T Clark Ltd,
59 George Street, Edinburgh EH2 2LQ, Scotland

This edition published under license from T&T Clark Ltd by
Trinity Press International
P.O. Box 1321
Harrisburg, PA 17105

Trinity Press International is a division of The Morehouse Publishing Group.

First published in USA 1999

Library of Congress Cataloging-in-Publication Data is available
ISBN 1–56338–288–1

Typeset by Waverley Typesetters, Galashiels
Printed and bound in Great Britain by Bell & Bain Ltd, Glasgow

Contents

BOOK ONE

1. An Introduction to the Debate between Science and Religion

Section A: Outlines of the Debate (1.1–1.11)

1.1 Two views of the conversation between science and religion – 1.2 Important sources, figures and developments – 1.3 Typologies of the relationship – 1.3.1 Natural theology vs theology of nature – 1.4 Further typologies – 1.5 Two crucial points – 1.5.1 Science and religion, or science and theology? – 1.6 The metaphor of the maps – 1.7 Critical realism in science – 1.8 Critical realism in theology – 1.9 The central role of model and metaphor – 1.10 Consonances – 1.11 Was religion necessary to the rise of science?

Section B: Three Historical Examples of Tensions as Science and Theology Developed (1.12–1.15)

1.12 Copernicanism and the Galileo Affair – 1.13 The love affair gone wrong: the eighteenth century – 1.14 Early conflicts over Darwinism – 1.15 A contemporary instance of consonance and conflict (Big Bang cosmology)

Section C: Key Principles for Developing Theology in the Light of Science (1.16–1.20)

1.16 Different types of causation and explanation – 1.17 Determinism, indeterminism and their implications – 1.18 Developing theology in the light of science – 1.18.1 The interdependence of different aspects of a model – 1.19 Three attributes of models of God, humanity and the cosmos – 1.20 Questions of value

102896

BOOK TWO

[1] NB: Islam is considered separately in Chapter 9.

BOOK FOUR

BOOK FIVE

Figures and Tables

Exercises

Contributors

DR CHRISTOPHER SOUTHGATE, the Co-ordinating Editor, trained originally in research biochemistry. He is now a poet and editor, and part-time Lecturer in Theology at the University of Exeter. His previous book was *A Love and its Sounding* (University of Salzburg, 1997).

DR CELIA DEANE-DRUMMOND is currently Senior Lecturer in Applied Theology at University College, Chester. She has doctorates and teaching experience in both plant physiology and the theology of Moltmann. Her most recent book is *Theology and Biotechnology: Implications for a New Science* (Geoffrey Chapman, 1997).

PAUL D. MURRAY, Senior Lecturer in Theology at Newman College, Birmingham, also serves on the Faith and Culture Committee of the Roman Catholic Bishops' Conference of England and Wales. He is currently finishing a doctorate at Cambridge on the truth of God in pragmatist perspective.

DR MICHAEL ROBERT NEGUS, a biologist, is the Head of Science at Newman College, Birmingham, and also holds qualifications in Computer Science and Islamic Studies. His recent published papers are in the areas of ecological biology and the roles of science and scientists in Islam.

LAWRENCE OSBORN holds a degree in astronomy and a doctorate in theology. He is the author of a whole range of books and articles on subjects ranging from the nature of time to New Age spirituality and the Gaia Hypothesis. He was recently Templeton Post-doctoral Fellow at Ridley Hall, Cambridge.

MICHAEL POOLE is currently Visiting Research Fellow in the School of Education at King's College, London. With a background in science education, his research interests have centred on the interplay between science and religion with special reference to its educational context. He is the author of several books and some fifty articles and papers on the topic.

DR JACQUI STEWART began her career as a population geneticist, but has been involved with theology for many years. She has doctorates in both subjects, and lectures in Theology and Biology at the University of Leeds, where she is also Co-Director of the Centre for Science and Religion.

THE REVD DR FRASER WATTS is Starbridge Lecturer in Theology and the Natural Sciences at the University of Cambridge, Fellow of Queens' College, and Vicar-Chaplain of St Edward, King and Martyr. He was formerly at the MRC Applied Psychology Unit, working on cognitive aspects of emotional disorders, and has been President of the British Psychological Society.

How to Use this Book

Although it should be of considerable interest to the general reader, this book is designed principally as a resource for teachers and students on undergraduate-level courses. No scientific background is presumed. It is expected that most students will have some theological background, but where a technical theological term is used for the first time an explanation is provided. The index enables the reader to refer to these definitions.

The book is designed to be read as a whole or to be used in its individual sections, or its individual chapters:

BOOK ONE introduces the science and religion debate, giving key historical examples (Chapter 1), and then provides a philosophical analysis of science and theology as related rational enterprises (Chapter 2).

BOOK TWO proceeds to a detailed examination of how three types of science – physics (Chapter 3), evolutionary biology (Chapter 4) and psychology (Chapter 5) – interact with theological and religious claims.

BOOK THREE explores further the theological resources available for making a model of God, humanity and the cosmos (Chapter 6) and how those resources can be applied to a description of divine action in the light of contemporary science (Chapter 7).

BOOK FOUR takes up the question of science's place in society. First we look at science education and the role it can play in relating science to values, social and religious (Chapter 8). Then we consider the Islamic tradition and how that can give rise to a different perspective on the place of science (Chapter 9). Science has also been a major contributory factor in the development of technology. We review this historically and theologically in Chapter 10. Chapter 11 concentrates on 'biotechnology' – genetic modification and cloning – considered theologically and ethically.

Finally in BOOK FIVE we speculate on how the debate between science and religion is likely to develop (Chapter 12).

The sections within each chapter

These are all numbered. The main sections carry the number of the chapter and the number of the section – e.g. 7.4 *How to think about providential agency*. Sections going into a particular issue in more detail are shown by a three-digit number, e.g. 7.4.1 *Relation to the mind–body problem*. An initial skip-read of a chapter, or a summary reading for revision purposes, might concentrate on the two-numbered sections. More detailed work would include the three-numbered sections.

Footnotes

These have been kept to a minimum for a book of this kind. So they are well worth consulting when they do appear!

Bibliographical references

Wherever possible actual page references have been given. So section 1.4 introduces Ted Peters' classification of possible relations between science and religion, to be found in pages 650–54 of Peters, 1997a, which the main Bibliography shows to be Peters' article in *The Modern Theologians*, edited by David Ford and published in Oxford by Blackwell.

Foreword

In one sense, of course, issues of 'faith and culture', 'faith and reason' and 'science and religion' are as old as the Christian faith itself. Many have discovered this with surprise, indeed a sense of *déjà vu*, as they have gone back in time to try and grasp the ever-evolving intellectual process that has defined these crucial issues so differently in different epochs.

But those of us who have been part of the developing conversation about theology and science during the past fifteen years now find ourselves in the middle of shifts in paradigm and intellectual changes so profound that suddenly the whole world looks different.

Not so long ago the troubled relationship between religion and science could still be seen as the specialised, and often inaccessible, domain of a privileged few intellectuals who cared passionately about these two very diverse and often conflicting cultural forces. Today, however, everything has changed: not only has the 'theology and science' debate come to symbolise much more comprehensively the face of today's 'faith and culture' and 'faith and reason' debates, but what was formerly a private and specialised conversation has now burst onto the public scene in ways which would once have been unthinkable. Not only is the science-and-religion debate alive and well in many parts of the world, but a number of centres and societies have sprung up, and the debate is finding a permanent place in schools and colleges as well as in seminaries and universities. This highly visible public profile is further enhanced by a veritable explosion of books, papers and conferences on this fascinating topic.

This amazing phenomenon is still of course embedded in the complexity of our Western culture, with its ambivalence not only about the status of the debate, but about what we mean by 'science' and 'theology'. Most of us accept today that we have inherited from modernity a troubling and challenging dichotomy in which 'science' is taken to have emerged triumphantly as a superior form of rational thinking, and 'religion' is taken to have faded into a rather privatised form of subjective (if not irrational) experience. The ramifications of this modernist heritage have been all-consuming, and certainly devastating for religion: the divisions between science and religion (and theology, as a reflection on religious practice) led to sharp distinctions between objective descriptions and subjective experiences, between scientific and symbolic uses of language, between scientific truth and religious opinion, and finally to an all-consuming world-view in which science was taken to be more enduringly true precisely because it is empirically based on observation and repeatable experimentation. In the face of this superior paradigm of human rationality, which steadily accumulates knowledge, and even aspires to a 'theory of everything' which might even yield a complete account of all that is genuinely knowable, religion has often been forced to retreat into symbol and art as expressions of personal and communal experience.

This dichotomy left theology still firmly embedded in the stark modernist separation between knowledge and opinion, explanation and understanding, natural and human sciences, epistemology and hermeneutics. Part of the complexity and ambivalence of our culture's appropriation of the 'theology and science' issue has therefore been precisely the image of an enduring 'conflict' between science and religion. This conflict image extended to some stark differences and hostilities on philosophical and historical issues, as well as on issues of content.

Theologians and believing scientists to this day try to resolve these differences through attempts to construct wide-ranging typologies – trying to 'name' the sort of relationship one might want to see between these dominant and apparently conflicting forces in our culture. The ongoing conversation about the relationship between religion and science is also, however, revealing some important nuances in this age-old relationship: it has become increasingly clear that, contrary to some popular misconceptions, the dialogue is not only about conflict and dissensus. The image of perpetual conflict is increasingly seen as an invention of the late nineteenth century, and scholars in the field are realising that the truth about the historical relationship has always been much more complex (cf. Gregersen and van Huyssteen, 1998:1ff., Watts,

1998:2f., and Sections 1.11–1.14 of *God, Humanity and the Cosmos*). Moreover, for many participants in this discussion the whole idea of a 'conflict' has become something of a moot issue, given that science and religion often seem to be answering such different questions rather than giving different and conflicting answers to the same questions (cf. Watts, 1998:2).

Whilst an important part of the current ambivalent state of affairs represents the enduring attempt to maintain science's alleged priority as the paradigmatic way of establishing true knowledge, the continuing embeddedness of our contemporary culture in modernist epistemic values is by no means the entire story.. Our culture is being radically redefined and challenged by a new, all-pervasive mood which we have come to know as postmodernity. The confusing co-presence in our intellectual culture of both superior (modernist) notions of natural scientific rationality and pluralist postmodern views which radically reject all notions of scientific superiority has emerged as the defining challenge to anyone trying to come to terms with the values that shape the rationality of theological and scientific reflection today. Postmodernity has given us a cultural context which has been deeply affected by what many see as the complete fragmentation of knowledge, and even as rampant pluralism and relativism.

This gives new urgency to the question whether a more affirmative reading of postmodernity might leave scope for an intelligible, cross-disciplinary conversation between theology and the sciences today. Some postmodernists consider conventional definitions of academic disciplines simply as remnants of modernity and directly question the viability of strict boundaries between the natural sciences, social sciences, humanities, art, literature and religious reflection. Even more important, though, is that the reasons, arguments and value judgments employed by the community of scientists – like those of communities of theologians – are now seen to be fundamentally grounded in social practices. The very criteria and norms that traditionally guided and defined scientific and theological activities thus become open and vulnerable to criticism. In what seems to be a complete loss of any meta-standpoints from which to reflect on a possible interdisciplinary relationship between theology and science, all our interpretations of theology and science now seem to be reduced to the local context within which we operate. At the end of the day the postmodern challenge seems to leave theology in just the same place where modernity left it – isolated, and out in the cold.

In a recent and provocative paper this radical contemporary revisioning of the theology and science question is anticipated in an intriguing way. John Bowker asks: what would happen if we looked at the relationship between science and religion in an entirely different way? Bowker then proceeds to argue that this relationship looks entirely different when one realises that the really persistent issue between religion and science is not so much about different kinds of knowledge claims, but rather one of power (cf. Bowker, 1998:116f.) Although he never identifies this important shift as a postmodern one, it is clear what some of the ramifications of this epistemic shift might imply for a possible interdisciplinary relationship between theology and science. For Bowker the real challenge of science to religion and theology is not so much a conflict of competing propositions and world-views, but rather a ruthless challenge to the independence of religion's own authority. In doing this, science is taking over areas where religion traditionally had its authority and control.

Against the background of this argument Mary Hesse has recently asked whether science and technology in some sense represent 'the new religion'. (Hesse, 1998:120ff). By asking this Hesse too wants to alert us to issues of power and authority as crucial for thinkers trying to rescue a sense that religion has an essential function in human life (a function which cannot be allowed to be taken over by the increasing power of scientism). The power of science today is certainly overwhelmingly present in the technology without which our society would almost certainly collapse. But the focus of the power of science is certainly still found – in spite of the postmodern mood – in its claims to rational authority (cf. Hesse, 1998:122).

In addition, of course, postmodern pluralism makes it almost impossible to speak generically about 'science', 'religion', and 'theology' today. Both postmodernity's epistemic pluralism as well as modernity's marginalisation of religious meaning have therefore been very successful in deconstructing our attempts to find a space for meaningful dialogue between disciplines as diverse and different as theology and science.

I have argued elsewhere that the only way out of the confusing 'double challenge' presented by modernist as well as postmodernist themes in contemporary culture is to probe the interdisciplinary possibilities and shared resources of the ongoing conversation between theology and the sciences (cf. van Huyssteen, 1998). It is precisely on this point that Chris Southgate and his excellent and capable team of co-authors have been so remarkably successful. They have together produced a textbook on the current theology and science dialogue which is very different from other works currently available.

Not only is *God, Humanity and the Cosmos* directly addressed to teachers and students, and as such manages to be remarkably accessible; it also carefully addresses all the contemporary issues in the field, but in such a way that it moves the theology and science debate to the cutting edge of the current conversation, and in so doing brings their readers to the frontier of one of the most exciting explorations of our time.

This book represents a strong and quite remarkable move beyond some of the ubiquitous generalities of the religion and science dialogue. It is the living proof that the theology and science conversation 'works' if we contextualise it to specific issues in specific sciences and specific kinds of theologies in specific religions. In this sense the book will appeal to those of us with qualified postmodern sensibilities, and goes beyond much of what is out there in the current literature. The student and teacher using this work will very soon learn the far-reaching educational impact of the fact that the evolving relationship between different sciences and any one religion will be different at any given time, and will keep changing through history.

Moving beyond stereotypes of 'science' and 'the scientific method' the authors of this book also acknowledge the complexity of both scientific practice and theological discourse. What is developed clearly is that any focus on science is always a focus on practice and reflection, with all-important implications for science education. Similarly any focus on theology is, or should be, a focus on the models, the metaphors and the propositions that give theology its rational framework – these always, however, deeply embedded in religious practice. What emerges from this is the book's most important leitmotif: scientific and theological descriptions of our (one) world are like different maps of reality, maps which can rightly claim a profound degree of independence, but which are fundamentally interrelated because even as radically different discourses they share the resources of human rationality. The authors of this book thus succeed eminently in creating a space for true interdisciplinary reflection, and in doing that give a strong answer to both modernist and postmodernist challenges to the ongoing dialogue between theology and the sciences.

In reading this book students will quickly learn that both theology and the sciences are to be seen as more complex activities than merely a realist search for progressively truer data. At the same time the authors very convincingly show how science – on this point remarkably like theology – needs to be seen as exemplifying the activities of communities of motivated believers, holding core assumptions, and testing out new possibilities. Even more importantly, though, an awareness is created of just what kind of theology is being done in the light of contemporary science. One of the most important themes of this book emerges precisely around a sustained argument against any cultural or epistemic isolation of theology as a discipline. On this view a pattern emerges which finds a careful balance between highlighting the public voice of theology, on the one hand, while at the same time never just narrowly focusing on theological reflection as a mere acquisition of knowledge; the Christian faith, and Christian theological reflection, is also, indeed first and foremost, about conformity to Christ. An integrating force in this book is, therefore, the holding together of the reflection on epistemological issues of theory and belief with an analysis of how these theories and belief grow out of, and are permanently embedded in, practice. This leaves us with a strong sense of how the continually evolving Christian tradition unfolds in new and creative ways as a direct response to a culture so definitively shaped today by science and technology.

The basic thrust underlying the central argument of the book is therefore found in the strong conviction of the various authors that it is both possible and fruitful to seek to bring the insights and concerns of the sciences and religion together in a mutually constructive interchange. As such it boldly addresses interdisciplinary issues and even moves them into the more complex field of interreligious dialogue, while at the same time pointing to what the future may hold for the ongoing dialogue between religion, science and technology. What unfolds from this is a clear and unambiguous answer to the ambivalent cultural challenge to theology and science today: nothing in our world – even in our science and technologies – has been understood adequately until it has been understood from within its relationship to God as Creator of that world.

J. WENTZEL VAN HUYSSTEEN

James I. McCord Professor of Theology and Science
Princeton Theological Seminary

REFERENCES

GREGERSEN, NIELS H. and VAN HUYSSTEEN, J. WENTZEL (eds) (1998) *Rethinking Theology and Science: Six Models for the Current Dialogue* (Grand Rapids: Eerdmans)

VAN HUYSSTEEN, J. WENTZEL (1998) *Duet or Duel? Theology and Science in a Postmodern World* (London: SCM Press)

The essays referred to by JOHN BOWKER, MARY HESSE, and FRASER WATTS are all to be found in:

WATTS, FRASER (ed.) (1998) *Science Meets Faith: Theology and Science in Conversation* (London: SPCK)

Editor's Note and Acknowledgements

This book is unusual among the many emerging on the science–religion dialogue in that:

- it offers a depth of exploration between popular accounts and specialised research publications;

- it presumes little background knowledge, but signposts students to the forefront of the debate;

- it draws on the expertise of eight different authors, all experienced teachers and researchers. Each chapter, therefore, reflects the scholarship and teaching experience of one or more writers well versed in and particularly committed to that area of study.

Five of the authors (Christopher Southgate, Paul D. Murray, Michael Robert Negus, Lawrence Osborn and Michael Poole) acted as editors and co-authors of Chapters 1–4, 6–9 and 12. The principal drafters of the chapters were as follows:

Chapter 1 – Christopher Southgate, with text on explanation and value from Michael Poole. Chapter 2 – Paul D. Murray, with some input on positivism from Michael Poole. Chapter 3 – Lawrence Osborn. Chapter 4 – Christopher Southgate, with some text, especially on human evolution, from Michael Robert Negus. Chapter 6 – Christopher Southgate, with the sections on Eastern religion written by Michael Robert Negus. Chapter 7 – Christopher Southgate. Chapter 8 – Michael Poole. Chapter 9 – Michael Robert Negus. Chapter 12 – Christopher Southgate. Each chapter, then, is not only the work of a specialist but involves the intensive editorial input of the group as a whole.

Chapters 5, 10 and 11 are in a slightly different category. They were individually written by Drs Watts, Stewart and Deane-Drummond respectively (in each case with editorial feedback from within the core group).

As Co-ordinating Editor I take this opportunity to thank all my colleagues for the patience and diligence with which they went about this complex collaboration – also Professor Wentzel van Huyssteen who kindly contributed the Foreword. Other scholars helped us in various ways. Dr Arthur Peacocke was a great encouragement in the early stages of the project. He, and Drs Bob Russell and Janet Martin Soskice, kindly supplied manuscripts of material not yet published. Professor Mary Midgley kindly sent information on 'the metaphor of the maps' (Section 1.6).

Most of the critical comment came from within the editorial team itself, but we would also like to thank Dr John Martin of King's College, London, for comments on Chapter 3, Dr Andrew Robinson for a chastening critique of Chapter 4, and Dr J. C. L. Austin, formerly of Durham University, for checking the specialised Islamic material in Chapter 9. Louise Hickman, Cherryl Hunt, and Kate Taylor kindly acted as first readers of material in Chapters 4 and 6. Richard Skinner valiantly checked the whole of the first proof. More general thanks go to the many winners of Templeton Foundation Course Awards who offered comments on an early synopsis of the book.

We thank also The John Templeton Foundation itself, which generously provided a grant towards the costs of the project.

Finally it is a pleasure to thank the publishers for their painstaking and ever-courteous help in seeing the manuscript through the press.

Copyright permissions. We acknowledge the following: the Association for Science Education, in whose journal Figure 1.3 first appeared; University Science Books for permission to reproduce Figures 4.1 and 4.2; Cambridge University Press for permission to reproduce Figure 4.3.

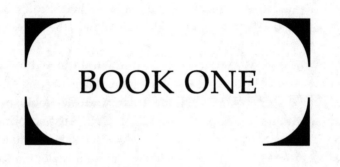

BOOK ONE

Chapter 1

An Introduction to the Debate between Science and Religion

SECTION A:
OUTLINES OF THE DEBATE (1.1–1.11)

1.1 Two views of the conversation between science and religion

> Whenever theology touches science, it gets burned. In the sixteenth century astronomy, in the seventeenth microbiology, in the eighteenth geology and paleontology, in the nineteenth Darwin's biology all grotesquely extended the world-frame and sent churchmen scurrying for cover in ever smaller, more shadowy nooks, little gloomy ambiguous caves in the psyche where even now neurology is cruelly harrying them, gouging them out from the multifolded brain like wood lice from under the lumber pile. (Updike, 1986:32)

> By encouraging openness between the Church and the scientific communities, we are not envisioning a disciplinary unity between theology and science like that which exists within a given scientific field or within theology proper. As dialogue and common searching continue, there will be growth towards mutual understanding and a gradual uncovering of common concerns which will provide the basis for future research and discussion. Exactly what form that will take must be left to the future. What is important, as we have already stressed, is that the dialogue should continue and grow in depth and scope. In the process we must overcome every regressive tendency to a unilateral reductionism, to fear, and to self-imposed isolation. (John Paul II, 1988)

3

A caricature, crisply phrased by a leading novelist, and an excerpt from a papal letter to the Director of the Vatican Observatory. We begin with this juxtaposition, because these two extreme viewpoints will be with us throughout this look at the interactions between the sciences and religion.

The character in Updike's novel talks of theology in progressive and inevitable retreat before the dominance of science. There is a conflict in which one subject is overwhelming the other, forcing it off its territory.[1] The tone of the Pope's letter is very different, implying a common territory on which may take place exploration and dialogue. He renounces the idea that theology might seek to preserve itself from the 'harryings' of science (*qua* Updike) by seeking isolation.

1.2   Important sources, figures and developments in the field of science and religion

The Pope's letter was published at the beginning of the proceedings of a Vatican Conference held at Castelgandolfo in 1987, marking the tercentenary of the publication of Newton's *Principia*.[2] Since then a series of conferences have offered leading articulators of the debate between science and religion an intensive opportunity to compare positions. The resultant proceedings, edited by R. J. Russell and others (Russell *et al.*, 1988; 1993; 1995; 1998), are invaluable guides to the cutting-edge of the debate, particularly on the vexed question of God's action in the world science describes. We take up that question in Chapter 7. Another important collection of research positions appeared in 1996, edited by W. Mark Richardson and Wesley J. Wildman (Richardson and Wildman, 1996).

Much of the literature in this field builds on the pioneering work of Ian Barbour, who brought out *Issues in Science and Religion* in 1966 and *Myths, Models and Paradigms* in 1974. His Gifford Lectures of 1990, published as *Religion in an Age of Science*[3] and *Ethics in an Age of Technology*, gave a valuable overview of the field. Two English

---

[1] The conflict or warfare hypothesis was much furthered by two books originating in the 1870s: *History of the Conflict Between Religion and Science* by John William Draper and *A History of the Warfare of Science with Theology in Christendom* by Andrew Dickson White. See Welch, 1996 for a discussion of these.

[2] On the significance of Newton's work see **3.2–3.4**.

[3] Republished in an enlarged form as *Religion and Science* (Barbour, 1998).

theologians who are both Anglican priests and former research scientists have also done much to bring the science–religion debate to wider attention. Arthur Peacocke's Bampton Lectures of 1979, *Creation and the World of Science*, still read very well, and his *Theology for a Scientific Age* (1993) continues to be an important text. Sir John Polkinghorne, former Professor of Mathematical Physics at Cambridge and since then a vigorous and articulate apologist for Christianity as compatible with science, has brought out an extraordinary number of books, of which the most adventurous and important is his *Science and Providence* (1989). His *Science and Christian Belief* (1994) is the most comprehensive statement of his position, important for his coverage of eschatology (see **7.17**).[4]

Just as the development of the Chicago Center for Religion and Science (directed by Philip Hefner) and the Center for Theology and the Natural Sciences at Berkeley (directed by R. J. Russell) were most valuable in establishing the academic integrity of the science–religion debate, so the endowment of the James I. McCord Chair at Princeton Seminary (1990) and the Starbridge Lectureship at Cambridge (1994) marked other important landmarks in the debate's development. Fraser Watts, the first Starbridge post-holder, contributes our Chapter 5, and has also edited the most recent guide to the conversation, *Science Meets Faith* (Watts, 1998c). Oxford University will shortly appoint the first holder of the Andreas Idreos Chair in this area.

Two other figures not normally thought of as theologians have also done a great deal to stimulate the debate. The first is the physicist Paul Davies, who has been drawn towards theism by the directions he has seen his scientific field take, and who has written of this journey in books such as *God and the New Physics* and *The Mind of God* (Davies, 1990; 1993). The second is the biologist Richard Dawkins, whose vigorous dismissals of the claims of religion (see **4.10**) have had a most stimulating effect on believers interested in dialogue with science. Had Dawkins not existed, the Christian Church might have found it necessary to invent him.

One of the ways sometimes used to try and characterise the relations between science and religion is to interview practitioners in the different fields. A short but very rewarding book of this type is *Science and*

---

[4] Polkinghorne has surveyed the contributions made by himself, Peacocke and Barbour in *Scientists as Theologians* (Polkinghorne, 1996a).

Wonders (Stannard, 1996).[5] Two others well worth consulting are *Cosmos, Bios, Theos* (Margenau and Varghese, 1992) and *Cosmic Beginnings and Human Ends* (Matthews and Varghese, 1995). Very many other books have emerged in the last ten years which are important in particular areas – these are cited at the relevant points in the text. *For convenience there is a single alphabetical list of references and bibliography at the back of the book – though it might seem large and daunting, students are urged to make use of it.* It is of the nature of this book that it functions quite largely as a signpost to more specialised material.

To produce a textbook in this field, which draws on so many areas in philosophy and theology as well as on the material of a number of different sciences, is a massive task. Hence this volume draws on the expertise of eight authors, each writing in their own specialist areas. However, even such a team is very reliant on the best of what has been written by others, and two books in particular stand out – John Brooke's historical survey *Science and Religion* (Brooke, 1991) and Willem Drees' *Religion, Science and Naturalism* (Drees, 1996). Brooke shows clearly how much more complicated and fluid the relation between Western science and the Christian world has been than had often been thought.[6] Drees applies an intensely intelligent, theologically sceptical approach to a wide variety of topics.

However, the present authors consider that more can be said of the positive overlap between scientific and theological positions than Drees allows. We write from within a Western Christian perspective, which we clarify in more detail below. The book however also surveys a wide variety of Christian thought in **6.1–6.6.1**, and outlines some very different patterns of thought, deriving from Taoism, Hinduism, and Buddhism, in **6.9–6.12.1**. Chapter 9 is devoted to Islam, a monotheism in some ways closely related to Christianity but leading to a very different set of relations with the world of science.

We have mentioned the great explosion of work there has been in this area, much facilitated in various ways by the work of the John Templeton Foundation, which has commissioned lecture series, funded courses and sponsored workshops which have greatly furthered dialogue between educators working in the field. It is in considerable

---

[5] Stannard interviews both Dawkins and another arch-opponent of theism, the Oxford chemist Peter Atkins.

[6] Brooke, in the company of another eminent historian, Geoffrey Cantor, has recently updated his explorations in *Reconstructing Nature* (Brooke and Cantor, 1998).

part due to Templeton funding that there are at least 300 courses running in this interdisciplinary subject area in the USA, and probably almost as many again in universities in the rest of the world.

1.3   Typologies of the relationship between science and religion

One of the features of this movement has been a search for typologies of the relationships between science and religion. Again Barbour has taken a lead, proposing a four-fold scheme with subdivisions (Figure 1.1).

FIGURE 1.1

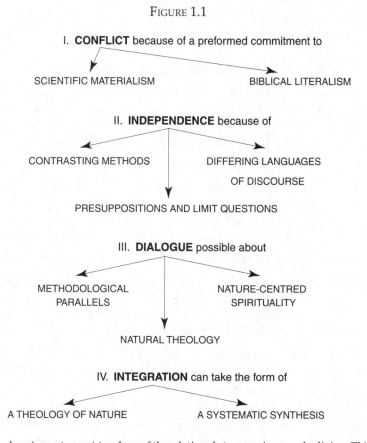

Ian Barbour's most recent typology of the relations between science and religion. This is a slight revision of the scheme in his 1990 Gifford Lectures, and is thoroughly discussed in Barbour (1998:Ch. 4).[7] Here we merely note a distinction within his Category IV.

[7] For a series of articles on Barbour and his Gifford Lectures see *Zygon 31 (1)* (1996).

1.3.1   An important distinction – natural theology vs theology of nature

What does Barbour mean by these two similar terms? *Natural theology* is traditionally understood as the consideration of what can be known about God without the aid of revelation, i.e. from consideration of the created world in general, aided by reason. Whereas Barbour's *theology of nature* 'starts from a religious tradition based on religious experience and historical revelation. But it holds that some traditional doctrines need to be reformulated in the light of current science' (Barbour, 1998:100). The framing of a theology of nature is in fact what most of the contemporary writers in the science-and-religion field are engaged upon, and what this book will encourage students also to attempt (see **1.18–1.19** and **6.4.3** on models of God, humanity and the cosmos).

Most Christian natural theology has stemmed in one way or other from the work of Thomas Aquinas. Two of his arguments for the existence of God have stimulated particular interest among those concerned with science: *the cosmological argument* (that all change must stem from a necessary, self-existent being who is the First Cause of all phenomena in the universe) and *the teleological argument* (that order and intelligibility and apparent purpose in nature imply a rational designer). Much of the science done in the late seventeenth and the eighteenth centuries was motivated by a desire to learn more of the nature of this ordering designer-divinity (see **1.13** below, also Brooke and Cantor, 1998:Ch. 5). However, the teleological argument was the subject of a devastating attack by David Hume (1711–76), who pointed out for example that our experience of the world does not rule out its order having arisen by chance, or indeed there being not one but many designers, and so forth. Arguments for the existence of God from apparent design in nature persisted, but were finally laid to rest by the work of Darwin (see **4.4** – also Brooke, 1991:181–89, 192–225).[8] The cosmological argument has also received much critical scrutiny from the time of Immanuel Kant (1724–1804) on, and it must be accepted that what we know about the universe can never demonstrate whether it has a cause, or whether its existence is ultimately inexplicable.

---

[8] Arguments for a different sort of divine designer then developed, but they were arguments *from* presuppositions about God, rather than attempts to *prove* God's existence or character (see Brooke, 1991:310–17)

The demise of natural theology, and its partial rebirth as 'a philosophical theology or new style natural theology' are well analysed by Macquarrie (1977:Ch. 2). The central point to note is that those authors claiming to revive natural theology tend to do so in a way which is 'descriptive instead of deductive' (Macquarrie, 1977:56). A good example concerns the 'anthropic balances' which will be discussed in **3.19–3.23** and **7.11**. Commenting on the notion that the universe appears to be fine-tuned so as to produce life, John Polkinghorne calls this not a demonstration of the existence or the nature of God but merely 'a fact of interest calling for an explanation' (1991:78).

The boldest attempt to reinvoke natural theology in our own time is that of Richard Swinburne who claims not that what we know of the universe demonstrates God, but that it renders theism more *probable* than not. We analyse Swinburne's approach in **2.5**.

1.4   Further typologies

Barbour's scheme at least maps out the territory, but in practice students often experience a lot of difficulty in applying his categories with any precision, or aligning themselves wholeheartedly with any particular one. A related scheme is that of John Haught, who in his ingenious book *Science and Religion: From Conflict to Conversation* (1995) addresses a series of key issues from the standpoints of *conflict, contrast, contact* and *confirmation*. This is a more helpful approach than Barbour's because the categories are not simply mapped out in the abstract, but applied to particular questions. Ted Peters offers eight possibilities for understanding the relation between science and religion, varying 'from pitched battle to an uneasy truce' (Peters, 1997a:650). His categories are:

- *scientism* – religion is outdated, science tells us all we need to know;

- *scientific imperialism* – science can give us good information even about what were formerly religious questions (see, for example, Tipler's 'physical eschatology' mentioned at **3.22** and **5.7**);

- *ecclesiastical authoritarianism* – the Church should have authority over science (effectively the Roman Catholic Church claimed this until the Second Vatican Council in the early 1960s);

- *scientific creationism* – geological and biological data attest to biblical truth. Peters points out that creationists are usually seen as anti-science, but scientific creationists see themselves as within science;

- *the two-language theory* – 'peace through separation' – the two disciplines speak in their own discourse and shared understanding is impossible;

- *hypothetical consonance* – the two disciplines do raise questions of concern to the other, and should be open to subjecting their assertions to further investigation (see also **1.10**);

- *ethical overlap* – theology has a vital role in speaking to questions of value raised by science and technology, especially in respect of the ecological crisis (see **1.20**, Chapter 6 *passim*, **10.9–10.11**, **11.8–11.9**);

- *New Age spirituality* – a term covering certain recent attempts to fuse science and spirituality (see **6.9**, **6.13–6.14**).

(cf. Peters, 1997a: 650–54)[9]

Oddly, Peters' scheme does not develop the nuances of the crucial area between 'two-languages' (Barbour's 'independence'), and 'hypothetical consonance' (Barbour's 'dialogue / integration'). Peters does however clarify the nature of positions at the extremes.

1.5   Two crucial points about the science–religion relationship

Any investigation of the possible relations between science and religion – and a consideration of what relation is most appropriate – must take account of two most important points:

(i) *The relations between different sciences and any one religion – even any one branch of any religion – will be different at any given time, and will alter through history.* That a given science can dramatically alter its character is shown by the sense some physicists had in the 1870s that the subject was coming to an end – the young Max Planck was advised against doing physics on the grounds that everything to be discovered would shortly have been discovered.[10] Fifty years later (partly because Planck ignored the advice) the subject underwent such changes that there was a golden age of conceptual advance, a time 'when second-rate men did first-rate work' (Paul Dirac, quoted in Polkinghorne, 1990:14).

Clearly the self-image of a scientific community will have enormous effect on its attitude to theological claims which seem to relate to its

---

[9] See also Peters, 1998:11–39.

[10] See **3.4** *re* Lord Kelvin's similar advice and the two 'clouds' he noted on the horizon of classical physics.

subject area. The 'cruelly harrying' effect of neurology as described by Updike (**1.1**) – as instanced by the sense evinced by such scientists as Francis Crick that it will be possible at some stage to describe all human activities in neurophysiological terms – this effect is testimony to a science whose experimental techniques are rapidly expanding its data-base (especially through PET and MR scanning). The effect of Darwinism on 'the world-frame' of biology, especially when coupled first with Mendelian genetics and then with molecular biology (see **4.4– 4.6, 4.7.1**), has led to a science which is still expanding under the influence of a great unifying set of ideas – much as physics did in the two hundred years after Newton. We look at some resultant reductionisms in **4.9–4.13, 4.17**.

Contemporary cosmological physics seems to be in a rather different place – very conscious of limits both to its experimental and its theoretical purchase on the ultimate questions which it tends to raise. As we shall see in **1.15**, the most ingenious quantum-cosmological speculations, going far beyond what could ever be tested experimentally, cannot answer the metaphysical question as to whether the universe had an underlying cause – why, in other words, there is something and not nothing. But the fundamental structure of the universe has led some physicists like Paul Davies to express themselves in quasi-religious terms, as here:

> I belong to the group of scientists who do not subscribe to a conventional religion but nevertheless deny that the universe is a purposeless accident. Through my scientific work I have come to believe more and more strongly that the physical universe is put together with an ingenuity so astonishing that I cannot accept it merely as brute fact. There must, it seems to me, be a deeper level of explanation. Whether one wishes to call that deeper level 'God' is a matter of taste and definition. (Davies, 1993:16 – see also Davies quoted in **3.19.2**)

Psychology is in a different place again in relation to religion (see Chapter 5). So John Brooke's conclusion is of the first importance:

> There is no such thing as *the* relationship between science and religion. It is what different individuals and communities have made of it in a plethora of different contexts. Not only has the problematic interface between them shifted over time, but there is also a high degree of artificiality in abstracting from the science and religion of earlier centuries to see how they were related. (Brooke, 1991:321)

Some of the 'discoveries' of the appropriate relation between science and religion proposed in recent years are reminiscent of the 'special relationship' 'that has always existed between our two countries' invented by Winston Churchill in his efforts to woo the US into the war with Hitler. Indeed there had been all sorts of relationships between Britain and the States in the preceding two hundred years: empire–colony, empire–rebellion, naval powers at war, distant economic power awaiting the result of civil war, belated allies against the Kaiser. And indeed there has always been a relationship of a special kind between the advance of different types of knowledge of the natural world and religious understandings. But this 'special relationship' has been just as diverse and as ambiguous as the one Churchill invoked!

(ii) In their important collection of papers *Religion and Science: History, Method, Dialogue* Richardson and Wildman write:

> At times it has seemed as if theology and science had nothing in common at all. At other times they have been regarded as only partially distinguishable aspects of a single kind of intellectual inquiry. (Richardson and Wildman, 1996:84)

That last sentence reflects the fact that our understanding of the relation between science and religion will depend on our understanding of what it is that human inquiry, human rationality *consists of*. That understanding has itself been subject to major changes even within the last fifty years. These we examine in Chapter 2.

1.5.1   Is the important relation that between science and *religion*, or science and *theology*?

One of the most important analyses of the relation between science and religion is that of Willem Drees in *Religion, Science and Naturalism* (1996). Drees stresses two points which have received too little attention in the debate:

(a) That religion contains a number of elements other than the cognitive-propositional (the effort to express in conceptual and analysable terms understandings of the nature of reality). In particular much of the content of religion rests on *religious experience* (which we consider in more depth in **5.8–5.12**) and *tradition*. So Drees proposes a much wider scheme of 'areas of discussion concerning the relationship of religion and science' (Table 1.1).

TABLE 1.1

CHALLENGE POSED BY SCIENCE	CHARACTER OF RELIGION		
	1. Cognitive	*2. Experience*	*3. Tradition*
(a) New knowledge	(1a) Content: i Conflicts ii Separation iii Partial adaptation iv Integration	(2a) Opportunities for experiential religion? Religious experience and the brain.	(3a) Religious traditions as products of evolution.
(b) New views of knowledge	(1b) Philosophy of science and opportunities for theology.	(2b) Philosophical defences of religious experiences as data.	(3b) Criticism and development of religions as 'language games'.
(c) Appreciation of the world.	(1c) A new covenant between humans and the Universe?	(2c) Ambivalence of the world and implications for the concept of God.	(3c) A basis for hope? Or religions as local traditions without universal claim?

(Drees, 1996:45)

This broadens the debate helpfully, and shows that the categories that have received most attention, Drees' '1a. Content', form only one aspect of a complex matrix. These categories concern science's propositional claims and the way they impinge upon the cognitive claims developed by *theologies*. Drees shows that these interactions do not exhaust the content of science's interaction with *religions*, or the challenges science poses to them.

Where Drees' analysis is itself too limited is in not acknowledging that the 'science' which gives rise to challenges to religions has itself all sorts of different components. Sciences themselves have their traditions. As well as their cognitive claims they have imaginative, indeed aesthetic, components which are important in the generation and evaluation of novel hypotheses and models. Drees himself in an earlier book mused that 'a metaphysics informed by a religious perspective might determine the criteria for theory development and appraisal' (Drees, 1990:7). The matrix of interaction, then, has extra dimensions beyond those represented in Table 1.1, which only concern the *challenge* of science (viewed as a homogeneous whole) to various aspects of religion.

While this present volume is predominantly concerned with Christianity, indeed with Christian theology as an enterprise of rational exploration within a Christian commitment, we recognise that other traditions have much to contribute to the debate. We show in **6.9–6.12** how the scriptural teachings of Eastern religions offer radically different ways of thinking about divinity and the cosmos – some of which may prove to be a source of new models and metaphors within science. We also consider in Chapter 9 the framework of Islamic thought, in which the challenges posed by scientific theories (such as evolution) may receive a very different theological reception from that which is typical of the relation between the sciences and Western Christianity.

(b) Drees also recognises clearly that *religion is itself a phenomenon in the evolution of human culture*. As such it is an object of scientific study.[11] We show in **4.10** that seeing religion as an aspect of human evolution has led some to dismiss its truth-claims, whereas Drees himself recognises that this inference need not be drawn. A significant study which sees religion as an evolved phenomenon is Gerd Theissen's *Biblical Faith: An Evolutionary Approach* (1984). This book is important not least for a fine 'history-of-religions' account of the rise of Hebrew monotheism, but even within that account one can see the problems associated with Theissen's attempt to hold to an evolutionary epistemology,[12] to knowledge as a form of adaptation to reality. Within such a scheme, a religious or scientific explanation is only more or less successful than its competitors. But when he reaches the climax of his description of the evolution of Hebrew religion, Theissen cannot forbear to speak of 'the *discovery* of the one and only God' (1984:64, emphasis ours). Two pages later he has reverted to 'the *development* of the one and only God, [with which] a radically new environment opened up with completely new "demands for adaptation"' (p. 66, emphasis ours). But either such a God in some sense *constituted* the ultimate environment of human culture and the physical world alike, and was however partially and provisionally 'discovered', or there is not and never has been such a God, and the belief merely 'developed'. As van Huyssteen shows, Theissen is actually putting forward the former view, a 'critical-

---

[11] It is less evident, though equally important, to note that the activities of scientific communities are properly the subject of theological and ethical critique. What values do the communities *actually* evince? Are they committed to disinterested enquiry, or merely to a self-perpetuating search for funding? Does their source of funding constrain what results they can admit to obtaining [as in the case of those epidemiologists employed by the tobacco industry, or those climatologists employed by oil companies]? We look further into this in **1.20**, and in Chapter 11.

[12] *Epistemology* is the study of the nature of knowledge – how and to what extent we possess different kinds of knowledge.

realist epistemology'[13] under the guise of his evolutionary descriptions (van Huyssteen, 1997:Ch. 10).

Theissen's difficulties with terminology reflect the fact that the evaluation of scientific descriptions of religion as an evolved phenomenon will necessarily depend on the religious position of the evaluator. It is easy to concede a point made years ago by D. T. Campbell (1976:167–208): religion *may* have served to facilitate the transition from a human society dominated by biological evolution to one in which tribes were knitted together by holding certain common propositions about reality. Cultural, rather than biological, evolution then became dominant.[14] But the belief that religion is also able to anticipate future possibilities to which cultural evolution has not yet attained, because it represents a process of adaptation to the-way-things-really-are, is a much more contentious one. It will be held inside believing communities, but will be largely opaque to those outside.

Our concern throughout most of the present volume will be with *theology* – with the network of models, metaphors and propositions which give a religion its rational framework. But in examining in Chapter 2 the respects in which that framework is related to that of a scientific community we also indicate how theology must be integrally related to religious praxis (how a believing community acts out its faith within society). Indeed we see theology, ethics and action as intimately bound up together with an understanding of the world as the natural and social sciences describe it, as in Figure 1.2 (page 16).

1.6   The metaphor of the maps

It will be clear from the preceding sections that we recommend abandoning the search for any sort of 'philosopher's stone' of a definition of a perfectly appropriate relation between science and religion. A more helpful way to think of the relationship might be in terms of the metaphor of different 'maps' of the one world. Mary Midgley has used this recently in arguing for an approach to consciousness which is neither reductionist nor dualist.[15] She argues that different sorts of mental phenomena – and aspects of humanity dependent on our

---

[13] We take up the issue of critical realism in **1.7**.

[14] For a more developed discussion of these themes see Bowker (1995:3–150).

[15] Midgley (1996a and b). For an analysis of reductionism see **4.11**. For a rejection of dualism between mind and brain see **5.4**.

FIGURE 1.2

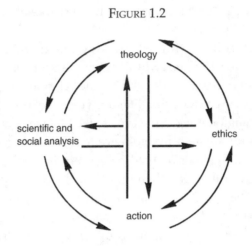

The 'Bossey Circle'. A World Council of Churches diagram,
taken here from Gosling (1992:65).

consciousness, such as society – can be described using the analogy of different maps (political, demographic, climatic, etc.) – of the (one) world. These different maps are no less accurate or genuine than the 'physical' maps of that world in terms of atoms and forces. Furthermore, Midgley insists that consciousness, and indeed society and politics and the like, *are not any less real* than the atoms of which they are made, and the maps drawn of them should not be regarded as inferior. 'Neither houses nor quarks ... are more real than mental items' (Midgley, 1996a:513).

The image of different maps of reality has been used by a number of philosophers – Midgley (1996b:58) mentions the discussion by John Ziman in *Reliable Knowledge* (1978), but suspects the idea goes back to Wittgenstein. It seems to us a most appropriate metaphor for the ways scientific and theological descriptions of the (one) world operate. It connotes a degree of independence, and yet a degree of relationship. It allows for the possibility of dialogue, and the likelihood of 'border disputes'. And as we have noted above, each science will have its own map, and its own relation to the maps theologians draw (of which there will be a diversity even within one religious tradition).[16]

---

[16] See our study of two closely-related Anglican theologies, those of Arthur Peacocke and John Polkinghorne, in **7.7**.

1.7   Critical realism in science

Consideration of the metaphor of a map is also particularly thought-provoking, since it provides a useful introduction to the vexed philosophical debate about what science *is* and whether theology operates at all in the same way. This we take up in much more detail in Chapter 2, but here we give an outline of some of the main areas of contention. (In **2.13** we indicate possibilities for a nuanced position which we consider offers many of the advantages of the different positions described here.)

We start by considering how *science* operates. We dismiss the position known as 'naïve realism', which simply holds that every scientific discovery directly corresponds to a truth about the world. Scientific views always depend on particular preconceptions about the world and particular ways of measuring it; they are moreover in a continual state of change, and in some cases undergo radical correction – these considerations are enough to rule out naïve realism. Equally, however, the success of the various sciences seems to suggest that they *do* manage to articulate something of the complexity of reality, in a way which is open to ever-new discoveries. So we rule out also any of the more extreme forms of 'idealism' which promote the notion that mental concepts are somehow more real than the physical world.

We revert to assessing a more sophisticated form of realism, frequently referred to as 'critical realism'. The critical realist recognises that we hold our views of reality *provisionally*, that we cannot simply read off the nature of the world from scientific data. The theories and presuppositions with which we approach our studies are acknowledged to affect our selection of what data we count as important to collect, as well as the ways in which we interpret these data. For example, simple *measurements* using something as basic as an electricity meter *rest upon commitments to theories* about interactions between current-carrying conductors and magnetic fields. Experimental data are never other than *theory-laden*, and *there are never enough data totally to demonstrate every element of a theory*. Other reasons for adopting a critical approach take into account the fact that observations themselves affect the character of an entity as it is observed (most markedly in quantum mechanics, see **3.10–3.14**).

Although it is unclear how we could be sure whether we had arrived at the best fit between scientific data and reality, it is widely agreed that there are criteria for our theories which can be taken as pointers to such a fit. They are:

- the *comprehensiveness* of the theory in taking account of all known data deemed relevant;
- the *consistency* of the theory – being devoid of internal contradictions;
- the *compactness* of the theory – its economy in not doing 'with more what can be done with fewer', a principle known as Ockham's razor.

These three can be seen as interrelated aspects of a 'coherence-based' approach to the assessment of truth (see **2.12, note 14**). A fourth criterion should be added – that of whether a theory possesses a quality of 'comeliness' – 'elegance' would be a better word though it doesn't begin with 'c'! Scientists are often influenced by a sense of the neatness and elegance of a particular formulation (cf. Derkse, 1993).

An alternative to a *realist* position is the claim made by what is referred to as the 'strong programme' of the sociology of science – that science is simply a social construction, rather than an attempt to describe a real world. Such a claim appears to suffer from major defects. For one thing it runs counter to what almost all practising scientists think they are doing. Its main problem, however, is that of *reflexivity*. If it *were* the case, then no human analysis could be more than a social construction, so the social scientists who made this claim would have to face up to the implication that *their* analyses and conclusions suffered from the same problem of being socially constructed. These analyses would not be saying anything true about how the world is or about what scientists are actually doing, but only reflecting the results of the sociologists' own social conditioning. (To reject the validity of a thorough-going relativism is not however to decry the importance of social and political factors in determining the course of science, not least in determining what research will be funded. See **2.10** on Thomas Kuhn's work for a fuller exploration of this.)

The most profound challenge to critical realism in science comes from views coming under headings such as 'instrumentalism' or 'constructivism'. These focus on the impossibility, already mentioned, of detaching data from the instrumental and experimental design which produced it. Given that we can neither think nor speak nor engage with the world at all except through language, theory, and concept, there can be no way to step beyond our theoretical frameworks and assess directly how adequate any particular theory is to the complexity of reality. It should be noted moreover that science undergoes major periods of change in which old theories are discarded and radically new ones adopted. Consequently many philosophers of science have argued that it is better to make no realist claims at all, but merely to regard scientific data as, however successfully, a function of the instrumentation, and of the conceptual constructs, by which science functions. To return to our starting metaphor, this view would hold that our map gets us about on the particular contrived journey that is science (just as a map of the London Underground gets us around the city) but we have no real idea what the streets are like which surround our path.

- The major problems, then, for realists, even critical realists, are *the theory-ladenness of data, the underdetermination of theory by experiment,* and in particular *scientific revolutions* in which supposed points of reference to reality have to be discarded because a radically new 'paradigm' takes over within a science (see **2.10**).

- The major problem for instrumentalists is *the sheer success and apparent progressiveness of science.* Its maps seem to work, in general, astonishingly well. It is hard to credit that an electron is an instrumental fiction, even though no-one has ever seen one directly, since so many phenomena have been observed in accordance with the behaviour and properties of electrons.

To follow this debate in more detail see in particular Laudan (1977) and Banner (1990). Particularly important to critical realism is the concept of *inference to the best explanation*. Granted that we cannot be sure that data correspond in any simple way to reality, we can nevertheless consider a variety of explanations of the data, and elicit the one that best fits our criteria of comprehensiveness, consistency, and compactness. For a recent defence of inference to the best explanation see Clayton (1997b).

1.8   Critical realism in theology

A very influential array of scientist-theologians[17] have argued that theology is also a critical realist discipline, which considers data, draws inferences to explanations, and submits these to testing closely analogous to that outlined for a scientific hypothesis. This is a problematic

[17] Such as Barbour (1998:118–20), Polkinghorne (1991:Ch. 1), Peacocke (1993:11–19) and Bowker (1995:42–46). For a summary of the debate between the first three see Polkinghorne, 1996a:Ch. 2).

claim. What are the 'data' of a religion which correspond to those of a science? Some might argue that they are the Scriptures of that faith, others the liturgy, others religious experience. Again, can it be said that there is a genuine critical element which can lead to theories being discarded, or are religious data privileged against falsification?

Willem Drees dismisses the claim of theology to be regarded as a realist discipline like the sciences. In his view theology shows no parallel with the spectacular success of science. With the science of the last three hundred years there is a cumulative success, an ongoing fertility in the development of new theories, which is simply absent from theology (cf. Drees, 1996:141–42). Polkinghorne concedes that 'One could not assert that (theology) has been characterised by the same power of its community to reach conclusions, which is such an impressive feature of the cumulative advance of science' (1996a:17). He points out that 'Theology depends for its moments of transparency to the divine upon events and people that are unrepeatably unique' (p. 18). So its data are going to be more precarious and less testable for that reason alone.

Working from the proposals of Imre Lakatos (see **2.12**), Nancey Murphy wants to claim strong parallels between science and theology as rational explorations. But she rejects critical realism in theology, on the grounds that it makes too great a claim as to our knowledge of elements of reality beyond our ordinary human ways of knowing (Murphy, 1990:197). Van Huyssteen, however, takes issue with Murphy, claiming in effect that we can make inferences to the best explanation even in matters close to the core beliefs of theism (1997:48–51). Roger Trigg dismisses critical realism as no more than 'a vague umbrella concept' (1998:86). So critical realism, as a way of thinking about the claims of either science and theology, or science alone, is a position towards which many in the field are drawn. Its philosophical usefulness remains a matter of keen debate. For a recent analysis see McGrath (1998:Ch. 4).

We can understand more about the similarities and differences between claims to realism in science and in theology by looking at the role played by model and metaphor in these two rationalities.

1.9   The central role of model and metaphor

One of Ian Barbour's great contributions to the science-and-religion debate was to indicate as long ago as 1974 in *Myths, Models and Paradigms* how central to both scientific and religious frameworks is the role of models (Barbour, 1974:Chs. 3 and 4; 1998:Ch. 5). A model in science can be thought of as a means whereby the human imagination can engage with and depict the aspect of nature under investigation. A good example is the one Barbour himself uses (1998:116) – the picture of the atom developed by Niels Bohr. At a time at which atomic structure was proving very baffling, Bohr produced a model in which the negatively-charged electrons orbited the positively-charged nucleus in a way which was like – and yet not like – the way the planets orbit the sun (see **3.10.3**). The model proved a fruitful heuristic device – that is to say, it promoted further exploration, and allowed various predictions to be made and tested. As a result of that work, earlier models – from Democritus to Rutherford – have long since been discarded. A refined form of the Bohr model is still a valid way of imagining the atom for certain restricted purposes. But a new structure of concepts and theories – based on the Schrödinger Equation – overtook the Bohr model. This mathematical formulation, though much harder to picture, is now the basis on which predictions about the atom are made.

If we now consider as an example of a model in Christian theology one of Augustine's 'psychological' models of the Trinity – the relationship between Father, Son and Spirit being seen as like – but yet not like – the relation between memory, understanding and will in the human mind – we can see all sorts of similarities with the part models play in science. The model emerged in a situation of difficulty and controversy – this time over how to imagine God. Augustine's was one of a number of attempts to picture how God might be like – but yet not like – three co-equal entities in relationship. Again, it was a model which greatly stimulated theological debate and led ultimately to a new conceptual framework.[18]

But these similarities should not be allowed to disguise differences. Augustine's model remains just one of a range of ways of stretching the imagination towards the mystery of the Trinity. No great advance has superseded it, yet it does not hold sway. More importantly, a whole range of *earlier* understandings of the relationship between Father, Son and Spirit remains alive for the Christian community though the Scriptures. The whole spectrum of titles for Jesus remains just as important as it was before the work of the Fathers of the fourth and fifth centuries.

---

[18] Mackey points out that Aquinas (in his great thirteenth-century system) 'did little more . . . than systematize Augustinian thought on this matter' (Mackey, 1983:586).

As well as Barbour, Janet Martin Soskice and Sallie McFague have written importantly on model and metaphor in religion (Soskice, 1985; McFague, 1982; 1987). McFague in particular stresses the role of metaphor in the development of imaginative formulations – all metaphor contains an is / is not – in some respects a crafty statesman may 'be' an old fox, in other respects he clearly is not. In the foregoing paragraphs we saw the 'is / is not' operating in the Bohr atom and the Augustine's Trinity. Theology, for McFague, operates between poetry and philosophy, so metaphor is indispensable. A model, for her, is 'a metaphor with "staying power"', a pattern which allows relatively comprehensive and coherent (though still exploratory and open-ended) explanation (McFague, 1987:Ch. 2). Both in science and religion human exploration requires both the imaginative and metaphorical on the one hand and the conceptual and systematic on the other. Models are what connects them. They are necessarily provisional and heuristic in character.

Polkinghorne, a former theoretical particle physicist, wants to draw a sharper distinction than many between model and metaphor. He writes: 'In my opinion, when scientists use apparently metaphorical language – as in talk of "black holes" or the "genetic code" – they are using these terms as picturesque shorthand for ideas they can more readily and more adequately convey in precise scientific language, and they are not using them as imaginative resources for the generation of ideas in a truly metaphorical way' (1996a:20). This remark is an important corrective to an over-romantic view of science, but does not do justice to the way metaphors determine what can and cannot be thought, even in a highly mathematical science such as physics. We discuss what can and cannot be thought in science when we look at Kuhn's concept of a 'paradigm' – see **2.10**. One of Kuhn's points is particularly relevant here – he notes that a science does not teach its students, to any great extent, the classic texts of the past, however seminal they might have been (Kuhn, 1970b:165). In a religious tradition old models and the metaphors that inform them remain part of the currency of the tradition. And whatever metaphors or narratives continue to inform the worship of a religious community will continue to influence its theology, in a way which has no parallel in science.

We argue in Chapter 2 that theology has to be seen as a more complex activity than merely a realist search for progressively truer data, and at the same time we are able to show how science, like theology, needs to be seen as the activity of a community of motivated believers, holding core assumptions and testing out new possibilities. On realism this will bring us out close to the position defended by van Huyssteen, a so-called 'weak form of critical realism' (van Huyssteen, 1997:51). Addressing reality is the goal of the rational explorations of sciences and religions, but our *confidence* as to which elements of our models do refer to real entities will vary across a discipline and over time. What we do retain is a strong sense of the ultimately *practical* nature of theological work. For example, for the believing Christian theologian the work is not only weighing the world in the light of Christ but also living within it in the power of the Spirit. This is the stance of the authors of this book, though we explore other emphases within Christianity and also in various other faiths.

1.10   Consonances

We noted above parallels between the methods of exploration in science and theology, but methodological parallels do not of themselves establish any particular relationship as to *content*. However, we also suggested that both disciplines manifest a sort of realism – however tentatively they expect their concepts to *refer* to elements of reality. To return to our previous metaphor (**1.6**) the disciplines are maps of the same world. We might therefore expect that 'following the coastlines', as Mary Midgley suggests (1996b:57), might enable us to see 'consonances' – places where the descriptions of reality offered by the two types of mapping seem to show a particularly close relation, when they (to change the metaphor) 'chime together'. For Ernan McMullin the Christian '*must* strive to make his theology and his . . . cosmology consonant in the contributions they make to (this) world-view' (quoted in Drees, 1990:26).

At once this notion sounds certain 'warning-bells', as follows:

(i)   In respect of the history of natural theology (see **1.3.1** and **1.13**). If science fails to 'show us God' by matching a piece of coastline with that drawn by theology, or if a piece of science we took for a sign of God loses its consonance (see **1.15**), does that make God non-existent, or less probable?

(ii)   The claims made by sciences and religions must both be recognised as a function of their cultural contexts, as being in some sense 'constructed' by those contexts. So as Drees has emphasised, consonances are also constructs (1990:29).

Polkinghorne has also discussed consonance (see his 1991:80–84). He is clear that the position is complex in respect of Big Bang cosmology (see **1.15**). He finds a more rewarding consonance in respect of the physical world being shaped by an interplay between chance and physical law (see **7.3.1**). (Note however that Jacques Monod places a very different construct on the presence of so much chance [see **4.10**].) Concerning eschatology there seems to be no consonance – scientific cosmology predicts that the universe will end in a state devoid of structure or meaning; Christianity cherishes a final hope of redemption (see **3.17, 7.17**).[19]

In our view Peters has assessed the situation correctly when he writes:

> 'Consonance' in the strong sense means accord, harmony. Accord or harmony might be a treasure we hope to find, but we have not found it yet. Where we find ourselves now is working with consonance in a weak sense – that is – by identifying common domains of question-asking. (Peters, 1997a:652)

Indeed even if we find from time to time glints of the 'treasure' we may not be able to glimpse them for long, since both the sciences and theology move on. Even McMullin, an early proponent of consonance, recognised that it would be 'in constant slight shift' (quoted in Drees, 1990:26). What consonance often seems to mean in practice is that theology is asked to redraw its map in order to fit its coastlines to new scientific understandings (as we shall see in **4.16.2** in respect of the doctrine of the Fall).

But if the scientific cartographers are the powerful ones now, it is often claimed that they could not have acquired this power except in the context of a theistic society. So we turn now to look at the history of the 'special relationship', beginning with the question as to whether religion was necessary to the rise of science, and going on to examine occasions when the map-makers have been in conflict.

1.11   Was religion necessary to the rise of science?

It is often claimed, particularly by those who want to emphasise the positive relations between science and religion, that Western science could only have arisen in the context of the three great monotheisms,

---

[19] R. J. Russell has called attention to this as an example of *dissonance* (Peters, 1997a:662).

Judaism, Christianity and Islam. This is a very complex issue, but it is possible to set down certain markers. For example:

- The first thinkers ever to ask, in anything like their modern form, such radical and demythologised questions as 'what is the world made of?' and 'how does it change?' were the Pre-Socratic philosophers of Ancient Greece (operating between roughly 600 and 400 BCE). Their intellectual ingenuity and daring remains one of the great landmarks in human achievement. It gave rise to an atomic theory, Pythagoras' Theorem, and geometric techniques good enough to obtain a reasonable estimate of the circumference of a (spherical) Earth. *Nevertheless the Greeks did not go on to invent experimental science*. This is partly because their philosophy became dominated by two patterns of thinking, both extremely ingenious, but neither propitious for science:

  (i) Plato's idealism, the conviction that a perfect abstraction is more real and worthier of study than a physical entity which may crudely imitate the abstraction, and

  (ii) Aristotle's theory of causation, which included not only material causes (what things are made of) and efficient causes (what past events affected them) but also formal causes (to what pattern the matter in them conforms) and final causes (towards what purpose or end are things being attracted).

- To say that Plato and Aristotle of themselves do not lead to experimental science is not however to deny their enormous contribution in framing and training the patterns of thought of the Western world from their own time until now. For instance, Aristotle's texts on logic, metaphysics[20] and the structure of the world were a major spur to intellectual development in the late Middle Ages.

- These great Aristotelian texts *entered Western Europe through the work of Islamic commentators*. We explore in Chapter 9 the relation between science and Islam, and note some tensions which may have prevented the Golden Age of Islamic enquiry into the world from going on to give rise to a scientific tradition such as the one that flowered with Galileo and Newton.

- *A belief that the world is fundamentally ordered and reliable is essential to science*. It seems clear that, of different kinds of religious beliefs about

---

[20] The very term *metaphysics* was originally the title given to the books of Aristotle which followed his *Physics*. It refers to questions about reality which 'lie beyond or behind those capable of being tackled by the methods of science' (Blackburn, 1994:240).

creation, the conviction found in the Hebrew Scriptures that the world is 'good' in itself – the work of one God, a Creator who does not keep changing the rules – is very favourable to a belief in an ordered world.

- *The belief that God brought the world out of nothing as an act of free creation*, which is the main line of the Christian doctrine of creation, *implies (a) that the world is not itself part of God, and is not therefore itself holy, and (b) that God could have created a different world*. Hence in order to discover what harmonious, faithful and ordered work God did do – a plausible task for natural theology and philosophy – *it is both permissible and necessary to 'put the world to the test'* in Francis Bacon's memorable phrase – to conduct experiments.

Beyond this, seventeenth-century Puritanism may have provided the perfect climate for science to grow, since, as Janet Martin Soskice has pointed out, both Puritanism and natural science appealed to living experience rather than merely accepting received tradition, and both drew on sources they considered had been neglected (in the one case Scripture, in the other experiment) (Soskice, 1993a). She goes on to claim that the relationship between science and religion in Britain in the seventeenth and eighteenth centuries was 'almost a rapturous love affair' (1993a:71).

We have come a long way from the quotation from John Updike with which we began! But we would want to stop short of the trite conclusion that Christianity was both a necessary and a sufficient condition for the rise of science. After all, the 'experiment' of the rise of Western science has only run once. Sweeping hypotheses about the history of thought neglect the complexity and contingency of history. To what extent, for instance, did the final cohering of the scientific tradition depend on the particular genius of Galileo, the first man to bring together mathematics, observation and experiment in a combination such as modern science employs? To what extent was the history of the world changed by the fact that the precocious and almost entirely self-taught genius of Newton was able to come to fruition in a country at peace?

Mention of 'rapturous love affairs' should not blind us, moreover, to the tensions that *have* existed. These we examine in the next few sections. The irony is that the two most famous conflicts – between Galileo and the Catholic Church of the early seventeenth century and between the early Darwinists and certain members of the Anglican Church in the mid-nineteenth – have both occurred when the relevant branch of the Christian Church was taking a vigorous role in promoting the type of scientific research in question.

Newton's post at Cambridge was for many years under threat because of his beliefs. This however was not a reflection of his science – rather of the non-Trinitarian theological schemes to which he devoted much of his time. More famously and significantly, Galileo spent the last years of his life under house arrest, and this *did* stem from his convictions about the structure of the solar system.

SECTION B:
THREE HISTORICAL EXAMPLES OF TENSIONS AS SCIENCE AND THEOLOGY DEVELOPED
(1.12–1.15)

1.12   Copernicanism and the Galileo Affair

The origin of Galileo's notorious dispute with the papal authorities came long before the Italian astronomer's birth. Aristotle had placed the Earth at the centre of the universe, not because it was the most important place, but because it was the coldest, most impure place in the cosmos and it would therefore fall as far as it could – to the centre. The celestial bodies were made out of a very pure and perfect element and travelled on the surface of spheres, the most perfect geometric shape.[21] The mediaeval Church adopted this system, and for Christians the Earth was central as being of the place of the world's salvation. Not surprisingly astronomical observation of the planets fitted only erratically with this Earth-centred (geocentric) scheme and complicated explanations were devised to overcome these anomalies. These were refinements on the general system of Ptolemy (second century CE) (Figure 1.3(a), page 28). In the 1530s the Polish mathematician Nicolaus Copernicus (1473–1543) began to challenge the Ptolemaic model and suggest a sun-centred (heliocentric) model (Figure 1.3(c)); this was only published as Copernicus was dying (in his *De Revolutionibus* of 1543).

---

[21] These conclusions of Aristotle's about the shape of the cosmos and the place of the Earth are fine examples of Greek reasoning – *deductive* from general principles (some of them philosophical and aesthetic rather than astronomical in the ordinary sense) rather than *inductive* from observations to theories.

There followed a period of what Kuhn has called 'paradigm shift', a crisis in the (newly developing) scientific community, in which two radically different models were in competition. Nor was it clear that Copernicus was right – his circular orbits gave no better fit than its best geocentric competitor – that of the Imperial mathematician Tycho Brahe.[22] This is because the planetary orbits are in fact ellipses, a model first proposed by Johannes Kepler (1571–1630), who was one of the very few thinkers other than Galileo to adopt Copernicanism before 1600.

FIGURE 1.3

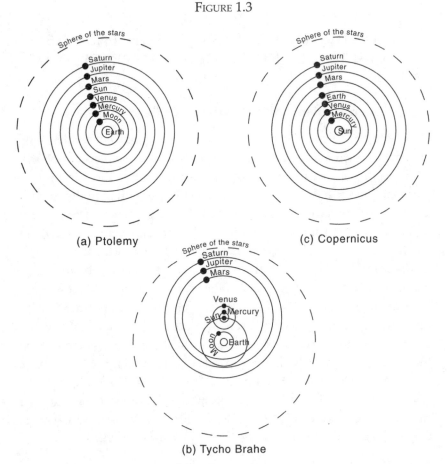

(a) Ptolemy   (b) Tycho Brahe   (c) Copernicus

Three competing models of the solar system (early seventeenth century) from Poole (1995:105).

[22] Brahe (1546–1601) had proposed a scheme in which the planets revolved around the sun, but the sun itself revolved around a stationary Earth (Figure 1.3(b)).

Enter then Galileo Galilei, whose career can be briefly summarised as follows:

1564   Born in Pisa

1592–1610   Taught mathematics in Padua, a city under the protection of Venice. Convinced from early on of the truth of Copernicanism.

1609   Obtained the principles of the telescope, constructed his own, and observed the craters of the Moon, the phases of Venus and the moons of Jupiter, none of which was predicted by the Ptolemaic model.

1610   Went to work for Cosimo de' Medici in Florence, insisting on the title 'first philosopher and mathematician'.[23]

1613   Wrote to Benedetto Castelli about the compatibility of Copernicanism with Scripture – this letter later developed into 'The Letter to the Grand Duchess Christina' (1615).

1616   Cautioned by Cardinal Bellarmine in Rome not to teach Copernicanism as a *fact*, though *De Revolutionibus* was republished in 1620 with the heliocentric view treated as a *hypothesis*. Cardinal Maffeo Barberini of Florence was instrumental in ensuring the book's republication.

1632   Galileo published his *Dialogue Concerning the Two Chief World Systems – Ptolemaic and Copernican*. This passed the ecclesiastical censors, and indeed did nominally present the systems as alternatives, but actually it was heavily pro-Copernican. Moreover, it appeared to ridicule the Aristotelian views of Barberini, by then Pope Urban VIII.

1633   Galileo was interrogated, and abjured his views under pressure. Put under house arrest until his death in 1642 (though he continued to be vigorously engaged in astronomy and other scientific work, including suggestions as to how a clock might be governed by a pendulum).

To understand how Galileo came to be on trial it is necessary to know a little more about the man himself. As Kuhn pointed out, Galileo saw falling bodies, and swinging bodies, pendulums, 'differently from the way they had been seen before' (Kuhn, 1970b:119). (Eventually, indeed, he was able to see a pendulum, a feather dropped from the Tower of

---

[23] This was an important addition to his status (and hence to the weight of influence perceived to be carried by his views) – mathematicians were technicians; philosophers were those who could establish truth.

Pisa, and the Earth itself, all as examples of falling bodies.) This was partly because he was not brought up solely on Aristotle's ideas of motion, but was already familiar with the 'impetus' theory of the fourteenth-century scholars Buridan and Oresme.[24] But also Galileo was blessed with an extraordinary clarity of thought which enabled him, for example, to discern a truth which had never been observed on Earth (because of friction) – that a body in motion will continue in the same motion unless a force acts on it. He was also possessed of a great curiosity about the world, which fired him to construct one of the earliest telescopes and observe the solar system in unprecedented detail.

Furthermore, Galileo had a strong religious faith and was keen to relate his discoveries about the world to his Christian understanding. But he was a disputatious and difficult character, impatient of those who failed to follow the power of his arguments. These were all important ingredients in his relationship with the papal authorities.

The Galileo affair has had intensive study in recent years. For an accessible account see Poole (1995:Ch. 6). For other corrections to the standard caricature of the merely-blinkered Church against the noble scientist, see Brooke and Cantor (1998:Ch. 4), Drees (1996:55–63), Brooke (1991:82–105), or Gingerich (1982). For a more specialised investigation see Finocchiaro (1989).

One of the most important documents in the case is Galileo's letter eventually issued as 'The Letter to the Grand Duchess Christina'. Recently Howell (1996) has analysed the type of case Galileo was making, drawing a parallel with the arguments of Augustine about the reading of the Book of Genesis, as follows:

(i) distinguishing matters of science from matters of faith – Galileo begins from the dictum that Scripture was given to show how to go to heaven rather than how the heavens go. But if it is not conceded that science and biblical interpretation are separate, Galileo's fallback is

(ii) that the interpretation of Scripture should not go against demonstrated truths in science. But if his opponents will not concede either that Copernicanism is a demonstrated truth, or that such truths can oppose a Scriptural text (such as the description in the Book of Joshua of the sun standing still

---

[24] By which 'the continuing motion of a heavy body is due to an internal power implanted in it by the projector which initiated its motion' (Kuhn, 1970b:119)

only by the mighty action of God) then Galileo has a second fallback, that

(iii) actually Copernicanism is closer to literal Scripture than the Ptolemaic model.

So Galileo's own position was multifaceted, and very much rooted in the hermeneutics[25] of one of the great doctors of the Church. We have seen too that Pope Urban had defended Copernicus' book despite disagreeing with it. Moreover Cardinal Bellarmine, chiefly responsible for dealing with Galileo for the Vatican until his death in 1621, was not a bigoted cleric either, but an open and thoughtful one, keenly concerned with astronomy. His approach emerges in passages like this one from a letter to Foscarini:

> I say that if there were a true demonstration that the sun is at the centre of the world and the earth in the third heaven, and that the sun does not circle the earth but the earth circles the sun, then one would have to proceed with great caution in explaining the Scriptures that appear contrary, and say rather that we do not understand them than that what is demonstrated is false. (Quoted in Finocchiaro, 1989:68)

This complex affair, then, was influenced by a number of factors:

- the scientific, yes, but it is worth pointing out that because Galileo ignored Kepler's work his model still fitted the data no better than its best geocentric competitor. It also suffered from the great problem that it predicted stellar parallax, which had not then been observed;[26]

- the epistemological – what, in the terms of the passage quoted above from Bellarmine, constitutes a 'demonstration'? How should Bible-reading astronomers understand their data, and their Bibles, in the interim phase when a scientific model has been proposed but is not yet established?;[27]

---

[25] *Hermeneutics* is a study of the principles of interpreting the meaning of written texts. It includes the whole question of how a particular text is 'received', especially considerations such as discerning the author's intentions as well as understanding the social context and the thought-forms of the period.

[26] The reason for this, as Copernicus had guessed, is that the solar system is a relatively tiny place enormously far from even the nearest stars. Stellar parallax is therefore very small. It was not observed until 1832.

[27] Gingerich has shown moreover that Galileo's own logic was not always of the soundest in his efforts to demonstrate his case (Gingerich, 1982:123).

- the hermeneutical – how should Scripture be read, how should that reading affect or be affected by science? Above all, who should have the authority to determine the range of permitted readings?;[28]

- the political – it was a stage in the Counter-Reformation at which the Vatican felt the need to assert its central authority.

- the personal – Galileo pursued his cause with an arrogant lack of tact and diplomacy which in the end forfeited the patience even of those inclined to sympathise with his view.

Small wonder that when the trial is 'rerun' in classes on science and religion Galileo is often the loser!

The utter triumph of heliocentrism that followed ended forever any prospect that a religious group could exercise the sort of hegemony over an area of scientific inquiry that the Vatican tried to assert in suppressing Galileo. It showed moreover that a scientific theory could *gradually* gain in comprehensiveness and coherence until it displaced another, without requiring a strict *logical* demonstration.

1.13   The love affair gone wrong: the eighteenth century

We noted above (**1.3.1**) that the period from around 1680 to 1800 saw the great flourishing of natural theology. The great explanatory power of the new science, especially of Newtonian mechanics, was pressed into service to investigate how the Creator had worked and was working. In the process more and more purely scientific explanations were given of natural phenomena.[29] At first this was not in tension with a strongly theistic position – Newton himself regarded God as directly mediating the force of gravity. Newton's successors developed the idea of the mechanical universe which accepted action-at-a-distance without the need for divine mediation, but neither was this necessarily in tension with the narrative of God's creative action. Rather the mechanical model was regarded as constituting the 'how' of the great Architect's work, and was therefore a source of understanding of God's character. The 'Book of Nature' could be read alongside the 'Book of Scripture'.

---

[28] The Council of Trent, in tightening the structures of the Roman Church, had ruled in 1546 that 'no one should dare to interpret Scripture "contrary to the unanimous consensus of the Fathers"' (Brooke, 1991:97). (Though as we have seen Galileo did in fact follow the hermeneutical method of Augustine.)

[29] As Kaiser makes clear this was a process which had been going on at least since the twelfth century (Kaiser, 1996:185–97).

The great irony of this period is that as Brooke puts it: 'the God *known* through science would prove most vulnerable to being *overthrown* in the name of science' (1996:10). The atheist Anthony Collins remarked that it would never have occurred to anyone to doubt the existence of God if theologians had not tried so hard to prove it. Mechanistic explanations of natural phenomena, not involving miraculous intervention, were suggestive of true objectivity. They were celebrated by Robert Boyle and his successors, the 'physicotheologians', as descriptions of the Creator's activity. But they were equally attractive to 'deists', who confined God's work to the initial establishment of the created order, and highly prized by the new movement of atheists which developed from the 1740s. Moreover the 'Book of Nature' could only give rise to generalised theistic conclusions about creation; over-focus on this aspect of theology tended to cut natural theologians off from the great strengths of Christianity in giving an account of redemption. Pascal had described seeing in his famous vision the '"God of Abraham, of Isaac and of Jacob", not of philosophers and scholars'[30] – a God who had been in saving relation to humans throughout history – but this perspective tended to be lost.

Brooke emphasises the complexity of this period (1991:Ch. 4; 1996:7–27, Brooke and Cantor, 1998:Ch. 5) but the radical nature of the change in the relation between the sciences and theology is unmistakable. A hundred years after Newton came Laplace (see **1.17**); a hundred years after Burnet's *The Sacred Theory of the Earth* came James Hutton's *The Theory of the Earth*. Gone from Hutton was Burnet's interpretation of Noah's Flood as an example of divine design – in its place came a theory based on endless cycles of mountain-building and destruction. But as Brooke insists, it would be wrong to see science as simply an *agent* of secularisation – rather scientific interpretations illustrated in a particularly vivid way the secularising effect of other forces – social, economic, philosophical. (The impact of David Hume is an example. We saw in **1.3.1** that Hume questioned the argument from design which was such an important element in natural theology. His sceptical empiricism in fact called into question not only talk about God, but also the regularities on which science depends. But because science was on the ascendant, the way Hume's writing tended to be received was as an attack on miracle, and hence a reinforcement of views which stressed the adequacy of scientific accounts of phenomena.)

[30] Pascal, 1966:309.

We go on to consider the conflicts that followed an immensely influential scientific proposal – Charles Darwin's scheme in *The Origin of Species* (1859), which finally put an end to any simplistic argument from design.

1.14   Early conflicts over Darwinism

Once again there is a prevailing caricature:

- that the Christian theologians of the time were all committed to a model in which God had designed every single creature exactly as that creature was known to the naturalists of the 1850s;
- that Darwin's book showed any belief in creation to be untenable; and
- that the Bishop of Oxford, Samuel Wilberforce, rendered himself ridiculous by opposing Darwinism at the British Association Meeting in 1860.

The story goes that Wilberforce, recognising that Darwin's scheme implied that humans too had evolved, from other apes, questioned Darwin's friend and champion T. H. Huxley as to whether he was descended from an ape on his father's side or his mother's. Huxley, supposedly, quipped back that:

> If then . . . the question is put to me 'would I rather have a miserable ape for a grandfather or a man highly endowed by nature and possessed of great means and influence, and yet who employs those faculties and that influence for the mere purpose of introducing ridicule into a grave scientific discussion' – I unhesitatingly affirm my preference for the ape. (Quoted in Drees, 1996:65)

The evidence now suggests that the legend of these exchanges grew to its final form long after the event itself. Again both Brooke and Drees record a much more balanced view (Brooke, 1991:40–42, Drees, 1996:64–67).

What the caricature ignores is that:

(i)   Wilberforce was Vice-President of the Association that year, and made his critique of Darwinism as a scientist rather than a theologian.[31] He had reviewed *The Origin of Species* – adversely, but in a way which Darwin acknowledged as perceptive (Poole, 1995:123–24).

---

[31] Brooke notes that between 1831 and 1865 forty-one Anglican clergy held office in the British Association; between 1866 and 1900 only three (Brooke, 1996:13). So it is true that the 1860 Meeting came at a transitional time, but the transition was not so much the dismissal of Christianity by science as the rise to influence of the professional scientists (of whom Huxley was an early exemplar) at the expense of the gentleman amateur.

(ii)   There were real scientific problems with Darwin's view, which were not lost on Bishop Wilberforce, a follower of Richard Owen's theory of archetypal patterns in vertebrates (see **4.2**).

(iii)   Christian responses to Darwin varied greatly – some, like Charles Kingsley's, were immediately affirmative (see **4.5**).

There were, then, just as in Galileo's case, scientists and theologians on both sides of the question. Personalities, such as that of Huxley ('Darwin's bulldog'), exacerbated conflict. And just as Galileo pressed the issue by asserting himself as a natural philosopher, claiming truth rather than mere effectiveness of calculation, so the new breed of nineteenth-century scientists used the Darwinian controversy to press their authority over their discipline in a way which took the clerical establishment by surprise. What needs to be stressed is the complexity of the interaction between science and religion, and the shallowness of the caricature. We explore the nature and impact of Darwinism in greater detail in Chapter 4.

1.15   A contemporary instance of the interplay between claims of consonance and claims of conflict

Today the hegemony lies with the scientific community. Science is a rational enterprise of unparalleled success (by its own lights – those of providing understanding of the physical universe – if not necessarily those of furnishing humans with wisdom as to how to live). Theissen claims that 'Nowadays religion is on the opposition benches and science forms the government. It would be good if religion could find a way out of its role as a smouldering opposition, and if science were less arrogant as the government' (Theissen, 1984:40). The Bossey Circle (Figure 1.2, page 16) all too often looks like one-way traffic – science sets the parameters for what can be believed about the world, religious doctrines have to fall in line. In later chapters we discuss the idea of a historical Fall (**4.16.2**), the possibility of resurrection and virginal conception (**7.7 (v)**), and the ultimate fate of the universe (**3.17, 7.17**). We shall show that in some cases, such as the Fall, science has restricted what it seems appropriate to believe, but in other cases, such as the end of the universe, it seems essential for theology to continue to assert hopes to which astrophysics is in no position to give support.

One particular case will be helpfully illustrative of a number of these themes, namely the question of the origin of the universe in a 'Big Bang'. We describe in **3.16** and **3.18** the development of the theory, and how it prevailed over the competing 'steady-state' theory of Bondi, Gold and Hoyle. Interestingly, one of Hoyle's motivations was aversion to the Genesis-like connotations of the Big Bang. He wrote: 'Unlike the modern school of cosmologists, who in conformity with Judaeo-Christian theologians believe the whole universe to have been created out of nothing, my beliefs accord with those of Democritus who remarked "Nothing is created out of nothing"' (Hoyle, 1982:2f.). *Here, then, we have an important example, albeit a negative one, of theory selection in science being influenced by theological stance!*

The Big Bang survived Hoyle's counter-proposal, and *it seemed to have a most pleasing consonance with the opening of Genesis, the dramatic beginning of the universe in an event of vast mystery.* The consonance was celebrated by no less a figure than Pope Pius XII (see **3.18**).

However, since around 1980 cosmological interest has shifted to the first ten million, billion, billion, billion, billionth of a second (10^{-43} second) of the universe's history, when the developing universe was so small as to be significantly affected by quantum theory. Stephen Hawking records that he was at a conference at the Vatican in 1981 at the end of which:

> the participants were granted an audience with the Pope [John Paul II]. He told us that it was all right to study the evolution of the universe after the big bang, but we should not inquire into the big bang itself because that was the moment of Creation and therefore the work of God. I was glad then that he did not know the subject of the talk I had just given at the conference – the possibility that space-time was finite but had no boundary, which means that it had no beginning, no moment of Creation. (Hawking, 1988:116)

The physicist continues, ironically, 'I had no wish to share the fate of Galileo ...'. However, Hawking has ventured various theological comments much more extreme than any uttered by Galileo, most famously that:

> So long as the universe had a beginning, we could suppose that it had a creator. But if the universe is really completely self-contained, having no boundary or edge, it would have neither beginning nor end: it would simply be. What place, then, for a creator? (Hawking, 1988:140–41)

Hawking is referring to his proposal, with Jim Hartle, about the very early universe. There is very substantial agreement as to the development of the universe from the first 10^{-43} second on (see Figure 1.4a). Traditional Big Bang theory allowed the space-time diagram to arise from a point, like an ice-cream cone (Figure 1.4b). This point was then a so-called 'singularity' at which values such as the density of the universe would go to infinity and the laws of physics could not hold. The Hawking–Hartle proposal allows the time dimension, the vertical axis of the diagram, to 'fade away', to be subsumed into the space dimensions. The diagram therefore originates not from a point but from a curved surface with no boundary or edge, like the surface of the Earth at one of the poles (Figure 1.4c).

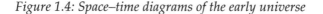

Figure 1.4: Space–time diagrams of the early universe

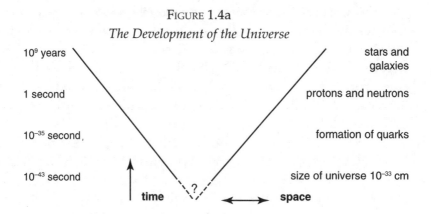

Figure 1.4a

The Development of the Universe

10^9 years — stars and galaxies

1 second — protons and neutrons

10^{-35} second, — formation of quarks

10^{-43} second — size of universe 10^{-33} cm

time   ? space

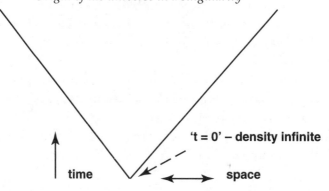

Figure 1.4b

Origin of the universe in a singularity

't = 0' – density infinite

time   space

FIGURE 1.4c

The Hawking–Hartle proposal – no 't = 0'

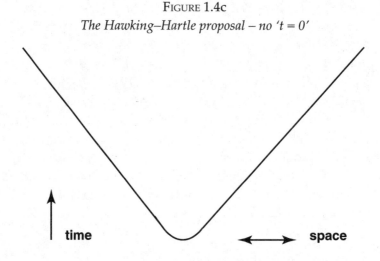

time   space

Hawking and Hartle's proposal is the most ingenious of the quantum-cosmological speculations which aim to overcome the problem of the singularity. These speculations as they stood at the end of the 1980s were reviewed by Drees (1990:Ch. 2). He points out that indeed at this early stage in the development of these theories a physicist *might* be influenced as to which one to pursue by a sense of their theological connotations (1990:67–68).

However, theologians of science are uniform in their rejection of the last-quoted comment of Hawking's, as well as the militantly atheistic programme of P. W. Atkins to the effect that: 'The only way of explaining the creation is to show that the creator had absolutely no job at all to do, and so might as well not have existed' (Atkins, 1981:17).

Atkins draws comfort from the notion that quantum cosmology has shifted away from the 'blue-touch paper' model, in which everything arose from a single inexplicable moment, towards various types of proposal in which space–time arises by chance out of a simpler state – Hawking's boundariless space, or a quantum vacuum, or some such.

Such views seem to show consonance not so much with theistic creation as in Genesis as with the view that the universe arose by some transition which had no purpose or meaning.

Keith Ward has rightly taken issue with the suggestion that quantum cosmology implies that the *reason* for the universe is pure chance (1996b:Ch. 2). He writes:

> On the quantum fluctuation hypothesis, the universe will only come
> into being if there exists an exactly balanced array of fundamental
> forces, an exactly specified probability of particular fluctuations
> occurring in this array, and existent space–time in which fluctuations
> can occur. This is a very complex and finely tuned 'nothing' . . . So
> this universe looks highly contingent after all, and a creator God might
> well choose to create a partly probabilistic universe by choosing just
> such an origin for it. (1996b:40)

Drees points out that in fact the Hawking–Hartle proposal accords
well with a theology which emphasises that every space is equally
created by God, '"sustaining" the world in all its "times"' (Drees,
1990:74). For more recent discussion of God and quantum cosmology
see Craig and Smith (1993); Worthing (1996:Ch. 3); and R. J. Russell's
fine essay in Richardson and Wildman's book, in which he shows
that at the core of the doctrine of *creatio ex nihilo* (divine creation out
of absolutely nothing) is the principle of ontological dependence.[32]
The discovery of an actual temporal beginning to this material
universe would serve only as a gloss on the doctrine (Russell, R. J.,
1996:201–24).

SECTION C:
KEY PRINCIPLES FOR DEVELOPING THEOLOGY
IN THE LIGHT OF SCIENCE (1.16–1.20)

We have considered examples of different sciences in different eras in
tension or in consonance with theology. We now examine some key
principles which help to determine what relationships can appropriately
exist between the two types of discipline. We look briefly at different
types of explanation, and at questions of determinism.

1.16   Different types of causation and explanation

We saw in discussing Aristotle that he had devised a very sophisticated
four-fold pattern of causation (**1.11**). However, Western physical science

---

[32] *Ontology* is the study of being, of how reality is in itself, as opposed to how we
might have knowledge of it (epistemology). Ontological dependence implies that all
creation owes its being, from moment to moment, absolutely and utterly to God.

only developed in its present form by refusing to discuss final causation – the ultimate purpose or end towards which an entity was attracted. A cannonball (or a feather) dropped off the Leaning Tower of Pisa is considered to fall not because it is seeking its natural end or *telos* in being united to the Earth but because there is a net force acting on it – that of gravity. The force, mathematically characterised and operative throughout the universe, is the efficient cause of the motion. This shift in understanding also resulted, eventually, in the removal of a divine purposing agent from any scientific explanation. Science deals in *non-teleological* explanations, which do not invoke some purpose acting from outside the system concerned.

Poole points out that:

> ... an object such as a thermostat might have a number of **compatible** explanations:
>
> *An interpretive explanation* A thermostat is a device for maintaining a constant temperature.
>
> *A descriptive explanation* A (particular) thermostat consists of a bi-metallic strip in close proximity to an electrical contact.
>
> *A reason-giving (scientific) explanation* Constant temperature is maintained because, when the temperature falls, the bi-metal strip bends, so making electrical contact. It switches on a heater which operates until, at a predetermined temperature, the bi-metal strip bends away from the contact, thereby breaking the circuit.
>
> *A reason-giving (motives) explanation* An agent wished to be able to maintain enclosures at constant temperatures to enable people to work comfortably, ovens to cook evenly, and chickens to hatch success-fully.
>
> ... It needs to be understood that there is no logical conflict between reason-giving explanations which concern mechanisms, and reason-giving explanations which concern the plans and purposes of an agent, human or divine. (Poole, 1994:48–49)

The success of science has been based on restricting itself to particular forms of non-teleological explanation – reason-giving (scientific) in the classification above. We saw above that natural theology went into retreat because such explanations of natural phenomena displaced explanations (for instance of how gravity could act) which relied on divine mediation. Science has also succeeded by concentrating as much as possible on measurable behaviour which can be reproduced by a range of different observers – on what Galileo called 'the primary qualities' of mass and motion, rather than 'secondary qualities' such as taste and smell (see **3.2**).[33]

In considering types of explanation it is important to clarify reason-giving explanations in biology. Biologists will often describe the 'purpose' of a particular entity – for example, the prehensile tails of some monkeys are 'designed' to enable them to swing through trees. By this however biologists are not giving a 'motives' explanation about the activity of a conscious, designing agent (though as Poole points out, motives explanations can co-exist with scientific explanations). Rather they are saying that the tails of these monkeys have evolved a property which helps the organisms survive and reproduce (by extending their mobility in their habitat). Descriptions of the extent to which a biological property fits an organism for its environment and 'improves its design' constitute a special category of description known as the 'teleonomic'.

1.17 Determinism, indeterminism and their implications

The physics of Newton proved an enormously powerful way of describing moving bodies (see **3.2–3.4**). A century later Pierre Simon de Laplace (1749–1827) showed among other things how the solar system could have arisen without divine intervention.[34] He went on to claim that an 'intelligence' possessing complete knowledge of the position and momentum of every body in the universe would be able to predict all future states of that universe. In other words, that the cosmos is *deterministic*. Laplace's 'intelligence' was a mathematical fiction. But it illustrated the problem of determinism, which challenges our instinct that we ourselves as humans are able to make choices about the future, that we are to some extent 'free' agents. Indeed determinism raises problems as to how God could either enter into any sort of real relationship with humans, or indeed guide the material world towards divine purposes.

---

[33] However, this latter success has tended to privilege physics, the science most concerned with fundamental forces, at the expense of biology. Some recent thinkers, such as Brian Goodwin (see his 1995:215–20), have called for a less mechanistic approach, especially in biology.

[34] When Napoleon remarked to him the absence of God in his models, legend has it that Laplace said he 'had no need of that hypothesis'. The mathematician was nevertheless a practising Catholic.

We explore this in more detail in Chapter 7. It is enough to note here the conviction of many thinkers in this field that this is not a wholly determined world, but one in which the laws and processes God has created can give rise to novel structures through the operation of chance, and that God can co-operate with those developments, and relate to the conscious beings to which evolution has ultimately given rise. So Ward writes:

> there can only be an open future if there is a degree of indeterminism. There can only be the sort of freedom that is morally important if there is an open future, at least sometimes. So indeterminism is a necessary condition of the later development of morally important freedom in rational beings. (Ward, 1996b:20)

1.18   Developing theology in the light of science

We are now beginning to see the sort of theology that is being done in the light of contemporary science. It is theology which treats scientific principles with great respect, while recognising how their emphasis may shift (see **1.15** above on the origin of the universe). It expects that there will be consonances between two disciplines which are both 'mapping' the same territory, albeit in different ways, but it handles these consonances gently, using them to ask further questions rather than celebrating them in themselves.

It is one aim of this book to enable students *to do such theology for themselves*. It is too often overlooked that one task of theology is to generate new, vital and creative ways of speaking about the relationship of God to human beings and the non-human creation, and students should feel free to generate such ideas. As we indicated above, we ourselves see this task as one of starting within a religious tradition (in our case the Christian, rooted in Scripture, tradition, reason and religious experience) and seeking to renew and refresh that tradition by contact with the methods and descriptions of science. We pursue, then, a 'theology of nature' in Barbour's sense (see **1.3.1**). We would encourage students to embark on that same model-making process – whether rooted in a particular tradition, or having no especial allegiance – and to do so creatively and imaginatively. (The corollary is that they also need to learn the skills of defending the rationality of their models.)

It cannot be stressed too strongly that such a model is always provisional, exploratory. A student should never be put off from beginning a model on the grounds that every position taken must be precisely accurate. The tradition of 'apophaticism' or 'negative theology' acts as a corrective to any precise attempt to describe God or the divine in relation to any other entity. (Apophaticism stresses that whatever description we assign to any aspect of God's nature, however coherent in itself, falls vastly short of encompassing that aspect of God.) But models of God, humanity and the cosmos, informed by the insights of contemporary science, remain a valuable heuristic tool. Such models would be expected also to be fruitful in terms of proposals for ethics and praxis (see Figure 1.2, page 16).

1.18.1   The interdependence of different aspects of a model

This will be familiar to students who have studied, for example, Christology and atonement theory. 'High' Christologies stressing the divinity of Jesus drew much of their momentum from the perception that only God could save human sinners – hence they tend to be found in company with objective theories of Christ's atoning passion and with eschatologies centred on the conviction that in the divine Christ all things will ultimately be reconciled (Col. 1.20). Likewise an Abelardian picture of the crucified Jesus as the supreme exemplar of love *can* (though it need not necessarily) be held with 'lower' Christologies of Jesus the God-centred man. One doctrinal choice will affect a number of others.

   We can extrapolate this into a more general model of the relation between God and humanity. Much will depend on the attitude taken to human beings. Are they to be viewed, initially, as 'little lower than the angels' (Ps. 8), the God-commissioned organism *par excellence*, vice-regent of creation, or is the starting point for thinking of humans to be that they are exceptionally highly culturally developed anthropoids, in whom the habit of worship and ritual practice has developed to a very marked extent? (See **4.15–17** for more on the evolution of humanity.) Once such a choice has been made as to which picture of humans the model will start from, then that picture has to be meshed with the chosen model of God (see **6.1–6.6.1**). From there the model-maker must consider how the *relationship* between God and humans is to be characterised. Since humans are part of the creation, made out of elementary particles like all other entities, this relationship will in turn be affected by what stance is taken on the relationship of the divine to the material world. And so on. The exercise is exploratory, and each element in the model will be affected by understandings of what claims theology and science make in general, and what are the particular claims of different sciences in areas of special concern to theologians.

Chapter 2 gives a background to how scientific rationality works, and various ways in which theology has responded, culminating in a proposal as to a way in which they may be seen to operate in parallel. Chapters 3–5 look at some of the key questions which touch on major narratives in different sciences and in theology – the origin, functioning and end of the physical universe, the origin and development of life and humanity, the nature of mentality and religious experience.[35] Chapter 6 provides an opportunity for students to look at a wide variety of models derived from Christian theologians – also some from Eastern thought. Chapter 7 provides an opportunity to test out models students may be developing on a theology of divine action. But it is helpful to stress three aspects of models at this stage.

1.19   Three attributes of models of God, humanity and the cosmos

   (i)   As we indicated above, different elements in the model will be *interdependent* – the effect of one choice has to be evaluated in terms of its coherence with the other proposals that are being made. Thus a model of God as intimately and vulnerably related to every entity in the non-human creation would sit distinctly oddly with an ethic which allowed humans to do whatever they chose to the environment.

  (ii)   Models may *derive from different metaphysical positions* – they may for example be critically realist with respect to both science and theology (see **1.7**), critically realist with respect to science and non-realist in respect of theology (see **2.3**), or instrumentalist (see **1.7**) with respect to both. Students who wish to propose models which involve no divine entity should not feel excluded from the exercise – they have still the task of giving an account of origins and ends, of the nature

---

[35] It may be asked why chemistry seems to have been omitted from our sequence of sciences! Chemistry finds mention only insofar as it forms part of consideration of one of the particularly acute questions for the interface between science and theology listed above. *Historically*, chemistry has of course had a vastly important part to play in the growth of human understanding. For some fine descriptions of relevant incidents in the history of chemistry see Russell, C. A. (1994).

and significance of humanity and of human relationships to the environment. (Furthermore, just as theists have to face the problem of evil – see **4.4, 6.1–6.6.1** and Chapter 7 *passim* – so atheists have to face 'the problem of goodness' and address questions about the surprising existence of beauty and intelligibility in the universe – also about the [much disputed] phenomenon of altruism.)

(iii) As will be clear from the above, models *are expected to give rise to ethics*, possibly indeed to proposals for action (see the Bossey Circle, Figure 1.2, page 16). Here Chapters 8–11 of this book are particularly important, since they indicate ways in which the effects of science are manifest in society, and areas where science might or might not be regulated to meet theological and ethical concerns. Here we begin that exploration by looking briefly at questions of value.

1.20 Questions of value

What humans count as valuable involves their *thinking*, their *feeling* and their *willing* – the *cognitive, affective* and *volitional* domains of their lives. The values humans hold because of their beliefs are often referred to as their dispositions or their commitments. These may arise from beliefs about major matters like the meaning – or otherwise – of life; values may also be attached to factors like the quality of objects as works of art, their irreplaceability and sale value, the stability given to society by traditional customs, the sanctity of life and so forth.

With a vast array of possible values, *value judgements have to be made.* These may be between the relative values of objects or organisms, or they might be between alternative courses of action in science or technology. If for instance we want to say that a piece of rainforest has value, we have to be able to say why. The sciences can provide certain data on rare species, biodiversity, etc. but they cannot of themselves provide the ethical basis for attaching value to an organism or a system. Likewise science and technology can help humans to judge the likely outcomes of particular courses of action, but cannot tell us whether those courses of action ought or ought not to be pursued.

However the scientific community *does* continually make decisions as to value, by selecting different priorities for research, and different methods of carrying it out. These selections, then, need to be a matter of public concern. Religious beliefs about right and wrong provide a source of these moral *oughts*, as do non-religious stances for living. Such beliefs are continually seen to interact with both science and technology, over matters like deciding whether to clone human beings, how long to keep patients who are in a persistent vegetative state on life-support machines, or indeed how much countryside is to be used up for roads.

Even a brief list of issues like this highlights one logical point: *'ought'* implies *'can'*. It would sound odd to say that the doctors *ought* to have saved the patient's life, if the illness was one for which there was no known cure. However, the converse, *'can* implies *ought'* is not true. Just because science and technology make something possible does not imply that it ought to be done. One only has to remember some of the bizarre experiments performed by Nazi concentration-camp doctors to see a grim illustration of that point.

As we indicate in Chapter 11, the possibilities presented by science and technology need to be assessed within a view of the world which seeks for *wisdom*. Daniel Hardy has recently written:

> wisdom designates more than the wisdom of human beings. It is the domain in which the dynamics of fundamental dimensions of the world and God are placed relative to each other, the domain . . . of relativities. Wisdom is therefore the *configuration* of insight – both theoretical and practical – into the multi-dimensionality of the world and God, *not only how they are related but how they should be related* (this emphasis ours) . . . Anyone who tried to understand how the world and God are related, and therefore how they are best approached, or how the various disciplines of human understanding are best related to each other, is involved in the search for, and finding of, wisdom. (Hardy, 1998:137)

In other words the making of models such as we have proposed, with their emphasis on relationality and on the ethical reflection that should result as to the *appropriate* relationships between God, humanity and the cosmos, is an aspect of a new search for wisdom, which humans so urgently seem to need.

1.21   Conclusion

In this chapter we have indicated the importance of moving beyond the trite caricature that science simply displaces religion from every aspect of life where the two meet. We have indicated important sources for exploring the 'special relationship', both historically and in the contemporary world. We considered, and moved beyond, some of the main efforts to narrow the relationship to a typological scheme. The metaphor of different maps of the same reality led us into a discussion of the claims of critical realism in science and theology, which prepares for our examination of their philosophical backgrounds in Chapter 2. We then considered whether religion was necessary to the rise of science, and some of the classic cases where conflict has been real. Clarification of different types of explanation, and of the importance of questions of determinism, enables the student to tackle the suggested task of making her or his own model of God, humanity and the cosmos.

FURTHER READING

BARBOUR, I. G. (1998) *Religion and Science: Historical and Contemporary Issues* (London: SCM Press)

BROOKE, J. H. (1991) *Science and Religion: Some Historical Perspectives* (Cambridge: Cambridge University Press)

BROOKE, J. H. and CANTOR, G. (1998) *Reconstructing Nature: The Engagement of Science and Religion* (Edinburgh: T&T Clark)

DREES, W. (1996) *Religion, Science and Naturalism* (Cambridge: Cambridge University Press)

PEACOCKE, A. (1993) *Theology for a Scientific Age* (London: SCM Press, expanded edn.)

PETERS, T. (ed.) (1998) *Science and Theology: The New Consonance* (Oxford: Westview Press)

POLKINGHORNE, J. (1994) *Science and Christian Belief: Reflections of a bottom-up thinker* (London: SPCK)

POOLE, M. W. (1995) *Beliefs and Values in Science Education* (Buckingham: Open University Press)

STANNARD, R. (1996) *Science and Wonders: Conversations about Science and Belief* (London: Faber & Faber)

VAN HUYSSTEEN, J. W. (1998) *Duet or Duel? Theology and Science in a Postmodern World* (London: SCM Press)

VAN HUYSSTEEN, J. W. and GREGERSEN, N. H. (eds) (1998) *Rethinking Theology and Science. Six Models for the Current Dialogue* (Grand Rapids: Eerdmans)

WATTS, F. (ed.) (1998) *Science Meets Faith* (London: SPCK)

Chapter 2

Truth and Reason in Science and Theology: Points of Tension, Correlation and Compatibility

2.1 Introduction

In Chapter 1 we saw that the 'conflict' model of the relationship between science and religion is only one possibility among many, and not by any means necessarily at all typical. Indeed we saw that monotheistic religion, especially Christianity, had had an important role in nurturing the roots of Western science (see **1.11**).

However, *it is still all too frequently the case that science and theology are thought of as two utterly distinct spheres of human interest with the relationship between them being viewed, at best, as one of uneasy tension.*

One might note the respective ways in which the words 'science' and 'theology' function in popular usage. 'Science' and 'scientific' are frequently appealed to as a means of bestowing respectability on a subject, bringing with them connotations of rationality, reliability and utility. How often in the media do we encounter the authoritative 'Science tells us . . .'? Interviewees when pressed riposte with 'We need to be scientific about this . . .', and advertisers attract us with such phrases as 'The appliance of science', 'The science diet' and all manner of goods which come with a supposedly scientific seal of approval. In contrast 'theology' and 'theological' have, for some at least, taken the place of the once popular 'metaphysical abstraction' as the standard terms of derogation: 'Theological nonsense' cries an MP across the floor of the British House of Commons, implying irrationality, confusion and irrelevance.

The theological problems occasioned by the rise of science extend then, it would seem, beyond particular disputes to a more pervasive sense that science stands as the measure of all valid knowledge – in a way which calls into question the notion that theology is a route to truth. This belief can take many forms:

- science is a truly modern form of knowing, whilst theology represents a pre-modern throw-back;
- science is useful, whereas theology promotes a disengagement from reality;
- science is value-free, whereas theology is compromised by personal commitment;
- science is open to falsification and renewal, whereas theology is dogmatically entrenched;
- science is based upon empirical data, whereas theology is a matter of pure speculation;
- in short, science seeks after objective truth, whereas theology deals only in subjective meaning.

We consider these assumptions to be as untrue to the reality of science as to the practice of theology. The present chapter explores the relevant philosophical background before considering the more constructive possibilities opened up by recent thought. As such, the chapter falls into three broad sections (A, B and C): the first is concerned to trace the high-water mark of scientistic rationalism in the logical positivism of the early part of this century, the constraints which this imposed on Christian theology, and the relative merits of some attempted responses; the second traces the unravelling of positivism in the middle part of the century; and the third explores more recent post-positivist accounts of science and their theological relevance – particular attention is given here to Nicholas Rescher's thought.

SECTION A:
EARLY TWENTIETH CENTURY – THE CHALLENGE OF LOGICAL POSITIVISM (2.2–2.6)

2.2   The verificationist criterion of meaning

In the early part of the twentieth century a group centred upon the University of Vienna articulated a formal theory of knowledge which established scientific propositions as the measure of all truth in a way which condemned all other kinds of propositions as meaningless. Heirs to the traditions of scientific positivism and British empiricism alike, the 'Vienna Circle's' views are generally referred to under the labels 'logical positivism' or 'logical empiricism'. A. J. Ayer's *Language, Truth and Logic* (first published 1936) is the standard English language presentation of their thought.

Following the lead of Kant, the logical positivists drew a distinction between 'analytic' and 'synthetic' statements. Under the category of the analytic they included statements of definition (e.g. 'All bachelors are unmarried', '2 + 2 = 4') and statements of logic (e.g. 'Something cannot be both true and false in the same respect at the same time') – statements the truth of which can be uncontroversially ascertained without recourse to empirical reality. In turn, the category of the synthetic included all statements which go beyond logic and definition alone to exert claims concerning what reality is actually like (e.g. 'The swan on the lake is white', 'There is a God'). According to the logical positivists' characteristic 'verificationist' principle of meaning, the class of meaningful propositions consists of analytic propositions, which are true by definition, and synthetic propositions which can be verified in a similarly empirical manner as was presumed to be the case with scientific propositions.[1] In the face of any given synthetic proposition, the logical positivists asked for the sensory data which might serve to verify the truth of that proposition. If no such data could be adduced then the proposition was to be classed as meaningless on the grounds that there was no means of distinguishing its truth from its falsity.

Whether the verification principle is actually capable of supporting scientific explanations (which are less concerned with particular descriptions than with general laws) is a moot point (see **2.7**). What is apparent, however, is that its rigorous application would condemn vast swathes of discourse as meaningless – in particular metaphysics, religion, aesthetics and ethics (Ayer, 1971:42). Take ethics as an example. Given that it is impossible to verify value statements in an uncontentious manner, the logical positivists concluded that they could not be classed

---

[1] As Ayer put it: 'We say that a sentence is factually significant to any given person, if, and only if, he knows how to verify the proposition which it purports to express – that is, if he knows what observations would lead him, under certain conditions, to accept the proposition as being true, or reject it as being false' (Ayer, 1971: 48).

as meaningful in any literal sense. At most they can be ascribed an emotive or evaluative meaning in the sense of expressing the preferences of those stating them – statements such as 'Theft is wrong' being understood along the lines of 'We reject the practice of stealing'. Likewise it was claimed that statements concerning the being of God cannot even be discussed, let alone affirmed, in any meaningful manner (Ayer, 1971:152).

As we discuss in **2.9,** the two central presuppositions of the logical positivist agenda (i.e. the analytic/synthetic distinction and the assumption that it is possible to verify propositions in a discrete manner) have each been subjected to rigorous challenge in subsequent philosophy. As a result the focus of contemporary interaction between theology and the philosophy of science has shifted to other very different places (see **2.10–2.13**). Nevertheless, the assumptions which logical positivism formalised continue to ripple through popular consciousness. It will therefore be helpful to pause in order to consider the range of possible theological responses. We will focus upon four. Whereas the first and third represent differing attempts to *accommodate* theology to the positivist challenge, the second and fourth represent differing attempts to *isolate* theology from it. The critical comments that we offer lay down certain markers for the more constructive case which will follow later (see **2.13** in particular).

2.3   Strict accommodation: non-cognitive accounts of religious belief

1955 saw the publication of R. B. Braithwaite's lecture 'An empiricist's view of the nature of religious belief' in which he sought to defend the meaningfulness of religious discourse whilst embracing a positivist perspective. He did this by evacuating religious assertions of any cognitive content concerning the nature of reality (i.e. of any claim to convey conceptual *knowledge* of reality) and then treating them as statements of purely ethical intent embroidered with illustrative stories. His argument hinges around two claims: firstly that 'Unless religious principles are moral principles, it makes no sense to speak of putting them into practice' and secondly that whilst 'A religious assertion will . . . have a propositional element which is lacking in a purely moral assertion . . . it is not necessary . . . to believe in the truth of the story involved' (Braithwaite, 1971:81, 84–95). The point of this was to suggest that religious assertions are to be accorded the kind of evocative or evaluative meaning attributed to ethical statements in a verificationist perspective rather than the more literal kind of meaning reserved for analytic and empirically testable propositions (p. 86).

R. M. Hare had already published a similar account of religious belief in 1951. For Hare as for Braithwaite, religious beliefs do not count as cognitive claims about the nature of reality. Rather they are to be understood as constituting what he terms a '*blik*', or overarching principle, which guides believers' lives and their interpretation of their experience.

The most obvious problem facing such strategies is the fact that their response to the positivist challenge is bought at the cost of an account of religious belief which few adherents would either recognise or wish to endorse. With regard to Braithwaite's proposed identification of religious and ethical statements, whilst most if not all theological statements can indeed be held to have practical implications, this is somewhat different from claiming that they are ethical statements without remainder. Within the Christian tradition, for example, it is widely held that the true force of Christian living consists not in the stoic observance of ethical codes but in a process of grace-filled conversion and conformity of life to the transforming reality of God in Christ and the Holy Spirit. This is certainly what we find in the epistles of Paul and again in Augustine's dispute with Pelagius. For each of them Christian life is rooted in convictions about the action of God and not simply the ethical intentions and imaginative faculties of humans. As such, there is an inescapably cognitive dimension to Christian faith which makes the strategy espoused by Hare and Braithwaite appear odd to say the least.

This point could be pressed further. Implicit within the claim that Christian faith is centred upon the action of God is the recognition that we do not, of ourselves, have the wherewithal to sort out the intractable messiness of the human condition and that hence, any genuine hope of transformation must be grounded in something more than human resources alone. Indeed, in a context where belief in God has ceased to have any literal meaning it could be argued that Camus' *La Peste*, with its portrayal of the heroic refusal of Dr Rieux to be overwhelmed by the futility of his actions, represents a more appropriate narrative ethic than does the kind of transposition of Christian stories advocated by Hare and Braithwaite.[2]

2.4   Strict isolation: Christian existentialism

The second of our four possible theological responses to logical positivism seeks to identify a realm of significant discourse quite different to the scientific, and hence distinct from anything that would figure under a positivist epistemology, with a view to claiming that this constitutes the true locus for a meaningful use of religious language. The key text is Rudolph Bultmann's 1941 essay 'New Testament and mythology', in which he claimed that scientific understanding had shown the need for what he referred to as the 'mythical world picture of the New Testament' to be demythologised if it is to speak to twentieth-century men and women. By this he did not simply mean the traces of the ancient three-storey picture of the cosmos which can be found there. He referred equally to the basic notion of the Earth as '. . . a theatre for the working of supernatural powers' (Bultmann, 1985:1). As he expressed it in particularly sharp form at one point, 'We cannot use electric lights and radios and, in the event of illness, avail ourselves of modern medical and clinical means and at the same time believe in the spirit and wonder world of the New Testament' (1985:4).

The larger point at issue here – as to the possibilities for making sense of a real divine action in the natural order within the context of contemporary scientific understanding – will be discussed in Chapter 7. We see Bultmann as having allowed his theological agenda to be dictated by an overly deterministic world-view which such developments as quantum theory (see **3.11–3.14**) were already placing in question at the time that he was writing. Bultmann's response to this situation was to draw a sharp distinction between the kind of empirical knowledge supposedly at issue in science and the more existential style of knowledge which he believed to lie at the heart of Christian faith. Where the former is concerned with causal connections in the world,

---

[2] As Nicholas Lash has commented in a somewhat different context, '. . . there are surely less cumbersome ways of being an atheist than to use the paraphernalia of Christian language and imagery simply to express the form of our alienation?' (1986:117). Substantially the same charge could be levelled against the more recent and more vigorous non-realism of writers such as Mark C. Taylor and Don Cupitt (see Murray, 1998a:165–66).

the latter is concerned with questions of personal meaning and significance. For Bultmann, any attempt to link God-talk with talk about physical happenings in the natural order confuses the categories of causality and existential significance in the way in which a mythical world-view did previously. Faced with such confusion, the task is to seek to demythologise the language concerned by extracting the underlying message from the imagery in which it is expressed. As he put it:

> The real point of myth is not to give an objective world picture; what is expressed in it, rather, is how we human beings understand ourselves in our world. Thus, myth does not want to be interpreted in cosmological terms but in anthropological terms – or, better, in existentialist terms. (1985:9)

Accordingly Bultmann reinterpreted all talk of God's action in particular events in terms of the way in which they open up new possibilities for understanding human existence when perceived with the eyes of faith. God's action is confined to the inner level of personal address and existential challenge rather than to the external level of factual explanation. Most notoriously, the resurrection narratives are understood as testimonies to the continuing possibility of finding faith and personal meaning in Jesus rather than as witnesses to the fact of God actually having raised the dead Jesus to a new state of life. To this extent, similar fault lines run through Bultmann's position as have been identified in the work of non-cognitivists such as Braithwaite and Hare. With them he shares the basic positivist assumption that the realm of facts is to be distinguished from the realm of values, with religious belief being placed firmly on the latter side of the divide. But as Nancey Murphy observes, 'If theological meanings are not grounded in theological facts – facts about the character and acts of God, in particular, then they are mere fairy tales, however comforting they may be' (Murphy, 1996:153).

In fairness to Bultmann it has to be acknowledged that he, unlike Hare and Braithwaite, did genuinely wish to think in terms of God's acting at the level of personal address in order to initiate the believer's transformed vision of things. Nevertheless Bultmann severely curtails the scope of divine transformative action when compared with traditional Christian claims concerning God's action in and through particular events in the historical order, most notably those surrounding the life, death and resurrection of Jesus. As such it would be as difficult to preserve the necessary cognitive dimension to such aspects of Christian faith on the basis of Bultmann's account of things, as it would on the basis of either Hare's or Braithwaite's. It would therefore be equally difficult to present an account of Christian faith which is capable of speaking to the depths of human need.

Finally, it could further be argued that Bultmann's attempt to immunise Christian faith from the challenge of scientific positivism is itself self-defeating. Implicit in Bultmann's strategy is the assumption that whereas an action of God within the external world would necessitate God's intervening in the continuum of natural causality, God can be thought of as acting in the inner life of the believer without any such problems arising. But such an assumption is by no means beyond question. If, as will be argued in **5.2–5.4**, mental states and neuronal activity are necessarily interrelated, then God's inspiring of altered mental states must be thought of as having a neuronal component to it also. Bultmann has not solved the problem of God's action so much as merely shifted it to a different level. As such his existentialist version of Christian faith appears to be as inadequate to the positivistic world-view which it assumes as it is to the tradition of faith that it espouses.

2.5   Relative accommodation: on the possible verification of Christian faith

Whereas our first possible strategy of theological response to the challenge of logical positivism (see **2.3**) shared the positivist assumption that religious belief is in principle unverifiable, a polar opposite strategy (but still one of accommodation) would be to claim that it is indeed open to such verification, or at least a form thereof. Two quite different forms of this strategy will be considered: the first, espoused by John Hick, appeals to the possible 'eschatological verification' of religious belief after death; the second attempts to reclaim something of the tradition of natural theology.[3]

Taking verification in its broadest sense as 'the ascertaining of truth by the removal of grounds for rational doubt', Hick noted that the fulfilment of predictions has a particular role to play (Hick, 1971:54–55). He told a parable (pp. 59–60): two men walk together along the

---

[3] See **1.3.1** for an introduction to natural theology and the problems it faces.

same road but with radically different beliefs about the road's terminus – one believes that it leads towards a Celestial City, the other that it leads nowhere (comparable to the positions of the theist and the atheist respectively). The point for Hick is that whilst neither of these interpretative frameworks gives rise to any testable predictions about events *in the course of* the journey, the controverted claim that the road leads to a Celestial City does itself represent a potentially verifiable prediction. To this extent there are matters of real substance at issue in the counter-claims of the 'believer' and the 'non-believer' in such a manner as makes it utterly inappropriate to think of them as non-cognitive *bliks* (**2.3 para 2**) lacking in any real content. Likewise, he argued that Christian faith is correctly to be viewed as having a cognitive dimension to it which is open to potential, albeit eschatological, verification in such manner as renders it meaningful even within the strict terms of the verification principle (1971:65–71).

Where Hick settled for the modest task of establishing that Christian faith could, on account of its *potential* verifiability, be meaningfully discussed within a positivist perspective, the second possible verificationist approach to religious belief would attempt the more ambitious task of establishing that such belief is open to actual verification *in this order*. More precisely, by exploiting a distinction which Ayer himself drew between 'strong' and 'weak' forms of the verification principle it might be claimed:

- firstly, that experience which renders a given proposition probable, rather than absolutely certain, is sufficient to verify it in the 'weak' sense (Ayer, 1971:50–51);

- secondly, that religious beliefs are indeed open to being verified in just such a 'weak' probabilistic manner (Swinburne, 1993:182).

In support of this latter claim, appeal might be made to certain implications deriving from the belief in God as Creator. This belief, in the Christian view, is more concerned to maintain the absolute and continuing dependence of all that is upon the creative and sustaining hand of God than it is merely to exert a claim about temporal origins (Aquinas, 1967:77–85; see **1.15**). More precisely, the belief in God as Creator is concerned to maintain that everything that exists (a) is brought into being through the Logos or self-reflected reason of God and (b) is sustained in being by the generative and transforming Spirit of God. As such, it implies that all that exists reflects in very diverse and particular ways something of the rationality and being of God (Soskice, 1993a:71, Aquinas, 1967:95). Such a stance readily lends itself to being employed in support of the claim that the observable data of the natural order bear the impress of the hand of the Creator within them. This in turn makes it possible to interpret them as indirect evidence for the existence of God.

Complementing this it might equally be argued that science itself provokes the need for a broader explanatory framework by raising questions which cannot be answered purely within its own terms (Murphy and Ellis, 1996:5, 15–18, 59–62, 250–51). For example, science has yielded unparalleled effective knowledge concerning imminent causal relations within the world, but is incapable of answering the question which this almost inevitably raises as to the possible ultimate cause of the entire causal order taken as a whole. This remains the case no matter how far cosmology penetrates into the first milliseconds of the cosmos, or even if it concludes that the origins of all that is lie in a boundariless singularity (see **1.15**). Still the question remains as to the possible cause lying behind even this – why is there something rather than nothing?

Putting this together, where a doctrine of creation might be taken as supporting the belief that there is evidence for the existence of God to be discerned within the world, the limits of scientific explanation might be taken as creating an opportunity for just such a conversation to occur. These two assumptions form the twin pillars supporting the attempt here being considered to ground religious belief on the basis of observation and experience. Where this approach differs from the eighteenth-century Anglican tradition of natural theology is that *it foregoes any hope of articulating a definitive proof of God's existence* and settles instead for *seeking to establish the greater probability of God's existence than not.*

Richard Swinburne is probably the best known advocate of this approach.[4] His thesis is that the various arguments are best taken jointly rather than individually, as together contributing to a many-sided cumulative, or inductive, case which serves, through the application of

---

[4] His 1979 *The Existence of God* stands as the classic text. In the Introduction he describes the book as 'concerned with whether the claim [that there is a God] is true; it is concerned to assess the weight of arguments from experience for and against this claim, and to reach a conclusion about whether on balance the arguments indicate that there is a God or that there is not' (1979:1; see also Swinburne, 1993:188).

probability theory, to establish that the existence of God is more likely than not (1979:13–14, 277–91). Basil Mitchell had already commended the benefits of a 'cumulative case' approach to the justification of religious belief.[5] The application of probabilistic confirmation theory is however Swinburne's own distinctive contribution to the task. This determines the particular form that his argument takes and lends to it an appearance of rational clarity and logical rigour which, he believes, serves to set it on a par with the examination of large-scale scientific theories (1979:2–3). However, whilst appearing attractive to those looking for a robust defence of theistic belief, to others it represents an inappropriate form of argumentation.

Much of the force of Swinburne's case lies in his adoption of an apparently neutral starting point. He presents an account shorn of rhetorical flourish and 'written in deep conviction of the possibility of reaching fairly well justified conclusions by rational argument' – the implication being that any rational person should be swayed by the case which he presents (1979:1). The problem however is that the underlying notion of a pure, neutral rationality untainted by perspective and commitment is now widely thought of as an elusive ideal at best and an unhelpful illusion at worst (see **2.7–2.13**). We are all always embedded in linguistic and conceptual frameworks, cognitive and evaluative commitments and shared practices which, rather than acting as an obstacle to rationality, actually constitute the contexts within which human reason appropriately functions. *Consequently, we each bring differing perspectives to the process of rational reflection in such a manner as rules out any chance of there being arguments which are equally persuasive for all.*

For example, pivotal to Swinburne's argument is the claim that 'the intrinsic probability of there being a universe such as ours and no God is very much lower than . . . the intrinsic probability of there being a God' (1979:288). But this is by no means an uncontentious claim. One sharing a different set of presuppositions to Swinburne could legitimately challenge his case at numerous points and arrive rationally at a different conclusion (Mackie, 1982). The broader issue, as Michael Banner has pointed out, is that probabilistic confirmation theory can at best offer 'a means whereby one encodes one's prior judgements in a more technical form' rather than a precise formula for neutral theory choice (Banner, 1990:144; see also Putnam, 1981:189–93). It would seem

---

[5] In *The Justification of Religious Belief* (1973).

then that not only is there no possibility of articulating a deductively certain proof of God's existence; there is no possibility either of presenting a probabilistic inductive case to which all people should feel themselves compelled to submit. Indeed the best writing in this tradition already recognises this fact (Mitchell, 1973:21–41, 59; Aquinas, 1964:29–33). The most that arguments such as Swinburne's can do is establish that, given certain presuppositions, a rational case can be made demonstrating a fit between belief in God and other aspects of human knowledge and experience. Reflecting this we suggest that rather than being articulated from a position of supposed neutrality, they are most appropriately set within an explicit faith context. Further, there are sound theological rather than merely philosophical reasons why this is so.

Intrinsic to Swinburne's case is the prioritising of what are presumed to be the common perceptions of general human reason over the particular commitments of Christian faith, the latter being relegated to the point of arrival rather than departure. As he has expressed it himself: 'In all my works on the philosophy of religion my approach has been to start from where secular humanity stands, develop a philosophy of that area of thought, and then show how that philosophy leads to a Christian understanding of things in some respect' (1993:197–98). The problem with this from a theological point of view is that it runs the risk of allowing the terms of the debate to be set without any reference to that which is distinctive about the Christian understanding of God (i.e. the belief that the character of God's presence and action in the world is demonstrated most clearly in and indeed is actually identified with the particular living unto death of the crucified and risen Christ).

More precisely, Swinburne starts out with the confident assertion that 'God is by definition an omnipotent (that is, infinitely powerful), omniscient (that is, all-knowing) and perfectly free person . . .' (1993:192; 1979:8). He thus displays no concern to wrestle with the difficult question as to whether this widely assumed philosophical concept actually matches with what is alleged by Christians to be revealed of God in the life, death and resurrection of Jesus. As such, Swinburne's case appears more as a defence of the 'God of the philosophers' than it does a justification of Christian faith itself. Indeed, some have argued that a related strategy was actually responsible for paving the way for modern atheism. Their claim is that it was the very shift in focus of theological reflection to general cosmological speculation which in turn provoked the naturalistic response which saw no need to invoke God in the chain of causal explanation (see **1.13**, also Buckley, 1987; Brooke, 1996:14–17; Jüngel, 1983).

2.6   Relative isolation: the Barthian emphasis upon the primacy of God's self-revealed Word

Horrified first by the support given to the Kaiser's war policy by liberal theologians in 1914 and then again by the ready submission of German Christianity to the allure of the Third Reich in the 1930s, Karl Barth denounced all attempts to establish Christian faith upon the basis of prevailing secular reason. For Barth such attempts inevitably serve to compromise the true focus of Christian theology (i.e. the absolutely free God revealed in Jesus as capable of challenging and transforming the created order) by conflating it with the terms of contemporary culture in such a manner as dulls its critical edge. From the publication of his epochal commentary on *The Epistle to the Romans* (particularly the 1922 second edition) onwards, Barth took it as axiomatic that Christian theology should be shaped exclusively in accordance with the 'wholly other' self-revelation of God in the life, death and resurrection of Jesus.[6] The force which this methodological tenet exerted over his theology is most evident in the complex spiralling form of the *Church Dogmatics* in which each interlocking theme is continually related back to what God has supposedly shown of God's self in the person of Christ (Hunsinger, 1991:28–29).

Donald MacKinnon has pointed to a certain parallelism here between Barth's trenchant emphasis upon the particular givenness of Christ as the self-disclosure of God and the positivists' emphasis upon the 'given' of empirical data as the privileged disclosure of natural reality.[7] This could be pressed further and used to justify the claim that whilst science represents the appropriate means of gaining knowledge about the natural world on the basis of empirical observation, this does not raise

---

[6] This principle received classic statement in the first article of the Barmen Declaration in 1934: 'Jesus Christ, as He is attested to us in Holy Scripture, is the one Word of God, whom we have to hear and whom we have to trust and obey in life and in death. We condemn the false doctrine that the Church can and must recognise as God's revelation other events and powers, forms and truths, apart from and alongside this one Word of God' (Barth, 1957:172).

[7] See MacKinnon (1968:66–69); for a related point see also Hunsinger (1991:32–35). For further discussion of the particular use which MacKinnon himself makes of Barth's Christocentric particularity, see Murray (1998b:particularly pp. 364–67).

any problems for theology which, as the 'science' of God, is focused upon the reality of God's dealings with the world as known through the scriptural witness to God's self-revelation in the person of Christ.

Whilst such a strategy would support a far more full-blooded version of theological truth than is at work in Bultmann's programme (in as much as it would resist the reduction of God's being in action in Christ and the Spirit to the purely 'interior' level of personal address), it would nevertheless stand with that project in espousing what amounts to a strategy of isolation. As with Bultmann the implicit claim would be that science and theology are focused upon different dimensions of reality and that, provided their boundaries are respected, there can be no undue conflict. In this regard it is significant to note that when Barth turned to the doctrine of creation in Volume III of the *Church Dogmatics*, he showed no apparent concern to reflect upon the theological signi-ficance of contemporary scientific thinking. The entire discussion, extending to well over two thousand pages in the English translation, is given over exclusively to the significance of the created order as viewed within a Christocentric perspective. As such, it exemplifies both Barth's overriding concern to forego all attempts to found Christian theology on the basis of general human reason – and the limitations in this project as Barth himself pursued it.

On the one hand we believe there to be something of lasting signifi-cance in Barth's concern to shape Christian theology in radical accordance with the disclosed truth of God in Christ, particularly so in the light of the now-widespread consensus that there is no possibility of attaining to a perspectiveless neutrality in human reason (see **2.5** and **2.10–2.13**). Put bluntly the point could be expressed as follows: if the hope for neutrality is illusory then why should theologians feel obliged to chase after it when it only serves to skew what is distinctive about Christian faith anyway?

On the other hand, however, we would equally claim that this legitimate Barthian sense of priorities requires to be matched by a more explicit concern to expose the particular commitments of Christian faith to the refreshing challenge of other traditions of thought and practice. Unless some such attempt is continually made then Christian faith is in danger of closing in upon itself in such a manner as would threaten to reduce the supposedly objective truth of God's self-disclosure to the level of a mere communal *blik*. As Wentzel van Huyssteen has put it:

> A positivistic theology of revelation that adopts a highly esoteric
> method makes it extremely difficult to convince others that the basic
> tenets of theology – God, revelation, Holy Scripture, inspiration,
> etc. – are not the basic constructs of subjective whim, whether
> personal or directed by an influential tradition. (van Huyssteen,
> 1989:22; see also Murray, 1998a:162–65)

Somewhat more positively, it could be argued that Barth's rearticulation of the belief that the entire created order relates to Christ
itself suggests a need in Christian theology. This is the need to adopt a
constant self-critical exposure to the challenge and refreshment of other
traditions of thought and practice. The point is that if the deepest
significance of all things is Christological in orientation, then it is
possible that *there are things to be learned about the reality of God in Christ
which can only be learned by allowing the insights of other aspects of human
understanding to refresh and renew the perspective of Christian faith.*

The contemporary renaissance in Barthian studies has revealed the
extent to which Barth himself acknowledged that his Christocentric
focus and starting point in Christian theology was by no means in
tension with a recognition as to there being truth (what he referred to
as 'other lights') outside the sphere of Christian faith (Barth, 1961:106–
09, 114–25, 139–43, 151–54, 156–65; Hunsinger, 1991:234–80). Further,
the fact that this was no mere late aberration on his behalf can be seen
by looking again at the first Article of the Barmen Declaration cited
earlier (see note 6 in this chapter):

> Jesus Christ, as He is attested to us in Holy Scripture, is the one
> Word of God, whom we have to hear and whom we have to trust
> and obey in life and in death. We condemn the false doctrine that
> the Church can and must recognise as God's revelation other events
> and powers, forms and truths, apart from and alongside this one
> Word of God. (Barth, 1957:172)

Upon which he later commented:

> We may notice that it does not deny the existence of other events
> and powers, forms and truths alongside the one Word of God, and
> that therefore throughout it does not deny the possibility of a natural
> theology as such. On the contrary, it presupposes that there are
> such things. But it does deny and designate as false doctrine the
> assertion that all these things can be the source of Church
> proclamation, a second source alongside and apart from the one
> Word of God. It excludes natural theology from Church procla-
> mation. (Barth, 1957:178)

Indeed, the tension which this discloses can be held to have characterised Barth's line of argument throughout (McCormack, 1995). As early as the very first part of the first volume of the *Church Dogmatics* we find surprisingly 'un-Barthian' quips about God speaking through Russian communism, blossoming shrubs and even dead dogs (Barth, 1936:60). Earlier still in *Romans* he had already referred to the 'faithfulness of God' as 'the divine patience according to which He provides, at sundry times and at many divers points in human history, occasions and possibilities and witnesses of the knowledge of His righteousness' (Barth, 1968:96). Immediately following this he referred to Jesus not as the *exclusive* locus of the knowledge of God but rather as 'the point at which it can be seen that all the other points form one line of supreme significance. He is the point at which is perceived the crimson thread which runs through all history'.

It seems then that the Barthian project is open to being extended into just the kind of rooted yet expansively self-critical theological rationality that is required. Given the uncompromising tones he adopted in the face of crisis and the relative lack of attention that he himself paid to the task of explicitly exposing the Christian tradition to the refreshment of other perspectives, it is not entirely surprising that Barth has frequently been interpreted as rejecting all possibility of such critical interaction (Pannenberg, 1976:265–76). More significant, however, is the fact that Thomas Torrance could not only expand the Barthian project in order to take explicit account of the findings of contemporary science, but that he enjoyed Barth's full support in doing so (Torrance, 1969; 1976:ix–xiii; 1985).

In the course of the present section we have already anticipated certain points which will feature as component elements in the approach to theological rationality that we ourselves most strongly favour. It will be readily apparent that our own sympathies lie far more with the claim that there is a great deal more to reason and truth than the positivists allowed for than it does with attempts to fit theology to the positivist agenda (see **2.5** in particular). This being said, however, it equally needs to be stated that, far from siding uncritically with any of the attempts which have been made to argue for a strict demarcation between rationality in the scientific and the theological domains (see **2.4** and our comments above on Barth), we see the need rather to hold these two spheres in tension and to seek for what Wittgenstein might have referred to as certain 'family resemblances' between them (Wittgenstein,

1967:32[e], 46[e]; 1969:17). In order to show something of the possibility of doing so, we turn in the next section to follow the unravelling of the logical positivist agenda in the middle part of the twentieth century. Along with this went the breaking of the stranglehold which it had exerted over both the philosophy of science in particular and the concept of rationality more generally. Before doing so, it may be helpful for you to pause awhile in order to reflect upon your own reactions to the material under discussion.

EXERCISE 2.1

1. Restate in your own words the essential challenge that logical positivism posed to claims for the rationality and truth of religious beliefs.

2. What is your assessment of the adequacy of the verificationist principle as a criterion of meaning and / or truth?

3. Outline the key differences between the four strategies here explored of possible theological response to the challenge of logical positivism.

4. Assess the respective strengths and weaknesses of these differing strategies. Which of them are you personally most in sympathy with and why?

5. What questions does all of this raise for you?

SECTION B:
MID TWENTIETH CENTURY – THE UNRAVELLING OF THE POSITIVIST AGENDA (2.7–2.9)

2.7 The problem of induction and Popperian falsificationism

Whilst the likes of Hare, Braithwaite, Bultmann and Barth were each writing against the backdrop of positivist accounts of science, philosophy of science was itself coming to view such an account as inadequate to the true character of scientific explanation. The problem, it was realised, is that whilst the available set of observations against which a proposition may be verified is always finite in extent, the propositions which most truly characterise the task of scientific explanation (i.e. all-embracing laws) are themselves universal in scope – they are more of the form 'All *x*'s are *y*' than of the form 'This *x* is *y*' (Popper, 1959:93–95). Even were it possible to extend the range of observations to include all actual cases of the relevant kind, this would still be insufficient for universal propositions, the scope of which extends to embrace not only the actual but also the hypothetical and hence as yet unobservable.

The irony then is that *a rigorous application of the verificationist criterion would have the effect of condemning the core language of science itself to meaninglessness* (Ayer, 1971:50–51). Alternatively stated, the 'strong' verificationist agenda founders on the problem of induction – that is, the question as to how one might validly move from a finite number of observations to the articulation of universal laws.

It was in response to this problem that Karl Popper (1902–94) articulated his falsificationist account of scientific rationality, at the heart of which is the belief that whilst any number of confirming instances of a given law still falls short of strict verification, even one counter instance falsifies it in just the way that it took only one sighting of a black swan to falsify the belief that all swans are white. For Popper it follows that whilst it is impossible to verify proffered laws beyond all possibility of future refutation on the basis of empirical observation, it is at least possible to distinguish between those which can be shown to be false and those which show themselves resilient in the face of all attempts to falsify them (Popper, 1959:42). This represents a reversal in the way in which scientific rationality is to be thought of as proceeding. Rather than moving inductively from observations to generalisations, the suggested way of proceeding is by deducing predictions from the available theories and then testing for them with a view to the possible refutation of the theory in question (1959:27–30; 1963:82). For Popper it is this falsificationist manner of proceeding which serves to demarcate science from non-science (1963:33–37).

More generally Popper's reversal of theory and observation marks a significant step in twentieth-century philosophy of science. It opened the way to a recovery of the more radical insight of Pierre Duhem to the effect that theory not only precedes the concern for empirical observation but actually helps to determine the character of what is observed in any given situation (Duhem, 1954, originally published in French in 1906). For example, one trained in the theory and practice of

X-ray plate interpretation observes something different when examining such a plate than does someone else without such training (Hanson, 1958). Nor was this general point lost on Popper. In *Objective Knowledge* he wrote:

> In science it is *observation* rather than perception which plays the decisive part. But observation is a process in which we play an intensely *active* part. An observation is a perception but one which is planned and prepared. We do not 'have' an observation (as we may 'have' a sense experience) but we 'make' an observation ... An observation is always preceded by a particular interest, a question, or a problem – in short, by something theoretical. (Popper, 1972:342)

We will return to the broader significance of this point a little later (see **2.9**). For the time being it is necessary to explore the possible theological implications of Popper's thought. At the outset it is important to note that whilst Popper used his falsificationist approach in order to distinguish science from non-science, he did not intend thereby to condemn all non-science to meaninglessness in the way in which the logical positivists had done (Popper, 1963:38).

2.8 Falsifiability, fallibility and theology

Whatever Popper's own intentions were in adopting falsification as a means of demarcating science from non-science, Anthony Flew in a famous essay first published in 1950 proceeded to draw the conclusion that theological statements were to be condemned as meaningless on account of their failing to meet the principle of falsification. His argument in effect was that believers normally respond to any potentially falsifying evidence by continually qualifying the expression which they give to their belief in a way which tends to evacuate their belief of any meaningful content.

Flew illustrated his point with reference to an extended version of a parable first introduced by John Wisdom concerning the differing reactions of two explorers upon encountering a clearing in which is growing a profusion of flowers. One is adamant that this must be the work of a gardener, the other sees no need to explain it in such terms. In the face of each piece of apparently disconfirming evidence (e.g. the lack of sight, sound and smell of any gardener) the believer continually makes some qualification to his belief in order to avoid having to abandon it, to the point of eventually provoking the reaction from his sceptical colleague: 'But what remains of your original assertion? Just how does what you call an invisible, intangible, eternally elusive gardener differ from an imaginary gardener or even from no gardener at all?' (Flew, 1955:96). Likewise:

> Now it often seems to people who are not religious as if there was no conceivable event or series of events the occurrence of which would be admitted by sophisticated religious people to be a sufficient reason for conceding 'There wasn't a God after all' or 'God does not really love us then' . . . Some qualification is made – God's love is 'not a merely human love' or it is 'an inscrutable love' . . . But then perhaps we ask: what is this assurance of God's (appropriately qualified) love worth, what is this apparent guarantee really a guarantee against? (1955:98–99)

Two points can be made in response to Flew, one concerning the character of theology in particular and the other concerning the way in which our theories and beliefs confront the bar of experience more generally.

To take the specifically theological point first: implicit throughout Flew's discussion is the assumption that it would be utterly contrary to the practice of theology for it to adopt a genuinely falsificationist or, perhaps better, fallibilist approach to matters of religious belief. This assumption is, however, by no means beyond question. More precisely, whilst Flew is indeed on solid ground in claiming that the theologian is concerned to scrutinise potentially falsifying arguments with a view to examining whether any credible responses might be made, the point is that this is only *part* of the task of theology. Equally important, as Nicholas Lash reminds us, is the task of acting as the bad conscience of faith – concerned to apply the tools of historical, philosophical and literary analysis to the realities of faith in a spirit of constant criticism, even to the point of their possible destruction (Lash, 1986:116; 1979:45–59). J. L. Mackie presses further in claiming that the fact and extent of evil in the world does indeed serve to falsify religious belief in such a manner as satisfies the falsificationist criteria of meaning (Mackie, 1971:92–104; 1982). Contrary to Flew then, there is no reason either *in principle* or *in practice* why theology should not be fallibilist in spirit and indeed every reason why it should be so (see **2.13**).

Granted this, Flew does seem to be correct in maintaining that individual theological propositions cannot be falsified in the straightforward manner presupposed in the falsification principle. It is always possible to salvage a particular theological proposition by making adjustments in the total framework of beliefs within which it is set (e.g. 'God's love is "not a merely human love" or it is "an inscrutable love"'). But perhaps this suggests more about the inadequacy of the falsification principle as a criterion of meaning than it does about the meaninglessness of theological propositions. This brings us to the second, more general, point that can be made in response to Flew, concerning the way in which our theories and beliefs face the bar of experience.

2.9 The Duhem–Quine rejection of thesis fallibilism

According to a thesis originally propounded by Duhem and later popularised by Willard Van Orman Quine it is no more true of scientific theories that they face the bar of experience in a discrete manner than it is of theological propositions. Rather they confront experience as an interrelated system of mutually supportive theories and auxiliary hypotheses. In Quine's terms: '. . . our statements about the external world face the tribunal of sense experience not individually but only as a corporate body' (Quine, 1953:41). And again, 'Taken collectively, science has its double dependence upon language and experience; but this duality is not significantly traceable into the statements of science taken one by one . . . The unit of empirical significance is the whole of science' (p. 42). Consequently it is never possible to point to one crucial experiment which serves to falsify a theory in a straightforward fashion for it is always possible to salvage it by making adjustments elsewhere in the overall framework of beliefs. It is worth quoting Quine's argument at length:

> The totality of our so-called knowledge or beliefs, from the most casual matters of geography and history to the profoundest laws of atomic physics or even of pure mathematics and logic, is a manmade fabric which impinges on experience only along the edges. Or, to change the figure, total science is like a field of force whose boundary conditions are experience. A conflict with experience at the periphery occasions readjustments in the interior of the field . . . Reevaluation of some statements entails reevaluation of others, because of their logical interconnections . . . But the total field is so underdetermined by its boundary conditions, experience, that there is much latitude of choice as to what statements to reevaluate in

the light of any single contrary experience. No particular experiences are linked with any particular statements in the interior of the field, except indirectly through considerations of equilibrium affecting the field as a whole. (1953:42–43)

In the light of this, the following conclusion is drawn, 'Any statement can be held true come what may, if we make drastic enough adjustments elsewhere in the system'. Likewise, 'no statement is immune to revision' and for this reason it is even 'folly to seek a boundary between synthetic statements, which hold contingently on experience, and analytic statements, which hold come what may'. In short, *in place of the image of knowledge as a superstructure erected on the basis of firm empirical foundations* (the strength of which can be tested in a piecemeal fashion), *the Duhem–Quine thesis suggests a non-foundational or post-foundational[8] image of knowledge as a complex flexible net (or web) the value of which must be determined in a more holistic way*. This points to what is arguably the most serious weakness in Popper's falsificationist account of scientific reason (and, along with this, in Flew's elevation of falsifiability to the level of a criterion of meaning): whilst Popper rejected the verificationist criterion of meaning, he continued to hold with the underlying positivist assumption that it is possible to confirm the negation of a proposition *in a discrete manner*.[9] With this in view we turn in Section C to explore the work of philosophers who have sought to articulate genuinely post-positivistic accounts of scientific reason and to reflect upon the possible

---

[8] 'Foundationalism represents the assumption that it is both necessary and possible to identify certain sure foundations for human knowledge (i.e. claims of knowledge the truth of which is absolutely certain) which underpin the rest of human knowledge by providing a firm basis upon which the ensuing edifice of human reason can be securely established' (Murray, 1998a:160 – see also 160–61). Correlatively, post-foundationalism refers to the now widespread assumption that such indubitable foundations are simply not available for real human knowing which is always rooted in and shaped, to some degree at least, by the particular contexts (historical, socio-political, psychological, linguistic, etc.) within which it operates.

[9] For the sake of accuracy it should be noted that at one point Popper does add the following rider to his thesis: 'In point of fact, no conclusive disproof of a theory can ever be produced; for it is always possible to say that the experimental results are not reliable, or that the discrepancies which are asserted to exist between the experimental results and the theory are only apparent and that they will disappear with the advance of our understanding' (Popper, 1959:50). However the broader implications of this statement do not figure in Popper's overall argument. Thomas Kuhn seems to be correct in stating: 'Having barred conclusive disproof, he has provided no substitute for it, and the relation he does employ remains that of logical falsification. Though he is not a naïve falsificationist, Sir Karl may, I suggest, legitimately be treated as one' (Kuhn, 1970a:14).

theological relevance of their work. Before doing so, however, it may again be helpful for you to pause in order to take stock of the material which has been under discussion in the present section.

EXERCISE 2.2

1(a) Can you summarise the weakness which Popper pointed to in the verificationist criterion of meaning?

1(b) What alternative strategy did Popper himself propose in place of verification?

1(c) To what extent do these differing approaches represent a contrast between inductive and deductive forms of argumentation?

2(a) How significant in your opinion is Flew's argument concerning the unfalsifiability of religious belief?

2(b) How important do you consider it to be that the discipline of theology should promote an active regard for the fragility and potential fallibility of all religious thought and practice?

3(a) How does the Duhem–Quine notion that our beliefs face the bar of experience collectively rather than discretely challenge the assumptions at work in both verificationist and falsificationist forms of positivism?

3(b) What is your reaction to the claim that it is not possible to identify any absolutely sure, certain and universally adequate 'foundations' for human knowledge?

3(c) Some assume that the lack of firm foundations makes all concern for knowledge and truth futile. Others believe that it helpfully promotes a more realistic understanding of the way in which the valid search for knowledge is always rooted, partial and fragile and hence constantly requiring to be renewed. With which of these positions do you at present find yourself most in sympathy and why?

3(d) Do you think that religious belief and the discipline of theology have more to gain or to lose from the shift to a post-foundationalist image of human knowledge? Why?

SECTION C:
LATTER PART OF THE TWENTIETH CENTURY –
REVOLUTION, ANARCHY AND RESISTANCE IN
SCIENTIFIC THEORY CHANGE,
AND THE NEED FOR TEMPERED POST-
FOUNDATIONALIST ACCOUNTS OF SCIENTIFIC
AND THEOLOGICAL RATIONALITY (2.10–2.13)

2.10   Thomas Kuhn's revolutionary account of scientific theory change

We have seen that whilst Popper replaced the overly confident image of science as dealing in proven truths with the more modest image of it as dealing in potentially refutable conjectures, he nevertheless left intact the assumption that science makes steady progress through the piecemeal testing of discrete hypotheses and theories. It is this widely held assumption that was in turn radically called into question in 1962 by the publication of Thomas Kuhn's *The Structure of Scientific Revolutions*, one of the most influential books in recent intellectual history.

Kuhn's central thesis is that scientific 'progress' over the long term shows more a pattern of occasional dramatic and total transformations in our understanding of the world (what he refers to as 'paradigm' shifts) than it does one of steady development within an enduring framework of understanding. The shift from the Ptolemaic geocentric view of the cosmos to the Copernican heliocentric world-view (see **1.12**) is one of Kuhn's favourite examples – another is the shift from Newtonian to relativistic physics (see **3.6–3.7**). According to Kuhn the effects of such paradigm shifts are so total as to be spoken of in revolutionary terms (Kuhn, 1962:92–110). Further, there seems to be no strictly logical or *reasonable* way (to continue with the image of revolutionary overthrow) in which to move from one paradigm to another (p. 94). As he wrote in his Postscript to the second edition of *The Structure of Scientific Revolutions*, 'There is no neutral algorithm for theory-choice, no systematic decision procedure which, properly applied, must lead each individual in the group to the same decision' (Kuhn, 1970b:200; see also Kuhn, 1970c:260). Each move from one paradigm to another is 'a conversion experience which cannot be forced' involving a total switch from one way of viewing the world to another, with no apparent middle state in between (Kuhn, 1962:151, 111–12, 85, 150).

Kuhn even went as far as talking of the subscribers to competing paradigms as working in different worlds with no possibility of direct communication between them (1962:121, 150; 1970c:275–76). By this he meant that they cannot even reach common agreement as to what the relevant data is, since the data itself is perceived differently within the competing paradigms (1962:94, 148–49; 1970b:199–200; 1970c:266–67). To take the case of a ball rolling along a flat surface and gradually slowing to stationary: whilst the Aristotelian philosopher perceives in this the natural propensity of a moving object to come to rest, the Newtonian physicist, in contrast, perceives the effects of friction impeding the natural propensity of a moving object to continue at uniform velocity in a straight line. Kuhn referred here to the '*incommensurability*' of competing paradigms – by which he meant that whilst they are not utterly incomparable, it is nevertheless impossible to compare them in any direct one-to-one manner.[10]

For Kuhn it is precisely this determining effect of paradigms over observation which renders them resistant to straightforward Popperian falsification. Indeed, rather than thinking of science as focused always upon the potential falsification of current paradigms, he viewed it, in its 'normal' state at least, as operating within the terms of an accepted paradigm, seeking to solve problems, explain apparent anomalies and extend the scope of its application (1962:23–42). Only when the number of anomalies reaches a critical level will a new paradigm begin to stand a chance of being widely accepted (1962:52–65). Even at this point there is likely to be much resistance (1962:150–52, 81); a resistance which will be compounded, moreover, by extra-rational factors such as formative training, personal investment of time and reputation, peer loyalty, professional patronage and the influence of ideological presuppositions, commitments and interests deriving from the broader socio-cultural milieu. For example, for an age which interpreted Scripture in a particular way and which was steeped in a metaphysic which placed the creation of humans at the centre of its cosmic story, it is not surprising that so many were initially opposed to the counter-intuitive idea that the Earth revolves around the sun (rather than *vice versa*).

[10] Cf. Kuhn, 1962:103, 112, 148; 1970c:267. The most helpful reading of what Kuhn did and did not intend in introducing this vexed notion is to be found in Richard Bernstein's *Beyond Objectivism and Relativism* (1983:20–25, 51–71, 79–93; see also Poole, 1995:44f.).

For Kuhn it is impossible for scientists ever to distance themselves completely from such factors and hence impossible for them to assess competing paradigms in a neutral fashion. To play upon the title of Thomas Nagel's book, there are for Kuhn no 'views from nowhere', only particular views from somewhere (cf. Nagel, 1986). The most that is possible is for scientists to seek to be aware of the anomalies in their own favoured paradigms and to be open to the task of applying commonly held values such as simplicity, coherency and empirical fruitfulness to the task of assessing, from their own standpoint, the relative merits of competing paradigms (Kuhn, 1970b:199; 1970c:261–62). As such, scientific theory change is held to come about less by strict rational proof than by a combination of growing discontent with the inadequacies of one theory and gradual persuasion, operating on a number of levels, that another offers a more fruitful way of looking at things.

2.11   Feyerabendian anarchism and the need for tempered post-foundationalist accounts of rationality

As Janet Martin Soskice has noted, there is a common assumption, shared both by those committed to the tenets of positivism and by those who espouse a thoroughgoing relativism, to the effect that the concern for rationality is inextricably linked with the hope of attaining to a purely objective, strictly neutral standpoint.[11] Where positivists believe that such a hope can indeed be realised, at least with regard to the empirical data of the hard sciences, relativists forego all such hopes as both illusory and oppressive and point instead to the myriad different ways in which humans creatively construe the world in word and deed (Rorty, 1979).

For those caught in this bind, Kuhn's challenge to the positivist agenda and his espousal of a holistic approach to 'paradigm' change readily located him amongst the relativists (e.g. Scheffler, 1967). The assumption was that if there is no neutral standard against which to judge the relative adequacy of competing paradigms then all is a matter of mere subjective preference (Stanesby, 1985:157). This situation was further exacerbated with the publication in 1975 of Paul Feyerabend's ominously entitled *Against Method: Outline of an Anarchistic Theory of Knowledge*.

---

[11] Soskice, 1993b:49; 1985:119–26. Bernard Williams has referred in this regard to the notion of an 'absolute conception of reality' (Williams, 1978:65–67 and *passim*).

Where Kuhn had challenged the image of science as progressing through gradual refinement and consolidation, Feyerabend challenged the more pervasive notion of there being any such thing as *the* scientific method which can be taken as the model for all human rationality. In place of this assumption Feyerabend spoke in flamboyant rhetorical tone of the history of science displaying a methodological 'anarchism' in which practically 'anything goes' which happens to contribute to the handling of specific problems (Feyerabend, 1993:27–28). Whether or not Feyerabend meant these words literally – he has since denied that he did (1993:vii, 231) – he was widely taken as claiming not simply that scientists find inspiration for their theories in the most surprising of places (cf. Popper, 1959:32), or even that all judgements are value-laden, contextual and hence partial (cf. Kuhn); more than this Feyerabend was assumed to be denying that reason and criticism perform any legitimate role at all in the practice of science and that, in contrast, all is a matter of ideological bias and perceived utility.

Throughout the controversy that has been generated by the combined effects of Kuhn's revolutionary account of scientific theory change and Feyerabend's dismissal of the notion of there being one uniquely successful and precisely definable method for organising our dealings with the world, Kuhn has consistently maintained that it represents a fundamental misinterpretation of their work to view either of them as abandoning all concern for rationality *per se* (Kuhn, 1970b:174–210; 1970c:231–78). Rather, they are to be seen as challenging an overly circumscribed model of rationality – one that does not fit even the practice of science – and as calling for it to be readjusted and changed in order 'to explain why science works as it does' (Kuhn, 1970c:264). That is, they are to be seen as pointing to the need for what we have referred to as viable post-foundationalist[12] accounts of rationality which are capable, in Bernstein's terms, of opening a way beyond the false dichotomy of a narrow objectivism on the one hand and an unconstrained relativism on the other (Bernstein, 1983). In Kuhn's own words:

> if history or any other empirical discipline leads us to believe that the development of science depends essentially on behaviour that we have previously thought to be irrational, then we should conclude not that science is irrational but that our notion of rationality needs adjustment here and there. (Kuhn, 1971:144)

[12] See note 8 above. Mary Hesse has termed this type of account of rationality 'post-empiricist'. For her account see Hesse (1980:167–86).

We have already seen the need for a comparable revisioning of theological rationality (see **2.6**). What is required is a way of holding together on the one hand a sense of the perspectively particular character of Christian faith with, on the other hand, a recognition of the need for that faith to be constantly exposed to the challenge and refreshment of other insights. Indeed we claimed that without such a concern Christian faith is in danger of appearing as a self-enclosed communal *blik* which is incapable of supporting its traditional claim to represent *the* perspective within which all aspects of reality can truly be set (cf. Aquinas, 1964:5–9, 25–27). More particularly we claimed that the central Christian beliefs concerning God's action in Christ and the Spirit require constant rethinking in dialogue with the best of contemporary scientific understanding of the processes operative in the natural order if they are not to degenerate to the level of merely inspirational myths (see **2.3** and **2.4**).

The main limitation of Kuhn's work, and even more so of Feyerabend's, is that whilst they have exposed the inadequacies of narrowly objectivist accounts of rationality, neither of them has really complemented this with a more positive account of how rationality might actually function in the more fragile, humble and partial mode which they point to. Accordingly in **2.12** and **2.13** respectively we turn to explore two such attempts to reconfigure human rationality in the light of the post-empiricist, post-foundationalist perspective which we have seen to have been opened up by the work of Quine, Kuhn, Feyerabend and others. In each case we are equally as concerned to reflect upon the possible theological relevance of the particular approach to rationality that is in view, as we are to address the question of its relevance to the scientific context.

EXERCISE 2.3

1. In what ways have the respective discussions of Kuhn's and Feyerabend's work furthered your understanding of some of the challenges which can be levelled at foundationalist/objectivist accounts of human reason?

2. What is your reaction to these challenges?

3. How might concerns to continue with a rational quest for truth best be taken forward in this context?

2.12   Imre Lakatos' account of the methodology of scientific research programmes and Nancey Murphy's theological appropriation of Lakatos

As a former student of Karl Popper and a friend of Paul Feyerabend, Imre Lakatos was well placed to seek to achieve the kind of dialectical overcoming of the objectivist-relativist dichotomy called for above. His concern was to take full account of the thesis-holism espoused by the likes of Quine and Kuhn, whilst seeking to tie this into a much stronger emphasis upon the rationality of scientific theory change than he found in Kuhn's language of incommensurable paradigms and scientific revolutions.

In place of Kuhn's somewhat vague notion of competing scientific paradigms, Lakatos set the central concept of differing collaborative 'research programmes' enduring through time and guiding the practice of different communities of scientists. *At the heart of each such research programme is a 'hard core' theory which determines its shape and identity.* Whilst revision of this 'hard core' is by no means inconceivable, such revision would amount to the abandonment of the particular research programme in question. *Surrounding the hard core and protecting it from premature abandonment is a safety belt of lower level 'auxiliary hypotheses'* which mediate between the hard core and what is deemed to count as relevant data within the purview of a particular research programme. In one direction the auxiliary hypotheses serve to define and to support the core theory and are themselves explained with reference to that core; in the other direction they guide the interpretation of appropriate data.[13]

As with Quine's account the image which suggests itself is that of an interrelated web of theories, some of which are more firmly embedded than others (the 'hard core') but none of which is open to discrete verification or falsification. It is the web as a whole which hangs together with the data that it interprets. Like Quine, Lakatos emphasised that potentially falsifying data can be accommodated within research programmes by making appropriate adjustments in the protective belt of auxiliary hypotheses in such manner as allows the central core to remain intact (Lakatos, 1970:133). The important thing for Lakatos,

---

[13] This is particularly so in the case of what Lakatos referred to as 'theories of instrumentation', by which he meant theories which are involved, either implicitly or explicitly, in the construction, use and interpretation of data-gathering instruments.

however, is that whilst this ability to preserve the hard core of any given research programme serves to slow the pace of change between competing programmes, it does not make of such changes the kind of irrational affairs which he presumed Feyerabend and Kuhn to imply. The key for Lakatos here is the fact that *research programmes do not represent mere ways of interpreting the world. Rather, they represent programmes of action which seek both to explain the available data and to guide future research*. More specifically they make predictions which can in turn be tested. On this basis he allowed a distinction to be drawn between what he referred to as 'progressive' and 'degenerative' programmes of research (1970:118).

According to Lakatos a programme is to be deemed progressive if the auxiliary hypotheses that are adopted not only serve to defend the hard core against some potentially falsifying data (what he refers to as the 'negative heuristic') but also allow for the prediction of hitherto unexpected 'novel facts'. In contrast, a programme is degenerative if all or most of the auxiliary hypotheses are added in a purely *ad hoc* manner with a view to avoiding potential disconfirmation and without themselves predicting any new facts. For Lakatos a research programme can be thought of as being pursued rationally to the degree to which it yields predictions which either are actually confirmed, or which hold out the realistic possibility of finding some significant confirmation following further investigation of new data (or the reinvestigation of existing data).

The most obvious objection that could be raised against Lakatos' position is that he nowhere specified how long it is appropriate to seek to hold to an apparently degenerating programme in the hope that further research might yield some new significant data. Without this it becomes more difficult to distinguish between progressive and supposedly degenerating programmes in any clear and unambiguous manner. One of Lakatos' own favoured examples itself illustrates this point. Prout formulated his theory to the effect that the atomic weights of all chemical elements are whole numbers as early as 1815. There followed, however, a considerable stretch of time during which there were periods when, in Lakatosian terms, it could easily have been abandoned as degenerative. Indeed, it was only on account of the perseverance and tenacity of its advocates that it eventually succeeded in establishing itself (Lakatos, 1970:138–40). This point could be pressed further: the attraction of Lakatos' approach is that it appears to point to a mechanism for rational adjudication between competing research programmes; on closer inspection, however, it becomes apparent that Lakatos no more provides a precise formula for rational theory choice than is to be found in the work of Kuhn or Feyerabend.

In response it could be argued that to find Lakatos wanting in this regard is to miss the real point of what he was seeking to do. It is clear from the role that he attributed to 'auxiliary hypotheses' in the interpretation of 'data' that he fully accepted that research programme adoption, adaptation and potential rebuttal is a matter of holistic judgement rather than precise formulation. As such he is best viewed not as one searching for a guaranteed algorithm with which to escape the ambiguity of judgement but rather as one seeking to expand the range of resources available for guiding this process in a rational manner. His own particular contribution was to argue that the somewhat negative move of adapting a research programme in the face of potentially disconfirming data can be complemented by the more positive move of seeking for a progressive coherence with 'novel facts' which it can be held to predict. As such he has made a significant contribution to the search for a viable post-foundationalist or post-empiricist rationality.

For this reason, were it possible to transpose Lakatos' thought into the theological sphere then it might be expected to make an equally significant contribution there as it has already been found to make in the scientific sphere. At the very least such a transposition would show that there are significant family resemblances between the ways in which rationality functions in the respective domains of science and theology, and hence good reasons for believing that the insights and concerns of these two disciplines can be brought together in a mutually constructive interchange. Nancey Murphy has sought to achieve just such a theological transposition of Lakatos' thought in what is continuing to develop as one of the most exciting 'research programmes' in the contemporary theology-and-science landscape.

The most extended presentation of Murphy's case is to be found in her *Theology in the Age of Scientific Reasoning* (1990). Her strategy is two-fold: firstly, to indicate the theological relevance of Lakatos' basic account of the structure of science by pointing to examples of 'coherent series of theories in theology that have the formal properties of a research programme' and secondly, to claim that some of these can be deemed empirically progressive in a manner comparable to that intended by Lakatos (Murphy, 1990:86, 183–92). For Murphy, talk of there being a 'hard core' to theological research programmes is best thought of along the lines of David Kelsey's notion of a '. . . "single, synoptic, imaginative judgement" regarding what Christianity is all about' which serves to give a particular theological project its distinctive shape and focus (Murphy, 1990:184). Where 'God is the God of the oppressed' might be taken as the 'hard core' of liberation theology, Murphy's own inclination at the time of writing *Theology in the Age of Scientific Reasoning* was to identify the hard core of Christian belief with the doctrine of the Trinity (1990:184; 1994:106). She has since given this a more practical slant by pushing it back to the more fundamental notion of the self-giving, kenotic character of God's being in action as revealed in Jesus (Murphy and Ellis, 1996).

Howsoever the hard core of Christian belief is defined, once it has been identified the next step in a Lakatosian theology is to evaluate the extent to which all other significant aspects of theology mediate successfully between the hard core on the one hand and what is judged to be the total range of relevant data on the other hand (Murphy, 1990:186–98). The rationale here is that where some of these lower level doctrines might appear almost exclusively concerned with the further conceptual clarification of the hard core – as does, for example, the *homoousion* ('of one substance') clause in Christology – others, most notably the doctrines of revelation and the Holy Spirit, relate equally closely to the identification, interpretation and discrimination of potentially relevant theological data. For example, a sufficiently broad doctrine of revelation would support the treating of data from practically any source whatsoever as being of potential theological significance. Murphy's own preference is to focus, in the main, upon data arising from the interpretation of Scripture and the discernment of God's presence and address in the life of the believing community (1990:188–89).

More precisely, she argues that theories of scriptural interpretation and of spiritual discernment function within theology in a manner comparable to the role performed by theories of instrumentation in the scientific context (1990:130–73; 1994:107–22). Indeed, in what is undoubtedly the most original part of her argument, she claims that such theories can be put to work in order to yield significant new data against which it is possible to test the accuracy of certain predictions arising from particular theological programmes. For example she signals that the claim that it is appropriate to address the Holy Spirit as *she* might be tested against a widespread process of communal Christian discernment as to whether or not this is indeed the will of God (1990:167–68). More generally, the image which this suggests is one of Christian communities as living laboratories in which theological hypotheses can be put to the test (1990:166; 1994:121).

Murphy's Lakatosian account undoubtedly makes a significant contribution to the search for a viable post-foundational approach to theological rationality. As with Lakatos, her particular contribution is to extend an essentially coherence-based approach to rational judgement[14] beyond the mere concern to maintain overall coherence in the face of potentially disconfirming data. Her approach complements this with the need also for progressive coherence with certain predicted 'novel facts'. Vital though it is, however, the rational testing of theological positions by no means constitutes the entirety of theological activity and hence cannot be thought of as an exhaustive account of theological rationality. The point is that the testing of theological positions presupposes their prior articulation. In this regard Christian theology is constantly facing new challenges and new situations (e.g. the challenge posed by the rise of feminism) which require the tradition to be rethought and reworked (see Chapter 6). Further, this reworking does not represent a merely reactionary concern to maintain the tradition at all costs; rather it goes to the very heart of the Christian understanding of the truth of God in Christ and the Holy Spirit as a living truth which continues to impact on new situations in ever new ways.

When viewed in this light, the task of Christian theology is seen to be rightly focused as much upon an expansive exploration of what possibilities are open for the refreshment, renewal and rearticulation of the tradition, as it is upon a rigorous testing of the ensuing proffered positions. Accounts of theological rationality must therefore attend to

---

[14] As the name suggests, coherence-based approaches to truth and reason typically emphasise the relevance of the degree of overall coherence which pertains within a given body of beliefs to questions concerning the truth-status of that body of beliefs. See **1.7** for coherence as an overall term for a variety of criteria of theory-comparison. Where some would view truth as actually consisting in propositional coherence, others settle for viewing such coherence as the most reliable means of testing for truth as correspondence to reality (see Rescher, 1973).

each of these aspects of theological work. Accordingly, we believe that Murphy's proposal, valuable though it is, requires to be set within a more rounded account of theological rationality as a whole; one that pays equal attention to both the constructive and the critical / evaluative moments in Christian theology. Related to this, we believe that it also needs to be complemented by a more explicit appreciation for the essentially practical focus of theological work. Our earlier dismissal of non-cognitivist accounts of Christian faith was rooted in the conviction that at the heart of the Christian tradition is the reality of God's action rather than a set of merely human ideas or ethical ideals (see **2.3**). It was suggested there that *Christianity consists neither in a mere way of looking at the world, nor simply in a way of living within it, but in a lived process of deepening conformity to the transforming action of God in Christ and the Holy Spirit.*

This point has direct bearing upon the function of theology within the Christian tradition, for it suggests that the constructive dimension of theological work referred to above should never be driven by a mere concern to renew Christian *concepts* alone (as opposed, more funda-mentally, to Christian living also) in the light of contemporary ways of *thinking*. Rather it should be driven by the ultimately practical concern always to understand better how to respond to, and so manifest more cogently, the living truth of God. As Murphy herself states, 'The point of being a Christian is not first of all to acquire knowledge, but rather to be obedient to Christ' (1990:196). Again, as is clear from the impact of feminist theory on Christian circles, the task of theological analysis in both its constructive and its evaluative modes must be held in close relationship with the need for constant ecclesial renewal. Anything less threatens to reduce Christian belief to the level of a mere ideology detached from material reality.

When viewed in these terms, Murphy's otherwise excellent appli-cation of Lakatosian methodology to the rational assessment of theological programmes appears somewhat truncated as an account of theological rationality in the round. Whilst she acknowledges that Christian faith is more about conformity to Christ than it is the mere acquisition of knowledge, when she turns her attention to the task of theology she defines it purely in terms of the analysis of beliefs. As she states, 'I suggest that theology is a *rational reconstruction* of the beliefs of a Christian community. Its job is to examine the community's belief system in order to display the relations among its parts and its justification relative to whatever else there is' (1990:196). Whilst this is right, in so far as it goes, the problem is that it does not go far enough. More specifically, we would suggest that Murphy's notion of Christian theology as being focused upon the rational assessment of beliefs in turn requires complementing with a more explicit emphasis upon the way in which such beliefs may already be called into question by live issues concerning the adequacy of the practices which they promote. *What is required is a model of rationality which is capable of holding together the assessment of theory and belief on the one hand with the analysis and evaluation of practice on the other.*

Alternatively stated, what this points to is the need for a broader account of theological rationality than can be supported by a transposition of Lakatosian methodology alone. Lakatos stands with the majority of philosophers of science in assuming a more or less strict demarcation between the question as to the rational justification of theoretical frameworks on the one hand and the ethical evaluation of their potential applications on the other. Consequently, for all the contribution which he made to the rational assessment of competing research programmes in a post-foundationalist perspective, his work offers little or no help with the larger and arguably prior task of assessing the value of such programmes (i.e. whether they should be pursued at all)[15] in terms of the practices which they support.

Somewhat in contrast to this received view, Chapter 10 explores the work of philosophers who argue for the recontextualisation of science and technology within a prior, explicitly ethical debate. Indeed it is to be noted that Murphy in her most recent work, written in collaboration with George Ellis, argues for just such a location of science within a wider context of explicitly ethical concern. The implication is that there is just as much need for the kind of extended vision of rationality in the scientific context as we have pointed to in the theological: that is, one which combines the standard *cognitive* concern for the assessment of theory and belief with an *ethical* concern for the analysis and evaluation of practice, and which pursues each of these concerns in a genuinely post-foundationalist manner. The work of the Pittsburgh-based philosopher Nicholas Rescher presents us with just such an account of rationality.

---

[15] See **1.5.1 note 11, 1.20**.

EXERCISE 2.4

1. How helpful do you find Lakatos' account of scientific research programmes as a contribution to the task of seeking to articulate a constructive post-foundationalist account of human rationality?

2. What questions and difficulties does it raise for you?

3. What new insights does it open up?

4. How helpful do you find Murphy's attempted theological appropriation? Again, seek to identify the specific questions and/or new insights which it prompts for you.

2.13   Nicholas Rescher's pragmatic-idealist account of human rationality and its theological significance

According to Rescher, one of the best ways to gain an initial under-standing of a philosopher's work is to know who his or her philosophical heroes are. For Rescher, three stand out from amongst the many lesser others whose combined influence contributes to the distinctive combination of expansive *coherentism*, conceptual *idealism* and tempered *pragmatism* which characterises his work.[16] They are the German thinkers Gottfried Wilhelm Leibniz (1646–1716) and Immanuel Kant (1724–1804) and the American philosopher Charles Sanders Peirce (1839–1914).

Leibniz's influence manifests itself both in a commitment to the role of formal logic in the elucidation of philosophical problems. Also in an expansive, architectonic vision which views the task of philosophy as consisting in an ever-renewed attempt to present a coherent, systematic

---

[16] Even more so than is the case with the term 'coherentism' (see note 14 in this chapter), 'idealism' and 'pragmatism' are terms used variously to refer to a wide range of differing yet related positions. Where the central integrating assumption at work in all forms of idealism is that reality is somehow mind-dependent or 'mind-co-ordinated' (for more on this, see Rescher, 1992a:187–91), the central idea throughout the various shades of pragmatism is that questions of truth require to be held together with considerations of practical efficacy (for more on this, see Rescher, 1995:710–13). The combined influence respectively of coherentist, pragmatist and idealist emphases on Rescher's thought is signalled by the overall title that he gave to his three volume *magnum opus* – he calls his work in its vast interconnected entirety *A System of Pragmatic Idealism* (see Rescher, 1992b; 1993a; 1994).

account of the way in which, in Wilfrid Sellars' words, 'things in the broadest possible sense of the term hang together in the broadest possible sense of the term' (Sellars, 1963:1). For Rescher, there is nothing that is ultimately irrelevant to this task; there is no sense in which the expansive, systematic urge of philosophy can be thought of as being brought to a point of stasis and irreformable finality.

In turn, Kant's influence is at its clearest in Rescher's espousal of the idealist claim that our ways of understanding the world really are *our* ways; ways, that is, which might be quite different were our own composition in turn different to the way in which it in fact is. However, Rescher does not view this constructive role of the mind as operating without all constraint. Rather, *he views our conceptual frameworks and human rationality more generally, as being shaped by a process of successful evolutionary interaction with a world that is really there.* Nevertheless, he stands fully with the force both of Sellars' attack on 'the myth of the given' and Wittgenstein's analysis of language to the effect that there is no possibility of our attaining to a pre-conceptual, pre-linguistic understanding of reality and, hence, no possibility either of our successfully pursuing a foundationalist approach to rationality.

What marks Rescher out as significant for present purposes is the fact that he by no means equates this with a fundamental disavowal of rationality and truth *per se*. Rather his concern is to seek an approach to rationality and truth that is genuinely fitted to the exigencies of this situation. It is here that the influence of Charles Sanders Peirce is at its most evident. Like Peirce, Rescher intends to maintain a firm grasp on the cognitive dimension of truth. Whilst he accepts that truth cannot be directly assessed in terms of correspondential accuracy, he equally maintains that it should continue to be defined in such terms and this regardless of the fact that it must always function as an ideal to be aspired towards, rather than as a terminus at which one can know that one has arrived. Again like Peirce, Rescher looks to practical consider-ations as providing a reality principle against which it is possible to test the strength of our truth claims.

More precisely, whilst Rescher accepts that pragmatic benefit cannot be taken as a direct indicator of cognitive truth at the level of individual theses – false theses can after all support desirable consequences[17] – he

---

[17] Such as for example the thesis that 'unless conserved, all the Earth's non-renewable resources will be exhausted by 2005' or that 'enemies always give up their hate if they know themselves loved'.

maintains that it can be legitimately applied at the methodological level as a measure of whether or not a particular method is effective for the purposes for which it is intended. When it is recalled that our purposes in seeking after truth are both cognitive (i.e. to gain understanding) and practical (i.e. to better organise our dealings with reality), Rescher is left in no doubt that it is consistently the findings of coherentist methods of truth assessment which show such methods to be the most effective means of seeking after truth. More precisely, for Rescher, whilst the adoption of a coherentist approach to truth assessment cannot guarantee the attainment of truth, it does at least guarantee that one is moving in the direction in which truth (and that as traditionally defined in terms of correspondential accuracy) is best sought. So truth is to be *defined* in correspondential terms, but *assessed* in terms of the coherence of the rational framework which both attempts to describe reality and to indicate ways to respond authentically to that reality.

This brings us to the very heart of Rescher's approach to truth and rationality. For Rescher, pure objective neutrality and unassailable certainty are each impossible to attain. We are always already engaged in value-laden practices of knowing the world, the veracity of which are constantly called into question by the existence of other differently value-laden practices. Again, whilst Rescher's aforementioned emphasis upon the evolutionary adaptation of human reason to reality helps to reassure us, against radical sceptical concerns, that our value-laden practices of knowing do indeed have some hold on reality; the fact that he views truth as an ideal state which always eludes full and final attainment should equally serve to counteract any complacency concerning the adequacy of current states of knowledge. In contrast, it should act as a constant reminder of the partial, fragile, value-laden nature of all human knowing and of the consequent need for current states of knowledge to be constantly exposed to potential revision. For Rescher, it is precisely such an expansive, recursive, fallibilistic model of rationality which is in mind in his advocacy of coherentist approaches to truth assessment.

Thus far attention has been concentrated upon Rescher's treatment of the cognitive dimension of human rationality. Since the late 1970s he has progressively complemented this with a more adequate treatment of the evaluative and practical dimensions of rationality also. The result is that Rescher's mature thought presents an integrated and genuinely post-foundationalist account of the complex interweaving of human rationality in its cognitive, evaluative and practical dimensions. It is an account which retains a concern for the cognitive dimension of truth whilst setting this within the context of a strong sense of the human knowing subject as first and foremost an engaged agent in the world.

For such reasons the hope is raised that a theological appropriation of Rescher's thought will support just the kind of contextually rooted, yet dynamically expansive account of theological reason that was earlier held to be required by an authentic understanding of Christian truth and tradition (see **2.12**).[18] In the light of what has emerged in the course of the present chapter, however, any such appropriation will have to be clearly distinguished from what in present terms would appear as a theologically inappropriate and philosophically incoherent attempt to establish Christian theology on the basis of Rescher's post-foundationalist account of rationality. In other words, theologically speaking, the most appropriate kind of interaction between philosophical work, on the one hand, and the Christian tradition, on the other hand, will be one that unfolds as a subsequent drawing of Rescherian insights into an enriching conversation with resonant emphases already widely acknowledged as being intrinsic to the Christian tradition; the purpose being to seek by so doing to grant these emphases clearer voice in such a manner as will extend their shaping power over the practice of theology more generally.

Perhaps paramount here is the traditional emphasis upon the unknowability of God. As Rescher himself notes, it is the very reality of the object that is at issue in faith (i.e. the inexhaustibly rich mystery that is God) which itself serves to place in permanent question the adequacy of any attempt to give truthful expression to it (Rescher, 1993b:131). However, whilst this features as a traditional tenet of Christian belief, at the level of theological practice it is all too frequently smothered by a somewhat less humble tone rather more at home with certainties than it is with open questions. A theologically-focused engagement with Rescher's recursively expansive and determinedly fallibilist account of rationality at this point will help to restore something of the ethic of continual conversion and renewal by which Christian theology, as with the entirety of Christian living, should be distinguished.

---

[18] Some of what follows in the remainder of this section has already been published in Murray, 1998a:167–68. We acknowledge with thanks permission from *The Way* to reproduce the relevant material here.

Likewise, a theologically engaged reflection upon Rescher's vision of rationality as a dynamic interweaving of cognitive, evaluative and practical concerns (as prompted by specific questions and occurrences) will in turn promote a heightened sense of the ultimately practical focus of theological work. More precisely, it will promote a heightened sense of the way in which the theological concern to understand God, the world and the relationship between the two is most appropriately set within the prior context of the dual practical concern to weigh the world in the light of Christ and to live within it in the transforming power of the Spirit. Taken in conjunction with the previous point, it will promote the view of Christian tradition as not just a conservative, retrospective force but as equally a creative, prospective impulse which continues to unfold ever anew in diverse situations. Such an emphasis by no means excludes the possibility of certain parameters of thought and patterns of action becoming recognised as essential to the authentic continuance of Christian identity. Indeed correctly understood it can be held to require it. Nevertheless, it does represent a recovery of the sense in which the promised infallibility of the Church should serve to encourage Christian communities to risk discerning new answers to new questions and not merely to root them in what they inherit.

Alternatively stated, it suggests that the appropriate grounding of Christian thought and practice in what have become recognised as the distinctive patterns of Christian faith should never be allowed to justify the petrifying of theology into a self-enclosed discourse – a discourse which feels assured of its full and final adequacy, and which is immune from all challenge and criticism from without. On the contrary, the cosmic scope of the belief in the risen Christ's universally particular presence to all of created reality should itself impel Christian communities to adopt as expansive a vision in the theological sphere as Rescher advocates in the philosophical. This in turn holds implications for the range of contexts in which, and people by whom, this process of continuously renewed reflection upon the nature of Christian identity is properly pursued in a way which serves significantly to blur any supposed boundary between the *ecclesia docens* (the 'teaching church') and the *ecclesia discens* (the 'listening church'). Whilst all of this reintroduces an element of risk to the practice of Christian theology, sustaining it throughout should be the memory that the central Christian narratives themselves identify the very truth and purpose of God with the creative embrace of such risk and vulnerability.

EXERCISE 2.5

1. How helpful do you find the kind of approach to rationality that Rescher advocates?

2. What is your reaction to the claims made here for its potential relevance to the theological sphere?

2.14   Summary and conclusion

The present chapter started out with the caricatured assumption that science stands as *the* model of rationality in such a manner as leaves no place for theology to be understood as a rational discipline. This assumption was examined more closely in the guise of logical positivism, as also were the strengths and weaknesses of four differing theological strategies for responding to the challenge which it posed. The central section of the chapter traced the unravelling of the positivist agenda in the middle part of the twentieth century and the shift towards a more modest account of scientific rationality in the work of Karl Popper. This story was continued into the final section where we traced the rise of holistic accounts of scientific rationality in the work of Quine and Kuhn and the final disavowal, in the work of Paul Feyerabend, of the claim that there is any such thing as *the* scientific method which defines the essence of rationality.

Emergent from this discussion was the realisation that whilst the demise of positivism and the move beyond philosophical foundationalism served to re-open the possibility of taking explicitly tradition-bound discourses such as theology seriously; such a move equally requires complementing with viable accounts of how rationality should function in post-foundationalist perspective. Without such accounts, the move beyond foundationalistic objectivism appears simply to sanction a collapse into unconstrained relativism (Bernstein, 1983). In the hope of finding some guidance we turned in the final two sub-sections of the chapter to consider the work of Imre Lakatos and Nicholas Rescher respectively, each time with a view to the potential theological relevance of their work. We found that whilst they each make a real contribution to the search for a viable post-empiricist, post-foundationalist account of rationality, Lakatos' approach to the assessment of theoretical frameworks requires to be set within the broader vision of rationality espoused by Rescher.

In short, where the chapter started out with the positivistic assumption as to the exemplary rational character of science and the corresponding irrationality of theology, it drew to a close with two examples of the family resemblances which can be traced between the operation of rationality in each of these contexts when viewed within a post-foundationalist perspective (**2.12** and **2.13** respectively). *This in turn lends weight to the assumption underlying the entirety of this book: that it is both possible and fruitful to seek to bring the insights and concerns of these two perspectively distinct disciplines together in a mutually constructive interchange.* Indeed, the necessary self-critical openness to other traditions of thought and practice which has been seen to be such an essential feature of rationality in a post-foundationalist perspective itself demands such a mutual interchange.

Going beyond this, the present chapter has already highlighted certain aspects of science and theology which themselves prompt the need for a mutually constructive interchange. On the one hand, we have seen that whilst science is quite appropriately methodologically agnostic or naturalistic (in the sense that it leaves questions about the ultimate origin and end of things out of account), it nevertheless serves to raise questions which cannot be answered within its own perspective, in such a manner as itself suggests the need for them to be set within the broader perspectives of metaphysical and theological reflection (see **2.5**). Again, we have seen the need for science to be set within a prior context of explicitly ethical debate in such a manner as provides renewed impetus to the need for constructive dialogue between science and religious traditions (see **2.12**).

On the other hand, we have seen that the distinctiveness of Christian theology consists not in its treating of God *as opposed* to any of the things which constitute the furniture of the world but rather in its treating of all that is within the perspective of God as its 'origin and end' (see **2.5** and **2.6**; Aquinas, 1964:27, 9). For this reason Christian theology must, by its very nature, be concerned with what can be known of creaturely reality on the basis of other disciplines. In accordance with this, it has been claimed that the openness to challenge, refreshment and renewal which this necessitates goes to the very heart of the character of God's continuing impact in Christ and the Holy Spirit on the diverse particularities of created reality. In turn, and related to this, it has been indicated that the credibility of these central claims concerning the reality of God's act in Christ and the Holy Spirit itself requires those claims to be thought through in dialogue with what can be known of the processes operative in the world in the purview of the natural sciences (see **2.3** and **2.4**). Each of these points will be treated more fully in subsequent chapters.

FURTHER READING

BANNER, M. C. (1990) *The Justification of Science and the Rationality of Religious Belief* (Oxford: Clarendon Press).

BERNSTEIN, R. J. (1983) *Beyond Objectivism and Relativism: Science, Hermeneutics and Praxis* (Oxford: Blackwell)

MARSONET, M. (1996) *The Primacy of Practical Reason: An Essay on Nicholas Rescher's Philosophy* (Lanham, MD: University Press of America)

MURPHY, N. (1990) *Theology in the Age of Scientific Reasoning* (Ithaca, NY: Cornell University Press)

SOSKICE, J. M. (1993) 'Bad language in science and religion', in *Explorations in Science & Theology: The Templeton London Lectures at the RSA* (London: RSA), pp. 69–78

—— (1993) 'The truth looks different from here, or: on seeking the unity of truth from a diversity of perspectives', in *Christ in Context: The Confrontation Between Gospel and Culture*, ed. by Hilary D. Regan and Alan J. Torrance (Edinburgh: T&T Clark), pp. 43–59

VAN HUYSSTEEN, J. W. (1989) *Theology and the Justification of Faith: Constructing Theories in Systematic Theology*, transl. H. F. Snijders (Grand Rapids, MI: Eerdmans)

BOOK TWO

Chapter 3

Theology and the New Physics

3.1 Introduction

In this chapter we shall look first of all at the powerful (and continuing) influence of Newtonian thinking (Section A). Then we shall consider two ways in which physics has parted company with the Newtonian world-view: through the rediscovery of time (Section B), and the rediscovery of the observer (Section C) – noting some theological implications. We go on to look at issues in modern cosmology – the beginning and end of the universe (Section D) and the possible rediscovery of purpose (Section E). Finally we consider the new science of chaos and complexity (Section F).

SECTION A:
CLASSICAL PHYSICS AND THE NEWTONIAN
WORLD-VIEW (3.2–3.4)

3.2 The scientific revolution

The century and a half from the middle of the sixteenth century to the end of the seventeenth is, with some justification, regarded as a watershed in the development of the natural sciences. Beginning with the publication of Nicolaus Copernicus' '*De Revolutionibus*' (*On the Revolutions of the Celestial Spheres*) in 1543 and culminating in the appearance of Isaac Newton's '*Principia*' (*Mathematical Principles of Natural Philosophy*) in 1687, a succession of radical thinkers revolutionised the disciplined study of the physical world. Among the main achievements of these early scientists were the establishment of a potentially simpler heliocentric model of the solar system in preference to the geocentric model favoured at the time (Copernicus, 1473–1543); the application of experimental method and mathematical analysis to the study of motion (Galileo, 1564–1642); the refinement and mathematisation of the heliocentric model (Kepler, 1571–1630); and the grand synthesis of these elements to show that all the situations under consideration, whether Earthbound or celestial, could be explained in terms of three mathematical laws of motion and a law of universal gravitation (Newton, 1642–1727).

Certain common assumptions regarding the nature of the physical world may be gleaned from this body of scientific work. The world as seen through the eyes of these men is ultimately simple. Natural phenomena may appear on the surface to be unimaginably complex but, according to classical physics, there is an underlying simplicity. Specifically, all the natural phenomena that really matter can be expressed in mathematical statements. The founders of modern physics were quite clear on what really mattered. They distinguished between primary and secondary qualities. The former (mass, extension and duration) can be quantified and measured accurately. They are, therefore, amenable to the combination of experimentation and mathematical analysis adopted by classical physics. Secondary qualities (such as colour, temperature and hardness), by contrast, could not be measured accurately and were, at that time, dismissed as subjective. The world they envisaged was well-ordered, stable and predictable. Indeed subsequent generations of classical physicists were prepared to argue that, in principle, the future motion of every particle in the universe is predictable given an accurate knowledge of their positions, masses and velocities at some arbitrary point in time (see our discussion of Laplace in **1.17**).

3.3   From method to world-view

This Newtonian paradigm had an impact that extended far beyond the methods of the virtuosi and the doors of the learned societies. According to Holton and Roller,

> So impressive were the victories of Newtonian mechanics that, in the early part of the 18th Century, there spread a mechanistic world-view which asserted that man's confident intellect could eventually reduce *all* phenomena and problems to the level of mechanical

interpretations. The development of this new view through the extrapolation of the findings of science to philosophy was carried out mainly by philosophers, and it had important effects on economics, the 'science of man', religion, and political theory. (Holton and Roller, 1958:207)

However, in order to understand why something as far removed from practical concerns as a law of gravity should so catch the public imagination, we must recall that science does not exist in a vacuum. The peculiar attraction of Newtonian mechanics becomes much clearer when it is set in its wider cultural context (a task which is dealt with in detail by Toulmin, 1990:45–87).

Europe had been divided on religious lines after the Reformation. After an initial period of hostility, efforts at reconciliation (or, at least, at finding some way for divided communities to co-exist) began during the sixteenth century, which proved to be a brief golden age during which the arts, the sciences, and indeed a revived magical practice all flourished. However, efforts at reconciliation between Roman Catholic and Protestant failed. The first two decades of the seventeenth century were marked by growing intolerance, culminating with the opening shots of the Thirty Years' War in 1618. In the wake of war came severe economic instability, famine and disease. Not surprisingly, apocalyptic speculation was rife, with Christ's return widely expected to occur before the end of the century.

This anarchy inevitably generated a desire for order and stability. But where were these to be found? Religion had been tried in the fires of the Thirty Years' War and found seriously wanting. The cultural and political leadership of Europe began to seek elsewhere for a secure basis for social order. A crucial part of their answer was the rationalistic philosophy of René Descartes (1596–1650). Perhaps human reason could succeed where religious tradition and authority had failed.

Rationalism offered the scientists of the seventeenth century a powerful device for underwriting the reliability and universality of their assertions. The mental discipline of subjecting their interpretations of nature to reason distinguished early modern science from competing ways of viewing the natural world. Classical physics, in turn, provided the exercise of reason (in conjunction with experimentation) with an early success story. The Newtonian paradigm in physics represented the successful adaptation of science to the new emphasis on universal truths of reason. And it did for the natural world what Cartesian rationalism promised to do for human society – it ushered in a new era of order and stability.

In the exhaustion that followed the Peace of Westphalia (1648), Descartes and Newton offered the intellectuals of Europe the hope of a new way forward. Within half a century their ideas dominated Western philosophy and science. The despair and hopelessness that led the intellectuals of 1650 to speculate about the imminent end of the world was swept away. In its place was a new vision – of a just society empowered by human reason, progressing towards an undefined goal in the future.

The success of the Newtonian paradigm in physics encouraged others to emulate it in other spheres. In particular, it offered the ruling élites a new and authoritative image for the ideal society. The modern nation state as it began to emerge in the eighteenth century was modelled upon the world of Newtonian astronomy. Like the solar system, it was centralised – a central authority (whether it be *le Roi Soleil*, a constitutional monarch, or a democratically-elected government) wielding authority over successive circles of subjects, all of whom knew their places. On a smaller scale this centralised pattern was reflected in the paternalistic family. Social Newtonians (notably Newton's staunch advocate Samuel Clarke) insisted that the order of nature indicated the rightness of the social order – that we should be content with our rulers and with our station in life. This is the outlook enshrined in that politically incorrect verse from 'All things bright and beautiful' by Cecil Alexander (1818–95):

> The rich man in his castle,
> The poor man at his gate,
> God made them high and lowly
> And ordered their estate.

According to Margaret Wertheim,

> The Newtonian society, like the Newtonian cosmos, was a lawful, stable, immutable, and supposedly God-given order. Just as the planets remained fixed in their respective orbits, human beings were to remain fixed in their respective 'stations' . . . It was thus humanity's moral duty to emulate in the social realm the order Newton had discovered in nature. And so, . . . Newtonian science in the eighteenth [century] was enlisted to justify the status quo. (Wertheim, 1995:132)

3.4   Change and continuity in the physical sciences

In the nineteenth century Newton's laws of motion proved to be equally valid for the motion of charged particles in electromagnetic fields, raising hopes that a complete description of the physical world could be achieved within the Newtonian paradigm. Indeed one of the most eminent physicists of the nineteenth century, Lord Kelvin, was so convinced of the completeness of Newtonian physics that he is reputed to have advised young people against a career in physics – all the really interesting work had been done; all that was left was the tidying up of loose ends.

Among those loose ends were two intractable problems which Kelvin himself admitted to be clouds on the horizon of physics. One was the failure of the Michelson–Morley Experiment to detect the motion of the Earth through the aether (the medium through which it was assumed light must be propagated). The other was the failure of classical physics to account for the colour of hot objects – the spectrum of black-body radiation. His identification of those clouds was almost prophetic – within a few years of his death they had grown into great storms. One gave rise ultimately to relativity theory; the other to quantum theory. Together these new theories amounted to a revolution in our understanding of the physical world.

However, while the content of the physical sciences may have changed radically, there remain underlying continuities. These continuities are highlighted by the marginal place of the new physics in elementary science education.[1] Critics sometimes deplore the fact that very little of the new physics appears in the average school science syllabus. But such criticisms betray a superficial understanding of science. Content is less important than method and attitude. For today's physics students, the role models are still men like Galileo, Kepler, Newton, Joule, Coulomb, Faraday, Maxwell and Kelvin. Einstein and Hawking may have become icons of science in the popular mind but they have so far had little impact on attitudes and methods. As for great women physicists, Marie Curie stands alone as a romantic figure in the popular mind – and her contribution to physics is still undervalued by a physics establishment that perpetuates the sexist

---

[1] For a discussion of new trends in science education as they relate to religion see Chapter 8.

myth that her husband Pierre was the creative member of the partnership.[2]

The formative assumptions of physics may be enumerated in a variety of ways. One example would be Coulson's account of the scientific method in his *Science and Christian Belief* (1958:42–83). He presents an idealised vision of the scientist as one who comes to his task with honesty, integrity, hope, enthusiasm, humility, singleness of mind, willingness to co-operate with others, patience and critical judgment – the gifts of the scientific spirit. Furthermore he highlights certain assumptions without which science would make little headway and reminds us of their roots in the Judaeo-Christian world-view:

> that common search for a common truth; that unexamined belief
> that facts are correlatable . . . that unprovable assumption that there
> is an 'order and constancy in Nature,' without which the patient
> effort of the scientist would be only so much incoherent babbling
> and his publication of it in a scientific journal for all to read pure
> hypocrisy; all of it is a legacy from religious conviction. (Coulson
> 1958:75)

Specifically, it is a legacy of the mediaeval synthesis, the world-view that informed Christendom. That the legacy continues to influence physics in the twentieth century will be a theme of the next section.

SECTION B:
THE REDISCOVERY OF TIME (3.5–3.9)

3.5   Classical physics and the exorcism of time

At first sight, classical physics appears to lend support to the commonsense view of time – that only present events exist; past events have ceased to exist, and future ones do not yet exist. In Newtonian physics time is linear and uniform with physical reality restricted to present events and things.

However, on closer examination we find that classical physics treats time as entirely external to and independent of the physical world. In spite of its apparent ontological priority, the present has no special status

---

[2] Wertheim (1995:173) cites comments to this effect made at a meeting of the American Physical Society in 1972.

in the Newtonian scheme. Indeed, far from explaining or integrating time into its theories, the first priority of classical physics appears to have been to eliminate it from consideration. Classical physics is characterised by the quest for laws that do not vary with time (or make no reference to time). This bias amounts to what Ilya Prigogine has described as an exorcism of time (Prigogine and Stengers, 1984:291f.) from classical physics.

This is not to suggest that physicists made a conscious decision to exclude time from consideration. Rather such an exclusion follows naturally (and unconsciously) from certain philosophical and theological assumptions that were widespread in seventeenth- and eighteenth-century Europe.

One of these assumptions was the sharp division of reality into two incommensurable realms. On the one hand, there is *res cogitans*: the intelligible realm, the province of subjectivity, of mind, soul and spirit (and, hence, of religion and supernature). On the other hand, there is *res extensa*: the material realm, the province of nature and science. According to Descartes, the entities of *res extensa* possessed no other properties besides spatial extension. It was a passive world amenable to the physicists' ideal of quantification.

The significance of this dualism for a physical account of time becomes clear in the light of the very close association between time and mind. As Genevieve Lloyd puts it, 'we cannot think consciousness without thinking time, or time without thinking consciousness . . . if we take away the thought of consciousness, time also vanishes' (Lloyd, 1993:2). The Cartesian elimination of mind from physical reality could only result in a similar elimination of time or, at least, its reduction to an external parameter. As a result, classical physics became the observation of a world characterised only by extension from the vantage point of a quasi-divine spectator, namely, from eternity.

Another factor affecting the classical physical treatment of time was the dominant interpretation of eternity in Christian theology. This tended to be treated either as timelessness or a present that does not pass away. Typical is the following passage from Boethius:

> Embracing the infinite lengths of past and future, it [God's knowledge] considers everything as if it were going on now in a simple mode of awareness. So, if you want to weigh the presentness with which he discerns everything, you will more rightly judge it to be not a foreknowledge as of the future, but the knowledge of a never

failing instant. Hence it is called pro-vidence rather than pre-vision, because it looks forth from a position far removed from things below as if from the highest summit of things. (Quoted in Sorabji, 1983:256)

Boethius portrays God's view of history as that of an observer on a mountain-top viewing the countryside all laid out equally below. Time is likened to space. From God's (true) perspective there is no passage of time in creation. And it was to these heights that the classical physicist aspired.

3.6 Relativity and the rediscovery of time

As physicists became more confident of their ability to model the world, they set their sights beyond the very simple mechanical phenomena that had been the foundation of Newtonian dynamics. Thus the idea of unvarying or time-free physical laws began to come under pressure during the nineteenth century with the development of thermo-dynamics. The more complex phenomena associated with heat transfer were simply not amenable to the same treatment as, say, a simple pendulum. As the Ancients realised, *ignis mutat res* – fire changes things. And change is a fundamental aspect of the commonsense view of time.

However, it is not thermodynamics that is commonly associated with the rediscovery of time in physics but Einstein's theory of relativity – the answer to the first of Lord Kelvin's clouds. Published in 1905, Albert Einstein's innocuously entitled paper 'On the electrodynamics of moving bodies' was first and foremost an attempt to explain anomalies arising from attempts to apply Maxwell's Theory of Electromagnetism to moving bodies. The velocity of light appears in that theory as a universal constant – but relative to what: the source, the intervening medium or the observer?

Drawing on our experience of objects moving at low speeds, we might expect the velocity of light to be constant relative to its source. However, this is not borne out by observation (e.g. it would significantly affect observations of binary star orbits). Thus attention turned to the second option: the velocity of light is constant relative to the intervening medium – absolute space – the aether. If so, it should be possible to detect the aether by looking for variations in the velocity of light caused by the Earth's motion relative to the aether. Failure to do so was one of the clouds that worried Lord Kelvin.

Einstein's extraordinary proposal was to treat the velocity of light as constant relative to the observer while, at the same time, insisting that 'the same laws of electrodynamics and optics will be valid for all frames of reference for which the equations of mechanics hold good' (Einstein, 1923:37f.) – his *principle of relativity*. These apparently irreconcilable postulates allowed Einstein to develop an alternative to Newton's laws of motion that effectively dissolved the anomalies that had troubled his predecessors.[3]

However, the new theory required a redefinition of the concept of simultaneity. In a Newtonian world there would be universal agreement that two events had occurred simultaneously. According to Einstein, one observer moving relative to another would not agree with the second that the two events were simultaneous. A corollary of this disagreement is that there can be *no universal present moment* – what is present to me may be past to one observer and still to come for another! Thus the principle of relativity rules out the possibility of a Newtonian universal 'now'. The universe may not be thought of as a succession of instantaneous spaces. Space and time are simply not separable in the manner envisaged by Newtonian physics.

3.7   Relativity and the spatialisation of time

Ironically, Einstein's revolution in our treatment of space and time is often interpreted as supporting the classical view of temporal passage as extraneous to physics. Many physicists maintain that the connection between time and space established by Einstein is of such a kind that time should be thought of as analogous to space – a fourth spatial dimension. For them, reality consists of the entire collection of events that ever have been or ever will be – past, present and future taken together in a static block (sometimes called the stasis theory of time). If so, our perception of time as passing is an artefact of human psychology rather than a physical reality. The following quotations are typical:

> The objective world simply is. It does not happen. Only to the gaze
> of my consciousness crawling upward along the lifeline of my body

---

[3] Russell Stannard's *Black Holes and Uncle Albert* (Stannard, 1991), though aimed at children, provides a very good introduction to the strange implications of Einstein's theory.

does a section of this world come to life as a fleeting image. (Weyl, 1949:166)

relativity physics has shifted the moving present out from the superstructure of the universe, into the minds of human beings, where it belongs. (Davies, 1974:2f.)

[The physicist] does not regard time as a sequence of events which *happen*. Instead, all of past and future are simply there, and time extends in either direction from any given moment in much the same way as space stretches away from any particular place. (Davies, 1990:124)

What these assertions (and many others like them) fail to make clear is that this is an *interpretation* of the special theory of relativity. It is not that relativity theory has somehow proven Boethius' analogy between time and space to be the case. Rather these physicists are reading relativity in the light of that analogy. Indeed it is an interpretation about which Einstein himself was ambivalent. On occasions he certainly wrote in a similar vein. However, when faced with Meyerson's critique of this interpretation, Einstein agreed that 'The element of spatial distance and the element of duration remain distinct in nature, distinct even in the formula giving the square of the world interval of two infinitely near events' (Einstein [1928] in Capek, 1976:366f.).

3.8   Time and space

What are the implications of accepting a strong analogy between time and space?

It would, to say the least, be odd to entertain the notion that the things and events located in some regions of space were somehow more real than those located elsewhere. By analogy, then, we must deny that present events are more real than past or future events. In other words, events at every temporal location must be equally real. All things and events coexist timelessly. I (LO) am ignorant of the events of 2010 only because of my location in 1998 (just as I am ignorant of events in Exeter while writing this chapter in Huntingdon). All future events are there to be read off as and when we reach the right spatio-temporal location. Nor do past events pass away into oblivion – they remain (timelessly) in spatio-temporal locations to which I (the conscious observer moving through spacetime) no longer have access.

If this is so, then we must admit the validity of certain strange locutions. For example, few people living in July 1998 would quibble with the assertion that 'Tony Blair is alive and well, and living in Downing Street'. But the theory that all entities and events exist timelessly (a 'stasis' view of time) requires us also to accept such assertions as 'John F. Kennedy is (timelessly) alive and well and living in 1958'. Of course, oddity does not imply that this is invalid. However, it does highlight the fact that this view of time is strongly counterintuitive.

3.8.1   Spacelike time and determinism

We generally believe the past to be determinate. For example, we may not have access to all the details of the Napoleonic Wars but we do know that a joint Anglo-Prussian force finally defeated Napoleon's army at the Battle of Waterloo. It simply is the case that this happened – nothing can change the fact (not even the most inspired historical reinterpretation). Conversely it is our experience that the future is not determinate in this sense. We do not know what the future will bring. However, we can make predictions based upon past trends and present knowledge. Our predictions generally take the form of a range of possibilities. We further believe that in certain cases it is possible to influence the outcome by acting in certain ways.

In direct contradiction of our experience of past and future, the spatial treatment of time asserts that future events are determinate in precisely the same way as past events. Advocates of this approach are quick to point out the mind-dependence of the experience described above. They argue that the apparent indeterminacy of the future is entirely explicable in terms of our psychological limitations. There is a *merely psychological* arrow of time that denies us access to knowledge of events which are located at spatio-temporal locations later than our own.

However, this has interesting physical implications. As we shall discuss in **3.11–3.14**, quantum mechanics is usually taken to imply indeterminacy – future states of the universe cannot be totally predicted, even in theory, from the present state.[4] But on a 'stasis' view where all future events are (timelessly) determinate, the most obvious candidate

---

[4] See also **1.17** on the significance of indeterminacy.

for an adequate interpretation of quantum mechanics would be some kind of hidden-variables theory, one in which the apparent indeterminacy of the quantum world is underpinned by a more fundamental determinism (see **3.13 (ii)**). Thus all uncertainty about the future is merely a product of our ignorance. Alternatively, we may opt for a many-worlds interpretation in which all possible future events are equally real but isolated from each other in parallel universes (see **3.13 (iii)**).

3.8.2   Spacelike time and causality

To say that A causes B is to say that A has some (significant) role in bringing B into existence. In our common understanding (with its implicit dependence upon a process theory of time), temporal location is usually implicated in such statements. A temporal relation of 'earlier than' is generally assumed to be a necessary but not sufficient condition for asserting a causal relation. Thus, when faced with the challenge to 'Discuss the influence of James Joyce upon William Shakespeare', an English undergraduate will either lapse into blank incomprehension or reinterpret it in postmodern terms as a request to explore the impact of Joyce's work upon all *subsequent* readings of Shakespeare.

If the stasis theory is correct, there is no warrant for our habit of attempting to explain the present in terms of the past. Temporal location should have no more significance for our investigations of causes than spatial location. And, if there really were a strong analogy between time and space, we might expect the cause of some event to lie in one particular direction rather than another!

In reality, of course, we observe a systematic distinction between past, present and future that is quite unlike the characteristics of space. On the face of it, time and space are distinct even though intimately related.

However the difficulties created by a spacelike view of time are by no means insuperable. One way out might be to assert the timelessness of all causal relations. There is clear precedent for such a move in the classical understanding of divine causality. Another (possibly preferable) option might be to relate causality not to temporal location as such but rather to the physical factors that lead to the apparent distinctions between past and future.

3.9 Space, time and theology

Is time essentially spacelike with all that implies for our understanding of freedom and causation? Or is it the fundamental determinant of being and non-being? *Contrary to popular belief, the new physics does not adjudicate between the rival interpretations of time that have been touched on in this section.*

Both interpretations are open to theologians. Indeed both have appeared in Christian theology, albeit under very different guises. By and large theologians have tended to adopt a more or less commonsense view of created time. Thus Emil Brunner is typical when he comments that,

> Everyone knows that time passes away. Everyone knows that the moment which was just now and is now gone never more returns. What men of all times and countries have been conscious of as the painful experience of time is the unceasing flow of the time stream, transience, the irreversibility and inexorability of this movement from the 'not yet' to the 'now' and onwards to the 'no longer' . . . The flow of time is inseparably bound up with transience, mortality, the not lingering, the not being able to return to what has once been, and just that constitutes the linearity of time. (Brunner, 1953:43)

However, when the same theologians try to imagine what the passage of created time might look like from God's perspective, the answer they often come up with is akin to the stasis theory of time described above. This is not to say that they conceive of God as possessing a kind of temporality akin to the stasis theory. Rather it reflects the observation that most understandings of eternity as kinds of timelessness seem to require a stasis theory of created time. In other words, the debate over the nature of time initiated by contemporary interpretations of relativity theory reveals a deep inconsistency in Christian theology with respect to created time. Much of Western theology has attempted to hold together a process view of created time with a doctrine of timeless eternity that implicitly requires a quite different understanding of created time.[5]

---

[5] For further discussion of different theories of time, especially of 'the block universe', a technical term for the 'stasis' view we have described, see Isham and Polkinghorne (1993:135–44).

EXERCISE 3.1

Consult the paper by Isham and Polkinghorne cited in the footnote, and then consider your own view of time in relation to the universe and to God.

SECTION C:
THE REDISCOVERY OF THE OBSERVER
(3.10–3.14)

3.10   The observational basis of quantum theory

Einstein's explanation of the null result of the Michelson–Morley experiment led to a radical revision of our understanding of space and time. If anything, the explanation for Lord Kelvin's other 'cloud' – the spectrum of black-body radiation – has led to even more radical changes in our understanding of the world.

3.10.1   The ultraviolet catastrophe

In line with Kelvin's warning, the first crack in the edifice of classical physics came with attempts to explain the colour of hot objects using classical physics and electromagnetism. The light from these objects is a mixture of different frequencies (colours). Observations reveal that such objects have a distinctive spectrum (pattern of energy distribution at different frequencies). However, attempts to explain this in classical terms failed abjectly – they predicted instead that the amount of energy would tend towards infinity at the high-energy (violet) end of the spectrum – an ultraviolet catastrophe.

Enter Max Planck. In 1900 he suggested that physics should abandon the assumption that electromagnetic energy is continuous and wavelike. If, instead, energy can only be absorbed and emitted in discrete packets (or quanta), theory can be made to fit observations exactly. However, while his suggestion certainly gave the right answer, its abandonment of a cherished assumption of classical physics gave it an air of contrivance that led to its relative neglect for several years.

3.10.2   The photoelectric effect

Another anomaly that concerned physicists at the beginning of the century was the ability of light to eject electrons from metal. The principle is simple – the light imparts energy to electrons which then effectively 'evaporate' from the surface of the metal. The classical analogy with the evaporation of water suggests that some degree of evaporation should occur regardless of the frequency of the light, provided it is sufficiently intense. In reality, there is a clear threshold frequency, which varies from metal to metal, below which the effect will not occur.

It was Einstein who, in 1905, rehabilitated Planck's quantum theory and explained this anomaly by assuming that the energy imparted by the light is packaged (quantised) in a manner that is related to the frequency of the light rather than spread evenly over the wavefront. Furthermore, he assumed that the way in which electrons absorbed that energy is also quantised – so that they can only acquire the energy necessary to escape if the light is of sufficiently high frequency. Light of frequencies lower than this threshold has no effect regardless of the intensity of the light source.

3.10.3   Collapsing atoms and spectral lines

In 1898 Becquerel had discovered an entirely new physical phenomenon – radioactivity. This growth area in physics rapidly led to the realisation that atoms were not simply inert billiard balls. On the contrary, they have an internal structure. By the end of the first decade of the twentieth century sufficient research had accumulated for physicists to be able to begin making models of this structure. It was clear that atoms had a very small, dense, positively charged nucleus surrounded by negatively charged electrons.

Rutherford proposed a planetary model for the atom – electrons in orbit around a nucleus like planets around a star. The fly in the ointment was electromagnetism. An electric charge moving in a circle emits energy. If electrons were classical particles emitting energy in this way, they would very rapidly dissipate all their energy and fall into the nucleus.

A solution was offered by a young Danish physicist, Niels Bohr, whose model of the atom was mentioned in **1.9**. Again the key was the abandonment of continuity in favour of quantisation. Bohr simply ruled out the possibility of electrons occupying every possible orbit. Instead they are confined to certain discrete energy levels. Although outlandish, his suggestion had the added attraction that it explained another anomaly – the fact that the light emitted by hot gases is emitted only at certain frequencies (spectral lines).

3.10.4   When is a particle a wave?

The above phenomena indicated that under certain circumstances light can behave in a particle-like manner rather than its usual wave-like manner. The next step in the development of a quantum view of the world was due to an aristocratic French physicist, Prince Louis de Broglie.

If light can sometimes be particle-like, might there not conversely be situations in which sub-atomic particles behave in a wave-like manner? De Broglie set out to search for such behaviour. He found that, if you take a beam of electrons and pass it through a pair of slits (a classical wave experiment), you get diffraction and interference – properties characteristic of a wave rather than a particle. If you reduce the intensity of the electron beam to a single electron at a time, the detector on the other side of the slits will still gradually accumulate a trace that looks like an interference pattern (see Figure 3.1). Explaining this in classical terms is impossible – if the electrons go through one slit or the other the pattern would look quite different.[6]

3.11   The quantum revolution

By the early 1920s, these anomalies had grown into a gaping hole in the fabric of physics. At the same time, the explanations proffered by physicists such as Einstein and Bohr held out the promise of a radical reconstruction. The task of integrating these insights into a coherent theory of sub-atomic physics fell to Werner Heisenberg and Erwin Schrödinger. Although they were working independently, their approaches were sufficiently similar to be formally merged into quantum mechanics. This new theory constituted a radical shift in the

---

[6] For a discussion of the two-slit experiment in terms of quantum theory see Davies, 1990:108–11.

FIGURE 3.1

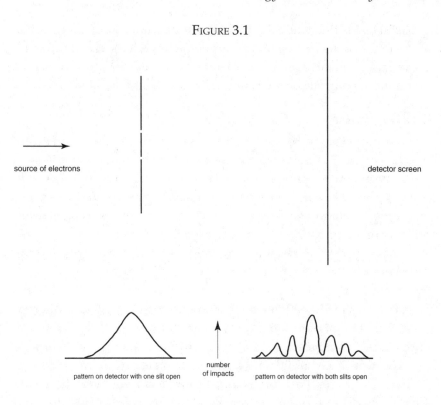

The double-slit experiment, used to illustrate wave-particle duality. If only one slit is open a scatter pattern, characteristic of particles, is observed. If both slits are open the interference pattern characteristic of a wave is observed. Even if only one 'particle' is in the apparatus, faced with two slits it still 'divides itself' to give wave behaviour.

Quantum particles, then, can exhibit two radically different behaviours depending only on how they are observed.

conceptual foundations of physics. We mention here three key aspects of quantum mechanics.

(i) Wave–particle duality

De Broglie's discovery of electron diffraction highlights one of the fundamental features of the new theory – wave–particle duality. This is one of the properties enshrined in the fundamental equation of quantum mechanics, the Schrödinger wave equation – so-called because it takes a mathematical form characteristic of classical wave equations. However, *this equation does not refer to physical waves but rather to probabilities, e.g. the probability of finding an electron in one location rather than another.* The final outcome may be determinate (an electron in a particular location), but the probability distribution of the possible outcomes has the mathematical form of a wave. This peculiar feature of a very successful equation has led to the intractable problem of how we should interpret quantum mechanics.

(ii) Uncertainty

Uncertainty is one of the best known implications of quantum mechanics. In 1927 Heisenberg argued that key physical quantities (e.g. position and momentum) are paired up in quantum theory. As a result, they cannot be measured simultaneously to any desired degree of accuracy. Attempts to increase the precision of one measurement result in less precise measures of the other member of the pair.

Take an electron, for example. We might try to determine its position by using electromagnetic radiation. Because electrons are so small, radiation of very short wavelength would be necessary to locate it accurately. However, shorter wavelengths correspond to higher energies. The higher the energy of radiation used, the more the momentum of the electron is altered. Thus any attempt to determine the location accurately will change the velocity of the electron. Conversely, techniques for accurately measuring the velocity of the electron will leave us in ignorance about its precise location. The conservative interpretation was that this was a limitation imposed by our measuring techniques. *However, Heisenberg himself took a more radical view – this limitation is a property of nature rather than an artefact of experimentation. This radical interpretation of uncertainty implies that quantum mechanics is inherently statistical – it deals with probabilities rather than well-defined classical trajectories. Such a view is clearly inimical to classical determinism.*

(iii) Radical interdependence

In spite of his crucial role in the early development of quantum mechanics, Einstein was very uneasy about its implications and, in later years, organised a rearguard action against it. His aphorism 'God does not play dice' highlights the depths of his distaste for quantum uncertainty. His strongest counter-argument was to call attention to a paradoxical implication of quantum mechanics now known as the Einstein–Podolsky–Rosen (EPR) Paradox.

Take, for example, a pair of protons whose quantum spins cancel out. Now separate them and measure the spin of one proton. Because they were paired, they had a combined wave equation. Measuring the spin of one proton 'collapses' that wave equation and determines the spin of the other. It appears that a measurement in one place can have an instantaneous effect on something that may be light years away.

For Einstein this was proof that quantum mechanics must be incomplete. To him this result only made sense if the spins were determinate (but unknown to us) before the protons were separated. In this case, measurement would merely tell what was always the case. But, according to the orthodox interpretation of quantum mechanics, it is not merely a matter of ignorance. The spin is not determined until it has been measured. In other words, the pair of protons cannot be regarded as separate entities until the measurement has been made.

Some years later, a quantum logician turned this paradox into a testable prediction that now bears his name – Bell's Inequality. This is an equation which should be true if two principles (assumed by Einstein and his colleagues in formulating the EPR Paradox) hold in the world:

> *The principle of reality*: that we can predict a physical quantity with certainty without disturbing the system, *and*

> *The locality principle*: that a measurement in one of two isolated systems can produce no real change in the other.

Taken together, these principles imply an upper limit to the degree of co-operation that is possible between isolated systems. In 1982 a team of physicists at the University of Paris led by Alain Aspect demonstrated experimentally that this limit is exceeded in nature. In other words, our physical descriptions of the world in which we live cannot be both real and local in the above sense.

What this means in practice is a greater emphasis on describing quantum-mechanical systems as a *whole*. This runs counter to the tendency of classical physics towards 'bottom-up thinking'– treating systems as collections of separate entities, and trying to reduce their properties to the individual properties of the simplest possible components. The quantum world, which deals with the simplest entities we know, seems to resist this reduction – it is in Karl Popper's famous phrase 'a world of clouds' as well as 'clocks' (quoted in Polkinghorne, 1991:44). 'Bottom-up' thinking has served science extremely well, we simply indicate here (and at **4.11**) that it has its limitations.[7]

3.12   Shaking the foundations

The quantum view of the world departs from classical assumptions in four main ways.

1. Determinism has given way to an emphasis on *probabilities*. We simply do not have access to enough information to make deterministic predictions. And this is widely held to be a feature of the world rather than an observational limitation.

2. Reductionism has given way to a more *holistic* approach to physical systems.

3. Closely allied to this, locality (the impossibility of information being propagated instantaneously) has given way to *correlation-at-a-distance*.

4. Most basic of all, the classical assumptions of continuity and divisibility (that between any two points there is an infinite number of intermediate values) have given way to *quantisation* – for certain physical quantities, the range of permissible values is severely restricted.

3.13   Schrödinger's cat and the meaning of quantum theory

The EPR Paradox described in **3.11 (iii)** introduces us to one of the basic problems of quantum mechanics – the relationship between measurement and reality. This is highlighted by a famous thought-experiment involving a hapless cat. The cat is in a box together with a canister of poisonous gas connected to a radioactive device. If an atom in the device decays, the canister is opened and the cat dies. Suppose that there is a 50–50 chance of this happening. Clearly when we open the box we will observe a cat that is either alive or dead. But is the cat alive or dead prior to the opening of the box?

---

[7] For a brief discussion of 'bottom-up' and 'top-down' thinking see Peacocke (1993:53–55). We take up the question of 'top-down causation' in **7.6**.

Interpretation (i) Quantum orthodoxy (Copenhagen interpretation)

The dominant view in quantum mechanics is that quantum probabilities become determinate on measurement – that the wave function is collapsed by the intervention of classical measuring apparatus. This means that the cat is neither alive nor dead until the box is opened. The cat is in an indeterminate state.

This interpretation is usually allied with a tendency to extreme instrumentalism (see **1.7**). On such a view the probabilities generated by the Schrödinger wave equation do not correspond to any physical reality. There simply is no reality to be described until an act of measurement collapses the wave function. Quantum mechanics is merely a useful calculating device for predicting the possible outcomes of such acts of measurement.

In spite of its dominance in the textbooks, this interpretation is hardly satisfactory. To begin with, it may be regarded as proposing a dualism in physical reality: two worlds – an indeterminate quantum world and a determinate classical world. Then there is the problem of what constitutes classical measuring apparatus. At what level does the wave function actually collapse?

The act of measurement that collapses the wave function cannot be limited to scientific instruments. After all, why should we assume that *our* scientific measurements are solely responsible for collapsing the wave function? This would give rise to a most peculiar world – one that was indeterminate until the evolution of hominids.

Some physicists, e.g. Wigner and Wheeler, have identified the classical measuring apparatus of the Copenhagen interpretation with consciousness. If so, they must be using a much broader definition of consciousness than is usual. What level of consciousness would be needed to make something determinate? Is the cat sufficiently conscious to determine the outcome of the experiment? Would earthworms do? What about viruses? The effect of pursuing this line of inquiry is to move towards a form of panpsychism – the doctrine that every part of the natural world, no matter how humble, is in some sense conscious!

An alternative might be to postulate a transcendent world observer – a divine mind whose observations collapse the wave functions on our behalf. In effect this would be the quantum-mechanical version of

Bishop Berkeley's idealism.[8] This is memorably summarised in a couple of limericks:

> There was once a man who said 'God
> Must think it exceedingly odd
>   If he finds that this tree
>   Continues to be
> When there's no one about in the quad.'

And the reply:

> Dear Sir, Your astonishment's odd:
> *I* am always about in the quad.
>   And that's why the tree
>   Will continue to be,
> Since observed by Yours faithfully, God.

The problem with this attractive solution to the measurement problem is that it proves too much. Invoking a divine observer leads to the question of why there should be any quantum measurement problem at all. Why should anything be left indeterminate for us to determine by our measurements? Is God only interested in those aspects of creation that are above a certain size?

Returning to the classical measuring apparatus, perhaps we should put the emphasis on 'classical' rather than 'measuring' – stressing not so much our *intervention* in the system as a *transition* from the world of the very small, in which quantum principles operate, to the everyday world of classical physics. This neo-Copenhagen interpretation has the merit that it avoids the absurdities of the consciousness-based approaches. However, we are still faced with the difficulty of identifying an acceptable transition point. One suggestion is that we choose the level at which physical phenomena become so complex that they are irreversible.

Interpretation (ii) Hidden variables (neo-realism)

Einstein was not alone in finding this interpretation of quantum mechanics objectionable. A handful of physicists has persisted in arguing that the statistical nature of quantum mechanics implies that it is only really applicable to ensembles of particles (just as an opinion

---

[8] George Berkeley (1685–1753) – a philosopher famous for his apparent denial of the reality of any external world.

poll is only meaningful if a reasonable sample of the population has been polled). In other words, quantum mechanics is an incomplete description of reality. They maintain that underlying this level of indeterminacy there is an objective foundation.

The best known hidden-variables theory is that of the physicist and philosopher David Bohm (see Bohm, 1980). What Bohm did was to distinguish between the quantum particle, e.g. an electron, and a hidden 'guiding wave' that governs its motion. Thus, in this theory electrons are quite clearly particles. When you perform a two-slit experiment, they go through one slit rather than the other. However, their choice of slit is not random but is governed by the guiding wave, resulting in the wave pattern that is observed.

The main weakness of Bohm's theory is that it looks contrived – which it is. It was deliberately designed to give predictions that are in all details identical to conventional quantum mechanics. His aim was not to make a serious counterproposal but simply to demonstrate that hidden-variables theories are indeed possible.

It is sometimes suggested that hidden-variables theories have been ruled out by the Aspect experiment (**3.11 (iii)**). This is a misunderstanding of the experiment. What it did was to show that attempts to explain quantum phenomena cannot be both deterministic and local. Hidden-variables theories, with their underlying determinism, must be non-local, maintaining the existence of instantaneous causal relations between physically separated entities. Such a view contradicts the simple location of events in both classical atomism and relativity theory. It points to a more holistic view of the quantum world. Indeed Bohm himself stressed the holistic aspect of quantum theory in his later years, after his conversion from Marxism to theosophy.

Interpretation (iii) The many worlds interpretation

The third main class of interpretations starts from the assumption that scientific theories ought to be self-interpreting. The Schrödinger wave equation in quantum mechanics is smooth, continuous and deterministic. There is nothing in it that corresponds to the collapse of the wave function.

In 1957 Hugh Everett surprised his more conventional colleagues by proposing that the Schrödinger wave equation as a whole *is* an accurate description of reality. There is no collapse of the wave function. Whenever there is a choice of experimental outcomes, all the possibilities are realised. Somewhere Schrödinger's cat will be really dead and somewhere it will be really alive. With each decision at the quantum level the universe splits into a number of isolated domains, each corresponding to a different outcome. In one universe the cat dies, in another it lives.

Most physicists find this extremely unattractive. One of the most venerable assumptions of the scientific method is Ockham's razor – *non sunt multiplicanda entia praeter necessitatem*; i.e. entities are not to be multiplied beyond necessity. In practice this leads to a very strong aesthetic bias in favour of the simplest possible explanation.

Only quantum cosmologists beg to differ. They attempt to apply quantum mechanics to the entire universe. Clearly this leaves no room for a separate classical measuring apparatus. In this context, a many-universes approach such as was described above may seem an attractive non-theistic alternative to the notion of a transcendent world observer. But one wonders which option requires the larger act of faith!

3.14   Quantum consciousness

In classical mechanics, with its close association with Cartesian dualism, the physical world was neatly divorced from the realm of conscious-ness. As far as classically-minded materialists were concerned, the latter was a mere side effect of biochemical interactions. However, as noted above, the dominant Copenhagen interpretation of quantum mechanics envisages a greatly expanded role for the observer. Granted the traditional association of temporal perception with conscious-ness, the rediscovery of time by modern physics may point in the same direction.

Such considerations have given rise to the suggestion that conscious-ness itself may be interpreted as a quantum phenomenon. Perhaps the best-known proponent of a quantum explanation of consciousness is Roger Penrose (1989; 1994; 1997). He rejects the currently popular view that human consciousness is essentially computational (that minds are analogous to computer programs) because, in his opinion, this model fails to account for intuitive problem-solving. The brain must be non-algorithmic (i.e. it does not operate by mechanically following a fixed set of procedures in the manner of a computer). Further he argues that classical physics is inherently algorithmic in its nature. Thus consciousness is not explicable in classical terms.

The obvious candidate for a non-algorithmic process in physics is the quantum-mechanical collapse of the wave function. Penrose suggests that the brain uses quantum collapse to solve problems non-algorithmically. But by what means? He pins his hopes on structures called microtubules that occur within cells, speculating that quantum effects within the microtubules may be co-ordinated across groups of neurones to provide the basis for such intuitive processes. However, as many physicists and neurophysiologists have pointed out, this is *highly* speculative – a weakness that Penrose himself acknowledges.

SECTION D:
MODERN COSMOLOGY AND UNIVERSAL HISTORY
(3.15–3.18)

3.15   The beginnings of scientific cosmology

The first step towards a scientific cosmology was taken in 1823 when the German astronomer Wilhelm Olbers discussed a paradox that has subsequently been associated with his name. He simply asked 'Why is the sky dark at night?' The paradox becomes apparent when you calculate the brightness that should be expected given the assumptions that were current about the overall structure of the universe. If the universe is infinitely large, Euclidean (i.e. the shortest distance between two points is a straight line) and stars (or galaxies) are distributed evenly throughout it, the sky should not be dark at all but as bright as the surface of the average star!

This might have been explained by arguing that the universe is relatively young so that light from distant stars has not had time to reach us. However, by the nineteenth century it was widely accepted that the Earth (and, hence, the universe) was very old. Thus a more popular explanation was that the universe consisted of a finite number of stars concentrated into a finite region of an infinite space – the island universe model of cosmology in which the Milky Way (our own galaxy) constituted a unique island of matter and energy in an infinite void.

In the 1920s astronomers were able to show that some nebulae (clouds of luminous gas and dust) were too far away to be part of the Milky

Way – they were island universes or galaxies in their own right. One of the discoverers of extragalactic objects, Edwin Hubble, went a stage further. In 1924 he announced the discovery that light from distant galaxies was systematically redder than light from nearby galaxies and that the degree of red shift was proportional to the distance. This provides a simple explanation for Olbers' Paradox: if light from distant galaxies is redder, it contributes less energy to the overall brightness of the night sky than light from nearby galaxies. Eventually there comes a point where a galaxy is so distant that it is simply invisible (the 'event horizon').

The simplest explanation for this red shift is that it is a case of the Doppler effect. This is the phenomenon that causes the pitch of a train whistle to vary as the train approaches or recedes. According to this explanation, the light is reddened because the galaxies are moving away from us. Since the degree of reddening is also a measure of the speed of recession, Hubble was able to show that more distant galaxies are receding from us faster than nearby ones.

3.16   The Big Bang

At first sight this observation might suggest that the Earth was located at the centre of some cosmic explosion. However, the fact that all motion is relative implies that observers elsewhere in the universe would make similar observations. This observation is consistent with an expanding universe. To illustrate this one might paint spots on a balloon and blow it up. As the balloon expands, the spots recede from each other and more distantly separated spots recede more rapidly.

Extrapolating backwards in time from the observation that the universe is expanding leads to the suggestion that there might have been a time in the distant past (about 10–20 billion years ago) when the entire universe was concentrated into a single point. This point would be unimaginably hot and dense. At this 't = 0' the universe would begin to expand rapidly, if not violently. As it expands and cools, matter as we now know it begins to appear. Small variations in the density of that matter lead to condensation and the eventual formation of stars, galaxies and planets. Gradually the mutual gravitational attraction of matter slows the expansion of the universe. The result is the basic picture of the universe as portrayed by modern cosmology.

3.16.1   Evidence for a Big Bang?

Taking the Big Bang as our educated guess about the origin of the universe, we naturally ask what would such a universe look like? Can we deduce potential observations from the hypothesis of a primordial fireball? The answer is 'yes'.

Since light travels at a finite velocity, observations of distant objects are also observations of conditions in the past. In the distant past, the universe was smaller and therefore denser than it is today. We would therefore expect distant objects to be closer together than those nearby – there is some evidence from radio astronomy that this is the case. We would also expect observations of very distant objects to be consistent with a younger, hotter universe.

In an effort to discredit this theory, Fred Hoyle and some colleagues calculated the chemical composition of a Big Bang universe. This is relatively straightforward since the bulk of the chemical elements would be generated in the first couple of seconds of violent expansion and cooling. Much to their surprise, the outcome of their predictions was very similar to the observed chemical composition of the universe (about 80 per cent hydrogen and 20 per cent helium – all the rest is a mere trace explicable as the result of supernova explosions at the end of the first generation of stellar evolution).

But the most convincing evidence for the Big Bang came from an accidental discovery in 1965. Two young American astronomers, Penzias and Wilson, were attempting to pioneer astronomy in the microwave part of the spectrum. They picked up a very faint signal which seemed to be coming from every part of the sky. At first they thought it was a problem with the telescope. Only when they had thoroughly checked all their equipment did the full significance of their observation became apparent. In the 1940s, George Gamow had predicted that the Big Bang should have left a trace of itself in the form of microwave radiation spread evenly across the sky. Furthermore, the predicted strength of this radiation was comparable with observed results.

3.17   The shape of things to come

The fact that mutual gravitational attraction is causing the expansion of the universe to slow down suggests three possible future scenarios, depending on how much matter there is in the universe. The more matter, the greater the gravitational attraction and the more rapidly the expansion of the universe will slow down. If there is sufficient matter, the gravitational attraction will eventually overcome the expansion and the universe will begin to collapse again. This leads to a family of so-called *closed* cosmological models. If the total mass of the universe is less than that critical mass, expansion will continue indefinitely – an *open* universe. At the critical mass itself, the expansion will cease in the infinitely far future.

Direct observations of galaxies suggest that the actual mass of the universe is only a few per cent of the critical mass. This would suggest an open universe. However many cosmologists postulate the existence of hidden (or dark) matter. Estimates of the amount of dark matter vary – it is not clear whether there is sufficient to bring about the ultimate collapse of the universe.[9] We discuss the implications of these predictions for theology in **7.17**.

3.18   Is the Big Bang a moment of creation?

Strictly speaking the point associated with the Big Bang itself is a singularity – a point at which our laws of physics break down. In itself, this does not imply an absolute beginning. Nevertheless, it is tempting to read the Big Bang as having theological significance. After all, it does seem remarkably like a moment of creation.

This temptation received strong papal endorsement in 1951. Pope Pius XII announced that 'everything seems to indicate that the universe has in finite times a mighty beginning'. He went on to claim that unprejudiced scientific thinking indicated that the universe is a 'work of creative omnipotence, whose power set in motion by the mighty *fiat* pronounced billions of years ago by the Creating Spirit, spread out over the universe'. To be fair, he did also admit that 'the facts established up to the present time are not an absolute proof of creation in time'.

Such pronouncements are guaranteed to provoke controversy. Even members of the Pontifical Academy of Sciences were divided over the wisdom of the Pope's remarks. While Sir Edmund Whittaker could

---

[9] At the moment of writing (summer 1998) the prevailing view is that the so-called 'cosmological constant' which would accelerate the universe's expansion (see Guth, 1997:37–42 for the history of this term) may be non-zero, and sufficiently large to guarantee an ever-expanding universe.

agree that the Big Bang might 'perhaps without impropriety' be referred to as the Creation, George Lemaître, one of the pioneers of the Big Bang theory, felt strongly that this was a misuse of his hypothesis.

Beyond the Christian community there was even greater unease. One of the fundamental assumptions of modern science is that every physical event can be sufficiently explained solely in terms of preceding physical causes. Quite apart from its possible status as the moment of creation, the Big Bang singularity is an offence to this basic assumption. Thus some philosophers of science have opposed the very idea of the Big Bang as irrational and untestable.

One popular way to evade the suggestion of an absolute beginning has been to argue that the universe must be closed (see **3.21**). If it will eventually return to a singular point, why should it not then 'bounce'? This is the so-called *cyclic* universe. Other astronomers opposed to the Big Bang, proposed instead a *steady state* theory. Fred Hoyle took a lead in this proposal. As we indicated in **1.15**, his motives were explicitly theological. The steady-state theory argued that, in spite of appearances, the universe was infinitely old and did not evolve over time. Although defended by some very able scientists, this theory suffered a number of major setbacks which led to its demise. In order to maintain a steady state in the face of universal expansion it was necessary to postulate the continuous creation of matter from negative energy – ingenious, but contrived. There was the embarrassment of Hoyle's failed attempt to show that the Big Bang could not account for the chemical composition of the universe (**3.16.1**). Finally, the steady state theory was not able to accommodate the new data that appeared – particularly the existence of the microwave background (**3.16.1**).

We discussed subsequent developments in the unfolding of cosmology, and its implications for theology, in **1.15**.

SECTION E:
MODERN COSMOLOGY AND THE
REDISCOVERY OF PURPOSE? (3.19–3.23)

3.19   Some contemporary cosmological enigmas

Modern cosmology offers us mathematical models of the possible large-scale structure of the universe. Like any other mathematical model, the actual features depend on the numbers that we choose to put in the equations. Thus in **3.17** we noted that different values of the total mass of the universe will give rise to very different cosmological models. In general, the overall structure of many physical systems is strongly influenced by the numerical values of a relatively small number of universal constants (e.g. the gravitational constant). Over the past couple of decades physicists have become increasingly aware that *the physical conditions that enable life to exist are very sensitive to the values of a number of these constants. If they had been only slightly different, life as we know it could not have evolved.*

3.19.1   The chemical composition of the universe

As we noted in **3.16.1**, the overall chemical composition of the universe was determined by physical conditions during the first seconds of the Big Bang. However, the elements on which life depends (such as carbon, nitrogen, oxygen, sulphur and iron) are the product of nuclear reactions within stars. In both situations the processes by which the chemical elements are formed are governed very precisely by the strengths of four fundamental physical interactions: gravitation, electromagnetism, and the weak and strong nuclear interactions.

If the relative strengths of these forces were different, the resultant universe would also be different. For example, increasing the strong nuclear interaction by 3 per cent relative to the electromagnetic interaction gives a cosmological model in which none of the known chemical elements could form. Conversely, decreasing it by 1 per cent gives a model in which carbon atoms would be unstable. Both scenarios would preclude carbon-based life. Other tiny variations in these forces might have given rise to a universe which was 100 per cent helium or one in which supernova explosions could not occur (since these explosions are thought to be the chief way in which the chemicals necessary for life are ejected from stars, this too would preclude the evolution of life). These 'precisions' in various parameters such as to give rise to life are known as the 'anthropic coincidences'.

3.19.2   The uniformity of the universe

Another of the remarkable features of the universe is that above a certain scale (about 10^{24} metres) it is highly uniform in structure.

However, this degree of uniformity is an embarrassment to cosmologists.

According to relativity theory, there should be no causal connection between points separated by distances greater than c multiplied by t (where c is the velocity of light and t is the age of the universe). Extrapolating this back to the Big Bang suggests that the primordial universe was partitioned into about 10^{80} causally separate regions (Barrow and Tipler, 1986:420). Nevertheless, all these disconnected regions had to expand at the same rate to maintain the observed degree of uniformity! Coincidence or co-operation? Small wonder that Paul Davies comments:

> It is hard to resist the impression of something – some influence capable of transcending spacetime and the confinement of relativistic causality – possessing an overview of the entire cosmos at the instant of its creation, and manipulating all the causally disconnected parts to go bang with almost exactly the same vigour at the same time, and yet not so exactly co-ordinated as to preclude the small scale, slight irregularities that eventually formed the galaxies, and us. (Davies, 1982:95)[10]

Davies' reference to small-scale irregularities highlights another feature of cosmic uniformity. According to current theories, galaxy formation depends upon the existence of small initial irregularities in the Big Bang itself. These are amplified by cosmic expansion to the point where gravitation can begin the process of stellar condensation (Barrow and Tipler, 1986:417). If the initial irregularities are too large, the result is the rapid and widespread formation of black holes instead of stars. If the initial irregularities are sufficiently small, the precise expansion rate of the cosmos becomes critical – too rapid and the irregularities will not be amplified enough for galaxy formation to occur; too slow and the cosmos will be closed with a lifetime too short to permit biological evolution.

3.20 Possible responses to the 'anthropic coincidences'

There is no obvious physical reason why the parameters mentioned in **3.19.1** should have the observed values. However, very small changes

---

[10] At the same time an inference to the existence of 'some influence capable of transcending spacetime and the confinement of relativistic causality' is very far from being an inference to belief in any established religion.

in any of these key parameters would have resulted in a grossly different universe; one in which life as we know it would almost certainly be precluded. The set of life-permitting cosmological models is a vanishingly small subset of the set of all theoretically possible cosmological models.

One response to these enigmas might be to adopt a hard-nosed empiricism and say, 'So what? It is meaningless to speak of our existence as improbable after the event.' However, few cosmologists seem prepared to ignore these cosmological coincidences in this fashion.

Another possible response would be to deny the contingency of physical laws and parameters. For example, some physicists speculate about possible developments in physics which would demonstrate that only this precise set of laws and parameters is possible.

A third type of response is to invoke what has been called the Anthropic Cosmological Principle. In its various forms, it offers a way of maintaining the contingency of physical laws while evading the theistic possibilities suggested by the above quotation from Paul Davies.

3.21　The Weak Anthropic Principle

The approach which does the least violence to conventional modes of scientific thought is to invoke a Weak Anthropic Principle (WAP). Barrow and Tipler describe it thus:

> The observed values of all physical and cosmological quantities are not equally probable but they take on values restricted by the requirement that there exist sites where carbon-based life can evolve and by the requirement that the Universe be old enough for it to have already done so. (Barrow and Tipler, 1986:16)

In other words, our existence as observers functions as a cosmological selection effect. There can be no observations without observers. Our observations must satisfy the conditions necessary for our existence.

However, the WAP does not take us very far towards an explanation of the observed coincidences. In conjunction with a conventional Big Bang cosmology, it still gives the impression that our existence is an accident of vanishingly small probability. *Thus, in practice, it usually appears in conjunction with a cosmological model which suggests that there is a sense in which all possible universes actually exist.* Three such strategies are to be found in the literature.

The first is to extend the closed Big Bang model to permit an endless series of expansions and contractions: the so-called *cyclic Big Bang* (see **3.18**). Each passage through a singularity is supposed to randomise the physical parameters which give rise to the anthropic features. In an infinite series of closed universes there will certainly be a subset whose physical features permit the evolution of life and the function of the WAP is to remind us that only in such an atypical subclass of universes could life evolve. The main difficulty faced by this scenario is justifying the assumption that, while the singularity randomises the laws and constants of nature, it leaves the geometry of spacetime untouched. If, as seems reasonable, passage through a singularity also affects the geometry of the universe, we should expect an open Big Bang after a finite number of cycles, thus putting an end to any hope of an infinite sequence of universes.

A second approach would be to opt for one of the recent sophisticated variants of steady-state cosmology. For example, one may envisage an *infinite chaotic universe* in which 'bubbles' of order appear and disappear at random. Thus our universe is merely a small local departure from the steady-state conditions. However, if spacetime is truly infinite in extent, we should expect every possible stable state to appear an infinite number of times!

The third and, currently, most popular strategy for relaxing the uniqueness of our universe is to adopt a *many-worlds interpretation of quantum mechanics* (**3.13 (iii)**). Again it is sufficient to invoke the WAP to 'explain' our atypical cosmos.

3.22   The Strong Anthropic Principle

For some cosmologists the WAP does not go far enough. Their response is to invoke the existence of rational carbon-based life forms as an *explanation* of the anthropic features of the universe. Thus, 'The Universe must have those properties which allow life to develop within it at some stage in its history' (Barrow and Tipler, 1986:21). The best known version of this principle is Barrow and Tipler's *Final Anthropic Principle* (FAP): 'Intelligent information-processing must come into existence in the Universe, and, once it comes into existence, it will never die out' (Barrow and Tipler, 1986:23). They believe that intelligent life-forms have cosmological significance by virtue of their future capacity to understand and manipulate matter on a cosmic scale.

This belief leads them to develop a non-theistic 'physical eschatology'. Tipler has amplified this further in his *The Physics of Immortality* (1995).[11] Humankind may not exist forever but human culture will persist, being preserved and developed by self-replicating intelligent machines. The transfer of our cultural software to alternative forms of hardware is one factor in encouraging the indefinite growth of the capacity to process information and to manipulate matter. They envisage the inevitable expansion of human culture to the point where it engulfs the entire cosmos. But let them have the final word:

> if life evolves in all of the many universes in a quantum cosmology, and if life continues to exist in all of these universes, then all of these universes, which include all possible histories among them, will approach the Omega Point. At the instant the Omega Point is reached, life will have gained control of all matter and forces not only in a single universe, but in all universes whose existence is logically possible; life will have spread into all spatial regions in all universes which could logically exist, and will have stored an infinite amount of information, including all bits of knowledge which it is logically possible to know. And this is the end. (Barrow and Tipler, 1986:676f.)

And, in a footnote, they add, 'A modern-day theologian might wish to say that the totality of life at the Omega Point is omnipotent, omnipresent, and omniscient!' (Barrow and Tipler, 1986:682 note 123).

In spite of the metaphysical tone of much of their discussion, Barrow and Tipler stress that the FAP makes clear predictions about the kind of universe we can expect to observe. Most importantly, they argue that, in order for life literally to engulf the universe, the universe must be closed. It must eventually begin to collapse under its own gravitation toward a final singularity.

3.22.1   Is it science?

Implicit in Barrow and Tipler's insistence on the predictive power of the Anthropic Principles is a claim that they be accorded scientific status. Predictive capacity is a keystone of Popper's well-known Criterion of Falsifiability. But what sort of scientific status is being claimed?

The SAP claims that the statement, 'Observers exist', in some sense constitutes a scientific explanation of the anthropic features of the cosmos. Two ways of interpreting this are possible.

[11] See also **5.7**.

It may be a claim that rational observers are the efficient cause of the universe. However, this would imply that time reversal is a reality on a cosmic scale and that in a very strong sense intelligent observers have (will have?) created their own reality.

Alternatively, the SAP may be read as a denial of the sufficiency of efficient causes as scientific explanations of certain physical problems. This implication of the SAP has caused some scientists and philosophers to reject it out of hand. However, it should be recalled that it was only with the rise of the mechanical model of the world that efficient causes were accepted as complete explanations in physics. Furthermore, the biological sciences have proved remarkably resistant to this view of scientific explanation.

By contrast, the WAP does not claim to be explanatory: it is merely a selection effect. However, like the SAP, it has a covert content. It is pointless unless it is used in conjunction with a cosmological model which postulates an ensemble of universes. Thus it functions as a way of commending to the scientific establishment certain speculative cosmologies which have so far failed to convince when restricted to more conventional forms of scientific argumentation.

3.23   Anthropic design arguments

As the earlier quotation from Paul Davies (**3.19.2**) suggests, the apparent fine-tuning of the cosmos is a rich source of material for new forms of design argument for the existence of God. Several such design arguments appear in recent theological (and scientific) literature.

Anthropic design arguments use aspects of cosmic fine-tuning as evidence that the universe was *designed* to permit (or, in stronger forms, to necessitate) the evolution of rational carbon-based life forms. There can be little doubt that, from the perspective of Christian faith, such features are suggestive of design. However, design arguments based on these features make certain assumptions that may make one cautious about placing too much reliance on them.

To begin with, they assume that the anthropic features of the cosmos are, in themselves, improbable. However, quite apart from the difficulties of assigning probabilities to these parameters, such an assumption is far from proven. As we noted earlier (**3.20**), it is conceivable that future developments in physics might render these very features quasi-necessary. In such a situation, this entire class of design argument would collapse. There is a hint of the God of the gaps about such arguments:[12] the universe appears to be a highly improbable structure: we cannot give a rational explanation of these cosmological features: therefore, they constitute evidence of an intelligent designer. And, like the God of the gaps, the role of this deity shrinks with the expansion of scientific understanding.

A second assumption of anthropic design arguments is that the ultimate goal of creation is the existence of rational carbon-based life forms (i.e. humankind). This is in agreement with the dominant view of Western Christian theology. However, it is arguable that the anthropocentricity of western Christianity is derived from sources other than the Christian revelation. For example, instead of presenting humankind as the end of creation, Genesis 1 may be read as insisting that the end of God's creative activity is his Sabbath rest in the presence of all his creation. A move towards less anthropocentric readings of the Bible (and Christian tradition) is a common feature of contemporary theologies of creation (see Chapter 6). The blatant anthropocentricity of these design arguments is hard to reconcile with this trend in ecologically-sensitive theologies of creation.[13]

EXERCISE 3.2

Consider which of the interpretations of the anthropic coincidences you prefer, and why this might be. *Then* look at a recent assessment of the arguments such as Polkinghorne, 1998:18–22, or Worthing, 1996:43–47.

SECTION F:
THE REDISCOVERY OF COMPLEXITY (3.24–3.27)

3.24   Introduction: 'Newtonian' limits to Newtonian physics

From the perspective of Newtonian physics, reality could be exhaustively understood in terms of particles moving in well-defined

---

[12] See 7.3 for more on 'the God of the gaps'.

[13] Here there is a polite difference of emphasis among the authors, CS considering that the unfortunately-named 'anthropic' coincidences are those which permit carbon-based life, and need not necessarily be thought of in association with the potential for *human* life. A universe which gave rise to a planet on which could arise organisms as complex as bacteria would still be a wonderfully fruitful universe.

ways under the influence of certain forces. Of course it was recognised from the outset that real life was more complex than that. Many everyday situations involved too many factors to be amenable to such straightforward treatment. In such cases physicists had to be satisfied with approximations. Nevertheless it was assumed that, in principle, these awkward cases could be treated exactly.[14]

Take, for example, the motion of planets round the Sun. Using his laws of motion, Newton was able to provide an exact solution to the two-body problem – the case of two physical bodies interacting gravitationally but isolated from other influences. However, Newton's successors were unable to create exact solutions for larger ensembles of bodies (e.g. the Solar System or even just the Sun, Earth and Moon considered in isolation from all the rest – the three-body problem). Instead they had to adopt a method of approximations – beginning with the simple case, they asked how the presence of an additional element might perturb the orbits of the two bodies, then they calculated the effect of that change on the third body, then corrected the original calculations in the light of that, and so on to higher and higher degrees of accuracy.

It was not until the end of the nineteenth century that astronomers finally abandoned the search for an exact solution to the three-body problem. In 1889 a young mathematical physicist, Henri Poincaré, won a competition sponsored by the King of Sweden with an essay demonstrating the impossibility of such a solution.

3.25   Recognising chaos

Poincaré may justly be called the father of chaos theory. In addition to demonstrating that there were physical systems which could not be precisely analysed using Newtonian physics, he was among the first physicists to comment on the extreme sensitivity of many physical systems to small variations in initial conditions. Little notice was taken of his remarks when he made them in 1903 but, since then, physicists have become much more conscious of the extent to which such chaotic behaviour is to be found in the physical world. This new awareness of chaos and complexity is not so much a recent discovery as a gradually changing perception resulting from a range of factors.

---

[14] See **1.17** on Laplace and the determinism of the Newtonian universe.

The research that has resulted from Poincaré's own work on perturbation theory is one of these factors. This has revealed the existence of
chaotic behaviour in simple isolated systems. Take, for example, the
motion of balls on a snooker table. It can be shown that their motion is
so sensitive to external factors that in order to predict the position of
the cue ball after a minute of motion (and collisions), one would have
to take into account the gravitational attraction of electrons on the far
side of the galaxy! Even something as apparently simple as the tossing
of a coin or the motion of a water droplet on a convex surface is so
sensitive to minute variations in the environment as to be unpredictable.

A second area of research that has encouraged physicists to take
chaos more seriously is that of turbulent flow in fluids. Its relevance
to engineering and meteorology ensured that this was a growth area
in research. Unlike the simple situations described above, turbulence
is not merely a matter of uncertainties in the system created by
random motion at the molecular level. That aspect of fluid dynamics
can be handled statistically. The real issue is the sudden emergence
of random motion on a macroscopic scale – eddies and currents involving large collections of molecules. Such situations are bounded
but unstable – in many such cases we are now able to generate
equations that tell us the boundaries within which the motion will take
place. Inside those boundaries, however, the particles involved are
subject to irregular fluctuations quite independent of any external
perturbation.

A third aspect in the development of chaos theory has been the
availability of more and more powerful electronic computers. They have
allowed physicists to extend classical perturbation theory to situations
that previously were too complicated to calculate. As a result more and
more situations have been revealed to be chaotic.

Finally, the widespread acceptance of quantum theory may also have
played an important part in changing the attitudes of physicists to
unpredictable situations. This is not to suggest that quantum theory is
directly relevant to chaos at an everyday level.[15] However, the
acceptance of quantum uncertainties may have made it easier for
physicists to accept a degree of unpredictability about the physical world
at other levels.

---

[15] Except in that Heisenberg's Uncertainty Principle (**3.11 (ii)**) sets a limit on the
precision of our knowledge of *any* system.

3.26 Coming to terms with chaos

This new awareness of complexity implies a profound change in the way in which many physical scientists view the world, a new perception of the relation between freedom and necessity. This can be summarised in the apparently paradoxical statement that chaos is deterministic. The situations described above are not completely anarchic. On the contrary, we are dealing with ensembles of bodies moving at the everyday level where Newtonian laws of motion still hold sway. The behaviour of these chaotic situations is generated by fixed rules that do not involve any elements of chance. Many of the physicists of chaos would insist that, in principle, the future is still completely determined by the past in these situations. However, these are situations which are so sensitive to the initial conditions that, in spite of the determinism of the associated physical laws, it is impossible to predict future behaviour. *Deterministic physics no longer has the power to impose a deterministic outcome.* According to one of the classic papers on the subject, 'There is order in chaos: underlying chaotic behaviour there are elegant geometric forms that create randomness in the same way as a card dealer shuffles a deck of cards or a blender mixes cake batter' (Crutchfield *et al.*, 1995:35).

At first glance this may seem entirely negative. The admission that chaos is far more widespread than previously realised appears to impose new fundamental limits on our ability to make predictions. If prediction and control are indeed fundamental to science then chaos is a serious matter. On the other hand, the deterministic element in these chaotic situations implies that many apparently random phenomena may be more predictable than had been thought. The exciting thing about chaos theory is the way in which, across many different sciences, researchers have been able to take a second look at apparently random information and, while not being able to predict exact outcomes, nevertheless explain the random behaviour in terms of simple laws. This is true of meteorology. It can also be applied to dripping taps or to many biological systems (e.g. the mathematical physics of a heart beat).

3.27 Implications for the philosophy of science

As we have just hinted, the emergence of a science of chaos has profound implications for our understanding of what science is and can do.

One may disagree with the notion that the *raison d'être* of science is prediction and control. Nevertheless, prediction still retains a central place in the scientific method. How else are we to test our scientific models? The classical approach is to make predictions from the model and devise experiments to test those predictions. Here, however, we are faced with situations in which such predictions seems inherently impossible. In fact, what is required is that we take a more subtle approach to prediction. What we observe may well be random (or pseudo-random). However, the deterministic element in mathematical chaos implies that the random observations will be clustered into predictable patterns.

A second important implication of chaos theory has to do with the continuing tendency to reductionism in the sciences. Chaos and complexity highlight the fact that only in the very simple systems that formed the backbone of classical physics is it true that the whole is merely the sum of the parts. Chaotic systems simply cannot be understood by breaking them down into their component parts and seeing how they fit together again.

Closely allied to this challenge to reductionism is a question about the possibility of completeness in physics. The reality of chaos undermines the hope that such completeness can be achieved by an increasingly detailed understanding of fundamental physical forces and constituents. It also provides a physical basis for the concept of emergence that is so important in philosophical and theological perspectives on the life and human sciences. The behaviour of chaotic systems suggests that interaction of components at one level can lead to complex global behaviour at another level – behaviour that is not predictable from a knowledge of the component parts. Indeed some chaos scientists suggest that 'chaos provides a mechanism that allows for free will within a world governed by deterministic laws' (Crutchfield *et al.*, 1995:48).

However, we consider caution is needed at this point. Chaotic randomness is not complete randomness. True, we are unable to predict the detailed outcome of a chaotic scenario. However, the mathematics of chaos does permit us to predict the limits of the possible outcomes. This is randomness within constraints – deterministic constraints. In fact, chaos theory allows us to extend our physical understanding of the world into new areas specifically by applying deterministic covering laws to situations that were previously thought to be completely random. This could be taken as evidence that determinism really works.

On the other hand, the fact that the equations we use are deterministic does not necessarily mean that nature is deterministic. The equations are maps, not the reality. It could be that the apparent determinism is an artefact of the particular way in which we have chosen to map reality – in terms of mathematical physics.

3.28 Conclusion

We have seen that, though Newtonianism remains very influential, in a number of areas modern physics has broken with the Newtonian paradigm. It has given rise to questions of interpretation which relate directly to theology – in the areas of quantum theory and chaos theory (*re* determinism), the Big Bang origin and final fate of the universe, and the question of evidence for design. A number of these areas will be considered again in our discussion of divine action in Chapter 7.

FURTHER READING

DAVIES, P. (1990) *God and the New Physics* (Harmondsworth: Penguin)

—— (1995) *About Time* (London: Viking)

GLEICK, J. (1988) *Chaos: Making a New Science* (London: Cardinal)

POLKINGHORNE, J. (1990) *The Quantum World* (Harmondsworth: Penguin)

—— (1991) *Reason and Reality* (London: SPCK)

WERTHEIM, M. (1995) *Pythagoras' Trousers: God, physics and the gender wars* (New York, NY: Times Books)

WORTHING, M. W. (1996) *God, Creation and Contemporary Physics* (Minneapolis, MN: Fortress Press)

Chapter 4

Theology and Evolutionary Biology

4.1 Introduction

We saw in the quotation from John Updike in **1.1** that the caricature of this relationship is one in which the development of evolutionary theory has been enough to sweep aside the claims of religion. In this chapter we shall review the science of biological evolution as it has developed since the pioneering work of Darwin. We shall indicate the challenges Darwinian thought posed to Christian theology of creation in the nineteenth century. We shall then discuss how evolutionary theory has developed, noting that contemporary Darwinism has given rise to new prophets of conflict: in particular Richard Dawkins, but also E. O. Wilson and other sociobiologists. We shall note the merits and limitations of different forms of reductionism. Finally, we outline the evolution of humans, and discuss how this relates to descriptions of human origin and status in Genesis. The challenge of synthesising evolutionary and theological narratives will be taken up in more detail in Chapter 7.

SECTION A:
THE IMPACT OF DARWINISM (4.2–4.5)

4.2 Early evolutionary ideas, and the importance of Darwin

The development of evolutionary theory up to the time of Charles Darwin (1809–82) took place against the background of powerful philosophical attacks on natural theology, and in particular the argument from design (see **1.3.1** and Brooke [1991:Chs. 6–8]. As Brooke shows (pp. 240f.) Charles Darwin was not the first naturalist to think that organic evolution might have occurred. Important predecessors of Darwin included his own grandfather Erasmus Darwin (1731–1802) and Jean-Baptiste Lamarck (1744–1829). Lamarck's scheme in particular was very influential (not least on Darwin), but he failed to perceive:

(a) *the importance of extinction*. In his scheme species sometimes became transformed into other species on an (inevitable) ladder of progress, but Lamarck rejected the notion of widespread extinction;

(b) *that heritable characteristics are not, typically, acquired during an individual organism's life*. The son of a bad-tempered tennis star might possibly inherit a predisposition to bad temper, but would not inherit the expanded racket-forearm a tennis pro develops after years of play.

Strangely, evolutionary ideas were more popular with the lay public than with the scientific establishment. 'Those who were best informed about biology, and especially about classification and morphology, upheld most strongly ... the constancy of species' (Mayr, 1964:ix). The furthest most scientists would go towards evolution was Richard Owen's view that closely related creatures were different implementations of a single divinely given archetype. The conventional belief remained that plant and animal species were more or less fixed in the form in which they had been created.

Darwin published *On the Origin of Species by Means of Natural Selection* in November 1859, by which time he had been developing the theory of evolution by natural selection for at least twenty-two years. For an account of this development, and the fluctuations in Darwin's own religious belief, see the biography by Desmond and Moore (1992). The importance of the *Origin* is that Darwin (a) presented a vast amount of evidence for evolution and (b) proposed a mechanism by which it could give rise, given time, to the vast variety of life-forms he had observed.

4.2.1   Influences on Darwin

Darwin derived his ideas from a combination of sources:

(i) *an extensive study of nature*, especially on his famous voyage on HMS *Beagle* in 1831–36. His observations on the Galapagos Islands were a key ingredient in his later reflections. Each island had a different environment, and its own combination of wildlife. Darwin collected a range of birds which seemed to resemble finches. Each had different characteristics appropriate to the different island habitat in which it lived. At first Darwin gave them little attention. But his thought was greatly spurred on when John Gould, who dissected the Galapagos finches back in London, told him that the different finch-samples belonged to different *species*. The most likely explanation was that they derived from a small number of finches of one species blown across the ocean from South America, and that they had developed differently in their different island habitats. (The story of the Galapagos finches is given a compelling update by Weiner [1994].)

(ii) *a study of artificial breeding techniques*, for example the selection of different attributes in pigeons, dogs and horses, each of which are mentioned in the *Origin*. Darwin wrote 'here, then, we see in man's productions the actions of what may be called the principle of divergence, causing differences, at first barely appreciable, steadily to increase, and the breeds to diverge in character both from each other and from their common parent' (Darwin, 1859:156). Having established a model for the origin of species Darwin applied his theory to the interpretation of both the fossil record and the geographical distribution of organisms.

(iii) *his wide reading*. Originally Darwin had been intended to take Orders in the Church of England. At Cambridge he read William Paley's *Natural Theology*, and noted the amazing properties of adaptedness that living things seemed often to possess. (However, his proposal of natural selection was utterly to supersede Paley's argument from design. See Desmond and Moore, 1992:90, and Dawkins, 1991:Ch. 1.) On the *Beagle* voyage Darwin took the first volume of Lyell's *Principles of Geology*, with its insistence that the Earth's rocks were formed by processes of gradual change over very long periods. And at a crucial juncture in his thinking on species he read Malthus' *Essay on the Principle of Population*, which claimed that in the struggle for resources weak and improvident humans would be eliminated.

4.3   The core of Darwin's theory

Darwin set out his main arguments in Chapters 2 and 3 of the *Origin*. He stressed a number of key aspects: the struggle for existence, variation, natural selection, extinction and species divergence. These ideas are woven into a very readable and perceptive text which gives an account of his biological knowledge and his experience of the breeding techniques of pigeon fanciers and farmers.

A few short quotations from the *Origin* are given below which give the core of the theory. They are taken from Darwin's first edition of 1859:

> Owing to the struggle for life, any variation, however slight and from whatever cause proceeding, if it be to any degree profitable to an individual of any species, in its infinitely complex relations to other organic beings and to external nature, will tend to the preservation of that individual, and will generally be inherited by its offspring. (Darwin, 1859:115)

> The preservation of favourable variations and the rejection of injurious variations, I call Natural Selection. Variations neither useful nor injurious would not be affected by natural selection, and would be left a fluctuating element ... (Darwin, 1859:131)

> It follows that as each selected and favoured form increases in number, so will the less favoured forms decrease and become rare. Rarity, as geology tells us, is the precursor to extinction. (Darwin, 1859:153)

> According to my view, varieties are species in the process of formation, or, as I have called them, incipient species (Darwin, 1859:155)

This results in a 'branching-tree' view of evolution, rather than a step-ladder of progress, or a series of isolated 'special creations'.

4.3.1   A note on the word 'evolution'

*Darwin did **not** use the noun 'evolution' to describe his theory in the* 'Origin'; in fact he only used the word 'evolved' once in his book (Darwin, 1859:460, and cf. Ridley, 1993:8). The pre-Darwinian connotations of the word concerned a predictable unfolding of possibilities, as seen for example in the processes of embryonic development. *Darwin would not* *have chosen the word because his theory is based upon variants which occur in an **undirected** way, and are then selected for or against by an environment which may also alter irregularly, **not on a ladder of progress**.* However, by the time of the publication of *The Expression of the Emotions* in 1872, he *had* started to use the term.

4.4   Darwin's challenge to theological positions

It is important to an understanding of the development of the 'special relationship' between evolutionary theory and theology to understand what it was about Darwin's scheme which challenged nineteenth-century theological descriptions:

(i) It refuted, virtually at a stroke, the notion that creatures had been individually designed by God, and hence any suggestion that one could argue *directly* from the ingenuity of their design, or the exquisite nature of their adaptation to their environment, to point to the existence or the ingenuity of such a Being.[1]

(ii) It cohered with the geological proposal of Lyell that the Earth was very old, compared with the chronology suggested by Genesis, and that therefore no literal reading of Scripture could accord with the scientific account.

(iii) It implied that apes and humans share a common ancestor; rather than humans arising by any distinct act of creation which might guarantee their theological uniqueness. This received little emphasis in *The Origin of Species* but is very clear in Darwin's later *The Descent of Man* (1871).

These three conclusions now form the accepted background from which most theology reflects on the biosphere. If, however, it is simply asserted that God has used the processes of evolution to further the divine purpose of creating a world in which there could be creatures like ourselves, then a further problem arises which was already known to Darwin, namely that evolution seems to contain such cruelty, waste and ugliness as to make it hard to defend as the means to a divine end. One of the strengths of Darwin's theory was that it explained, without

---

[1] Though theologians could and did argue for a different sort of designer God (cf. Brooke, 1991:310–17).

the need for any *ad hoc* hypotheses, both aesthetically appealing adaptations, such as the beak of the woodpecker, and the 'ugliness' of species like the *ichneumonidae* – wasps whose larvae are implanted within the body of a caterpillar and eat it alive from the inside. We explore the ugliness and waste in evolution as a continuing problem for theology in **7.15**.

EXERCISE 4.1

Consider to what extent these challenges remain problems for a contemporary faith. How might Christian theological schemes address these problems?

4.5　Theological responses

It is important not to over-stress the static nature of Christian theology at the time of Darwin. As Welch points out, before 1850 Schleiermacher and those following him had already questioned whether the doctrine of creation implied any particular point of temporal origin, whether the Fall implied a particular event in early human history, and whether God was immutable in the traditional sense (Welch, 1996:34). Probably the greatest challenges to the mainstream of the Christian tradition in the nineteenth century came from biblical criticism rather than natural science. However, the controversy over Darwin's scheme is one of the great moments in the history of the 'special relationship' (see **1.14**). But it is *a* moment in history. It is important to grasp just how much both Christian theology and evolutionary theory have changed since the British Association Meeting of 1860.

There were those Christian thinkers who immediately celebrated evolution. Frederick Temple, who preached the official sermon at the British Association Meeting in 1860 'was … said by one observer to have espoused Darwin's ideas fully' (Brooke, 1991:41). Charles Kingsley found that it was 'just as noble a conception of Deity, to believe that He created primal forms capable of self development … as to believe that He required a fresh act of intervention to supply the lacunas which He Himself had made' (quoted in Desmond and Moore, 1992:477). Kingsley saw that the new science might redirect the all-important balance in Christian theology between God's transcendence and the divine indwelling of creation (immanence) in favour of a greater emphasis on immanence.

Moreover, as we shall see in Chapter 6, theology in the light of the great success of science, and the great tragedies to human civilisation of the World Wars and the Holocaust, has become much more willing to describe a God who suffers, and whose continual creative activity is within a universe characterised by processes of law and chance, processes which God rarely, if ever, sets aside. The imagery of God the Sovereign Lord, the King of Kings, the Creator *ex nihilo*, the potter who creates according to an inscrutable will, has now to be weighed against descriptions of God 'the fellow-sufferer who understands' (see Chapter 6, especially **6.2–6.3**, **6.5.1–6.5.3**).

SECTION B:
DEVELOPMENTS IN EVOLUTIONARY THEORY
TO THE PRESENT DAY (4.6–4.8)

4.6   Mendelian genetics, leading to neo-Darwinism

One of the great difficulties of Darwin's theory was that, knowing nothing of the mechanisms of heredity, he thought parental characteristics were transmitted in the blood. Rare variants, however successful, would therefore be likely to be diluted out. This is no doubt why Darwin continued to admit the 'laws of use and disuse' – direct influence of experience on inheritance in the way that Lamarck had proposed (see **4.2**) – as well as natural selection. The problem was certainly a factor in the lack of acceptance of Darwinism in the late nineteenth century.

The solution lay at hand in Darwin's own lifetime. In 1866 Gregor Mendel (1822–84), a monk in Brün, Moravia, published a paper on the inheritance of attributes ('characters') in the garden pea. His work remained in obscurity for more than three decades, but in it he showed that characters were transmitted as units. Each higher organism had a pair of units (which we now call 'genes') for each inherited character. A particular gene (for example for blue eyes) may be expressed or lie dormant, but it is not simply diluted out as Darwin feared.

The first supporters of Mendelian genetics, from about 1900, rejected Darwinian evolution, because they argued that the proposed accumulation of minute variations, suggested by Darwin, were contradicted by the much larger changes observed by Mendel. Nevertheless, with time, the science of genetics became linked inseparably with Darwin's theory. By 1942, the date of the publication of Julian Huxley's book *Evolution: the Modern Synthesis*, the developing science of genetics and a recasting of the proposals of Darwin had been combined in the theory known as *neo-Darwinism*. 'The essence of neo-Darwinian argument is that the adaptation of organisms to their environment is brought about by natural selection acting upon small inherited variations, most of which are initially non-adaptive. Mutation [see **4.7.3**] is the ultimate source of new variation and it is preserved and transmitted by the mechanism of particulate inheritance' (Dowdeswell, 1984:157).

4.7   Discussion of the central characteristics of life

Those patronising 'The Eagle' pub in Cambridge in the last forty years may well have been told the story that on a memorable day in 1953 Francis Crick and James D. Watson burst in shouting that they had found the secret of life. Indeed their work on DNA was of the greatest importance, and did, in a sense, found a new science, and a highly successful one, called molecular biology.

But what *is* life, anyway? In Genesis 2 it is an attribute specially and distinctively imparted to a shape (which God had formed from the dust of the ground) by the divine *ruach* (breath, or spirit). But what is it *scientifically* that is shared by 'men, moulds and marigolds' (Cairns-Smith, 1990:2)? Life proves to be curiously difficult to define, but all lists of the properties common to all living organisms would include:

> being actually or potentially capable of reproduction, and
>
> having a boundary within which is an environment far from chemical equilibrium.

The most basic unit of life is a cell (see Figure 4.1 for a diagram of what some cells look like).

FIGURE 4.1

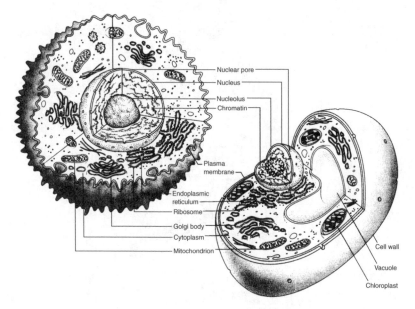

Nuclear pore
Nucleus
Nucleolus
Chromatin

Plasma
membrane

Endoplasmic
reticulum
Ribosome
Golgi body
Cytoplasm
Mitochondrion

Cell wall

Vacuole

Chloroplast

A diagram of a typical cell from an animal (left) and a plant (right)
(reproduced with permission from Berg and Singer, 1992:12).

For now we shall concentrate on the first property listed – reproduction. In the argument that began in 1996 over whether particular
structures in meteorites could be signs of life on ancient Mars, the clues
scientists particularly looked for were traces of structures in the process
of reproduction. If the shapes seen in the rock were once cells, we might
hope to see some in the process of division, a new cell budding off from
an old. Living things, characteristically, make copies of themselves. How
this is achieved is one of the central areas of study in biology. It is helpful
to understand it in some detail.

4.7.1   How DNA codes for information and enables it to be copied

The first step is to understand that most of the functions in cells involve
proteins, which provide much of the structure, and also catalyse (speed
up) and regulate the chemical reactions by which cells maintain themselves, grow and divide. Each protein must be made to a very precise
sequence of amino-acids.

FIGURE 4.2

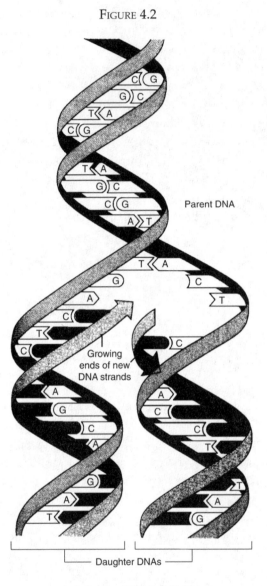

A replicating DNA molecule
(reproduced with permission from Berg and Singer, 1992:47).

Now look carefully at Figure 4.2, which shows the famous 'double
helix' of DNA unfolding and being copied to generate two 'daughter'
helices. This is the essential step by which cells give rise to copies of
themselves, each containing the genetic information to programme their
activity.

Note that on the inside of each strand of the helix (hence in a relatively stable position chemically) is a component, a 'base', which may be of one of four kinds: A, T, G or C. Each of these is a slightly different shape (the actual shapes are more subtle than the diagram indicates, but the principle is the same). So a strand of helix is like a series of letters in a four-letter alphabet. Just as the nine-letter word 'moonstone' has a different meaning from the word 'monotones', so in DNA language ATTGCGATG has a different meaning from AGAGTCGTT. Each strand, then, is a carrier of information in a four-letter alphabet. What is vital, though, is that the information can be reproduced. This is possible because each of the 'letters', bases as they are called, sticks to one and only one other base. A pairs only with T, G with C. So, reading down Figure 4.2, one strand reads CGTCTGCA. It can therefore only pair as shown:

C	G	T	C	T	G	C	A
G	C	A	G	A	C	G	T

with 'GCAGACGT'.[2]

When individual bases are brought up to the growing strands, each one can only be paired with the base complementary to itself. So the blacked-out base being paired with C on the right-hand strand in the Figure must be a G. When a strand is copied, then, it gives rise to a copy with the complementary sequence (with G's wherever there was a C in the parent, T's wherever there was an A, and so on). When the daughter strand is copied, the original sequence is restored.

A DNA strand, then, is a stable, copiable string of 'letters', arranged into groups called 'genes'. A typical gene might be 600–3,000 letters long in DNA language. The function of each gene is to code for a protein, which is also a long molecule built up of a sequence, like a sequence of letters.

The sequence in a protein, however, is in a twenty-letter alphabet, composed of the twenty different amino-acids. One DNA base from a choice of four would not provide enough variety to specify one of twenty amino-acids. A one-letter 'word' will not do to stipulate which amino-acid is to be put into the protein. Three bases are required.

---

[2] For the technically minded, the daughter strand runs in the opposite direction to the parental strand. It still constitutes a complete copy of the four-letter-coded information from the parent.

The first great period of modern molecular biology, 1953–64, established the following:

1. the structure of the genetic material DNA, which explained its information-carrying role and its ability to be copied.
2. the so-called 'central dogma' that:
   (a) DNA is (usually) the primary carrier of genetic information, which is copied from one generation to the next.
   (b) DNA is 'transcribed' into a secondary information-carrier, a 'message' of the closely related chemical RNA.
   (c) that message is then 'translated' into protein, according to a three-letter code known as the genetic code. Thus, the RNA 'word' CGG codes for the amino-acid arginine, and the 'words' AAA and AAG both code for the amino-acid lysine. All organisms on Earth use almost exactly the same code, evidence in itself for the view that all organisms are descended from the same group of primitive cells.
   (d) information, then, can pass from DNA to protein, but not the other way round.

Summary of **4.7.1**: A strand of DNA can be compared to a string of letters, which can be copied to make more DNA, or interpreted to make proteins for the cell's structure and function. For a slightly more extended, but still non-technical, account of the basics of molecular genetics see Bowker (1995:18–25).

4.7.2   Aside: elegance in biology and physics

One interesting feature of the development of molecular biology parallels that of particle physics. In 1932, with the discovery of the neutron, it was thought that there were precisely three sub-atomic particles. There are now thought to be in the region of 160. In 1964 there was thought to be a very simple relation between DNA sequence and functional protein in a cell, and that relationship is now known to be very complex and diverse, depending on hitherto unexpected phenomena. (For instance, a gene may occur not in one string, but in a series of sections ['exons'], separated by non-coding sequences ['introns'].) Science *sometimes* gives rise to extraordinarily elegant, simplifying steps forward, but other phases render the picture of a subject more and more intricate. And scientists' sense of what *is* elegant also moves on with the subject.

4.7.3 Questions arising about DNA – the importance of mutation

Two questions arise from this account of the functioning of the genetic material:

(a) How can a system based on such faithful copying be subject to change?
(b) How could such a complicated system, full of independent components (for all the processes we have described are dependent on the function of enzymes and cellular structures, in turn coded for by genes) have arisen in the first place? This is the ultimate chicken-and-egg problem!

Question (a) leads us directly to evolution at the molecular level, which we address below. Question (b) remains a profoundly difficult one for science, though hints of an answer may be coming from the work of complexity theorists such as Stuart Kauffman (see **4.8.2**).

Question (a) can be answered directly by reference to the chemistry of DNA. Although the sequence of letters is very stable, it is not absolutely stable. Although the copying of the strands is very accurate, it is not absolutely accurate. So the information can be 'mutated'. Variations are always creeping in. And whenever there is a range of variants being reproduced, processes of natural selection operate. Variants which promote survival and reproduction survive – others die out. It is important to realise that mutation is not necessarily harmful to a species – indeed it provides the variation without which natural selection cannot operate.

The simplest form of mutation is a 'point' mutation where a single base of DNA is changed, like a single mistyped letter. Many of these changes have little or no effect on the function of the protein that is made from them – others will be ruinous, others may enhance the protein's present function, or enhance another function which may later develop. It is now known that mutation can also occur through sections of DNA moving around (like paragraphs being moved around in word-processing). Again, the effects will often be deleterious, but sometimes they will confer some selective advantage. The great evolutionary advantage of sexual reproduction is that it makes possible a further shuffling of genes called 'recombination'.

4.8   Some recent debates about evolution

The *details* of evolutionary theory are hotly debated. But it has developed from Darwin's original proposal into a theory of enormous explanatory power – it fits to a very marked degree Barbour's criteria for a successful scientific theory: agreement with data, coherence, scope and fertility (1998:113). It is for this reason that we do not consider here schemes which seek an alternative science in order to defend a literalist reading of Scripture.[3] However, there are vigorous debates within Darwinism; we outline some of the main ones in the paragraphs following. For a detailed technical discussion see the two books edited by Depew and Weber (1985; 1995).

4.8.1   Punctuated equilibrium and radical contingency

Darwin supposed that variation would involve very small changes that might be difficult to detect and would initially appear to have little significance for natural selection. The idea that evolution proceeds by such small steps and never makes jumps, is a key 'dogma' in neo-Darwinism. It is called *gradualism*. There have been some challenges to this belief but the most significant have been by Eldredge and Gould, stemming from a paper in 1972. They stated that there was strong evidence in the fossil record for long periods of *stasis*, during which virtually no evolution occurred. These long periods of several million years were *punctuated* by relatively short periods of rapid evolution, over periods of 5,000 to 50,000 years, which is very brief in geological time. This view has more or less been integrated into neo-Darwinism.

The work of Gould in particular remains important, through his resolute resistance to Dawkins' genetic reductionism (see below), his insistence that evolution cannot be equated with progress, and his emphasis on historical contingency. In his beautiful book *Wonderful Life*, on the fossil evidence of the Burgess Shale, a sediment in the Canadian

---

[3] See Burke (1998:51–54) for some discussion of 'creation science' – also Barbour (1998:83–84 and notes thereon).

Rockies, Gould emphasises that it would have been impossible, inspecting the range of organisms of 500 million years ago, to say which would survive into later eras, yet all the vertebrates we know are thought to be descended from a single, insignificant-seeming type of worm called *Pikaia*. So running the tape of life again would be very unlikely to give rise to creatures like ourselves (Gould, 1991, especially Chapter 5).

The status of Gould's conclusions in *Wonderful Life* has recently been challenged by Simon Conway Morris in his *The Crucible of Creation* (1998).[4] Conway Morris, one of the principal investigators of the Burgess Shale, takes issue in particular with one of Gould's main points – that the last 500 million years have been characterised much more by the 'grim reaper' of extinction than by the continual branching of the tree of life. Different analyses of the data can give a very different conclusion – that evolutionary innovation has persisted, and shown continual evidence of convergence (the same characteristics arising by different evolutionary paths). Conway Morris infers from this that it was extremely likely that some form of complex life, such as humanity, would have evolved (1998:13–14, 199–205). For further discussion of these probabilities see **7.15.1**.

4.8.2   Self-organisation and the development of complexity

Here the most important figure is Stuart Kauffman, whose ideas are most accessibly presented in his *At Home in the Universe* (1995). Kauffman's work stems principally out of his analysis of non-linear systems – the mathematics of chaos, as modelled on the modern computer and applied to biological systems. In a sense his conclusions complement Gould's:

Gould's stress is that the evolution of higher organisms is not a matter of inevitable progress to greater sophistication, but rather that higher systems are always vulnerable to environmental change (most famously when a massive impact from space, 65 million years ago, made, it is thought, a major contribution to the extinction of the dinosaurs).

Kauffman has made use of work by Ilya Prigogine on complex chemical systems held far from equilibrium. The surface of the early Earth contained many such systems (because energy was continually pouring in from the sun and upwards from the hot interior). It is now

---

[4] For other rebuttals of Gould see Dennett (1995:300–08) and Dawkins (1998:193–209).

known that these systems are always likely to give rise to greater complexity. So the particularly elaborate systems that are self-replicating cells were, Kauffman alleges, very likely to arise.[5] Not merely that, but such evolving systems will tend to move to a special ordered state near to 'the edge of chaos', representing the ideal balance between stability and propensity to explore change.[6] So one of the properties that organisms may be expected to evolve is 'evolvability' – the capacity to try out new properties without prematurely losing the benefit of the old. Although the course of evolution will always be influenced by selection, and radically altered by any sudden climatic or geological change, it will be much influenced by the mathematics of self-organisation. Yes, evolution does depend on all sorts of chances, but also yes, a thermodynamic system like the surface of the Earth will keep throwing up the possibility of complexity.

An extension of the concept that organisms evolve evolvability is the perception that they develop information-processing systems which can analyse the environment and respond not just to stimuli which have occurred in the past but to conditions not met before. The immune systems of higher organisms would be an example, but in a sense the clearest case is the human intellect itself – a product of natural selection which is so versatile and creative that its activity affects the environment of millions of other species.

4.8.3   The rhetoric of Darwinism

Gould has suggested that Darwin deliberately stressed the reductionistic, physicalist aspects of his theory in order to eliminate any hint of the involvement of a designer or a vital force in his explanation of the development of living things (see Depew and Weber, 1985:253). Rather the rhetoric of Darwinism is of a 'force' (selection) acting upon essentially passive objects considered in isolation (organisms). It is the rhetoric of physics. And physics has also profoundly influenced molecular biology;[7] genes are described as strings of chemicals to which

---

[5] It should not be supposed that Kauffman has solved the very difficult chicken-and-egg problem we posed at **4.7.3**. The *details* of how a system as intricate as a single cell arose remain frustratingly obscure. What Kauffman has shown is that autocatalytic systems (where each of the components speeds up the reaction of the others) can become self-sustaining and therefore become the first self-replicators.

[6] See also Bak (1997) on 'self-organized criticality'.

[7] See **4.11** on the physicist Erwin Schrödinger's seminal lectures on the nature of life.

mutations happen. It may be, however, that the rhetoric of evolution in the next century will be much more in terms of Kauffman's work, of interdependent organisms exploring together the possibilities of greater complexity.

4.8.4 Evolution as a science of the unrepeatable past

Antagonists of the theory of evolution reject it on the basis that it is unprovable. It is true that the theory of evolution cannot be completely verified by direct observation of every part of the process. This is true of all theories that provide explanations for processes that involve immense periods of time. Peacocke (1986:35) comments: 'the postulate of past biological evolution cannot be falsified in the sense of Karl Popper,[8] by performing repeatable experiments whose outcomes are inconsistent with the postulate [that evolution has occurred] – nor can most theories of geology and of cosmology'.

Evolutionary biology, then, is akin to Big Bang cosmology, and much of astrophysics, in that it offers models to explain processes which are historically particular, and could never be duplicated in a laboratory. (In the case of cosmology this is because the energies involved are too high; in the case of evolution, because the timescales are too long.) Such sciences have an especially broad scope for dialogue with descriptions of the Christian God. The reason is that those descriptions tend to emphasise a Being who cannot be put to experimental test, but who is everywhere creative, and active in every part of history. (See **1.15** for discussion of the shifting dialogue between Christian theology of creation and Big Bang cosmology. See Chapters 6 and 7 for examination of proposals on God's nature and activity.)

SECTION C:
CAN REDUCTIONIST PROGRAMMES RULE OUT THE TRUTH OF RELIGION? (4.9–4.14)

4.9 Conflict revived: defining our terms

In contrast to the view given above, a number of contemporary thinkers have supposed that – far from being in dialogue with theology – Darwinism has utterly disproved the claims of religion about the

---

[8] See **2.7** on Popper and falsification.

ultimate nature of reality. Evolutionary thinking has given rise to a renaissance of explicit conflict between scientific and religious claims. In order to understand this renaissance it is important to distinguish three intellectual endeavours – naturalism, physicalism and reductionism – in their relation to theism. So we begin by defining these terms:

- *Naturalism*: 'a sympathy with the view that ultimately nothing resists explanation by the methods characteristic of the natural sciences' (Blackburn, 1994:255).

  As Blackburn points out: 'The central problem for naturalism is to define what counts as a satisfactory accommodation between the preferred sciences and the elements that on the face of it have no place in them' (1994:255).

- *Physicalism*: 'the view that the real world is nothing more than the physical world' (1994:287). This is a better term than 'materialism' because matter itself is described by physics in terms of energies and forces.

- *Reductionism*: a process of re-describing one area of discourse in terms of the explanations of another, more fundamental level of discourse.

Let us look at these different programmes of thought interacting in the contemporary debate between evolutionary biology and theology.

4.10 Conflict revived: Jacques Monod, Richard Dawkins and E. O. Wilson

The sorts of mutations of the genetic material we described above are not predictable; indeed a point mutation is an event directly influenced by quantum states, and therefore intrinsically indeterminate (see **1.17**, **3.11–3.12, 7.6 (iv)(b), 7.15.1**). It is this irreducible element of chance of which the great molecular biologist Jacques Monod wrote:

> Pure chance, absolutely free but blind, [is] at the very root of the stupendous edifice of evolution . . . (Monod, 1972:110)

> The ancient covenant is in pieces; man at last knows that he is alone in the unfeeling immensity of the universe, out of which he emerged by chance. (Monod, 1972:167)

These much-quoted sentences reveal much about the debate between biological atheists and those who want to defend a theistic account.

Monod, on the basis of his own existential presuppositions, makes a large step from the existence of chance within a process to asserting that the process is determined by nothing other than chance. He confines the categories of possible explanation to the natural, and then infers that there is no super-natural meaning to the world. Those scientist-theologians who wish to defend a theistic account are quite prepared to acknowledge the existence of chance, indeed to see it as a positive ingredient in an unfolding creation. Polkinghorne says: 'The role of chance can be seen as a signal of the Creator's allowing his creation to make itself' (1996a:47). D. J. Bartholomew in his major study *God of Chance* wrote that 'chance offers the potential Creator many advantages which it is difficult to envisage being obtained in any other way' (Bartholomew, 1984:97). We shall take up this question of a God who works with indeterminate processes in more detail in Chapter 7.

The proposal that Darwinism can eliminate the need for theology has been advanced in particular in the writings of Richard Dawkins, the 'selfish gene' theorist and first Professor of the Public Understanding of Science at Oxford, E. O. Wilson and his fellow sociobiologists, and Francis Crick. These thinkers have in common a rejection of the possibility that religious propositions about creation could have any validity. They see ideas of God as no more than phenomena in the history of human evolution.

Science is an aspect of Western culture which has been very successful in giving certain groups of human beings power over their environment. This gives credibility to attempts by scientific thinkers to *reduce* religion itself to a phenomenon for examination within the discipline of their science (see **1.5.1**). (These attempts receive much more attention than theological examinations of the bases of scientific exploration.) At the most polemical end is Dawkins, developing his idea of a 'meme', a complex of ideas evolving within a human culture:

> Consider the idea of God. We do not know how it arose in the meme pool. Probably it arose many times by independent 'mutation' ... Why does it have such a high survival value? ... What is it about the idea of a god that gives it stability and penetrance in the cultural environment? The survival value of the god meme in the meme pool results from its great psychological appeal. It provides a superficially plausible answer to deep and troubling questions about existence. It suggests that injustices

in this world may be rectified in the next. The 'everlasting arms' hold out a cushion against our own inadequacies which, like a doctor's placebo, is none the less effective for being imaginary. (Dawkins, 1978:207)

Any possibility that human ideas of God might reflect in however partial a way the *existence* of such a being is discounted. So also Wilson:

[W]e have come to the crucial stage in the history of biology when religion itself is subject to the explanations of the natural sciences ... sociobiology can account for the very origin of mythology by the principle of natural selection acting on the genetically evolving material structure of the human brain.

If this interpretation is correct, the final decisive edge enjoyed by scientific naturalism will come from its capacity to explain traditional religion, its chief competitor, as a wholly material phenomenon. (Wilson, 1995:192)

Compare this with the much more measured and less polemical approach of Willem Drees:

Theologians ... have to take into account that religious beliefs and interpretations arose in various historical and pre-historical circumstances. That such beliefs arose in certain circumstances *does not imply that they must be wrong* [emphasis ours], but their historical contingency in relation to human history and human nature raises the question of why we would consider particular beliefs of an earlier epoch as serious candidates for truth or as existentially relevant insights, worth reformulating in our time. Translating theological convictions into new terms by finding new models and metaphors is, in my opinion, inadequate if questions concerning the evolved, historical character of human religious traditions are passed by. (Drees, 1996:4)

[H]umans and their cultures, languages, aesthetic and moral codes, and their religious practices can be seen as results of a natural evolutionary process ... The actual history of morality and religions and their actual functioning in the web of genes, mind and culture are very complex, and therefore not clear. The complexities of culture and mind should not be glossed over in short-cuts from genes to human behaviour and social institutions. (Drees, 1996:212–13)

EXERCISE 4.2

Look at the passages from Monod, Dawkins and Wilson quoted above, preferably going back to the original sources. Examine the presuppositions of the writers. How do they compare with your own presuppositions about religious belief? Is humanity 'alone' in the universe, or 'at home'?

In Monod we saw the baldly stated conclusion that a universe containing chance occurrences is a universe without meaning. He moved from the naturalistic descriptions of science to a physicalist metaphysic, a clear sign that he began from a physicalist premise.

Dawkins and Wilson are both genetic reductionists – they both see a wide range of behaviour in humans and other higher organisms as attributable to the functioning of genes, and hence a manifestation of Darwinian selection. (Though Dawkins at least admits a higher level of selection, the unit of cultural inheritance or 'meme'. Furthermore he admits the possibility that genes will cease to be the important level of evolutionary selection in humans.)

4.11   An examination of reductionism

To understand their positions, and the 'new conflict' in the area of biology and religion we must look more closely at reductionism. Peacocke in a rather elaborate account (1986:1–30) makes the important point that not all reductionism is prejudicial to the science–religion debate. Indeed, a form of reductionism is intrinsic to all scientific explanation:

> The breaking-down of unintelligible, complex wholes into their component units, the determination of the structures of those pieces and what functions they can perform, and then the fitting of them together as best one can, hypothetically at least, in order to see how they function together in a complex whole, are such common ploys in experimental science that most practising scientists would consider it scarcely worth remarking upon. (Peacocke, 1986:6)

Again, science has made great progress through assuming that for experimental purposes living things can be described in terms of atoms and molecules – science need consider no extra fundamental ingredient which makes them living, contrary to the thinking known as *vitalism*. However, this very basic physicalist assumption is of strictly limited importance. All human beings are made of the same sorts of atoms, indeed the same sorts of chemicals. We *do* consist of 'nothing but' these constituents in the restricted sense that if those chemicals were taken away there would be nothing left. Yet there is clearly more to be said about different human beings than that.

When Francis Crick proclaimed that 'The ultimate aim of the modern movement in biology is in fact to explain *all* biology in terms of physics and chemistry' (quoted in Peacocke, 1986:12), he was seeking to replace one set of scientific descriptions by a more fundamental set. (This is 'bottom-up' thinking, which views 'higher-level' descriptions as special cases of more basic science. In discussing quantum mechanics in **3.10– 3.14** we saw that 'bottom-up' thinking runs into limitations at the smallest level of things, but this does not take away its attractiveness in other sciences.)

Three questions may be asked to discover whether Crick's project has succeeded:

(i)   do the laws of physics and chemistry apply to the atoms and molecules of living things?

(ii) are the interactions of atoms and molecules according to physics and chemistry sufficient to account for biological phenomena, or are other kinds of interaction needed?

(iii) can biological theories be deduced logically from the theories of physics and chemistry?

The answer to the first two is yes, but to the third no. Although biology involves the same matter, and the same forces, as physics and chemistry, new levels of description are needed to do justice to biological systems. So the reduction has not succeeded.[9]

The complement to science's natural tendency to reductionism is *emergence*. An emergent property is one describing a higher level of organization of matter, where the description is not epistemologically reducible to lower-level concepts (Peacocke, 1986:28–29). A classic example would be that of an ecosystem. In order to understand

---

[9] For a (fairly technical) application of this approach to reductionism in the area of evolution see Ayala (1985:65–77).

organisms coexisting together we need this concept, and cannot reduce it out of our understandings. (Come to that, the concept 'multi-cellular organism' is itself emergent – simply to describe an animal as a collection of cells living together is to miss a great many properties characteristic of the way those cells co-operate.)

Two notes of caution:

(i) We are not here referring to *temporal* emergence – a more complex system developing *over time* from a simpler, but to emergence within our levels of description.

(ii) The sort of reductionism on which we have just been concentrating concerns epistemology, the state of our ability to describe a subject. This is subject to change, and it is indeed conceivable that a property regarded at one time as emergent might later be deduced from the properties of a simpler system.

What actually happened in the history of molecular biology was most interesting. A number of scientists, Crick included, first began to consider questions of the chemistry of life because of a series of lectures given by the physicist Erwin Schrödinger in Dublin in 1943, and published as *What is Life?* The remarkable success of the investigations of such figures as Pauling, Perutz, Crick and Watson gave momentum to this programme of redescribing biology in terms of physics and chemistry, but has not effected a *reduction* of the one to the other. *Rather all sorts of emergent properties have been recognised at the interface between biology and chemistry* (see **4.7.2** on introns and exons, non-coding and coding DNA). Crick's aim has not been realised. He himself, after his groundbreaking work with DNA and the genetic code, moved on to another reductionistic programme – the redescription of mental events in terms of neurophysiology (see **5.3**).

4.12 The particular case of genetic reductionism

Dawkins and Wilson are genetic reductionists, in that they have picked a particular level of scientific explanation, that of the functioning of genes, and downplayed the claims of higher-level descriptions. This is a vastly tempting reduction, because we understand, in principle at least, a great deal about genes and how they function. We understand far less about organisms, how they grow and develop, what determines their behaviour.

Two points are important here:

- Genetic reductionism, as a theory, is much criticised within science. Dawkins in his book *The Selfish Gene* (Dawkins, 1978 – first published 1976) popularised a theory that the behaviour of whole organisms can be understood in terms of genes 'seeking' to reproduce themselves. The organisms themselves can be seen merely as 'vehicles' for the behaviour of genes. This ingenious way of thinking does explain certain elements of behaviour in certain organisms, but it does not do justice to evolution as a whole. Natural selection 'sees a five-foot tall plant as a five-foot-tall plant, not as a five-foot-tall plant with genotype *g* ... [the] phenotype[10] will screen off any intrinsic property of the gene (or the genotype) from its level of reproductive success' (Brandon, 1985:90). Or as Brian Goodwin colourfully puts it: 'As the spots disappear, so does the leopard' (see Goodwin, 1995:28f. and Rose, 1997:213f. for two recent critiques of selfish gene theory).

  We take up the claims of sociobiologists such as Wilson below – here it is enough to note that we are very far from being able to say that a particular gene directly codes for a particular human behaviour. Even behaviour with a strong genetic component is almost certain to derive from interaction between the products of many different genes. At the very most all we can say is that particular genes may have some effect on individuals' predisposition to the learning of some life-patterns rather than others.

- Genetic reductionism, as an attitude, leads to significant ethical concerns. The massive Human Genome Project to map every human chromosome will shortly be completed, a great advance in our knowledge. But it carries with it the danger that we may oversimplify our view of the human being. A one-dimensional string of code is a long way from a complete account of a person. The most obvious problems raised are:

  (a) those within the insurance industry, since knowledge of a person's DNA could lead to predictions as to what illness they *might* have in twenty years' time, irrespective of the character of the person or the nature of their lifestyle;

  (b) the temptation to suppose one could necessarily produce a 'better' human being by altering the genes of an embryo and implanting it into a mother (currently a prohibited practice in the UK) – thus

---

[10] The term 'phenotype' refers to how an organism manifests itself (as a result of the expression of its genes in the context of its internal structures and external environment).

altering forever the genetic inheritance of that person. As Barbour points out, 'Some of the indirect consequences of (such) intervention might be harmful, delayed and irreversible' (1992:196).

See also **11.8–11.9** on genetic reductionism considered in relation to the ethics of biotechnology.

4.13   'Cross-explanatory' reductionism

What we see in Monod, Dawkins and Wilson goes beyond a mere preference for a certain level of scientific explanation. They are also what might be called 'cross-explanatory reductionists', in that they assert that naturalistic explanations, interpretative and descriptive in nature, *render unnecessary* explanations of a reason-giving (motives) kind (see the categories described in **1.16**). To them theistic truth-claims are unnecessary and misplaced, and the underlying reasons for them must be sought in terms of behaviours which were adaptive at earlier points in the history of humanity. *This cross-explanatory reductionism presumes not simply that lower-level, gene-based description is adequate, and other explanations such as the religious are therefore redundant, but that the lower-level, the scientific, is adequate and that therefore the religious must be **wrong**.* Dawkins develops this via his attack on the argument from design in *The Blind Watchmaker* (Dawkins, 1991, first published 1988). He works from the same premise as Monod – *that only one sort of explanation is acceptable* (see also **5.4**).

The weakness of this sort of argument should be evident. It could be accepted only if its particular, often unstated, presuppositions were also accepted. Dawkins' presuppositions are well analysed by Poole (1994) and Ward (1996b:96ff.). Ward lists them as:

- that only material entities have any existence,
- that the universe lacks purpose or meaning,
- that scientific explanations are the only proper explanations (p. 99).

EXERCISE 4.3

Ward asserts that theism has presuppositions no more far-fetched or less testable. Could you list three analogous to the list above?

4.14   Is a 'hard' naturalism the best basis from examining points of contact between biology and theology?

Drees' *Religion, Science and Naturalism* is an attempt to push a naturalistic programme as far as it will go. Drees himself describes his approach as one of 'hard' or 'reductive' naturalism, attempting 'to view human behaviour in an "objective", "detached" light as events in nature' (Drees, 1996:11, drawing on the categories of Strawson). But as the passages quoted above indicate, Drees is well aware of the limits of our present understanding. We cannot say that religious beliefs 'must be wrong', nor are we in any sort of position to say exactly how or why human evolution has given rise to them. Naturalism does not have to be defended by cross-explanatory reductionism, whether this arises out of genetic reductionism in biology (see above) or eliminative materialism in neuroscience (see **5.2–5.4**).

Drees sets out his postulates with great clarity, not leaving them unexamined as in so much of Dawkins' writing. Three are helpful to note:

(i) ontological naturalism: 'The natural world is the whole of reality that we know of and interact with; no supernatural or spiritual realm distinct from the natural world shows up *within* our natural world, not even in the mental life of humans' (Drees, 1996:12);

(ii) constitutive reductionism: 'Our natural world is a unity in the sense that all entities are made up of the same constituents' (1996:14);

(iii) conceptual and explanatory non-reductionism – a recognition that some phenomena have to be described in terms of concepts beyond those of physics (1996:16).

Drees' proposal is, in effect, that if one accords the maximum status to the conclusions of science, including those sciences that analyse the functioning of religion, whatever points of contact are left with theology will be intellectually robust. Points of contact between a naturalistic description of the world and a picture of that world as dependent on a transcendent Creator will tend to involve 'limit-questions' in fundamental physics and cosmology (Drees, 1996:18). However, as Drees himself realises, it would be hard to give reasons for believing in such a God, since no evidence from the world, or from human mental functioning, could be admitted.

Our approach in this book is that there is a spiritual aspect to reality which is not adequately described by naturalism. Drees would see this as a rejection of the first of his fundamental postulates listed above. We are drawn to this view by the conviction that Christian descriptions of reality, like scientific ones, also exhibit agreement with 'data' (in the sense of the experience of the Christian community in worship and prayer, reflection on its history and reading of Scripture), coherence, scope and fertility. As Polkinghorne in particular has indicated (e.g. in *Serious Talk* [Polkinghorne, 1995a]), such a world-view can be in rich conversation with a view which takes scientific descriptions, including a certain element of reductionism, seriously, but stops short of the derisive anti-religionism of Dawkins or the hard, exclusive naturalism of Drees.

As we indicated in **1.5.1**, Drees is right to point out that religious understandings of reality must recognise that religion itself arose at an early stage in the evolution of humankind. We recognise too that religious understandings of human beings (theological anthropologies) need to take into account that humans are evolved beings. However, we also saw in **1.5.1** how difficult it is for the theist and the non-believer to agree on the significance of religious claims as they evolved. There needs to be a conversation between evolutionary and theological anthropology, and it is to that conversation that we now turn.

SECTION C:
HUMAN EVOLUTION (4.15–4.17)

4.15   The evolution of hominids

We begin by considering scientific accounts of the origin of modern humans. The fossil record of the hominids (*Homo sapiens* and its relatives) is sparse, with many long gaps (since fossils only tend to be found where the process of fossilisation occurs most readily). The evolution of the hominids is therefore not well understood in detail and new fossil finds are still causing significant changes to the proposed lines of descent. We present in Figure 4.3 (page 164) the present consensus on early hominid evolution.

FIGURE 4.3

	Homo habilis (small)	Homo habilis (large)	Homo erectus	'Archaic Homo sapiens'	Neanderthals	Early modern Homo sapiens
Height (m)	1	c. 1.5	1.3–1.5	?	1.5–1.7	1.6–1.85
Physique	Relatively long arms	Robust but 'human' skeleton	Robust but 'human' skeleton	Robust but 'human' skeleton	As 'archaic H. sapiens', but adapted for cold	Modern skeleton; ?adapted for warmth
Brain size (ml)	500–650	600–800	750–1250	1100–1400	1200–1750	1200–1700
Skull form	Relatively small face; nose developed	Larger, flatter face	Flat, thick skull with large occipital and brow ridge	Higher skull; face less protruding	Reduced brow ridge; thinner skull; large nose; midface projection	Small or no brow ridge; shorter, high skull
Jaws/teeth	Thinner jaw; smaller, narrow molars	Robust jaw; large narrow molars	Robust jaw in larger individuals; smaller teeth than H. habilis	Similar to H. erectus but teeth may be smaller	Similar to 'archaic H. sapiens'; teeth smaller except for incisors; chin development in some	Shorter jaws than Neanderthals; chin developed; teeth may be smaller
Distribution	Eastern (+ southern?) Africa	Eastern Africa	Africa, Asia and Indonesia (+ Europe?)	Africa, Asia and Europe	Europe and western Asia	Africa and western Asia
Known date (years ago)	2–1.6 million	2–1.6 million	1.8–0.3 million	400,000– 100,000	150,000– 30,000	130,000– 60,000

Distinguishing features of early human species
(reproduced with permission from Stringer, 1992:251)

4.15.1   The Neanderthals

Neanderthal man existed from at least 150,000 years ago – perhaps as much as 230,000 – to about 30,000 years ago. The Neanderthals seem to have become adapted for life in cold environments associated with periods of glaciation. Their migrations south, into the Middle

East, may have been to escape particularly cold winters, or perhaps to follow game, since they were efficient hunters. They were very heavily built, with an average height of up to 1.7 metres, and had powerful muscles, making them much stronger than modern humans. They had pronounced brow ridges, a receding forehead, pronounced jaw and a bulging back to the head. Brain size was slightly *greater* than that of the modern human.

In the Middle East the north-based Neanderthals and the more southerly-based 'modern' humans came into contact. It was once suggested that the two species were so closely related that they could interbreed. However a comparison between DNA from mitochondria (energy-producing components within cells) from modern humans and fossil bone of Neanderthals indicates that *Homo sapiens* and *Homo neanderthalis* were two entirely separate species, incapable of interbreeding, that diverged from a common stock between 550,000 and 690,000 years ago (Krings *et al.*, 1997:25).[11] There is no convincing explanation of why the Neanderthals disappeared about 30,000 years ago – no evidence of antagonism between Neanderthals and 'modern' humans; rather there seems to have been peaceful, though separate, co-existence.

There is evidence of 'religious' practice amongst at least some Neanderthal populations [the embryonic position and east–west orientation of some burials, burial with grave 'goods' such as flint tools, the possible scattering of flower blossoms – grape hyacinth, hollyhock and grounsel and boughs of pine – over the dead, the circling of a grave with six pairs of goat horns (cf. Shreeve, 1996:53)].

It is assumed that both the Neanderthals and modern humans evolved from *Homo erectus*. The earliest 'modern' human beings, *Homo sapiens*, are found as fossils at sites in Africa and in the Middle East. These fossils have been assigned dates that range from 70,000 and 120,000 years ago (Rasmussen, 1993:84). Two limestone caves in Israel, one at Skhul on Mount Carmel and the other on Mount Qafzeh, have provided some of the oldest 'modern' human remains (Bar-Yosef and

---

[11] DNA in mitochondria descends through the mother and does not undergo the shuffling associated with the pairing of parental DNA. It therefore has a slow and even mutation rate, and is used to date species divergence. Recent mitochondrial evidence also tends to confirm the theory that humans had a single origin in Africa. For a readable but detailed account of the geographical emergence of *Homo sapiens* (one which questions the implicit racism of earlier accounts) see Stringer and McKie (1996).

Van-Dermeersch, 1993). The Qafzeh Child skull (Qafzeh XI), belonging
to a ten-year-old is so modern that a caste of it could be easily confused
with a twentieth-century skull.

4.15.2   The paradox of the development of modern humans

Jared Diamond has written that:

> by 100,000 years ago many or most humans had brains of modern
> human size, and some humans had nearly modern skeletal
> anatomy. Genetically, those people of 100,000 years ago may have
> been 99.99% identical to humans today.

But

> The only features qualitatively distinguishing human behaviour
> of 100,000 years ago from the behavior of animals were the wide-
> spread use of . . . crude stone tools, plus the use of fire. (Chimpanzees
> also use stone tools, but less frequently.) At that time we were not
> even especially successful animals. (Diamond, 1995:45–46)

Clearly there is a great deal to explain about this crucial and still not-
well-understood period. The following are very marked in modern
human beings:

(a) *large, very intricately interconnected neural circuitry in the fore-
    brain*, associated with a high degree of learning and problem-
    solving ability.

(b) *the capacity for language*. This resides not just in the brain but
    in the 'design' of the vocal tract. The extensive work (for
    example by Savage-Rumbaugh, 1993) carried out in the
    United States on teaching common and pygmy chimpanzees
    to communicate by means of signs and visual 'icons', have
    indicated that language comprehension probably preceded
    the appearance of vocalised speech by several million years.
    *This means that the potential for the distinctively human feature of
    language is sophisticated vocalisation*. There is no way of being
    certain when the modern human vocal tract reached a form
    which enabled it to produce the range of sounds required to
    speak any of the 1600 different languages of the world.
       *But it does seem that vocalised speech was a decisive evolutionary
    step, perhaps as little as 50,000 years ago, which allowed the
    development of such characteristic human activities as art, music,*

technology (specialised tools, rope, boats, sewn clothing) *and the long-distance transport of precious objects* (Diamond, 1995:47). Language is also extremely important in the development of religion, since it provides such a powerful medium for symbolic expression and communication.[12]

(c) *the capacity for self-awareness.* We are not merely conscious of our environment but of ourselves, and of our having a past and a future (including an eventual death).

(d) *the development of science and technology.* We know at least in outline 'the common creation story' of our cosmic and evolutionary origins (McFague, 1993:104); we investigate and alter the whole surface of the planet.

However, it is important to exercise a degree of scientific caution, particularly in the area of language – other species also communicate. Vervet monkeys may only have ten grunt-words for predators (Diamond, 1995:50), but dolphins and whales seem to have much more intricate signalling systems. Chimpanzees do have a certain language-learning ability. And it is impossible to pronounce definitively on another creature's self-understanding, even a human's(!) – the so-called 'problem of other minds' (Gregory, 1987:161). Moreover, the account of Neanderthals given above makes clear how fine these distinctions are, anthropologically. Proto-religious behaviour seems not to be confined to *Homo sapiens.*[13]

4.16 The relation of various religious views to the scientific account

The evolutionary description of human origins may be seen as a challenge to biblical literalism and as challenge to some definitions of human dignity. Biblical-literalist Christians, scientific creationists and the great majority of orthodox Muslims reject the evolutionary view (see **9.10**). The Roman Catholic Church distinguishes between the evolution of the body and the special creation of the soul. Jones (1991:18–19),

---

[12] For a recent discussion of the importance of symbol in human evolution see Deacon (1997). Astonishingly neither 'religion' nor 'God' appears in his index.

[13] If it is hard to say what another human's self-understanding might consist of, it is all but impossible to say what might have been the significance for a Neanderthal of being buried with flowers and goats' horns.

summarises the Catholic position by reference to *Humani Generis*, the encyclical of Pius XII. Jones argues that the Catholic Church does not forbid the theory of evolution as an explanation of the origin of the human body, but rejects the notion that the soul was not created *directly* by God. This kind of language, however, poses problems in the debate with science because it smacks of vitalism, the incorporation of an ingredient in our natures which is not subject to scientific test.

In this account we have preferred to speak of a spiritual *aspect* to human existence. We have, in effect, chosen to use 'soul' as an adjective akin to 'spiritual', an attribute of a living person, rather than 'soul' as a noun suggesting a separate entity (see also **5.7**).

4.16.1   'Made in the image of God'

Genesis 1.26 describes humans as made in the image and likeness of God, the only creatures to which this direct connection with the divine is attributed. *Theologically, then, the Christian tradition has asserted a radical discontinuity between humans and other creatures. Scientifically, the differences between humans and other animals are ones of degree, rather than a radical discontinuity of nature.*

A Darwinian account of humanity can find no place for the notion that the species suddenly acquired a property called 'the image and likeness of God'. Human distinctiveness evolved gradually. Can theology frame its understanding of the *imago Dei* in such a way as to take account of this perception? There are three main possibilities for grounding this concept :

- the classical one that the image of God is in human rationality;
- the 'image' being grounded in other common characteristics – love, uprightness, dominion, creativity;
- the 'image' being understood in terms of capacity for authentic relationship (an understanding particularly attractive to certain Trinitarian theologians).

This last possibility seems the most fruitful, and is certainly in tune with the notion that the divine image developed only when culture – including and especially religion – enabled human altruism to transcend that of the immediate family group (for a discussion of altruism see the dialogue between Irons and Hefner in Richardson and Wildman's book – Irons, 1996 and Hefner, 1996). A modern description of the *imago Dei* should probably also emphasise creativity[14] which again is clearly an evolved characteristic.

4.16.2 The doctrine of the Fall

The second creation account in Genesis (Gen. 2.4–3.24) gives more emphasis to the origin of the human race than does the first account. It includes a number of key assertions upon which the Christian understanding of salvation is based. These include the unity of man and woman, the unity of the human species, the sin of our first parents and the consequences of the fall from divine favour. The story thus provides a mythological explanation of the current and fallen state of humanity.

The story emphasises that 'God fashioned man (*adam*) from the dust of the soil (*adamah*)'. We do not suggest that those who told and re-told this story ever had any evolutionary understanding in mind; they were no doubt thinking in terms of a clay image into which God then breathed life. Nevertheless, we could regard the phrase as providential, and accept it as an abbreviated and 'poetic' expression of the Earthly evolution of humankind. It is a serious error, however, to try to interpret either Genesis 1 or 2 in terms of evolutionary theory, not only because our understanding of evolution will undergo changes in the future, but because of the need to respect the intentions and world-views of the biblical authors.

It would be an equally serious error to try and rescue from the 'Fall' story in Genesis 3 a historical paradise of total vegetarian harmony. There have been various efforts to understand the reasons for the myth of Eden – it could even lie so deep in the human unconscious as to reflect the retreat of the forest which forced the most primitive proto-hominids to exercise what ingenuity they could out on the African savannah. But there is no evidence that hominids were ever in an idyllic, predation-free relationship with the non-human creation.[15] The importance of the Fall story must be that it describes that peculiar sense of alienation that seems to characterise the life at least of technological humans, a sense that we cannot wholly settle in our ecological niche or

[14] See Hefner (1993) on the human as 'created co-creator', also Ward (1998) and Habgood (1998) for thorough analyses of theological and scientific understandings of human personhood.

[15] Readers should not be confused in this regard by mention in the literature to 'mitochondrial Eve', which is a reference to our likely common ancestors in Africa, rather than to any Edenic conditions in which they might have lived.

network of relationships, a sense that we yearn for something other but cannot grasp it.

The need to move away from the historical Fall has been strongly emphasised by the scientist–theologians (see for example Polkinghorne, 1991:99–104, Peacocke 1993:222f.). Peacocke takes the argument in a helpful direction when, drawing on his idea that relationship with God and right perception of our environment represent the highest-level 'emergent' in the biological hierarchy, he argues that humans' ecological niche includes a right relationship with God, which for all sorts of reasons – some genetic, some cultural, some as mysterious as the appearance of evil in Genesis 3 – continues to elude us.

4.17   The sociobiological critique of religion

The quotation from E. O. Wilson given in **4.10** continues: 'Theology is not likely to survive as an independent intellectual discipline. But religion itself will endure for a long time as a vital force in society' (Wilson, 1995:192). Dawkins regards religion as one of many 'viruses of the mind',[16] something which has pervaded human affairs, but, having no truth-content, should be done away with. Wilson does see religion's utility, although he regards it as nothing more than a survival-strategy which has become embedded in our genes.

The first, trite rebuttal to this is to point out that if some of our beliefs about reality are to be described as Darwinian gene-schemes, then others are not exempt. Neo-Darwinism itself could be regarded not as a fact about reality, but as an evolved survival-strategy. If we doubt humans' capacity to derive truths, as opposed to following evolutionary strategies, then the 'fact' that Darwinism has, according to Wilson, 'point for point in zones of conflict, defeated traditional religion' (Wilson, 1995:192), does not make Darwinism any the more true. If this defeat *were* a fact, it would only show that at a particular juncture Darwinism was more *adaptive* than religious belief.

It is much more reasonable to suppose that humans *do* have the power to elicit conclusions about their environment largely independent of their genetic inheritance (though quite strongly influenced by their culture). This brings us to the second point, which is that the socio-biological case for very strong control of genes over culture simply

---

[16]   The title of a lecture he gave to the British Humanist Association in 1992.

cannot be sustained for humans. As we saw above, the proportion of the human genome which separates us from the early savannah-dwelling *Homo sapiens* may be as little as 0.01 per cent, and we know next to nothing of *how* so few genes could exert such an enormous effect on culture as to programme us to be modern humans. Moreover our present experience of the rate of cultural change suggests that gene changes could not possibly account for the pace at which human culture changes, or respond at an adequate rate. Bowker has made a very careful analysis of the claims of sociobiology in respect of religion (1995:1–118, especially 37–46), and concludes that critical realism is sustainable both for science and religion. We *can* make inferences about the universe as it happens to be, and about its God, beyond what is programmed in our genes.

4.18   Conclusion

We have shown that Darwinism, coupled with modern developments in genetics, molecular biology, palaeontology and complexity, is an immensely powerful theory for explaining change in living things. It would be fair to say that modern physics has seemed to many to be suggestive of theism (see **1.15**, **3.23**), but that Darwinism is not so suggestive. Indeed, as a way for a creator to work, it poses problems in respect of apparent waste and undoubted suffering. These we address in **7.15**.

However Darwinism need not be in conflict with religious claims as long as the bases of each description are understood, and dismissive reductions (on either side) avoided.

FURTHER READING

BOWKER, J. (1995) *Is God A Virus? Genes, Culture and Religion* (London: SPCK)

BROOKE, J. H. (1991) *Science and Religion: Some Historical Perspectives* (Cambridge: Cambridge University Press)

DARWIN, C. (1859) *The Origin of Species* ed. by J. W. Burrows (Harmondsworth: Penguin Books, 1985), which contains the full text of Darwin's first edition.

DAWKINS, R. (1991) *The Blind Watchmaker* (Harmondsworth: Penguin, reprint with appendix)

DESMOND, A. and MOORE, J. (1992) *Darwin* (Harmondsworth: Penguin)

GOULD, S. J. (1991) *Wonderful Life: The Burgess Shale and the Nature of History* (Harmondsworth: Penguin)

HABGOOD, J. (1998) *Being A Person: Where Faith and Science Meet* (London: Hodder & Stoughton)

HEFNER, P. (1993) *The Human Factor* (Minneapolis, MN: Fortress Press)

KAUFFMAN, S. (1995) *At Home in the Universe* (Harmondsworth: Penguin)

PEACOCKE, A. (1993) *Theology for a Scientific Age* (London: SCM Press, expanded edn.)

Chapter 5

Psychology and Theology

5.1 Introduction

The dialogue of theology with psychology, as with most other scientific areas, tends to be a rather one-sided one. Theologians are more concerned with what scientists have to say than *vice versa*. Though one might regret the one-sided nature of the dialogue, this chapter will inevitably reflect the way in which the relationship between psychology and theology proceeds in practice. It will therefore be largely concerned with the theological response to psychology. The key question is whether theology can be happy with contemporary psychology. There is often a sense of conflict between psychology and religion, a feeling that psychology is saying things that the religious traditions cannot be happy with. However, I will suggest that this is misconceived.[1]

It is essential to make a distinction between what is really established by scientific research in psychology, and what is sometimes claimed by way of extrapolation from that research. I will argue that there are no securely-based research findings in psychology that conflict with religious belief. However, there are many unwarranted extrapolations from psychological research which, if they were accepted, would raise conflicts with religion. It is essential to maintain this distinction between what is securely established and more speculative extrapolation. The sense of possible conflict arises, either from some psychologists saying more than, as psychologists, they really have any right to say; or from religious people assuming that psychologists are saying more than they actually are. I will be arguing that, when

---

[1] This chapter was solely drafted by Fraser Watts; he is the 'I' of the text.

everything is clearly understood, there is no conflict between psychology and theology.

This implies that there are limits to what psychology can properly say, but there are two different ways of setting out such limits. One is to divide up the territory, and say that there some things that psychology can study and other things that are outside the scope of psychology and should be left to theology. Those who advocate that approach might regard morality, aesthetics, and religion itself, as being outside the scope of psychology. I reject that view. There *is* a valuable psychology of religion, morality and aesthetics. (The psychology of religion will be discussed in this chapter, though there will be no space to discuss the psychological study of morality and aesthetics). However, I *do* claim that psychology never exhausts all there is to be said about what it is studying. There are other things to be said, from other points of view. It is in that sense that psychology is inherently limited.

The dialogue between psychology and theology falls into two main areas: the first is concerned with human nature generally, the second is concerned with 'religion'. This chapter will consider both areas in turn.

SECTION A:
HUMAN NATURE (5.2–5.7)

5.2   Perspectives on human nature

Even when psychology is not explicitly concerned with the religious or spiritual aspects of human nature, it often seems to be taking such a limited view of human beings that it is bound to come into conflict with the more open view of the potential of human beings in the religious traditions. A theological view of human beings emphasises that they are made in the image of God (*imago Dei*, see **4.16.1**). Sometimes this has been formulated in terms of human beings having a soul, though this terminology can cause confusion (and will be discussed later in **5.7**). However, whether or not soul terminology is used, the religious traditions would want to emphasise, in some way or other, the relatedness of human beings to God. A theological view of human beings also emphasises their potential, that they are capable of having a distinctive kind of relationship with God and to some degree growing towards the likeness of God. This is something that has been particularly important in the Eastern tradition of Christian thought. The views of the different religious traditions about being human are discussed by Ward (1998).

It is incompatible with the religious view of human nature to take a very reductive view of human beings. Such reductive views of human beings arise at various points in psychology, and they are often expressed in 'nothing but' language. For example, evolutionary psychology might suggest that human beings are nothing but survival machines for their genes. Similar issues arise when the basis of consciousness and personality in the brain is concerned; it can be suggested that we are 'nothing but' our central nervous systems. Artificial Intelligence (the enterprise of programming computers to simulate the intelligent functions of human beings) is another area where strongly reductive ideas arise, with the suggestion that the mind is 'nothing but' a computer programme. Genetic reductionism has already been discussed in the last chapter. The reductionist claims of neuroscience and artificial intelligence will be reviewed here. (For a somewhat fuller discussion see Watts, 1998a; also Ward, 1992.)

Issues about reductionism have also already been considered (**4.11–4.13**). The most important distinction here is between:

(a) 'methodological' reductionism, which refers to the pragmatic spirit in which science seeks to explain higher-level phenomena in terms of lower-level ones as far as possible; and

(b) 'strong' reductionism that insists that this programme can be carried through to the point where higher-level phenomena are completely explained in terms of lower-level ones.

As there are no examples of reductionist explanations being carried through to a point of complete success in the biological sciences, strong reductionist claims are always speculative, and no more than an act of scientific faith.

I will try to show that, though work in neuroscience and artificial intelligence is surrounded by an outer belt of speculative ideas that conflicts with the religious traditions, the core scientific work in these fields does not do so.

5.3 Brain and consciousness

Human consciousness is currently the focus of a huge amount of research activity; it is sometimes claimed to be one of the last great, unsolved mysteries. A central question is whether, and how, human consciousness can be 'explained' in terms of the functioning of the physical brain. There is a good review of the philosophical assumptions of the neurological explanation of consciousness in Flanagan (1992). More polemical, reductionist views of somewhat different kinds can be found in Churchland (1986), Dennett (1991) and Crick (1994).

The debate about the neurological explanation of consciousness is muddied by confusion over what is (or ought to be) meant by 'consciousness'. At least three different layers of meaning can be discerned (Copeland, 1993:Ch. 8). First, there is a baseline sense of 'consciousness' in which it refers to the capacity to experience the external world through sense organs and to perform cognitive operations on that sense experience. Secondly, there is a reflexive kind of consciousness in which people monitor what they experience and know. Thirdly, there is what Copeland calls 'the ineffable FEEL of it all', what in the technical language of philosophers are called 'qualia'. It is this last sense of consciousness that is most controversial, with some people such as Dennett (1991:Ch. 12) dismissing it as a mirage. At present, science is grappling with explaining how the more basic kinds of conscious experience arise. As a matter of scientific strategy that is clearly the place to begin; the more complex issues that will arise in studying higher aspects of consciousness are hardly yet in sight.

What makes the study of consciousness such a lively area of debate at the present time is that we are not just discussing *how* consciousness can arise from the brain, but the more basic question of *whether* consciousness can be explained in physical terms at all. For a long time, it was assumed that it could not. For example, in the seventeenth century, John Locke (1632–1704), argued that because consciousness is inherently immaterial, it could not arise from matter (Locke, 1960). Certainly, the qualitative difference between consciousness and the physical brain constitutes a problem. It is a real challenge to see how the brain could give rise to something so qualitatively different from itself (e.g. Nagel, 1974). Despite the problem of seeing how the 'gap' between the nervous system of the physical brain and human consciousness could be bridged, it is hard to see how else consciousness might arise, except from the brain. The strong, contemporary presupposition is that consciousness *must* be grounded in the physical brain, and it is only a question of discovering exactly *how* it arises.

At present, we only have very speculative ideas about this. For example, Penrose (1994) has suggested that consciousness arises from quantum indeterminacy in the 'microtubules' of the brain (as discussed in **3.14**). However, this is a highly speculative idea which as yet has no direct research support. In contrast, Crick (1994) has suggested that it arises from synchronised electrical rhythms in particular parts of the brain. This is perhaps a more promising idea, but also highly speculative. However, the fact that we don't yet have a convincing theory of exactly how consciousness arises from the physical brain in no way supports the conclusion that it could not do so.

5.4 Theological concerns about neuroscience

Now, the question arises of what, if anything, is at stake theologically in the attempt to explain consciousness in terms of the brain. There are some like Crick who claim that neuroscience can provide a complete explanation of consciousness, personality and soul, and that this disproves the claims of religion. However, there are many problems with this argument (see Watts, 1994). Once the exaggerated polemics of people like Crick are set aside, there is not as much at stake theologically in neuroscience as some people imagine.

As I have already indicated, one of the fundamental Christian assumptions about human beings, and indeed of most religious traditions, is that they are 'spiritual' creatures. By that I mean that they have a capacity for self-transcendence, and can form a conscious relationship with God in a way that is not possible for other creatures. Rahner (1989) is one twentieth-century theologian who has set out this view. It is a view of human nature that theology would wish to safeguard. Theology will always want to oppose any attempt to take a limited, almost demeaning, view of human beings that denies the reality of our higher attributes. In opposing such views, it is standing up for common sense, at least as much for its distinctively religious view of human nature.

Moreover, the higher aspects of human nature are not called into question simply by looking for their physical basis. This again raises issues about reductionism, and there are two further aspects of reductionism that it is important to distinguish here, one to do with explanation, the other to do with 'reality'. It is one thing to explain higher attributes in terms of lower-level processes. However, it is a quite separate (and unnecessary) further step to say that such explanation means that the higher-level phenomena are somehow not real. (The term 'real' is often the focus of philosophical confusions; and it is always wise to ask what it is being contrasted with.) The reality of the higher attributes is not called into question by explaining how they arise from lower-level ones. Provided the reality of higher human qualities of consciousness (and 'soul') is fully recognised, there is no religious objection to looking for their explanation in terms of neurological processes.

The assumption that human beings have distinctive attributes is as compatible with the investigation of their neurological basis as it is with the study of their evolutionary origin (see **4.15–4.16**). In the course of evolution, new attributes can and do arise. Indeed, from a theological point of view, I would want to suggest that it is central to God's creative purpose that, out of the natural world, creatures such as ourselves should arise who are both natural and spiritual. Having arisen, we are capable of entering into a conscious relationship with the God from whom the natural order itself arose. Though Christianity wants to insist that human beings are spiritual creatures, in the sense of being made in the image of God and having a conscious relationship to God; it has no reason to deny that we are also natural creatures.

Another theological issue that arises here is the role of mind and brain in discerning God's revelation to us. The mind and brain sciences have been emphasising the close intertwining of mind and brain. They are not two different things, but rather two different aspects of the same thing. We do not have any experience which is purely mental in the sense that the physical brain is not also involved; all experience is underpinned by the human brain. This also applies to our experience of God, which must be linked to brain processes as much as any other kind of experience. There is no possibility of God influencing private experience in a way that bypasses the natural processes of the brain. This underlines the point made in **2.4** about existentialism, that there is no scope for suggesting an experiential relationship to God which somehow bypasses the natural world. Human experience is, in this sense, inextricably intertwined with the natural world.

5.5   The scope of artificial intelligence

Artificial intelligence (AI) is another scientific area that sometimes seems to imply a view of human nature that is incompatible with the

Christian one. It is essentially the enterprise of programming computers to simulate the intelligent activities of human beings. There is a good discussion of the philosophical assumptions of AI in Copeland (1993:Ch. 9). A well-argued account of what has been achieved in AI so far can be found in Johnson-Laird (1988), and the last two chapters on the boundaries of AI in relation to consciousness, emotion and free-will are especially interesting. On the other hand, a trenchant critique of AI can be found in Edelman (1992, especially the Critical Postscript.)

The assumption of 'strong' artificial intelligence is that *all* intelligent human activity can be simulated in computer programmes, and hence that the computers of the future will be able to do anything that human beings can do now. That seems to imply that human beings are merely machines, and not the spiritual creatures that the Christian tradition assumes. One of the key issues here is how much progress artificial intelligence is likely to make. From the outset, very bold claims have been made. Actual progress has lagged behind. However, there is no doubt that considerable progress *has* been made in AI. For example, computers are now extremely good at playing chess.

Sometimes, general arguments are advanced for why AI will or will not be able to simulate human intelligence completely. However, such arguments often turn out to be inconclusive. For example, it might be claimed that any rule-governed intelligent activity can be simulated in the computer, but that begs the question of to what extent human intelligence is rule-based. Arguing in the other direction, some, such as Penrose (1994), have tried to invoke Gödel's Theorem to show that human intelligence could not be computable. However, Gödel's Theorem is concerned with mathematical systems, and there are serious doubts about whether extrapolations from it to other areas are legitimate.

If we set aside such attempts to argue from principle, we are reduced to looking at what progress has and has not been made in artificial intelligence so far, and trying to extrapolate from that. This is a hazardous business. For example, it used to be claimed that computers could never 'learn'. However, we have already reached a point at which computers can be programmed to 're-programme' themselves in the light of experience, which is a kind of learning. Moreover, that has been rendered feasible by the development of a new and radically different approach to computer programming known as Parallel Distributed

Processing, or 'connectionism' (see Copeland, 1993:Ch. 10). Over the decades and centuries to come, there will no doubt be many such new approaches to programming, and it would be foolish to be too dogmatic about what will and will not become possible.

However, there are certain things which at the moment look likely to remain insurmountable problems for AI. One is inner experience. An instructive example here is to consider how far a computer could go towards having emotions. Different emotions arise in human beings in fairly predictable circumstances; and there should be no difficulty in principle in programming a computer to know when a particular emotion would be appropriate. It would also be possible to programme some expression of emotion. For example, appropriate sentences could be composed and spoken through a voice box. However, it is a crucial feature of human emotions that we actually *feel* angry, guilty, sad or whatever. It is hard, at present, to foresee that computers could ever have such inner experiences.

Some enthusiasts for artificial intelligence might concede this, but try to argue that 'having an emotion' consists of nothing more than being able to express an emotion in appropriate circumstances. However, we see here an example of a recurrent tendency to talk-up the achievements of computers by redefining downwards the criteria which they have to meet. There is more to intelligence than following the rules of a computer programme, and there is more to being emotional than showing an appropriate emotional display.

Another limitation of computers that at present seems insurmountable is their lack of individuality. As Edelman (1992) has forcefully pointed out, computers are standard off-the-shelf pieces of hardware, and in that respect quite unlike brains, which are individual. Also, each person is the result of their quite different developmental history and social context. Computers might, through the limited learning of which they are capable, come to have some individuality in their software. However, it is difficult at present to see how computers might ever acquire the kind of radical individuality that humans possess.

5.6   Theological issues about artificial intelligence

Now let us focus more specifically on the theological issues raised by the claims of artificial intelligence. There are useful introductions to these in Puddefoot (1996) and Foerst (1996).

Note, first, that it is the *claims* of artificial intelligence to which theology will particularly want to respond. The programming and use of computers, in itself, does not really cause theological debates. There may, of course, be ethical and practical issues associated with the changing lifestyle that the computer age will increasingly bring, but that is another matter.[2] Note also that it is not the computers of the present day which raise theological problems. It is the claims of artificial intelligence about the computers of the future which draw a theological response.

Let us suppose, for the sake of argument, that computers are developed which simulate all the intelligent functions of human beings (though my scientific judgement is that it is unlikely that will happen). Should Christians be concerned about the possibility of computers that simulate human beings?

There might be a feeling that, in making humanoid machines, we would be 'playing God' and usurping the functions of the creator God. However, that would not really be the case. There would still be an important sense in which God would be the 'creator' of any humanoid computers that we might build. The Christian belief is that God is creator 'of all things, visible and invisible', which implies that it would be impossible for anything to exist, even a computer, without its being dependent on God for its existence. That would not be affected by the fact that human beings had made it. MacKay (1991:Ch. 8) has suggested that making such a computer would be an act of 'procreation', but would not usurp the functions of the creator God any more than biological procreation does.

One important difference, of course, between parents having a child and the making of a humanoid computer is that, in the latter case, we would be making something absolutely to our own specification. It would raise ethical issues rather like those that arise with genetic engineering (see Chapter 11), but on a much bigger scale. To many people there seems something sinister about the idea of having some kind of equivalent to a human being which was absolutely determined by its maker. However, I think the unease here stems in part from linking two ideas which are actually incompatible. Human beings are assumed to have a measure of free will and not to be wholly determined by their genes or by anything else. Either an advanced computer would have

[2] See **10.10**.

such free will or it would not. If it did not, it would be only a robot, certainly nothing like a human being. However, if we were able to build a computer that really had free will and responsibility, it would not be under our control, despite the fact that we had made it.

Nevertheless there is something disconcerting about the wilder fringes of speculation and prediction in the artificial intelligence movement, of which Moravec's book *Mind Children* (1988) is a good example. He sets out a powerful vision of computer-creatures, built by us, equivalent to us, but superior to us, which is the stuff of 'sci-fi' dreams. I think Christians are right to sense something unwholesome in the spiritual tone of such fantasies. People such as Moravec seem to be intoxicated with the hope that they will be able to 'play God'. That intoxication is something that invites theological comment, and it is a separate issue from whether they would in fact be able to accomplish all the things they boldly predict. In fact, I believe that in the wilder fringes of AI speculation, we are dealing, not with science, but with implicitly religious thinking in secular, scientistic disguise.

5.7   Immortality

A key area where the assumptions of both neuroscience and AI interface with theology is immortality. (For a general survey of religious ideas about immortality, see Hick, 1976; on resurrection in relation to modern science, see **7.7**, also Polkinghorne, 1994:Ch. 9.)

I suspect that one reason why some Christians are uneasy about accepting the physical basis of consciousness and personality is its implication for immortality. We have become accustomed to thinking of the Christian hope of eternal life in 'dualistic' terms, which assume the separateness of soul and body. Once you start thinking in these terms, it is natural to see eternal life in terms of the survival of the soul. Moreover, if the soul is to survive after the death of the physical body, it seems essential to assume that the soul is independent of the body, rather than being grounded in the physical processes of the brain.

While this way of thinking about immortality is indeed part of the Christian tradition, it is not the only way of thinking about eternal life. There is another strand in the tradition which emphasises the resurrection of the body rather than the immortality of the soul. It has often been claimed that it is Greek thought that has led to the idea of the immortality of the soul, whereas Hebrew thought, which emphasised the psychosomatic unity of human beings, focused more on the resurrection of the body. However, in the Christian tradition, the two are not really alternatives; those who have maintained the resurrection of the body have usually also maintained the survival of an immortal soul as a prior step. Also, an emphasis on the resurrection of the body hardly makes the Christian tradition any easier to reconcile with modern, scientific views of the person.

I would not want to argue for the survival of a disembodied soul, but neither would I see the solution as being a strong focus on the resurrection of the body. The key corrective that needs to be entered from the Christian point of view is that eternal life is seen as a gift from God, not as the automatic consequence of how human beings are constituted. On this view, if there were no God, there would be no hope of eternal life. Theologically, the distinctive thing about human beings is that they are able to establish a conscious relationship with God in a way that does not seem to be possible for the rest of natural creation. Eternal life, I would want to suggest, should be seen arising from this relationship, rather than being the consequence of human beings possessing a potentially disembodied soul.

There is the further question of how and in what form this gift of eternal life is granted by God. One possibility is that we exist within the mind or memory of God. However, it is necessary to emphasise that our eternal life is likely to be so different from our present mortal life that the scientific investigation of mind and brain are of little relevance to understanding it. A resurrection body would be wholly unlike a mortal body; equally a continued spiritual existence in some kind of unity with God would be very different from the continuation of our present mental life without the physical body.

How we think about these things may come to be influenced by future research on 'out of the body' experiences (Ring, 1980). Of the various aspects of 'near-death' experiences, out of the body experiences are particularly interesting scientifically in that they are open to verification. If it is indeed the case that human beings, in certain unusual states of consciousness, are able to make observations that could not be made from the vantage point of the physical body, we will have to learn to think in more flexible terms about the relationship between consciousness and the body. However, the scientific investigation of these matters is still far too incomplete to enable any specific theological inferences to be drawn.

The Christian tradition has been inclined to reify the soul, i.e. to talk about it as though it were a 'thing' of some kind. Post-Second World War philosophy of mind has been helpful here in teaching us the pitfalls attendant on talking about the mind as a thing; similar lessons apply to talk about the soul. Just as it is more appropriate to say that we have mental attributes than to say that we have a thing called the mind, so it is more appropriate to say that we have spiritual qualities than to say that we have a thing called the soul (see also **4.16**). There is a richer variety of thinking about soul in the Christian tradition than many people are aware of, and alongside the Platonic tradition, which can readily see the soul as disembodied, there is also the Aristotelian tradition, found for example in Aquinas, which sees the soul as the 'form' of the body (see **1.11**).

Ideas about immortality have also surfaced within AI, though the issues here are quite different. One of the strange features of AI is the way in which it has taken up the 'dualistic' assumptions of separation between soul and body which have all too often become intertwined with Christianity (Cotterill, 1989). In fact, the Judaic tradition, to which Christianity is heir, is of the human being as a psychosomatic unity, an 'ensouled body'. However, Tipler interprets the Christian vision of immortality in terms of the survival of a disembodied soul, and sees computer programming as a means to achieve that. It is one of the stranger assumptions of AI that it might be possible to achieve full human mental functioning outside the context of a physical body, an assumption that sits very uneasily with contemporary neuroscience.

This strange vision of immortality realised through AI has found its most conspicuous expression in Tipler's strange book *The Physics of Immortality* (1995) (see **3.22**), which holds out the vision of the personality of each one of us being immortalised by being captured in a computer programme. This is pseudo-science in the guise of religion. Tipler both distorts theological thinking and strains scientific credibility in bringing the two together. It is a wild extrapolation from the current achievements of AI to claim that the essential personality of each individual could be maintained in computer form, divorced from their normal somatic and social context. It is also strange, theologically, to tie thinking about immortality so exclusively to a kind of disembodied soul, and to separate it from the gift of God.

SECTION B:
RELIGION (5.8–5.12)

5.8   Psychological approaches to religion

In the second part of this chapter, we will turn from the relationship between scientific and theological views of human nature to examine more specifically how they intersect over matters of faith and the religious life.

The psychology of religion draws on many other areas of psychology. It includes, for example, the different approaches to religion associated with different personality types, the development of religious faith and understanding in children, the brain mechanisms underlying religious experience, and the group processes involved in church life. Nearly every branch of psychology can be applied to the study of religious life. A good, short introduction to the psychology of religion is Brown (1988). More thorough accounts of empirical research in the psychology of religion can be found in Hood *et al.* (1996) and Beit-Hallahmi and Argyle (1997). A survey of the various different approaches that have been taken to the psychology of religion can be found in Wulff (1991).

Whether you think that religion can be studied scientifically depends on what you mean by 'science'. There has been a growing realisation that science is a family of methodologies, rather than a single methodology applied in a uniform way across different disciplines. Within the sciences, there is a broad distinction to be made between sciences that study aspects of the 'natural' world, and the human sciences that study aspects of personal and cultural life. It is one of the interesting features of psychology that it is partly a natural, biological science, and partly a social science. Different branches of psychology need to draw on and integrate different scientific methodologies.

I see no basis for trying to claim that religion is a 'no go' area for scientific study. The concern arises from the idea that if you study religion psychologically, it will all be 'reduced' to psychology and there will be nothing left. I believe that that concern is misplaced. We are here dealing again with the issues about reductionism raised earlier in the chapter (5.2). Accepting that psychology can contribute to the explanation of religious life does not mean acceptance of the strong reductionist claim that religion can be completely explained in terms of psychology.

The key point is that, at least with human beings, there is room for different explanatory discourses to be developed in parallel. We are complex, multi-faceted creatures, and many human phenomena need to be approached at different levels. Depression is a good example. There are biological aspects of depression, including the genetic predisposition and the biochemistry associated with depression. There are also developmental aspects, such as the early experiences which predispose people to depression. Then there are social aspects, such as the ways in which depression can distort personal relationships, and be maintained by them. No account of depression that focuses on one of these strands alone can hope to be adequate. All are needed.

The same is true of religious life. However, I would want to claim here, not only that different psychological approaches are necessary to understand religious life, but that the theological approach is relevant too, and can sit alongside the psychological approach as a complementary perspective (see Watts, 1998b). Whereas psychological approaches generally do not concern themselves with the truth of Christian doctrine, a theological view of religious life presupposes Christian truths.

Though the relationship of theological and psychological accounts of religion to one another is somewhat analogous to the relationship between different kinds of psychological account, the analogy clearly has its limitations. It is in the nature of particular psychological approaches to religious life that they narrow the focus, and deal in detail with one particular facet of things. However, it is in the nature of a theological approach that it takes the broadest possible perspective, focusing on God who, in his nature, is seen as the source of all that there is. Theological and religious approaches to religious life are in a sense complementary, but that doesn't mean that they operate in parallel ways, or that they are concerned with exactly the same kinds of question about religion.

This assumption that psychological and theological interpretations of religious life are consistent with one another and are complementary is not universally shared. It implies a rejection of two more exclusive alternatives:

(a) the strong reductionist view that religion can be explained completely by psychology (perhaps in conjunction with other social sciences) and that a theological view of religious life is redundant and misplaced;

(b) the strong opposite view that religious life should be considered exclusively in theological terms, and that the human
sciences have no contribution to make.

These exclusive views seem to rest on the assumption that
phenomena can be divided up into those that are the concern of theology
and those that are the concern of the human sciences such as psychology.
If that assumption is accepted, the debate is about whose territory
religion falls in.

There are others who try to blend psychology and theology into some
kind of hybrid discipline, incorporating theological and psychological
elements in a way that scarcely discriminates between them. This
happens most commonly in the area of pastoral psychology. Lake's
Clinical Theology (1966) is an example of this kind of seamless integration.
In contrast I would want to suggest that psychology and theology have
quite distinctive vantage points, functions and characteristics, and
cannot simply be fused (see Hunsinger, 1995). Psychology and theology
are distinct, but consistent with one another, and complementary to
one another.

Having set out this general approach, I will now apply it to some
more specific examples:

(a) I will re-evaluate one of the best known, and apparently
'reductionist', psychological approaches to religion, that of
Freud, from this point of view, and

(b) I will consider more generally how psychological and theological approaches can complement our understanding of
phenomena such as religious experience.

5.9   Freud's critique of religion

Freud's is one of the best-known psychological approaches to religion.
It presents a hostile critique of religion, and many have assumed that
this is the form that all psychological approaches to religion must
necessarily take. It is an interesting psychological approach to religion
to re-examine, and we will see that it is not necessarily as hostile as
at first appears. (One of the best books on Freud's psychology of
religion is that of Meissner, 1984; there is also a good account in Palmer,
1997.)

In fact, Freud had several different theories of religion. However, the clearest and simplest is that set out in *The Future of an Illusion* (Freud, 1928). As the title suggests, the basic proposal is that religion is illusion. However, 'illusion' is, for Freud, a technical term, meaning wish fulfilment. The suggestion is basically that people accept religious ideas simply because they want them to be true. Freud assumes that the essence of God, in fulfilment of our wishes, is that he is both loving and all-powerful. Moreover, the need to have such a figure arises, Freud thinks, from the pervasive human experience of helplessness. He thinks that it assuages that feeling of helplessness to have a powerful, all-loving God.

A related proposal is that God is a 'projection' of the human mind. However, even in Freud's own terms, it is clearly an unusual kind of projection. Projection normally refers to the human tendency to attribute to other people, for our own psychological reasons, attributes that they do not really possess. However, in suggesting that God is a projection, Freud is assuming that we 'make up' a being who does not exist at all, and project on to him the attributes we wish him to have. It is worth noting that this theory of religion as projection was not an original idea of Freud's. Essentially the same idea can be found in Feuerbach. However, Freud develops the idea in more specific form, casting it within a detailed psychological theory which includes a general understanding of how projection and wish fulfilment operate.

Some religious believers, upset by the implications of Freud's theory of religion, want to rebut it entirely. That is not the approach I will take here. I am happy to accept that Freud's approach makes a useful contribution to the understanding of religious life. However, it is also important to understand the limitations of the theory:

(i) It should be noted that the general claims of psychoanalysis are, in fact, highly debatable, and there has been much discussion about whether it is a science and whether Freud's theories are really justified by his clinical data, or just an ill-founded and highly speculative superstructure built on top of them. (For example, see Webster, 1996.) In fact Freud's ideas about religion are some of his most speculative and least securely based on clinical observation. Even if Freud's general theory is accepted, it is not necessary to agree with

Freud's conclusions about religion, for which he offers no particular empirical evidence.

(ii) As Freud admitted, the theory does not deal with the *truth* of religious claims. Strictly, as Freud makes clear, it is one thing to say that religion is 'illusion' (or wish fulfilment), but quite another whether religion is a 'delusion' (or error). What Freud is arguing is that religion arises from human wishes, and meets them. However, when being careful, he admits that it is outside the province of psychology to assess the truth of religious claims.

(iii) Freud's is not the only possible psychoanalytic theory of religion. Even Freud himself, on occasion, recognised this. It emerged in an interesting way from Freud's correspondence with Oskar Pfister, a Lutheran pastor with whom Freud apparently enjoyed a good relationship, and who early on saw the potential value of Freud's methods for the pastoral work of the church (see Meissner, 1984). Freud wrote to Pfister 'if I drew on analysis for certain arguments, that need deter no one from using the non-partisan method of analysis for arguing the opposite view' (Meng and Freud, 1963). That is no longer just an abstract possibility. The broad lines of alternative psychoanalytic approaches to religion are now in place.

5.10   Alternative psychoanalytic approaches to religion

One strand is a re-evaluation of the nature and function of 'illusion' (wish fulfilment) stemming from the work of the psychoanalyst and paediatrician, Winnicott (see Meissner, 1984; or, more briefly, Watts and Williams, 1988). He suggested that there was a domain of psychological life, which he termed the 'transitional', which was neither that of objective reality, nor of subjective fantasy, but something in between. He saw the play of infants, which he observed particularly carefully, as belonging to this transitional realm. However, he also saw much adult cultural life, such as art and religion, as also 'transitional'.

Far from being an unhelpful distraction from reality, he believed that this transitional realm made an important contribution to adjustment. We have here the outline of a psychoanalytic view of religion which still sees it as wish fulfilment, but nevertheless emphasises the constructive value of religion from the point of view of human adaptation. From this perspective, it is clear that the view that religion is wish fulfilment need not lead to a critical view of it.

Another strand in the revision of Freudian thinking about religion concerns the extent of its applicability. Even if it is accepted that *some* religion arises from wish fulfilment in the way that Freud maintains, this is not necessarily true of all religion. It was part of Freud's theory that the attributes of human parents are projected on to God. Though he sought no empirical support for this theory, others have done so, partly through statistical surveys of the attributes associated both with parents and with God, partly through very detailed clinical case studies. In some of these, there is such a far-reaching similarity between the way a particular person thinks of God and one of their human parents that it is difficult to write it off as a mere coincidence (see Beit-Hallahmi and Argyle, 1997:106–09).

However, this is not to accept that all concepts of God are 'nothing but' human projections. You can still believe in the possibility of moving away from human-based concepts of God to an apprehension of the true God that does less to distort his nature. This is, in essence, the view that Tillich (1952) takes at the end of his book, *The Courage To Be* (see also Homans, 1970). He argues for the importance of Christians moving beyond the 'transference God'.

Yet another strand in the more sympathetic application of psychoanalysis to religion emphasises that religion at its best, far from being a symptom of poor psychological adjustment, in fact requires a high level of adjustment. This was part of Pfister's early debate with Freud, and similar views have been advanced, for example, by Lee (1948). In Freudian theory, the principle functions of the ego are love and work. It is not difficult to argue that exemplary Christians, and indeed Jesus himself, far from showing poor psychological adjustment, showed a remarkable capacity for love and work.

This leads on to the question of how such advanced levels of ego-adjustment may be facilitated by the Christian life. Meissner (1987) has sketched out one possible answer to this within the framework of what is basically a Freudian theory of personality development. However, it is one in which he sees scope for the operation of the grace of God. In simple terms, the idea is that the grace of God provides the resources to overcome obstacles to psychological development that might otherwise be insurmountable.

Since Freud's time there has been a good deal of empirical study of the mental health of religious people (Beit-Hallahmi and Argyle, 1997:189–91; Loewenthal, 1995). It turns out to be quite diverse, and to depend on the approach to religion that people have. In broad outline, the picture is that people who have a merely conventional approach to religion may have poorer mental health than average. However, those who have a particularly committed approach to religion often have better mental health than average.

These various revisionist approaches to the psychoanalytic theory of religion make use of Freud's ideas up to a point, but put them in their place, not allowing them to be paraded as a valid theory of universal application, even less a theory that determines the truth of religion. Freud's approach to religion provides a good case study of how even an apparently hostile psychological theory can be seen as compatible with the assumption of the truth of religion once the theory is put into appropriate context and not allowed to make claims that go beyond its proper scope.

5.11 Complementary approaches to religious experience

The predominant assumption within the Christian tradition has been that there is a 'real' God, who seeks to reveal himself to humanity, and of whom it is possible for us to have some experience, however imperfect. This has been combined with an emphasis on the transcendent nature of God, and the impossibility of human beings coming to know him fully or through their own powers, but the tradition has normally maintained the possibility of some degree of apprehension of God's revelation through human experience. The main suggestion of this section will be that the available psychological data on religious experience is perfectly compatible with such assumptions, even though it does not presuppose them.

Contemporary approaches to religious experience have seen a strong emphasis on its cultural-embeddedness (e.g. Katz, 1978). The exact nature of religious experience often seems to depend on the faith-traditions of the people concerned. The tradition provides a set of expectations about religious experience, a language in which it can be described, and sometimes even a kind of 'training' that prepares people for it. Though there is clearly some validity in these points, it is also possible to argue that there are some core elements of religious experience that seem relatively universal and less shaped by tradition (e.g. Forman, 1990). Also, the empirical study of reports of religious experience indicates that descriptors of religious experience divide into two clusters, one relatively phenomenological, the other relatively belief-laden (see Hood *et al.*, 1996:258). However, we need not enter fully here into the debate about exactly how far religious experience is shaped by tradition. The main point is a more philosophical one, that the contribution of faith traditions to the shaping of religious experience is not incompatible with the assumption of a real God revealing himself through such experience.

A different kind of theory of religious experience can be advanced in terms of the unconscious 'psychodynamics' from which it arises. This is where Freud's approach to religion is relevant, directing us to look towards the role of psychological needs and wishes, the internalisation of parent figures, and so on. It is a plausible claim that religious experience often arises in the context of unresolved psychological problems. Survey evidence certainly confirms that powerful religious experiences often occur in the context of stress and unhappiness, though the striking finding is that they characteristically produce a state of calm joy (e.g. Hay, 1987; Hood *et al.*, 1996:Ch. 7).

Once again, different assumptions are possible. You can see religious experience as being *simply* a method of dealing with stress and unresolved psychological problems. However, it has also frequently been recognised in the Christian tradition that distress, and the accompanying sense of human inadequacy, creates a genuine sense of openness to God. It is perfectly compatible with the Christian tradition to assume that unresolved psychological problems provide a particular opportunity for God to reveal himself and bestow his grace.

Similar points can be developed in relation to various charismatic phenomena, of which much the best studied is glossolalia or 'speaking in tongues' (see Malony and Lovekin, 1985). Psychological and socio-logical research has given us quite a good picture of the conditions under which glossolalia is most likely to arise, though the picture is complex, and there seem to be different forms of glossolalia which arise in different circumstances. Such findings could be taken as providing a full and adequate account of why and how glossolalia arises. However, this understanding of the human context of glossolalia is by no means incompatible with the assumption that God can use this phenomenon as a particular means of bestowing his grace.

5.12 Neurological approaches to religious experience

There has also been interest recently in the neuropsychological basis of religious experience. The idea that has attracted most interest is that there is a similarity between the neural processes underlying religious experience and temporal lobe epilepsy. It was the focus of a recent newspaper report under the headline 'God Spot in the Brain'. However, the data supporting this theory are very weak (see Jeeves, 1997). Though there are some superficial similarities between religious experiences and the seizure experiences of those who suffer from temporal lobe epilepsy, the dissimilarities are very marked. For example, religious experiences are generally positive and often life-transforming, whereas seizure experiences are distressing and transitory.

The best current theory of the neurological basis of religious experience is that of d'Aquili and Newberg (1998), who see it as arising out of the operation, in a particular context, of two general-purpose cognitive operators in the brain. The first is the 'causal operator', which attributes events to causal processes and powers. The other is the 'holistic operator' which forms a unity out of fragments of experience. D'Aquili has made a plausible argument that religious experience can be seen as arising from these two operators, one having a special application in the discernment of God's action in the world, the other underlying the powerful sense of unity that is a function of many mystical experiences.

However, once again, such a theory is neutral concerning the assumption of a real God seeking to reveal himself through religious experience. D'Aquili's theory might provide a complete and adequate explanation of the brain mechanisms from which religious experience arises. On the other hand, it can equally well be seen as a theory of the brain processes through which experience of the real God is mediated.

The assumption for which I am arguing here of the compatibility of psychological and theological views of religious experience has been formulated clearly and carefully by Meissner in his psychological study of Ignatius of Loyola (Meissner, 1992). Ignatius was concerned to identify 'uncaused consolations', i.e. religious experiences for which there was no natural explanation and which should therefore be attributed to God. Meissner argues, in contrast, that there is no incompatibility between the role of natural causes, and the assumption of a divine origin and purpose in such experiences. There is no need to assume that God's grace bypasses all natural psychological mechanisms in its operation (see also Peacocke, 1993:Ch. 11).

5.13   Conclusion

This chapter has been concerned with one of the newer areas of dialogue between science and theology. The main focus in that dialogue so far has been on evolutionary biology, and the physical sciences, especially cosmology. However, it seems likely that debates about human nature and religion will now increasingly come to the fore. Psychology has been through a number of methodological twists and turns in this century as it has attempted to find a way of getting to grips with its rather elusive subject matter. However, the twin approaches of neuro-psychology and cognitive science (in which the computer model of mind has been dominant) are now yielding real scientific progress.

There is certainly scope for a sense of conflict to arise between psychology and theology, both in their general assumptions about human nature and in their approach to religious life. However, it has been argued here that such conflict only arises when psychology overreaches itself. There is nothing in psychological research on neuropsychology or artificial intelligence which is incompatible with Christian assumptions about human nature. However, it is nonetheless true that these scientific activities are sometimes surrounded by an outer belt of general assumptions which do conflict with the Christian tradition. The key task in evaluating the dialogue between theology and psychology is to distinguish between what is really supported by research and what is speculative background or extrapolation.

Equally, there is no reason in principle why there should be conflict between the psychology of religion and traditional theological assumptions of the truth of religion. However, it seems likely that there will be a growing *sense* of such conflict in the years ahead, and neuropsychological theories of religion will probably be central to this. However, as has been pointed out here, such theories are in no way incompatible with traditional theological assumptions. The key point is that the explanatory perspective of the neurosciences is not the only one, and is not incompatible with other perspectives of a very different kind. The sense of conflict between theology and psychology only arises when psychology asserts that it is providing a full and adequate explanation of religion, a claim that it is beyond the competence of psychology to make. When the psychology of religion is seen as one explanatory perspective amongst others, it is not incompatible with the theological perspective.

FURTHER READING

BROWN, L. (1988) *The Psychology of Religion: An Introduction* (London: SPCK)

HOLDER, R. D. (1993) *Nothing But Atoms and Molecules?* (Tunbridge Wells: Monarch)

JEEVES, M. (1997) *Human Nature at the Millennium* (Grand Rapids, MI: Baker Books; Leicester: Apollos)

PALMER, M. (1997) *Freud and Jung on Religion* (London: Routledge)

PUDDEFOOT, J. (1996) *God and the Mind Machine* (London: SPCK)

WARD, K. (1992) *Defending the Soul* (Oxford: Oneworld)

WATTS, F. and WILLIAMS, M. (1994) *The Psychology of Religious Knowing* (London: Geoffrey Chapman)

BOOK THREE

Chapter 6

Models of God in an Ecological Age

SECTION A:
MODELS OF GOD WITHIN CHRISTIANITY (6.1–6.6)

6.1 Introduction

In Chapter 4 we touched on changes in theological approach which have taken place since the days of Charles Darwin. In the present chapter we develop this by exploring responses made by various twentieth-century theologians to critiques of the Christian tradition. In particular, we ask what models of God and of God's relation to humanity and the non-human creation[1] are *both* faithful to tradition *and* appropriate to apply to a world understood not only in the light of science, but in the light of the Holocaust, and the work of the feminist and environmental movements. We also examine what contribution Eastern religion and spirituality make to the dialogue between religion and science, and to the ecological debate. As we indicated in **1.18**, the challenge offered by this treatment is that the student consider her or his own model of the relationship between God, humanity and the cosmos.

We begin by identifying and evaluating three pairs of theological developments of particular importance:

(a) process thought, and its relevance to the task of constructing a theodicy (an account of God's relation to suffering) after Auschwitz;

[1] We avoid the term 'nature' because it can be used in so many senses. Ruether lists four: that which is essential to a being; the sum total of physical reality; the sum total of physical reality apart from humans; and the created world apart from God and divine grace (1992:5).

199

(b) the critique of patriarchy, which we link with critique of anthropocentrism, and

(c) revived Trinitarianism, also associated with reflection on the suffering of God.

6.2 Process thought

Process philosophy arose out of A. N. Whitehead's effort to generate a radically new metaphysics which would unify the way we understand the world. In his 1927 Gifford Lectures, published as *Process and Reality*, Whitehead abandoned the notion, strong in Western philosophy since Parmenides and Plato in the fifth century BCE, that what is most unchanging is most real. Instead he conceived the structure of reality in dynamic terms (an approach which goes back to Heraclitus). Whitehead set out a radical metaphysics based not on entities but on events – on an infinite series of 'actual occasions'. All entities are 'momentary constituents of the processes of reality'; unchangingness is a property of what is 'dead, past, abstract or purely formal' (Pailin, 1989:51). The emphasis is on *becoming*, on development in time, rather than on static being.

Space does not permit a detailed analysis of this way of thinking, except to say that for process thought the central metaphor for understanding the world is that of organism, rather than that of machine. The formation of each event is a function of:

- the nature of the entities involved (as in, for instance, a physicalist scheme);
- their context and interdependence on a number of levels (in a way more characteristic of biological organisms than of inanimate objects);
- their 'experience' and their effort to 'fulfil their possibilities to the full' in the given event (language deriving not merely from biology but from the analogy of human mentality).

As Barbour describes, 'Each entity is a center of spontaneity and self-creation, contributing distinctively to the world' (Barbour, 1998:285). This assignment of quasi-mental subjective experience to all entities is known as panpsychism, or sometimes pan-experientialism. The best recent account of process thought is that of Pailin (1989). For briefer summaries see Fiddes (1988:40–45) or Barbour (1998:284–304, 322–28).

Note that the process scheme is neither consistent nor inconsistent with experimental observations – it does not of itself give rise to any empirically testable proposals.[2] Nothing in science attributes any sort of subjectivity to an entity like an electron, nor is such a postulate anywhere supported by experiment. Whitehead's scheme is true 'meta'-physics.

6.2.1   A 'dipolar' God

In the last chapter of *Process and Reality* Whitehead turns his attention to God, and develops his concept of a dipolar deity. By this is meant that God, who in strict process thought is one entity among others – not ontologically distinct from the rest of the cosmos – is (a) affected by the experience of all other entities (God's 'consequent' nature) *and* (b) constant in character as the ground both of order and of novelty (God's 'primordial' nature). This formulation of the character of God in terms of two types of attribute in tension – responsiveness and constancy – is known as 'dipolarity' (sometimes 'bipolarity'). Charles Hartshorne, the greatest theological exponent of process thought, developed a somewhat different form of dipolarity. For Hartshorne God is both necessary being in himself, God's 'abstract' pole, but contingent in the particular relationships into which God enters with contingent creation, God's 'concrete' pole. This is a very helpful way of overcoming some of the intrinsic paradoxes of theism (see Pailin, 1989:Ch. 4).[3] Dipolarity, then, allows God to be responsive to the world and yet remain God. The emphasis in process models of God is on a God who experiences the world's pain and struggle, and persuades it towards paths of creativity and fulfilment. In Whitehead's famous phrase God is the 'fellow-sufferer who understands' (quoted in Pailin, 1989:59).

---

[2] It is sometimes supposed that because Whitehead formulated his metaphysics at the time of the great developments in physics known as the second quantum revolution (Schrödinger's Equation was published in 1926, Heisenberg's Uncertainty Principle in 1927 – see **3.11(ii)**) and because both process thought and quantum theory require a somewhat unusual way of looking at the world, that therefore process schemes are particularly compatible with the new physics. But see Polkinghorne, 1994:22–23 against this view.

[3] Keith Ward wants to propose a different type of theism (see **6.6.1**), but sees clearly the helpfulness of dipolarity. He writes: 'The basic idea of divine dipolarity, with its associated place for temporality and possibility in God, may survive dissociation from general process metaphysics' (1996a:308).

6.3   Questions of theodicy

The fellow-suffering God, who does not coerce but merely seeks to persuade other beings in the direction of love, seems profoundly attractive in the light of the Holocaust. The massacre of Jews by a country at the heart of European Christendom stands as a devastating critique of images of God acting in power to bring his kingdom in through his chosen Church. (For indications of how theologians have tried to respond to this critique see Fiddes, 1988:3–5, Surin, 1986:116–32 and references therein.) *Process schemes subvert the notion of the omnipotence of God*, and therefore escape some of these tensions.

The extent to which process theodicy is a satisfactory resource for addressing human-inflicted evil is crisply addressed by Surin (1986:86–92) who doubts whether it is enough to tell the victim of torture that there is a passive fellow-suffering God who understands. *Where process schemes are at their strongest is in offering a single account of human-inflicted evil and so-called 'natural evil'* (such as earthquakes) – in both cases 'evil' arises from conflicts between the desire of different entities for self-actualisation. God lovingly suffers with all entities, and retains their experiences in God's eternal memory, but the process God does not 'fix' these conflicts for the benefit of one entity rather than another. Instead God tries to lure all elements towards the optimal blend of harmony and intensity. This is a particularly tempting scheme for addressing the theodicy problems of evolutionary creation, which were referred to in **4.4** and are explored in detail in **7.15**.

Process theology has influenced many thinkers in the science-and-religion debate to a greater or lesser extent. Some have allied themselves explicitly with the process camp, in particular Ian Barbour – also others such as Charles Birch, John Cobb, and Jay McDaniel.[4] Polkinghorne and Peacocke have adopted some of the rhetoric of a God who guarantees order and co-operates in the universe's exploration of possibilities, although neither theologian embraces the process scheme as a whole. We explore their concepts of God more fully in **7.7**.

6.4   The critique of patriarchy

This critique has focused on the whole complex of references to God as Lord, King and Father, and to men as 'his' particular representatives,

---

[4] See Barbour (1998), Birch and Cobb (1981), McDaniel (1989).

which so dominates the language of the Bible and the Christian Fathers. The aspect of the critique that most concerns us here is the strand of thinking known as 'ecofeminism'. This takes up the charge that patriarchal attitudes have led to the oppression and denigration of women, and connects this with the way humans have abused the natural world. Patriarchy, then, is seen on this view as the root of all patterns of domination and subordination. A masculine God is viewed as utterly separate and remote from the dependent believer. This dominating remoteness, it is claimed, is used to vindicate masculine power-figures dominating others deemed to be inferior and exploitable, whether they be women, or non-human creatures, or the land itself. Daphne Hampson, herself a 'post-Christian' theologian, regards the major task of feminist theology as being the reconceptualising of God – not merely the 'renaming' but the 'reshaping' of our whole understanding of divinity (1990:Ch. 5).

Ecofeminism overlaps with *the critique of anthropocentrism*, which alleges that systems of thought which emphasise the priority of humans over other species have greatly contributed to the present ecological crisis. In a seminal article in 1967 Lynn White Jr. described Christianity as 'the most anthropocentric religion the world has seen' (White, 1967:1205)[5] and laid the blame for humans' wholesale exploitation of the natural world on the combination of science and technology that this attitude engendered. He yearned instead for the sacramental view of the Earth he found in Francis of Assisi. White's is a (highly contentious) historical analysis, and as Colin Russell comments, it must be judged historically as well as theologically. Russell points out that 'It is a great over-simplification to posit "reverence" and "control" as mutually exclusive attitudes' (Russell, C. A., 1994:89). For a recent analysis of White's charge, and other factors behind the environmental crisis, see Northcott (1996:especially Ch. 2).[6]

There has been much discussion in recent years as to whether patriarchy and anthropocentrism are so prejudicial to the formulation

---

[5] It is not hard to find biblical texts to support this: two prominent texts on human domination are Gen. 1.26 and Ps. 8.6–8. Note however Brueggemann's point on Psalm 8 – that the dominion given to humans is framed in the context of doxology, the glorifying of God (Brueggemann, 1984:37–38).

[6] Those referring to Northcott should note that instead of 'anthropocentric' he uses the more etymologically correct but less common term 'humanocentric'.

of Christianity in an age of ecological crisis as to render the faith untenable. This is a conclusion arrived at both from radical feminism by such as Hampson and Mary Daly, and from radical environmentalism by many of the followers of the 'creation spirituality' movement pioneered by Matthew Fox. Christianity will not 'work' in our present situation and we must look elsewhere for myths and rituals that will.

Those ecological theologians staying within the Christian tradition have been inclined to follow this same pragmatist line. A good example is Sallie McFague, whom we discuss in more detail in **6.5.4**. Although McFague refers to herself as working within critical realism, theological as well as scientific (1987:193 note 43), her concern is to offer a plurality of models of God, based for example on the metaphors of God as Mother, Lover and Friend (McFague, 1987:97–180), and of the world as the body of God (McFague, 1993), which she hopes will *allow humanity to survive and to avoid the abuse of the Earth.*

This seems a far cry from the critical-realist approach to theology attempted by the 'scientist–theologians' Barbour, Peacocke and Polkinghorne (see Polkinghorne 1996a:14–25), which is essentially an effort to derive consonances both between the *methods* of Christian theology and of the sciences, and also between their *cognitive-propositional claims*. In other words, an effort to derive truth-claims, rather than survival-strategies.

6.4.1   The importance of the relation between ecological theology and the science–religion debate

Divergence of approach between these two types of 'research programme' – those which attempt a pragmatically-oriented remythologisation of our relationship to the Earth, and those which attempt to align the traditional Christian narratives with those of science – tends to leave both on the margins of theology. *It is our contention that ecological considerations are an aspect of the world that science describes, and form an important part of the data for a critical-realist theology which takes science seriously.* (Indeed science has a particularly ambiguous role in the ecological crisis – having both (a) contributed to the technology responsible for much environmental abuse and (b) been the main source of our awareness of the extent of the crisis.)

So 'green' theology must form part of our discussion of the relationships between religious and scientific narratives, and of any formulation of a model of God, humanity and the cosmos.

6.4.2   Consideration of the relation between 'realist' and 'pragmatist' approaches

The above discussion raises an important issue concerning models of God. Is the task of theology to respond to the data of revelation in a way which is coherent, comprehensive, and fruitful of further exploration (a view analogous to critical-realist descriptions of scientific activity)? Or is it rather to propose ways of understanding our relation to the cosmos and to the divine which might allow us to survive (an essentially pragmatist view)?

That in turn raises another fascinating question: are not those two approaches, when considered in an evolutionary view of religion, actually the same? Must not adaptation to what-is-really-the-case be the most realist and at the same time the most pragmatic of cultural strategies?

6.4.2.1   An evolutionary approach to 'realism vs pragmatism'

We consider this question first from an evolutionary standpoint, in two ways:

(i) First, one might question whether religious cultures have been able to evolve far in the direction of the highest calling of their faiths. In biological evolution it is possible for there to be adaptive solutions to particular 'problems' – such as how to fly, how to see, etc. which cannot be reached because earlier patterns have locked the organism's structures into pathways from which there is no sufficiently adaptive route to the new solution. Indeed, some would argue that patriarchy, or come to that monotheism, is just such a locked pathway, which cannot now lead to a faith which would be adaptive to our present situation. Others would see the failure of New Testament faith to transform human behaviour (to a greater extent than it has) as one more re-statement of the doctrine of original sin. Though a community based on self-giving and neighbour-love might be the most adaptive to ultimate reality, no paths have yet been found which allow a human society to evolve to that behaviour.

(ii) A second response is to note the sheer difficulty in evaluating the adaptiveness of a world-view. The cultural-evolutionary project of Western Christianity could have been seen, as late as 1940, as astonishingly successful – it had spread its religious, economic and political norms across a great deal of the inhabited world, and could therefore have been taken to be an evolutionary strategy of unparalleled success, and hence the strategy most closely corresponding to the way-things-actually-are.[7] Teilhard de Chardin, writing in China, could conclude that the project of Western Christianity was well on the way to flooding the Earth with 'mentality', the precursor to the final consummation of that world in Christ at the Omega Point (Teilhard, 1959, see also **7.15.1**). At the end of the century, however, although the number of Christians continues to rise rapidly across the world as a whole, the global-economic system Western culture has produced threatens the continued survival of the human project in anything like its present form – not only through the risk of nuclear war, but through the ever-more-evident risk of radical climate change. (So James Lovelock, a kind of latter-day anti-Teilhard, writing in Cornwall, can remark that it may well be that the planet will need to discard this most troublesome of species [1988:212] – see **6.8 (ii)**.)

So considerable caution has to be exercised in presuming a deep truth-content to a pragmatic scheme, and in assessing the survival-adaptedness of critical-realist approaches.

6.4.2.2   A theological approach to 'realism vs pragmatism'

It is also important to question a realist-pragmatist dichotomy on *theological* grounds. The truth of God in Christian tradition is not an idea but a dynamic being. Christianity is not about 'knowing what

---

[7] This claim has been made more recently, in a secular context, for so-called free-market economics.

God is like' but about living *within* the truth of God. So Christian theology is not primarily concerned with conceptualisations for their own sake, rather it is interested in discriminating the contours of the being of God in relationship to humanity and the cosmos in particular situations, so that Christians may better live in that relationship. *Christian theology therefore seeks **neither** for useful but merely fictive or mythical ideas, **nor** for mere conceptual truth. It seeks to know the truth of God's being in order the better to live in the context of urgent practical questions.* (So Jüngel: 'the essence of Christian faith is joy in God and so concern for a more human world' [quoted in Webster, 1986:4].)

6.4.3   The development and assessment of theological models

Before we begin to outline different models which have been proposed as to the relation between God, humanity and the cosmos, a comment is needed on the process of developing and assessing models. As an example, an ecologically informed critical-realist theology will need to take the data of scriptural revelation as of central importance, but will be willing to re-evaluate these data in the light of new perceptions such as those of feminism. To return to the Lakatosian language of Nancey Murphy (**2.12**), belief in a God who has revealed the divine nature particularly in the events, stories, myths and wisdom of Scripture will be a core element in such a research programme; issues about whether that God is appropriately described as King, Lord and Father will be auxiliary propositions which can and should be subjected to severe testing in the light of the assembled data available to the community working in that tradition. This body of data will comprise the community's reflection on Scripture, tradition, reason (including all the fruits of scientific reasoning) and religious experience. Such a Lakatosian testing will involve the criteria Barbour lists for hypothesis-testing within science: agreement with data, coherence, scope and fertility,[8] but in particular it will major on the proposals to which a model of God, humanity and the cosmos gives rise. What proposals

---

[8] See 1998:109, 113 for the emphases Barbour suggests are important in applying these criteria to the assessment of particular beliefs within a religion.

does it make in respect of ethics, especially environmental ethics? Are such ethics at all workable for a real human society?[9] The proposals of a programme in Christian theology will however be liturgical as well as ethical – they will concern the prayer and worship of the community, and will be tested by 'liturgy-assisted logic' (Polkinghorne 1991:18–19) – by the extent to which that prayer and worship is experienced as positive, transformative and productive of distinctively moral life. They will also be progressive, exploring new data, such as a speaking of the Holy Spirit as feminine (Murphy, 1990:167f.).

It seems inevitable that in the current era Christian communities will explore a wide plurality of programmes. The history of the tradition that has given rise to modern Christianity has been typified sometimes by diversity, sometimes by the perceived need to establish orthodoxy (as in the reforms of Josiah and Nehemiah, the fourth-century patristic Councils, and, putatively, the Council of Trent). These fights for orthodoxy have continued to exert a tremendous effect on our models of God. In the reflection of peri-exilic Israel the worship of natural features (and the use of cultic prostitution) were pronounced uncreative, unhelpful to the moral and spiritual life of the community. Radical monotheism came to be insisted upon. The fourth and fifth centuries after Christ were characterised by sharp conflicts over definitions of the nature of Christ and the Trinity. Credal forms of words were set in place by ecumenical council. But there seems little likelihood that this present age will be one in which a new orthodoxy will be established.

It is part of the aim of this chapter to encourage the individual student to consider what their own favoured approach, realist, pragmatic, or indeed non-realist[10] would be to reflection on the relationship between God, humanity and the cosmos. The aim, then, is in a sense to fill in the gaps in Figure 6.1, but it is important to note that there could be other ways to draw the diagram – as a circle, for instance, or a series of circles inside circles. What is of particular concern is not some effort to

---

[9] This question is especially important in 'green' theological thinking. Many fine-sounding schemes based on the radical equality of all species are questionably relevant to any real situation.

[10] Typically proposals will be either realist in respect of both science and theology, non-realist in respect of both, or realist in respect of science and non-realist in respect of theology. See **2.3** for reflection on non-realist theological positions – also Ward (1996a:113–22).

define 'God' or 'nature' in the abstract, but to characterise the *relationships* between the different entities, and how those relationships have changed and will change over the history of the cosmos.

FIGURE 6.1

GOD

origin of humanity?	creation *ex nihilo*?
humanity in the image of God?	making/emanation/embodiment?
fall/sin?	autonomy/evolution of creation?
providence/theodicy?	sustaining/guiding of creation?
incarnation?/redemption?	creation's praise of/response to God?
ultimate prospects for humans/resurrection?	ultimate destiny of creation?

HUMANITY   THE COSMOS

humans' understanding of cosmic history and ecological interdependence on Earth?

anthropocentrism/biocentrism/right relationship under God?

instrumental/intrinsic value of non-human creation?

human stewardship/priesthood of creation?

A framework for expressing a model of God, humanity and the cosmos.

EXERCISE 6.1

The Exercise of the whole chapter is to consider how the different thinkers presented would draw the diagram in Figure 6.1 – what emphases are strongest for them – what do they omit to cover? (You will need to consult the original texts.) You should then be able to give an account of where your own model would differ from those described. One of the objectives of the Exercise is that you gain a sense of the *interdependence* of doctrinal positions: what choice is made as to, for example, the nature of humanity, or the significance of the Incarnation, or the salvation of non-human creatures, influences all the other choices in the model. The most problematic and underconsidered area of Figure 6.1 is the relation of the divine to the non-human world. In considering the seven brief treatments that follow you should consider in particular their adequacy in addressing this aspect of theology.

6.5   Some models discussed

We consider two models of God stemming out of process thought, and two arising out of critiques of patriarchy and anthropocentrism. We look at three formulations of a new Trinitarianism, and at the end of the chapter we review resources outside the ambit of Christianity which may offer insights into the relation of religion to science and to the ecological crisis.

6.5.1   Model A: David Pailin in *God and the Processes of Reality* (1989)

Pailin's account is a reworking of process theism, deriving in particular from Charles Hartshorne and his concept of a Godhead containing both necessary and contingent attributes (see **6.2.1**). So God is necessarily, indestructibly divine, but God's actuality as Creator is contingent on God's choice to be the Creator of this particular cosmos (Pailin, 1989:68–69). *The model is* **panentheistic** *– it regards the whole universe as contained within God, and yet considers that this does not exhaust the divine being. Pailin considers the closest analogy to be that of a human self within a body.* Although God's knowledge of the world is far greater than ours of our bodies, there is nevertheless autonomy of process within the non-divine. As in all process thought there is a strong emphasis on temporality in God (see Pailin's Ch. 3 for a discussion), but Pailin's God is very much the Creator, the 'self-grounded ground of all else' (1989:127), not merely an ordering entity co-existing with the primordial chaos. This responds to a common theological criticism of Whitehead's scheme that he made creativity, rather than God, his ultimate.

As regards the narrative of Darwinism, Pailin would say that evolution illustrates the autonomy of process in the creation, and that God has not intervened within it. Divine influence on the non-conscious world is in terms of implanting 'a bias towards complexification' (1989:153) and enjoying the value of whatever emerges, rather than luring or persuading every entity towards the divine goals of harmony and creativity. This view, he says, is 'biologically tenable, metaphysically significant, theistically important and rationally credible' (1989:153). Pailin here parts company with the pan-experientialism and theology of divine lure mentioned in **6.2–6.2.1**. He thus deals with the great problem of the implausibility of a metaphysic based on electrons having anything akin to subjective experience, but he abandons that unity of description of God's interaction with all elements of the creation which is such a striking feature of process schemes. As Paul Fiddes has written:

> [p]rocess thinkers argue that something akin to the basic features of human experience – feeling and enjoyment – must be present everywhere. However hard it is to express the term of the analogy at the lower levels of creation . . . nevertheless I believe that process thought is on to something here. Some overall vision of the 'responsiveness' and 'resistance' of creation to the Spirit of God is needed for a doctrine of creative evolution, (and) for a proper theodicy . . . (1988:228)

Pailin, in trying to move process thought closer to a typically Christian emphasis on God as the ground of creation and away from the weirder aspects of Whiteheadian metaphysics, has actually ditched something very significant. Fiddes again: 'It may be that process thought is pointing in a direction whose destination we do not yet have the conceptual tools to map; if we cannot yet define the mystery we may need "mythologies" such as universal mentality to recognise it' (1988:228).

6.5.2   Model B: Jay McDaniel in *Of God and Pelicans* (1989)

McDaniel has reflected carefully on the relation between God and the non-human world, which is as we have said in many ways the most theologically problematic relationship in Figure 6.1. In particular, McDaniel considers the 'back-up chick' which some birds hatch as an 'insurance', but which is usually destroyed by its stronger sibling. The pelican is an example of a species in which such behaviour has evolved. McDaniel uses this as an illustration of the tensions (already noted at **4.4**) involved in supposing God the inceptor and sustainer of the evolutionary process, and at the same time the one by whom nature is inexhaustibly loved (1989:23). McDaniel sees a process view as the only one which might generate a theodicy adequate to these challenges.

Like Pailin, McDaniel is a panentheist, and he makes a distinction between 'emanationist' panentheism, in which the universe is God's body, the direct expression of the divine being, and what he calls 'relational' panentheism, which regards the world as having some degree of creative independence from God. Although we may question to what extent McDaniel's relational panentheism is more than a re-statement of God's immanence within all creation, his scheme does allow him to regard God as 'both agent in and patient of nature' (1989:30).

As against Pailin, McDaniel conforms more closely to the main emphases of process theology in stressing the cosmos as co-eternal with God, and advocating panpsychism. Where *he* breaks ranks with most process theologians is in following John Cobb (rather than Hartshorne) and claiming that a Whiteheadian scheme is consistent with a category of life after death (McDaniel, 1989:44–47). For Hartshorne, the ultimate purpose and consummation of life is to enrich the divine experience. McDaniel accepts this, but claims that his model is strengthened by admitting *also* some form of 'pelican heaven' – in which the products of evolution are all transformed after death to an improved state of existence.

McDaniel's other importance is in his pursuit of a biocentric ethic – that is, one which accords moral status to all life and not just to human beings. He concedes that there need to be different approaches for different types of creatures – domestic animals to be considered in terms of their individual rights, other living creatures as moral patients, the rest of the non-human creation in terms of its general intrinsic value[11] (1989:67–69). He asks what theological and spiritual resources can promote the practice of such an ethic, and draws the conclusion that beyond those of process thought the most important derive from Buddhism, especially the concepts of (i) non-harming – refraining as much as possible from the violation of other creatures' interests – and (ii) emptiness.

We consider what Eastern spirituality can contribute to the dialogue between religion and science further in **6.9–6.12.1**. But it is important to note the approach here – McDaniel asks: what spirituality will enable us to *act out* the theological convictions we have formed about God

---

[11] McDaniel's approach to animal rights is founded not on Andrew Linzey's approach, which seeks to accord 'theos-rights' to creatures (Linzey, 1994), or on Peter Singer's utilitarianism (Singer, 1990) but on Tom Regan's assertion that to be 'the subject of a life' is a sufficient criterion of the possession of moral rights (see e.g. Regan, 1990:73–87). For a summary of Singer and Regan, and a comparison with process thought as a basis for ethics, see Armstrong-Buck (1986), or more accessibly Northcott (1996:93–102,146–7). See also Palmer (1998) on process-derived environmental ethics.

and the world? In this he conforms very much to the view of theology we have been articulating in this book – also to the Bossey Circle (see page 16) Scientific and social analysis should inform contemporary theology – theology should inform ethics – theology and ethics, to be meaningful, must lead to praxis.

At the end of his book McDaniel offers the metaphor for God he feels is most helpful: God as Heart (1989:140–45). This is an image of God as the centre of the vital functions of the universe, the core of things, but also the centre of the feelings of sympathy, understanding and compassion. McDaniel's incorporations into a process-based scheme lead to an attractive model, but one which has still to meet fundamental criticisms of process thought, of which we now address three.

6.5.3   Fundamental criticisms of process thought

(i) Is dipolarity in God coherent and theologically productive? For a fierce critique see Clark, 1993:72–88, for a more careful analysis of alternatives see Fiddes, 1988:111f.

A Possible Response: It is difficult to escape the conviction that the God of the Bible has at one and the same time two types of attributes which must be held in tension, being both unchanging in character and purpose, *and* also deeply influenced by real personal relationships with humans. (See Model G, Section **6.6.1**.)

(ii) Is the attribution of experience to the smallest entities, 'panpsychism', or more helpfully 'pan-experientialism', at all meaningful?

A Possible Response: Fiddes is correct (in the passage quoted above) in supposing that some such postulate, however difficult to articulate or substantiate, is necessary. Within a biblical theology of creation it is hard to escape the notion that the stuff of the universe is at the very least *responsive* to God (cf. Ps. 19.1, Ps. 104.27–30).

(iii) Is the process God enough of a God? Hartshorne has insisted that his God could be the God who raised Jesus from the dead, but the general tenor of process thought is that God and the cosmos co-develop without any guaranteed grounds for belief in God's ultimate victory over evil. It is not immediately clear how such a scheme would be reconciled with contemporary cosmological predictions about the end of the present universe, which are that either a 'Big Crunch' or an infinite expansion will eventually lead to a state quite incompatible with life.

A Possible Response: Process eschatology emphasises the role of the divine memory. 'Our lives are meaningful because they are preserved everlastingly in God's experience, in which evil is transmuted and the good is saved and woven into the harmony of the larger whole' (Barbour, 1998:304). And since the matter of the present universe will not indefinitely support life, all eschatological schemes must depend on *some* category of existence within God. We take up questions of eschatology in **7.17**.

6.5.4   Model C: Sallie McFague in *The Body of God* (1993)

McFague sets out first of all what she calls 'the common creation story', the account science gives us of our origins over the (approximately) 15-billion-year history of the cosmos (1993:41–42). This is, she claims, the narrative that binds all human cultures and traditions together. Nevertheless this story does not tell us how to think about ourselves in the world of the ecological crisis. It does not of itself promote 'sustainability and livability' (1993:68). Nor can the scientific narrative speak of purposes, divine or human. In the light of the use of earlier God-language for purposes of oppression we have to devise new metaphors (as McDaniel does with 'God as Heart', and as McFague did in her earlier book *Models of God* [1987], writing of God as 'Mother, Lover, Friend'). McFague explores the viability of the metaphor of the world as God's body, a 'remythologisation' with 'ethical or pragmatic concern' (1993:81) which she hopes can link the scientific narrative with the data of Christian revelation.

Again, note the nature of this approach, which emphasises the pragmatic, the practical, the concrete, a tradition which McFague traces back to Aristotle (as opposed to the disembodied, static and absolute propositional truths of Plato). This pragmatic approach might seem to fit well with the concerns of feminism and other theologies of liberation. However, Daphne Hampson has criticised McFague's model-making as being no more than a dressed-up form of humanism, noting that 'The construction of models of God is predicated upon what one construes to be evidence for belief in God ... [McFague's] work lacks talk of such evidence' (Hampson, 1990:161).[12] *But for McFague our function as humans is not to think true thoughts about abstractions, but 'to live appropriately and responsibly'* (McFague, 1993:89). She advocates 'attention epistemology' (1993: 49), paying attention to 'inscape' – to other things in themselves and for themselves – this has similarities to McDaniel's talk of 'suchness' (for McDaniel's model see **6.5.2**; for its connection to Buddhist concepts of 'suchness' see **6.12.1**). When we pay attention to the planet we can see that it is vulnerable and fragile, and, moreover, not a hotel but our home.

Humans are seen, in this model, as utterly dependent on other parts of the 'body', and not by any means the only locus of value, but having a special role as those who know 'the common creation story', 'like it or not, the guardians and caretakers of our tiny planet' (McFague, 1993:109). It is idle to deny the differences that exist between species. Sin is defined, not as in most Christian theology in terms of deviation from the loving purpose of God, but as refusal to accept our place in the network of (embodied) relationships that is the planetary ecosystem.[13]

God is understood as embodied like ourselves, as the 'prime and prior psychosomatic unity', but divine action is not only 'organic', as of the self in the body, but also 'agential', as of spirit in body. (The difficulty of this language will be evident – we cannot give a clear scientific account of what conscious agency is, still less is it easy to agree to what it might mean to be moved by spirit.) This model like the previous two is panentheistic – *the universe as God's body enlivened and empowered by the divine spirit*. McFague regards this as a model both commensurate with the scientific data, and able 'to help us to act holistically' (1993:147). Science has been used to help rule out some models, such as God as monarchical father, but is not used to try and 'rule any models in'.

---

[12] The student looking into McFague's work will want to consider the extent to which her 'remythologisation with ethical or pragmatic concern' is open to such a charge.

[13] Definitions of sin are very good diagnostics of the character of models of God, humanity and the cosmos – since they provide an index of the ways in which the threeway network of relationships (Fig. 6.1) is understood to break down.

Rather the traditional Jewish and Christian motif of the special concern of God for the weak and the oppressed is invoked in respect of both humanity and the non-human creation.[14]

Both the phrases italicised above, 'the universe as God's body' and 'empowered and enlivened by the divine spirit' cause McFague problems:

(a) the analogy with our own embodiedness is weakened by the fact that our 'selves' are inextricably dependent on our lower functions, from which they have arisen through evolution, whereas God for McFague is 'embodied, but not necessarily or totally' (1993:150). Polkinghorne has criticised such models on the grounds that 'the body of God' is always too much in thrall either to God or to the world (1989:18–23).

(b) the divine spirit is not identified with the Holy Spirit, except in relation to human beings. This tends to complicate the model without escaping the theodicy problems of evolutionary creation (see **7.15**).

6.5.5 Model D: Rosemary Radford Ruether in *Gaia*[15] *and God* (1992)

Ruether's book is chiefly remarkable for the quality of its analysis of our difficulty in framing an ecological theology. She warns against trying to derive ethics purely from spirituality, which she says will tend to be a 'privatized intrapsychic activity' (1992:4) or simply trying to replace a male, transcendent deity with a female, immanent one. Rather it is important to realise how much our reception of the Hebrew accounts of creation has been influenced by Greek motifs – two in particular:

(i) the myth in Plato's *Timaeus* that the soul is a principle which aspires to become detached from its present, corrupt body;

---

[14] Somewhat like McDaniel, McFague finds herself grafting on an extra category, resurrection, into her theological scheme, in order to associate herself more closely with 'the Christic paradigm'. So she writes (1993:179–91) of the body of God as also the Cosmic Christ in a way which seems insecurely juxtaposed with her model as a whole.

[15] 'Gaia', a name derived from the Greek goddess of the Earth, is used by Ruether for the whole system of interdependent living beings on the planet. See **6.8** for more exploration of this term.

(ii) cosmologies where the Earth is the lowest, most corrupt point (see **1.12**). (Ruether, 1992:27–28)

It is easy to see how these motifs would work against our valuation of the material world.

EXERCISE 6.2

Look at the creation narratives in Genesis 1–2 and identify elements of the stories which might reinforce the motifs just listed, and elements which might suggest a different valuation of matter.

The ambivalence towards matter in the Christian tradition is further complicated by the New Testament emphasis on the 'Fall' of humanity (derived from Genesis 3), from which we are rescued by Christ. Humanity is somehow to blame for the world as it is, and is in need of rescue from that world; not even 'the forces that govern the universe' (Rom. 8.38, Cassirer's translation) can keep us from this rescuing love.

However, Ruether is not as naïve about these 'forces' as some writers on eco-spirituality. She recognises that the natural world was not originally benign for humans and is not capable of fulfilling our hopes for the good. Our impulse to loving care for others stands out from our mortal limits. We can promote this – to a certain extent we can even reshape the world towards this impulse, but only within the constraints imposed on us by our mortality and by the interdependence of all organisms. Ecological ethics, then, will be an 'uneasy synthesis' between 'the laws of consciousness and kindness' and 'the laws of Gaia' (Ruether, 1992:31).

Along with our impulse to kindness goes our experience that things are not as they should be, a sense of sin. Some of which, Ruether points out, is a function of humans' drive to improve things (which of course has been, in evolutionary terms, vastly successful). But there remains a truth that our relationships to each other and to the non-human world do tend to become distorted; we assert our rights to life and power as absolutes at the expense of other beings. There are clear parallels with McFague's definition of sin (see **6.5.4** above). Ruether advocates that instead we recognise that all beings are 'covenantally related' – 'one family united by one source of life' (1992:227). As we seem to be in some sense 'the "mind" of the universe, the place where the universe becomes conscious of itself' (1992:249) it is 'our urgent task to understand the web of life and live within that web as sustainers rather than destroyers' (1992:250), not absolutising the good but recognising that it means living within limits.

Much of Ruether's diagnosis of our crisis and the constraints that hold us back from engaging with it is very cogent, but there is a striking absence of any clear doctrine of God. The 'voices ... of God and Gaia ... are our own voices ... not in the sense that there is "nothing" out there, but in the sense that what is "out there" can only be experienced by us through the lenses of human existence ... We can ... intuit *the source of all life and thought that lies behind the whole* [our italics]. This contact, though humanly imaged, can be true. Its truth lies in the test of relationships; do our metaphors bear the fruits of compassion or of enmity?' (1992:254–55) Note again the pragmatism of the approach – theology is being tested by the ethics to which it gives rise. Insofar as there is God-talk it is of an implicitly emanationist kind: the divine is the source and matrix of what is (see the words italicised in the last quotation), but in no sense either ontologically distinct from the cosmos, or an agent within it. We must take leave to doubt if this is enough to ground Ruether within the Christian tradition, however profound her analyses of the roots of its difficulties.

6.5.6   Model E: Jürgen Moltmann in *God in Creation* (1985)

There is however a significant body of theological work trying to frame Christian theology which is responsive to the ecological crisis and to feminist critique, but within a more traditionally Trinitarian framework than we have yet discussed, with the incarnation of Jesus Christ being seen as central. Moltmann has been a most eloquent exponent of this type of approach.[16] His greatest contribution has been in stressing the real suffering and chaos to which God the Trinity is exposed at the Cross (see his *The Crucified God* [1974]). He is also a great exponent of the theology of kenotic creation – God as limiting God's self in allowing creation existence and freedom to develop.

---

[16] Eberhard Jüngel is another very important figure in this area. See Webster (1986) for a summary of his work.

Moltmann's most controversial use of this motif is in the image he uses for the first creative impulse of a Trinity which he describes in terms of a self-sufficient community of love from all eternity. In order that there *be* any other entities whatsoever the Trinity had to withdraw from a certain ontological space, to allow a primordial element of non-being. For this self-withdrawal Moltmann borrows Luria's term *zimsum*, connoting a process of 'concentration and contraction ... a withdrawing of oneself into oneself. An inversion of God ... sets free a kind of "mystical primordial space" into which God can ... enter and in which he can manifest himself ... Here we have an act in which Nothingness is called forth' (Moltmann, 1985:87). This is attractive in terms of Gen. 1.2, which pictures a pre-creation state having some existence but 'without form and void' – also in that it sees 'letting be' as an intrinsic element in God's creative activity. Such a description of creation will be particularly consonant with scientific descriptions of the universe developing through the interplay of chance and physical law. (But see below for some criticisms of Moltmann's formulations.)

God's initial kenotic self-withdrawal leads for Moltmann to a whole series of divine self-limitations, including the creation of humans bearing God's image, and the call and election of Abraham, and culminating in the divine Son going silent to the most degrading of executions. Cross and resurrection inaugurate a new age in which evolution is *redeemed* through God's preferential love for the weak and the oppressed. (Moltmann makes this clear only in his later book *The Way of Jesus Christ* where in an important passage he takes issue with Teilhard and Rahner for interpreting the future unfolding of evolution as a *working-out* of Christ's purposes [Moltmann, 1990:292–306].) Again we see, as with McDaniel and McFague, a theologian needing to introduce an extra category of divine–human interaction – be it redemption, resurrection, or pelican heaven – beyond what parallels an evolutionary account.

Moltmann's kenotic scheme, panentheistic like Pailin's, McDaniel's and McFague's, embraces some of the advantages of both classical and process schemes. He criticises Whitehead for making the world process co-eternal with God – and hence, in effect, itself an attribute of the ultimate. For Moltmann the world arises out of and is utterly dependent upon the love of the Trinity. But the development of the world is accomplished through the persuasive and sacrificial love of God, the God who became the Crucified One and works now through the

Holy Spirit, in part within the fallible functioning of the Christian Church.

At the same time Moltmann is much firmer than any process theologian about the eventual consummation of all things in the kingdom of glory. The Sabbath, God's rest within God's creation, a concept so much neglected in Christian practice, is both the crown of creation and the foretaste of the ultimate harmony of all things at the eschaton. Some other emphases in Moltmann's ecological theology include:

(i)   What can be known by us is only ever partial; we need to restore a belief in *heaven*, the unseen reality (1985:39), the 'side of creation that is open to God' (1985:163).[17] It is the kingdom of God's *energeia*, God's 'energies'.[18]

(ii) We perceive creation not as 'very good' (Gen. 1.31) but as 'groaning in expectation' (Rom. 8.19–21). 'To understand "nature" as creation therefore means discerning "nature" as the enslaved creation that hopes for liberty.' Anyone who understands this 'begins to suffer with that creation, and also to hope for it' (Moltmann, 1985:39).

(iii) Just as the Earth is thermodynamically an open system – that is to say that it receives energy from the outside, from the sun, and also gives off energy into space – so we may picture the whole universe as an open system, in communication with the 'extra-worldly encompassing milieu' of God (1985:205). And only an open system can give rise to true novelty, or experience real transformation.

Moltmann's is a powerful and persuasive model, recently reviewed by Deane-Drummond (1997c). Three principal criticisms can be levelled at his scheme.

---

[17] Moltmann here draws heavily on Barth's *Church Dogmatics* III/3.

[18] Here Moltmann invokes a distinction in Orthodox theology between God's *energeia*, which impart the divine will to the world, and God's *ousia*, the divine being as it is in itself, utterly unchanging and unchangeable. See Gregorios (1987:57–59), but see also Fiddes (1988:111f.) for an effort to get beyond such distinctions.

6.5.7   Criticisms of Moltmann

(i) The first is a general problem with all schemes which invoke a Cross-inaugurated redemption – simply that there is so little evidence that the two thousand years since the Cross of Christ have really been transformative of human nature, or even that the Christian Church could be said to be in the forefront of what transformation there has been. Moltmann writes in fine terms of the coming kingdom, but the signs of hope and liberation for the world are few. (Hence the lure of a process scheme, or one which regards the project of redemption as still in its earliest evolutionary stages.)

(ii) The second criticism of Moltmann is that talk of *zimsum*, which forms a perfectly coherent part of Jewish neo-Platonic thought, seems at odds with the scepticism Moltmann expresses elsewhere about speculative metaphysics. And *zimsum* does raise a deep question: how *can* the all-sufficient, all-encompassing Trinity give rise to 'an annihilating Nothingness' (Moltmann, 1985:88)?

(iii) The third objection to the scheme of the writer of *The Crucified God* is that the focus of God's suffering concern for the world is so much the historical events of Incarnation and Cross. Fiddes writes: 'Clearly, if God suffers universally, we cannot speak of the being of God as first becoming suffering love at the cross. God must always have been so' (1988:7).

This leads us to the next of our models of the relationships between the divine, humans and the non-human world which start from within the Christian tradition.

6.5.8   Model F: Paul Fiddes in *The Creative Suffering of God* (1988)

This is a dense study of the coherence of the concept of kenotic creation. Fiddes rejects process thinking as making creativity the supreme value by which even God is constrained. He wants to retain a theology of God's willing the creation (and his suffering within it), but he pursues the question of the reality of change and suffering in God further than Moltmann. Further even in a sense than the process theologians, since

Fiddes rejects dipolarity (1988:110–11, see **6.2.1**) – his God therefore has no perfect pole on which to fall back. Suffering is not merely an inward action of God, it is something that *happens to* the deity, something by which God is really changed (1988:62–3), something, indeed, which makes God more truly God. The world is therefore necessary to God (albeit through God's own choice). God both chooses God's self as Father, Son and Spirit, and chooses to come to fulfilment through free, open, vulnerable relation to humankind. Fiddes' contention is that these are one and the same choice.

At the same time a model of the Christian God must promise *victory* over suffering, 'he should not be overcome or defeated by suffering' (1988:100). Fiddes thus draws back from W. H. Vanstone's radical account of God's risk in *Love's Endeavour, Love's Expense*; God's risk in creation is a limited risk, because ultimately God *will* be all in all. But the character of God's eventual glory depends on the experience God shares with the creation, on a real exchange of feelings between persons.

Fiddes' main emphases, then, are two-fold:

- every element in God's creative work has involved God's self-limiting and suffering love – vulnerable encounter with a creation which has some autonomy and displays some resistance to the divine will;

- the nature of God's internal nature and God's relationship with persons is one of real mutual exchange, best characterised in terms of Trinity rather than the language of process.

6.6   Recurrent motifs: panentheism and the suffering of God

If we apply McDaniel's distinction between emanationist and relational panentheism to the thinkers that have been discussed, we find that only Ruether is a pure emanationist, in that she has moved away from any emphasis on God *acting* on the world. Although Pailin concedes that the analogy of self to body may be the best analogy to God's relation to the world, he is very far from saying that the world is a direct expression of God's being. And McFague's rather vague account of divine agency seems to belong to a relational model.

Carefully formulated, relational panentheism can answer Polkinghorne's concerns about God being too much in thrall to the world (see **6.5.4**). Indeed, it need not differ significantly from the traditional emphases on God's being both utterly transcendent and utterly immanent. Yes, God must be totally present to every entity in the universe (in a way which has perhaps been understated in much Christian theology). But also yes, that immanent presence cannot be taken to exhaust the being of God. Panentheism, seen in this light, is indeed simply 'a useful spatial model' (Peacocke, 1993:370–71).

The other emphasis found throughout these models is of God's suffering with the sufferings of the cosmos. This seems a necessary consequence of conceding that God is affected by the world and responds to developments within it. It remains a real difficulty to associate the *general* suffering of creation with the *particular* suffering of the Godhead at the Cross, and to speak of divine suffering as utterly authentic, something that 'befalls' God, in Fiddes' phrase, and yet assert that God's victory is assured.

It may be asked at this point to what extent evangelical Christian theology has responded to the critiques with which this chapter began. Has ecofeminism, or biocentrism, had much impact here? An interesting exercise is to turn up the index of a standard text such as Alister McGrath's *Christian Theology: An Introduction* (1994). Feminism does receive three pages to itself (McGrath, 1994:100–02), and informs the general discussion. However, the links that many writers have made between denigration of women and exploitation of the Earth are not mentioned, nor does 'ecology' appear in the index at all.

Insofar as evangelical theology has addressed the ecological debate this has largely been through restatements of humans' role as stewards of creation.[19] (Likewise Islamic thought, while expressing concern for the environment and awareness of the duty of humans towards it [see **9.4**] has not responded to the charge that images of deity and patriarchy might lie at the root of continued environmental exploitation.)

Assistance in developing a model of God rooted in Thomism (the system derived from Aquinas) but thoroughly informed by

---

[19] For a good introduction see Granberg-Michaelson (1990). Note also Clare Palmer's attack on the concept of stewardship in (1992:67–86). For an example of more recent writing from the evangelical tradition see Prance (1996).

To comment on the slowness of many parts of the Christian tradition to address the importance of ecological concerns is not to minimise the difficulty of the task. One reason why we struggle to find 'green' content in Christianity is that the religion began to attain its full character in persecution – and it looked back to the time of the Israelite exile to Babylon, to a time of saying 'despite our situation God can work'. Christianity has always been at its strongest and truest in persecution. And it has never had a model of going back to the land in peace and power to work out its inspiration. (Rather the Israelite exiles went back as a vassal state preoccupied with racial identity.)

contemporary science, by process thought and by the theology of Barth comes from the third Trinitarian model we present:

6.6.1   Model G: Keith Ward in *Religion and Creation* (1996)

In Parts III and IV of this book Ward offers an important philosophical analysis of how Trinitarian faith can be combined with an account of God as active in the world the sciences describe. Ward starts from classical Western-Christian formulations of the ways in which God can be described – for example Aquinas' description of God as the most perfect possible being, and Anselm's principle that God must possess every property which it is better to possess than not. But he succeeds in developing these in a direction so lacking in Augustinian–Thomist thought – towards a God who acts responsively in time to make possible the realisation of values within the creation which could not have existed had creation not taken place.

Ward wrestles long and hard with the question of whether God necessarily creates. Fiddes, anxious to distance himself from too process-dominated a view, took the line that God can *choose* whether the world be necessary to God (Fiddes, 1988:135). Ward rejects that as incoherent. After some discussion he comes to the view that 'some disposition to creative activity and loving fellowship, necessarily actualised at some time, is necessary to God being what God is' (Ward, 1996a:320). This necessary disposition does not however generate a scheme in which the cosmos is co-eternal with God – Ward's model of creation remains *ex nihilo*, by the Father through the Son in the power of the Spirit.[20]

As was mentioned above, Ward sees dipolarity in God as a helpful insight from process thought which can be incorporated into a more traditionally Christian scheme. He discusses John Macquarrie's 'triadic' distinction in the divine nature – as primordial, expressive and unitive. But he demurs from Macquarrie's equation of these 'poles' with the persons of the Trinity. Ward has a yet grander scheme which might be called 'tetrapolar' – God is at one and the same time eternal-primordial, originative-expressive, historical-responsive and eschatological-unitive

---

[20] Ward, like R. J. Russell (see **1.15**), is able to show that the non-singularity proposals of Hawking and others for the origin of the Big Bang need not be an obstacle to a theistic model of creation (Ward, 1996a:295–99). He is also able to dismiss the idea that special relativity leaves God no scope to act in time (pp. 300–03).

(1996a:338) – and in *each* of these God can be seen as constituted as Trinity. This is a remarkable fusion of the thought-worlds of Aquinas, Barth and Hartshorne, earthed in a sense that all Trinitarian thought arises from the divine self-disclosure in the events of the New Testament.

Interestingly a recent article by Janet Martin Soskice (Soskice, 1998) on the naming of God stresses the same objective we see lying behind Ward's study. Soskice points out how the extent to which late twentieth-century theologians have abandoned 'the God of the attributes' – omnipotent, eternal, immutable – as 'remote and unfeeling'.[21] But she holds to the importance of not jettisoning *either* the philosophical basis of Christian theism in the utter transcendence, omnipotence and omniscience of God (towards which the tradition of negative or apophatic theology [see **1.18**] makes such an important contribution) *or* the biblical conviction that God has acted and will act in the lives of human beings – that God has met us and given us names for the divine self. *Both* sets of motifs are strong in Christian revelation, reflection and worship – also in such seminal accounts of religious experience as Augustine's *Confessions*. So it is for such a fusion that a Christian model of God (containing always a measure of the unsayable) must search.

At the time of writing (1998) Ward's work and that of Fiddes represent, to our mind, the best new insights into a Trinitarian theology of creation. Both, then, are very helpful in the search for a model of God, humanity and the cosmos. Their focus, however, is very much on God, and their discussion sometimes distinctly abstruse. We would look to see development of this line of thought around the *whole* of Figure 6.1 – particularly in the direction of theological anthropology: what exactly, given our evolutionary origins (see **4.15–4.16.2**), *is* this humankind with which God desires special fellowship, and what are the ethical (human-world) implications of human nature? These models also need work in the direction of developing a language for speaking of the non-human creation in relation to God.

---

[21] Here she quotes from Moltmann's *The Trinity and the Kingdom of God* (1981).

SECTION B:
SOME RESOURCES FOR THEOLOGICAL THINKING ON GOD AND THE WORLD FROM OUTSIDE THE CHRISTIAN TRADITION[22]
(6.7–6.14)

6.7   Introduction

In the first section of Ward's book he looks at a thinker from Judaism (Heschel), Christianity (Barth), Islam (Iqbal) and Hinduism (Aurobindo), and claims to find a common strand in their understanding of divinity (1996a:Chs 1–4, especially pp. 100–06). Each, Ward claims, wants to emphasise the dynamic quality of the relationship of the divine to the cosmos to an extent greater than is typical in their traditions. Many however have questioned whether all these thinkers are genuinely representative of the mainstream of their religions, and how much Ward has forced the similarity between them. Nevertheless his study points to the fact that the relation of the divine to the world is a live theological issue in a number of faiths, and that thinking in one tradition may feed theology in another. So we now consider some resources from outside the Christian tradition.

We consider firstly the Gaia Hypothesis, then the contributions of Hinduism, Taoism and Buddhism, and then two movements much influenced by Eastern thought – deep ecology and 'new paradigm' thinking.

6.8   The Gaia Hypothesis

(i) The Hypothesis considered in scientific terms

Ruether's use of the name 'Gaia' (6.5.5) derives from the work of the scientist and inventor James Lovelock who since the early 1970s has been putting forward what is in its essence a scientific hypothesis – albeit a difficult one to test – that the presence of life all over the surface of the Earth has dramatically changed conditions on that surface, and caused them to remain remarkably stable in a range which allows living systems to continue.

---

[22] NB: Islam is considered separately in Chapter 9.

The basic data for the Hypothesis are those seen in Table 6.1, which shows how utterly different the Earth is from a planet of the same sort of size, composition and orbit, but without life.

TABLE 6.1

Atmospheric component	Venus	Mars	Earth without life	Earth as it is
Carbon dioxide	96.5%	95%	98%	0.03%
Nitrogen	3.5%	2.7%	1.9%	79%
Oxygen	trace	0.13%	0.0	21%
Methane	0.0	0.0	0.0	1.7ppm
Surface temperature (°C)	459	−53	240–340	13
Total pressure (bars)	90	0.0064	60	1.0

Planetary Atmospheres: Their Composition, Temperature and Pressure
(drawn from Lovelock, 1988:9) [ppm = parts per million].

Lovelock elaborates this in a particularly fascinating way in *The Ages of Gaia* (1988), tracing the proposed history of life on the planet and the way in which life might not just have altered the planet, but given rise to self-regulating mechanisms to keep it altered. As Osborn has pointed out, the existence of these mechanisms is highly controversial. Much of the stability of the terrestrial environment may be associated with systems not involving life (for a survey of proposals of this type see Osborn, 1992:29–32). However, Lovelock may well be right in emphasising the damage to 'Gaia' being done by practices which pollute the atmosphere and reduce biodiversity. He may also be timely in pointing out that the cycle of atmospheric carbon dioxide levels is at an extreme at present, and that humans' sudden stressing of the system might lead to a rapid move to a different stable state (Lovelock, 1988:158–59).

Throughout his work, Lovelock's rhetoric is of the planet as an organism, a 'living thing'. Certainly it is a bounded system far from equilibrium (see **4.7**), one moreover which contains interacting subsystems and undergoes processes of development and change. It is more difficult to see Gaia as being capable of reproduction – unless by the 'ecopoiesis' of Mars (1988:183–202) – still less of evolving in the Darwinian sense, since there is, as far as we know, no other comparable 'organism' against which it might be selected.

(ii) The Hypothesis considered in metaphysical terms

Lovelock also shifts periodically into a somewhat different mode of writing, encouraged perhaps by the name he gave to his hypothesis.[23] Sometimes Gaia becomes personified – Lovelock suggests for instance that 'she' might 'get rid' of humans if they were a 'nuisance' to 'her'. This does make an important scientific point about the very unusual and stable conditions that pertain on the Earth. The parameters that make this a life-supporting planet (temperature, atmospheric composition, etc.) are stable to a remarkable degree, but they are not held in any absolute or lasting way within the limits that have allowed human civilisation to thrive. Another ice age is not merely possible but likely. But these considerations also cause Lovelock to slide towards the language of Gaia as personal agent 'who' might 'decide' to 'punish' or 'eliminate' humans:

> Gaia, as I see her, is no doting mother tolerant of misdemeanors, nor is she some fragile and delicate damsel in danger from brutal mankind. She is stern and tough, always keeping the world warm and comfortable for those who obey the rules, but ruthless in her destruction of those who transgress. Her unconscious goal is a planet fit for life. (1988:212)

The key word here is 'unconscious', but the rhetoric of the passage makes it easy to overlook. The Gaia Hypothesis, as a scientific description couched in non-teleological terms, is a very telling proposal and a helpful way to think about the systems that make our life possible, their very long history, our ignorance of them, and our possible vulnerability to sudden shifts in their behaviour. But any extension of that proposal into describing Gaia as a purposive, personified agent would move the discussion into a different realm of explanation, in which other considerations about the nature of divinity would become important. (One very obvious example is that Gaia 'herself' is a function of this planet alone, and has no status in other parts of the universe. Another is that 'her' power is extremely limited. No Gaian feedback systems extend to the behaviour of the sun, small changes in which could completely disrupt all the systems that stabilise conditions on the Earth. So at most 'Gaia' could only be a petty deity of no great cosmic power.)

---

[23] The suggestion of 'Gaia', the Greek goddess of the Earth, came from the novelist William Golding.

We therefore regard the Gaia Hypothesis with some caution, seeing it as a potentially helpful refinement of the scientific narrative of the development of the Earth's environment (and a reminder of how unusual that environment is), but aware that Gaia could also be the source of some ill-considered spirituality. For further reading see Osborn (1992), Russell, C. A. (1994:Ch. 8) and Deane-Drummond (1996:98–114).

6.9   The contributions of Eastern thought

In recent decades there has been a considerable interest in the concepts contained in some of the religious traditions of Asia, insofar as they have seemed to offer an imaginative language for expressing some of the findings of modern science. This occurred first in physics, as a result of quantum theory, and later in biology, especially in the application of a systems approach to understanding the emergence and self-sustainability of living beings, ecosystems and the global biosphere. These seeming consonances between science and Eastern thought have in turn increased interest in these religions within Western culture.

By contrast with the concepts derived from Newton and Descartes, which present a world consisting of masses in space interacting according to fixed laws of motion in a mechanistic fashion, oriental mystical traditions emphasise fluidity, continual change and impermanence, a reality which is dynamic and alive. An early attempt to associate these ideas with twentieth-century science was Fritjof Capra's *The Tao of Physics*, first published in 1975. The overarching thesis of this book is that:

> The two foundations of twentieth-century physics – quantum theory and relativity theory – both force us to see the world very much in the way a Hindu, Buddhist or Taoist sees it ... Modern physics leads us to a view of the world which is very similar to the views held by mystics of all ages and traditions. (Capra, 1976:17)

Capra proceeds to assimilate modern physics to a strongly monistic (and very Western) synthesis of Eastern spiritualities. The observer-dependence of determinate observations implied by some interpretations of quantum mechanics (see **3.13**) gives Capra a basis for his mystical speculations. Not only is reality-in-itself indeterminate (like his description of the One in Eastern mysticism), but the observer plays a crucial role in creating determinate reality. We create our own reality or at least affect it in a very fundamental way by what we choose to observe. Thus he concludes that 'the structures and phenomena we observe in nature are nothing but creations of our measuring and categorizing mind' (Capra 1976:292).

Capra's account of physics as a spiritual path is open to criticism at a number of levels. It is highly speculative, and dependent upon a particular interpretation of quantum mechanics which may have a short currency. Students of Eastern spirituality have attacked Capra's approach to mystical experience for presenting a misleading picture of unity among a rich diversity of spiritual traditions.[24]

There is, then, much suspicion, some of it well founded, of this association of aspects of contemporary science – quantum theory in particular – with ideas or world-views derived from oriental religions (see Polkinghorne, 1988:93–94, and Lucas, 1996:Chs 1–4). But John G. Taylor, formerly Professor of Mathematics at King's College, London, though he sees 'a large amount of vague and woolly thinking contained in Eastern mysticism', concedes that 'if these mystical ideas are used as an entrée into modern physics they have value, but only if used as stepping stones to the greater precision of the real thing' (Taylor, 1991:114–15). Without conceding that a theological idea – or indeed a mystical insight – is necessarily less precise than a theorem in physics, we wish to develop this idea of stepping-stones.

The following three sections introduce in turn aspects of Hindu, Taoist and Buddhist thought, to enable the reader to consider these as possible stepping-stones between science and theology – in *two* senses:

---

[24] However, the work does raise interesting questions about the relationship of science and spirituality. Many commentators have assumed that *The Tao of Physics* is an *apologia* for spirituality (after the fashion of nineteenth- and twentieth-century natural theologies). However, there is another possibility which becomes apparent when we consider the readership of *The Tao*. It was originally published by a firm specialising in New Age literature and its original readership would have needed little convincing of the validity of the spiritual path detailed by Capra. On the other hand, this readership would include many people who are suspicious of physical science in general and particularly of atomic physics (with its dubious connections to the military-industrial complex). Given such a readership, *The Tao of Physics* looks more like an *apologia* for Capra's vocation. Capra presents physics in a new light as a spiritual path that can be followed with integrity to the same destination as the great mystics of the East. Unwittingly Capra has revived an important social function of older natural theologies which, while appearing to offer scientific evidence of God's existence and benevolence, actually commended science as a godly and socially valuable vocation.

- from science to theology, in the sense of providing additional resources for understanding the relation of the divine to the world which science describes;

- from theology to science, in the sense of offering images and metaphors which might feed the growth of models in the science of the future.

The sections are necessarily very brief and focus upon the mystical and metaphysical aspects of the traditions rather than upon mythology, ritual or popular worship. In the case of Hinduism the emphasis is given mainly to the metaphysical system known as the Vedanta, taught by Shankaracharya and elaborated during the seventh and eighth centuries CE. A useful discussion of the Vedanta, from a Christian point of view, is to be found in Ward (1987:1–29). Many translations of the Taoist *Tao-Te-Ching* are available; the one chosen here (Bryce, 1991) is that of Fr L. Wieger which, although lacking poetic beauty, is technically very precise. There is a multitude of books on Buddhism; a very useful introductory text is that of Damien Keown (1996).

6.10   The universe as seen in Hindu metaphysics

The meaning conveyed in Hinduism by the word *Brahman* is difficult to express. It is not exactly equivalent to God, as conceived in the West. It is rather the Principle that is 'beyond all distinctions (*nirvishesha*)' and 'beyond all qualities (*nirguna*)' that belong not only to this universe but also to the one personal God, who in Hinduism is called *Īshwara* (cf. Guénon, 1958a: 25). Capra explains that the '*Rig Veda* [a collection of ancient Hindu Scriptures chanted by priests], uses another term to express the dynamic nature of the universe, the term *Rita*. This word comes from the root *ri* – to move; its original meaning in the *Rig Veda* being the 'the course of all things', 'the order of nature' (Capra, 1976:199).

The relationship between *Brahman* and the creation is related to panentheism – indeed Peacocke makes this connection (1993:158). The panentheism of Hinduism is expressed in the words of the *Bhagavadgita*, the fifth century BCE religious classic and 'bible' to millions of Hindus. The words of the text are the enunciations of the God Krishna attempting to inspire Arjuna, who represents each one of us in a despondent and demotivated state. Krishna speaks on behalf of the Divinity itself.

From Chapter IX

(4) By Me all this universe is pervaded through My unmanifested form. All beings abide in Me but I do not abide in them.

(5) And (yet) the beings do not dwell in Me: behold My divine mystery. My spirit which is the source of all beings sustains the beings but does not abide in them.

(6) As the mighty air, moving everywhere, ever abides in ethereal space (akasha), know thou that in the same manner all existences abide in Me.

(7) All beings O Son of Kunti (Arjuna) pass into nature which is My own at the end of the cycle; and at the beginning of the next cycle, I send them forth.

(8) Taking hold of nature which is my own, I send forth again and again all this multitude of beings which are helpless, being under the control of nature (prakriti)

(9) Nor do these works bind Me, O winner of wealth (Arjuna), for I am seated as if indifferent, unattached to these actions.

(10) Under my guidance, nature (prakriti) gives birth to all things, moving and unmoving and by this means, O Son of Kunti (Arjuna), the world revolves.

Bhagavadgita IX, 4–10 from Radhakrishnan (1958:238–42)

Hindu panentheism is a very subtle concept. The key Sanskrit expression, translated as 'divine mystery' in verse 5 above, barely translates the depth of the idea. The Sanskrit words are *yogam aiśvaram*; these could be translated as 'an integrated state in which the possessions of all the divine attributes (*aiśvaram*) of Being (*Īshwara*) are yoked (*yoga*) together in a unity' (cf. Radhakrishnan 1958:239 footnotes).

It is clear from the quotation from the *Bhagavadgita* that Hinduism does not view the universe as having been created once, as in Semitic religions, with time and space coming into existence at a first moment. Rather the universe is endlessly brought into being and then destroyed, cycle after cycle, making an indefinite series of worlds. This process is sometimes described as the continual breathing of *Brahman*, each creative expiration followed by a period of persistence and then terminated by a destructive inspiration. The three phases are respectively governed by the gods *Brahmā*, *Vishnu* and *Shiva*, who can be regarded as the vice-regents of *Brahman*. The universe is thus lacking in permanence; in addition it has no reality independent from *Brahman*. Our apparently self-existent universe is thus the Great Illusion (*Mahā-Mohā*), because it appears to be independent from *Brahman*. This illusion is due to a 'property' called *māyā*, the illusion of separateness, which is inherent in the creative process. *Māyā* is thus the cause of the human experience of *avidyā* (literally 'non-sight', spiritual blindness, ignorance). In reality, in clear 'seeing' (*vidyā*), nothing is separate from *Brahman*. This is expressed in the metaphysical system of the Vedanta as *advaita* (non-duality), which is the state of *Brahman* and therefore the only reality of every being in the universe, including all human beings. From a more positive point of view *māyā* both veils and reveals the Divinity in nature.

One of the principal 'stepping-stones' in respect of Hinduism, then, might be in the area of developing a panentheism which emphasises the utter dependence of the world that science describes on the divine power.

6.11   Taoism: nature's innermost reality is also the spiritual way

The fundamental text of Taoism, the *Tao-Te-Ching*, is attributed to Lao-tzu (*c*.570–490 BCE). The title of the book literally means 'The Principle (*Tao*) Its Action (*Te*) Treatise (*Ching*)'. The words *Tao* and *Te* have complex meanings in a metaphysical context. *Tao* literally means 'Way' and is sometimes translated as 'water course way' indicating that it exists naturally rather than as an artefact. *Te* is a word with complex meanings; it is often translated as 'Virtue' (see Bryce 1991:10). René Guénon translates *Te* as 'uprightness' and writes that *Te* 'might be called a "specification" of the Way (*Tao*), in regard to a given being or state of existence; it is the direction that a being must follow in order that his existence may be accordance to the "Way", or, in other words, in conformity with the Principle (in the upward direction, whereas the descending direction is that in which the "Activity of Heaven" is exerted)' (Guénon, 1958b:40 note 4). Ninian Smart further explains the subtlety of these two important words: 'In Taoism the true nature of the cosmos was summed up as the Tao, a word that has many meanings clinging to it – the Way, or Principle, or Method. It was used in particular to mean the Way of the cosmos, the principle or spirit governing it' (Smart, 1995:55).

Taoism is *both* a description of the universe in terms of *Tao and* the proposal of a spiritual method for attaining to the reality of *Tao*.
From Chapter 21 of the *Tao-Te-Ching*

> A. All of the beings *which play a role* in the great manifestation *of the cosmic theatre,* have come from the Principle [*Tao*], through its virtue (its unwinding) [*Te*].
>
> B. Here is the nature of the Principle: It is indistinct and indeterminate. Oh how indistinct and indeterminate! In this indistinction and indetermination there are types. Oh how indistinct and indeterminate it is! In this indistinction and indetermination there are beings *in force.* Oh how mysterious and obscure it is! In this mystery, in this obscurity, there is an essence, which is reality. *That is the nature of the Principle.*

From Chapter 37

> A. The Principle is always non-acting (not acting actively), and yet it does everything (without seeming to participate).

From Chapter 38

> A. That which is superior to the virtue [*te*] of the Principle (the Principle itself, considered in its essence), does not act, but holds Virtue in a state of immanence within itself.

From Chapter 51

> A. The Principle gives life to *beings,* then its Virtue nourishes them, until the completion of their nature, until the perfection of their faculties. Therefore all beings venerate the Principle and its Virtue.
>
> B. No one has the eminence of the Principle and its Virtue conferred on them; they have it always naturally.
>
> C. The Principle gives life; its Virtue gives growth, protects, perfects, matures, maintains and covers (all beings). When they are born it does not monopolize them; it lets them act freely, without exploiting them; it lets them grow without tyrannizing them. This is the action of transcendent Virtue. (From Bryce, 1991)

The ontology of the universe, in Taoist thought, starts with non-being (*Wu*) or the formless (*huan*) mystery. These words also describe the *Tao* in a state when there were no sentient beings. The state is called *hsien t'ien* ('before heaven'). Within the essence of the *Tao* were two immanent properties, or 'two determinations' called *yin* and *yang*. It is by means of the interactions between these two polar determinations that the universe comes into being. 'All natural phenomena are manifestations of a continuous oscillation between the two poles [*yin* and *yang*], all transitions take place gradually and in unbroken progression. The natural order is one of dynamic balance between yin and yang' (Capra, 1983:18). *Yang* is an expansive tendency, whereas *yin* is contractive. The first manifestations of the pair were the celestial sphere or heaven and the Earth, respectively. However, in Taoist thought, there is no manifestation of pure *yang* or pure *yin*, although particular phenomena or beings have a preponderance of one property or the other, or can have a dynamic balance between the two. *Yin-yang* dominates all aspects of Taoist thought and spirituality, including the qualitative aspects of temporal cycles, especially birth and death which are seen to be two aspects of the same event. The spiritual 'task' of a Taoist is to discover the 'Invariable Middle' (*Ching-yung*) which is a state in which all the various components of the human being are harmonised. This is seen to be a permanent state and is described as *Cheng-jen* ('true man'). The human being (*jen*) in this state harmonises within him, or herself, heaven (*T'ien*) and Earth (*Ti*) (cf. Guénon, 1958b:122–26).

The importance of Taoism is that its paradigm of the universe is at the same time the operative context for a spiritual way. The *Tao* is *Reality*. By means of 'non-action' (*wu-wei*), which amounts to abstaining from acts that are 'out of harmony with the ongoing cosmic process' (Capra, 1983:20), the individual discovers the harmony of the *Tao*. 'Those who understand this mode of action of heaven … concentrate themselves in meditative peace, which is the source of natural action [i.e. *wu-wei*]'. 'Nothing tends more towards rest, towards equilibrium, than water.' 'Now just as rest clarifies water, it likewise clarifies the vital spirits [of the psyche], including the intelligence. The Sage's heart, perfectly calm, is like a mirror which reflects heaven and earth, and all beings' (from Chuang Tzu Ch. 13, section A, in Bryce, 1984:174).

One of the principal 'stepping-stones' in respect of Taoism, therefore, might be in the area of ecological spirituality – the power of non-action.

6.12 The contribution of Buddhism

The founder of Buddhism, Sakyamuni (d. fifth century BCE), is usually referred to as the Buddha (this word is actually a title meaning 'the awakened' or 'the enlightened one'; it describes his state of consciousness). Buddhism regards every human being as a potential buddha and provides the framework and methods that enables each person eventually to achieve full enlightenment. It is important to remember that before all else Buddhism aims firstly at clarifying the true nature of the ever-changing world (*samsāra*) and of the ordinary human state; the latter being controlled by desire, craving and consequential suffering. The unhappy state of the human being in an unfulfilling world is contrasted with a state of perfect happiness, *nirvāna*.

Buddhism seeks to identify the intrinsic cause of human suffering and explains that it can be overcome. It then provides the spiritual methods by means of which suffering gradually ceases and perfect happiness is gained. The method is set down in the Four Noble Truths:

1. The state of humans in the world is characterised by suffering (*dukkha*) relieved only by superficial, temporary pleasures.

2. The cause of *dukkha* is fundamentally an egocentric craving based upon the double illusion that the 'world of appearances' *samsara*, is real and that the ego is an enduring entity. The doctrine of 'absence of self' *anatta*, contrasts strongly with the doctrine of an enduring self/soul of other religions. Buddhism states that both the world and the 'I' are aggregates (*skandhas*) are not discrete entities (cf. Nairne 1997: 19–21).

3. Egocentric craving can be overcome by the extinction of the 'poisons' of desire, hatred and illusion.

4. Buddhism provides the means, known as the Middle Way, by which *dukkha* may be overcome and *nirvana* achieved.

The *Dhammapada* (literally the Teaching Path, which summarises the sayings of the Buddha), explains the Four Noble Truths as follows:

> He who takes refuge in the Way and journeys with those who follow it, clearly sees the great truths.

> Suffering, the cause of suffering, the ceasing of suffering 'and the eightfold path' [the Middle way] that leads to an end of suffering.

> Then at last he finds safety. He is delivered from suffering and is free. (Bancroft, 1997: The *Dhammapada* v. 190–92)

Buddhism stresses the need for individual effort and individual experience of its methods. The proof of Buddhism is in doing. Apart from the prescription for a life of detailed attention to morality and virtues Buddhism provides meditation to create inner peace, promote wisdom and help progress along the path to *nirvāna*.

A caring and compassionate attitude was engendered in *Mahāyāna* Buddhism by the Vow of the Boddhisattva, who refuses to enter the bliss of *nirvāna* until the last blade of grass has attained to enlightenment. So the everyday life of every Buddhist is governed by the ethical principle of *ahimsā* (non-harming – see **6.5.2** above), which manifests itself as a great respect for all life, total rejection of the practice of animal sacrifice and the adoption of a vegetarian diet. 'In some Buddhist cultures the practice of agriculture is frowned upon because of the inevitable destruction of life caused by ploughing the Earth. In general, however ... Buddhism ... regarded the destruction of life as morally wrong only when it was caused intentionally or as a result of negligence' (Keown, 1996:106).

Buddhist thought before the coming of the *Mahāyāna* included a view of the cosmos that included an atomic theory of matter. The fifth-century treatise known as the *Abhidharmakosha* includes a theoretical analysis of gross matter as being aggregates (*skandhas*) of atoms, called *paramanus* (literally 'extreme-minute'). These are described as the 'smallest part of matter, uncuttable, unable to be destroyed' (Sadakata, 1997:20). These atoms aggregate to form molecules (*duyanuka*) which consist of one core atom surrounded by six others. Three such molecules produce one visible particle of matter. The main effect of this theory is that Buddhists are predisposed to accept the modern scientific particulate theory of matter. It simply confirms for them their paradigm of the impermanence and non-substantiality of matter.

For the Buddhist the 'common sense' view of the world is an illusion, as is the belief in a separate individual self. The fourteenth Dalai Lama writes: 'Ignorance, the belief that things are real, is extremely powerful. But we should remember that it is nothing more than a mistake; it is merely a misunderstanding that we cling to but which in fact has no foundation whatsoever [because all things are "composites" (*skandha* or *khandha*), and are therefore subject to disintegration and a cause of sorrow]. Its opposite, the understanding that phenomena have no reality, is based on a consistent truth that stands up to all argument. If one familiarises oneself with this understanding, it can be developed indefinitely, since it is both true and a natural quality of the mind' (Dalai Lama, 1994:13). For the influence of Buddhism on Fritjof Capra's 'new paradigm' see **6.14**.

Buddhism exhibits certain consonances with modern science, such as:

(i) An atomic theory of matter: thus solid matter is just an appearance, created by the way the particles are put together and by the interaction of the perceived object with the sensory and cerebral system of the observer.

(ii) A theory of the 'absence of self' (*anatta*), that the ego is not real (see below).

The assertion that there is no unitary self, no enduring ego, is affirmed by some modern psychologists (cf. Lancaster 1991:83) and is supported in studies of some split-brain patients in the United States (Gazzaniga, 1989). In such cases it appears that the patient has two 'egos', one on each side of the brain. Gazzaniga suggests that there are several 'agents' working independently in the normal brain, but that these are domi-nated by the language centres in the left hemisphere, so long as the brain is intact; this gives the impression that there is only one agent, one 'I'.

6.12.1 Buddhist spirituality

The influence of Buddhism on the debate between Western science and theology is relatively small because of the non-cognitive nature of the claims of Buddhism, which is first and foremost a *practice*, rather than a metaphysics or a theology. Buddhism describes what will be experienced if the Way is followed. Nevertheless Buddhist *spirituality* has been a great influence on Christian thinkers, such as Thomas Merton,[25] Keith Ward[26] and Jay McDaniel (see **6.5.2** – also McDaniel, 1990, in which he develops the notion of God as the Zen contemplative of the world). We have already noted McDaniel's stress on the concepts of 'non-harming' and 'emptiness'. For the Buddhist 'emptiness' contains within it:

---

[25] E.g. his *Zen and the Birds of Appetite* (1968).
[26] Especially in *A Vision to Pursue* (1991).

(a) the idea of 'suchness' (*tathata*), which is a sort of poetic per-
     ception of the integrity of the entity perceived. Suchness is
     ever-present, and becomes known to the mind when the
     internal ego and external physical objects become fully
     transparent to each other.[27]

(b) the concept of dependent origination – all entities being
     understood to be dependent on each other – a concept also
     important in deep ecology (see below)

(c) a sense of impermanence, of the beauty and transience of
     each moment of our lives.

     (McDaniel, 1989:92–110)

The contribution of Buddhism, especially of this rich concept of non-
harming, to deep ecology and to the systems thinking of Capra is
touched on further in **6.13–6.14**.

6.13   Deep ecology

Deep ecology is a term coined by the Norwegian philosopher Arne
Naess in an article in 1972 in which he contrasted 'environmental fixes'
within the existing attitudes of modern society ('shallow ecology') with
a real change of mind-set in relation to the planet. Characteristics of a
deep-ecological mind-set would be:

1. Rejection of the man-in-environment image in favour of the
   relational, total-field image.
2. Biospherical egalitarianism.
3. Principles of diversity and symbiosis.
4. Anti-class posture.
5. Fight against pollution and resource depletion.
6. Complexity, not complication.
7. Local autonomy and decentralization.

   (Naess, quoted in Merchant, 1992:87)

[27] There are fascinating parallels between this view and the perception of nature
developed by the Catholic poet Gerard Manley Hopkins, who wrote of being able
occasionally to win through to a sense of the 'instress' of things, an immediate perception
of the essential nature of elements of the natural world in themselves (Hopkins, 1953:xx–
xxii). Within Hopkins' theology, however, the nature of a kingfisher or a kestrel was
always a nature bearing the marks of its creation by the Christian God.

The profound respect for all creatures inherent in (1), and especially in (2) – the conviction of the need for a 'biocentric' scheme which asserts that all species are of equal status[28] – has its roots in Buddhism (**6.12–6.12.1**). Naess however acknowledges that it is necessary to kill some fellow-creatures to live – this expedient should be kept to a minimum. Central to deep ecology is the concept of wilderness – areas of the planet which are as they would be if no humans ever went there. One can sense here the influence of such early American environmentalists as John Muir, and of Aldo Leopold's *A Sand County Almanac* (1949). If there is a deity of deep ecology it is wilderness.

For some writers the natural corollary of such thinking has been that there are far too many humans, and that reduction of the human population – to some notional 'carrying capacity' which the Earth could sustainably support – should be welcomed. (A figure sometimes used is 0.5 billion, as against a projected population for the year 2000 of 6.2 billion.) There is a strain of 'environmental fascism' about some of these comments, very far from the stark but visionary tone of Naess' original article. Deep ecologists' suggestions as to how humans might live in the future are often very radical. In the standard work on deep ecology by Devall and Sessions[29] they quote Paul Shepard's: that the Earth's population be stabilised at 8 billion by 2020 and that these be positioned in cities strung around the edge of the continents, with the interior allowed to return to the wild. The contact with this wilderness, so essential to our ecological health, would all be by journeys made on foot. (This would mean feeding the world on biotechnologically-engineered microbial food [Devall and Sessions, 1985:172–74].)

Deep ecology contains many contradictions, the central one of which is that humans are to be the one species which is not to express its nature in seeking to maximise its ecological niche. Nevertheless, as a

---

[28] Frameworks in environmental ethics may typically be divided into those which are anthropocentric (humanocentric) – attributing value to entities according to their relation to humans – those which are biocentric, and those which endeavour to be 'theocentric' – valuing entities in terms of their value to God. The crucial question tends to be whether non-human organisms or ecosystems have value in and for themselves – 'intrinsic value', or merely instrumental value for humans . For a brief introduction see Deane-Drummond (1996:70–78); for more detail see Northcott (1996), especially Ch. 4. On intrinsic natural values see Rolston (1994:Ch. 6).

[29] Devall and Sessions, 1985. For a more recent set of essays see Sessions (1995).

spiritual exhortation to individuals and societies whose impact on the planet is greatest (that of the *average* US citizen approaches 100 times that of the average Indian, and many Westerners' consumption is far higher) deep ecology will remain important (as McFague comments, 'for its poetic power more than its conceptual adequacy' [1993:125]).

6.14 'New paradigm' thinking

This is a concept particularly advanced by Fritjof Capra, who may be regarded as the hardest-headed and most scientifically-informed speaker for deep ecology. He has strongly emphasised the importance of 'systems thinking' – 'all natural systems are wholes whose specific structures arise from the interactions and interdependence of their parts. Systemic properties are destroyed when a system is dissected, either physically or theoretically, into isolated elements. Although we can discern individual parts in any system, the nature of the whole is always different from the mere sum of its parts' (quoted in Merchant, 1992:93). This is particularly important in complex emergent systems such as life: 'while it is true that all living systems are ultimately made of atoms and molecules, they are not "nothing but" atoms and molecules. There is something else to life, something non-material and irreducible – a pattern of organisation' (Capra, 1996:81).

Capra uses the two adjectives 'ecological' and 'holistic' in explaining his worldview. This 'new paradigm' is set against the metaphor of the 'world as a machine', 'brought about by the new discoveries in physics, astronomy and mathematics known as the Scientific Revolution and associated with the names of Copernicus, Galileo, Descartes, Bacon and Newton' (Capra, 1996:19). Capra's approach to understanding the cosmos enables him to draw together several areas of modern science into a paradigm that encompasses quantum physics, systems theories, chaos theory, the mathematics of complexity, models of self-organisation and Gaia theory. In each case the inadequacy of the clockwork universe, Newton's deterministic machine, is emphasised. The world in which we live is not composed of 'things', nor of 'objects', but of relationships. Thus we know that an electron is 'there' because it relates in a particular situation as a particle or as a wave. We know that a tree, a river or a table is 'there' because of the sensory and neural relationships we establish with them. The generation of these relationships is cognition (see below).

Perhaps the most interesting aspect of Capra's writings is the way in which his consideration of scientific paradigms (in for example *The Turning Point* [1983]) opens the way towards spiritual and religious considerations. In particular he has drawn heavily on Taoism and Buddhism in framing his view of reality. This is especially so when he writes about life and the nature of mind and cognition. According to the Santiago theory of cognition, proposed by Maturana and Varela (1980), life *is* cognition, in the sense that living systems operate by 'knowing' their environment. The relationships within the living system, and between the system and its environment, that are written in its patterns of organisation, express the cognition that the life-form has of itself and its environment. Thus life and cognition go together. Moreover the Santiago theory rejects the idea that cognition is a representation of an objective 'out there' world. Rather each individual 'brings forth' a world that is unique to that individual of whatever species. Note that it is *not* a mind that brings forth a world; in the Santiago theory 'a world' is identical with 'a mind'.

Capra and Varela (cf. Capra, 1996:287) denote the modern human condition as being characterised by 'Cartesian anxiety'. This is a state of frustration and anxiety caused by a hopeless grasping after an exterior world of 'separate objects that we see as firm and permanent, but which are really transient and ever-changing' (Capra, 1996:186). Likewise there is a anxious grasping after an internal ego-self which does not have any independent existence but is the result of our internal structural coupling (i.e. the cognition that arises from neuronal relationships).

These points of view, which seem to be a logical development within the 'new paradigm', are very similar to the Buddhist principles of *anicca* (impermanence) and *anatta* (absence of self-essence) (see **6.12** on the illusoriness of our commonsense view of the world). The first of the Four Noble Truths in Buddhism is *dukkha*, usually translated as suffering, although a better, more generalised meaning is 'unsatisfactory and unfulfilling' (Keown, 1996:48–49) (see **6.12**). Capra used the same Buddhist term *dukkha* to explain the consequences of 'trying to cling to our rigid categories instead of realising the fluidity of life', as such 'we are bound to experience frustration after frustration' (Capra, 1996:286). The solution to the problem of 'Cartesian anxiety' is to see the world as it really is, 'seeing things in their state of suchness (*tathatā*) or is-ness' (Suzuki, 1970:370). The illusory round of existence (*saṃsāra*) then becomes an enlightenment-experience of unlimited bliss (*nirvāṇa*).

Capra, then, is calling for a 'new paradigm' in which our view of reality will be altogether changed, indeed the whole idea of a realist science which discovers 'facts' about the world will be replaced by a sense of systems within systems, processes of continual mutual cognition which lose their identity when they are analysed in a reductionist way. Again, as with other deep-ecological proposals, this faces the twin dangers of (a) being seen merely as naïve, unrealistic as to the way science has to be done, and six billion humans have to live, or (b) being used in an authoritarian way. Stephan Elkins has commented that 'The systems-theoretical core of Capra's ecological paradigm could be appropriated, not as a source of cultural transformation, but as an instrument for the technocratic management of society and nature, leaving the prevailing social and economic order unchanged' (quoted in Merchant, 1992:104).

6.15   Conclusion

We have explored a great variety of ways in which modern theologians and other thinkers have sought to describe reality in a way appropriate to the contemporary human situation. We have stressed the importance of the theology of relationships between God, humanity and the cosmos, rather than mere characterisation of entities in isolation. There is a clear need perceived by many Christian theologians to talk of God in more relational terms as Trinity and in more responsive terms as Creator. There is call for equality between species, and for consideration of systems as a whole, derived from environmental thinking and reflection on the ancient Eastern religions. These proposals must be judged both by their faithfulness to the traditions from which they derive, and the spiritual, ethical and practical attitudes to which they lead.

FURTHER READING

CAPRA, F. (1996) *The Web of Life* (London: Flamingo / HarperCollins)

DALAI LAMA (1997) *The Buddha Nature: death and eternal soul in Buddhism* (Woodside, CA: Bluestar Publications)

FIDDES, P. (1988) *The Creative Suffering of God* (Oxford: Clarendon Press)

FLOOD, G. D. (1996) *An Introduction to Hinduism* (Cambridge: Cambridge University Press)

KEOWN, D. (1996) *Buddhism: A Very Short Introduction* (Cambridge: Cambridge University Press)

LANCASTER, B. (1995) *Mind, Brain and Human Potential: A quest for and understanding of Self* (Shaftesbury: Element Books)

LOVELOCK, J. (1988) *The Ages of Gaia* (Oxford: Oxford University Press)

MCDANIEL, J. (1989) *Of God and Pelicans* (Louisville, KY: Westminster / John Knox Press)

MCFAGUE, S. (1993) *The Body of God* (London: SCM Press)

MOLTMANN, J. (1985) *God in Creation*, transl. by M. Kohl (London: SCM Press)

PAILIN, D. (1989) *God and the Processes of Reality* (London: Routledge)

RAHULA, W. (1998) *What the Buddha Taught* (Oxford: OneWorld)

RUETHER, R. (1992) *Gaia and God* (London: SCM Press)

WARD, K. (1987) *Images of Eternity: Concepts of God in Five Religious Traditions* (London: Darton, Longman & Todd)

—— (1996) *Religion and Creation* (Oxford: Oxford University Press)

Chapter 7

A Test Case – Divine Action

7.1 Introduction

So far we have reviewed the nature of science and religion and seen something of the diversity of their relationship as particular sciences address such problems as the origin of the universe, the evolution of life, and the nature of mind. We looked in the last chapter at a variety of ways in which thinkers are seeking to understand the reality of God at the end of the twentieth century, and commented on the cogency of different models. In this chapter we use all this material to address the possibilities for making sense of a real divine action in the natural order within the context of contemporary scientific understanding – the question: how can God be considered to *act*, to *have acted*, and to be *going to act* in the course of the history of the cosmos. In a sense Chapter 6 addressed mainly the character of God as God, and the 'spatial' question of God's relation to the world. Here we concentrate on the temporal aspect of the relationship – what, in the world, God is doing (Section A – **7.4–7.9**), what God has done (Section B – **7.10–7.16**), what God will do (Section C – **7.17**).

Of the voluminous literature on the subject we particularly recommend Keith Ward's 1990 study *Divine Action*. Ward sets out a contemporary philosophical base from which to explore the subject.

EXERCISE 7.1

Compare Ward's 1990 position with his more process-influenced approach in *Holding Fast to God* (1982).

The exploration has been taken forward by three collections of essays deriving from the Vatican Observatory Conferences of 1991, 1993, and 1995, edited by R. J. Russell with others, and entitled *Quantum Cosmology and the Laws of Nature* (1993), *Chaos and Complexity* (1995) and *Evolution and Molecular Biology* (1998), each with the sub-title *Scientific Perspectives on Divine Action*. The first of these is especially important for its discussion of God and the early universe, the second for its engagement with questions of providence. The third, not published at the time of our going to press, contains among other things a valuable updating of Arthur Peacocke's position.[1]

For reasons of space we confine this discussion to the Christian tradition, but the reader is invited to reflect on the shape the discussion of divine action might have taken in respect of Judaism,[2] Islam (see Chapter 9) and the Eastern religions discussed in Chapter 6.

7.2   General comments

We acknowledge the extraordinary difficulty intrinsic in even beginning to speak of the transcendent Creator of the cosmos as acting in any particular way which we can describe out of our own experience as limited, contingent beings. It may therefore be asked why there has been such a focus on this part of the debate between science and theology. Part at least of the answer must be historical. As Kaiser points out (1991:193), Newton would have subscribed to the following six ways in which God was active:

1. the creation of matter and setting of it in motion in accordance with certain prescribed laws;
2. the formation of the present world system;
3. its continued operation;
4. its occasional reformation;
5. occasional spiritual intrusions in human affairs through the agency of natural phenomena (e.g. comets and epidemics);
6. miracles.

---

[1] We thank Drs Peacocke and Russell for sight of pre-publication versions of their contributions.

[2] On some recent thinking on the Hebrew doctrine of God see Ward, 1996a:3–36.

EXERCISE 7.2

Stop at this point and decide in how many of these ways you believe God to act. Compare your beliefs with others in your class. The combinations will reflect different positions in the historical debate (for a discussion see Brooke, 1991: especially Ch. 4).

7.3 God 'edged out'?

It is especially interesting to note that Newton himself did not hold the mechanical view of the universe to which his system led (see Brooke, 1991:144–48). Rather he thought of God directly mediating the force of gravity. Yet within a hundred years of the publication of his *Principia* in 1687 there were many who would have denied that any of these six aspects of divine action were operative. It was accepted that physical forces could act at a distance without mediation, divine or other. *Hume* had attacked the reasonableness of believing in miracle (see **7.7 (iv)**). *Laplace* had posited the complete determinism of a world governed by Newtonian mechanics (see **1.17**). And we saw in **4.4** how the simplicity and elegance of *Darwin's* scheme did away with the notion that individual living creatures need be the direct products of divine design.

Over a long period in Western thought God seemed to be progressively edged out of descriptions of the development and functioning of the world – both as described by physics and by biology. *In particular it was seen how difficult it was to sustain descriptions of the physical world in which God acted as a cause complementing physical causes – filling in a gap left by scientific narratives.* The phrase 'God of the gaps', coined by Coulson (1958:41), has become proverbial as a description of bad theologies of the activity of God. Explanation of phenomena in terms of regular, natural causes has been extremely successful since the rise of science, so the 'presumption of naturalism' (Clayton, 1997a:173) has grown in strength.

Three strategies seem to offer themselves in the face of this problem: God 'banished', God 'before', or God 'behind'. The first is to abandon talk of God's acting in the physical world. This is the strategy adopted by atheism, sometimes motivated by a form of positivism (**2.2**). For different reasons it was also the strategy of Bultmannian existentialism (**2.4**). The second strategy is some form of deism, God being described as the first cause of all things, but as not otherwise active in the unfolding cosmos. The rise of deism is discussed by Brooke (1991:especially 167–71); what is, arguably, a new form of the strategy is found in the formulations of Kaufman and Wiles (**7.5 (ii)**, **7.6 (ii)**). The third obvious strategy is to posit that God acts 'behind' the system of causation, at another level not susceptible to physical description. This goes back to Aquinas and his discussion of primary and secondary causation (Aquinas, 1956:226–35; 1975:75–79).

In the light of these 'safe' strategies, which are all forms of 'separate development' for scientific and theological description, it is striking how many recent theologians have wanted to pursue a fourth path – they have regarded the system of causation that physics offers us as *open*, containing inherent gaps which allow God to effect particular actions within the system of natural causes without being subject to the risk that science will close the gaps. *This strategy has a great deal to do with the contemporary perception that what happens in the real universe is the result of the interplay of physical laws and an ingredient of **chance**. We do not live in the deterministic universe of Laplace* (**1.17**), *but in one in which it is not even theoretically possible to predict in minute detail what will happen next* (**3.11 (ii)**, **3.12**, **3.25–3.28**). In order to proceed with our investigation we must first set down (a) what might be the relationship between physical law and divine action and (b) exactly what might be meant by 'chance', a word as problematic in this field as is 'nature' in green theology (see **6.1 note 1**).

7.3.1   Law and Chance

Law

Most accounts of divine agency within the Christian tradition are not content either with 'God banished' or with a God who is only 'before'. Rather they regard God as actively sustaining the order of the physical universe, in some way or other maintaining the regularity of the cosmos. This is an important aspect of divine action, sometimes overlooked. So, for example, theologians of physics such as John Polkinghorne or Russell Stannard no longer regard the solar system as in need of 'occasional reformation', as Newton did (see **7.2** above), because physics no longer has the problem he experienced with the stability of planetary orbits. But they would want to assert that God continues to sustain the laws which govern the equations by which the planets move.

Chance

The word 'Chance'[3] is generally used in one of three ways:

(i) *in respect of an event such as the tossing of a coin.* As Peacocke says, 'had we sufficient knowledge of the exact values of all the relevant parameters, the laws of mechanics would in fact enable us to say in any particular toss which way the coin would fall' (1979:90).[4] Thus to call such outcomes chance is to confess to the incompleteness of our knowledge of the relevant causative factors, it is not to deny that those factors exist or that they are sufficient to account for the event.

(ii) *in respect of combinations of events which seem to come from two different causal chains.* Peacocke again: 'Suppose that when you leave the building in which you are reading these pages, as you step on to the pavement you are struck on the head by a hammer dropped by a man repairing the roof ... the two trains of events ... are each within themselves explicable as causal chains. Yet there is no connection between those causal chains except their point of intersection' (1979:90–91).

If Laplace were right, and the whole course of the universe were theoretically predictable (**1.17**), then of course this hammer blow would also be predictable. This second meaning of chance would again be an expression of our ignorance.

(iii) *as a non-technical way of describing the outcomes of events at the quantum level* (**3.11–3.14**). Quantum mechanics, as usually understood, implies that these outcomes are *not* determinate until they occur – they can only be expressed in terms of probabilities. Not only is our knowledge of them limited by the Heisenberg Uncertainty Principle (**3.11 (ii)**),

---

[3] The subject of a major study from David Bartholomew, *God of Chance* (1984).

[4] Whether we could *ever* possess such knowledge of a system is highly doubtful, as shown by the example we give in **3.25** of a snooker table.

but there is an inalienable indeterminacy about the events themselves. Polkinghorne has argued that there is indeterminacy also in large-scale chaotic systems (1989:28–30 – see **7.6 (iv)a**).

Meaning (ii) has an enormous effect on how the world actually develops – most strikingly in the field of biological evolution. Classical Darwinism postulates that the environment, viewed as an independently changing entity, is at every moment selecting which variants (arising by a largely separate causal chain) will survive and prosper (see **4.3**). Contemporary thinking would recognise the situation as much more complex than that: the environment is itself being shaped by the activities of species as they evolve (most strikingly in respect of the Gaia Hypothesis, see **6.8**). But the point still has force – most dramatically in respect of the great extinctions. The trajectory of the massive object that collided with the Yucatan Peninsula 65 million years ago clearly belonged to a different causal chain from the one that had given rise to dinosaurs vulnerable to the extreme conditions resulting from the collision. So the course of evolution is highly unpredictable, much influenced by this sort of chance.

But it is meaning (iii) of 'chance' which offers the *ontological* indeterminacy, the openness to possible influence from outside the structure of physical law, that has been of such interest to theologians. It seems to offer a possibility other than God banished, before or behind: that is, the possibility of a God who is 'before' in the sense of being the initial cause of everything, 'behind' in the sense of sustaining the laws and regularities God has established, but also a God working *through* the openness and indeterminacy of the natural order.

The debate about divine action has to be taken as a whole – any Christian-theological account of God's activity must include reference to creation and to eschatological redemption – but there is a specific sub-debate, much aired in recent years, on the possibility of God's *particular* action in situations in the present. Clayton makes the important point that *any such particular action must be congruent with God's action in universal history as a whole* (1997a:177). We cannot postulate a God faithful in upholding the regularities of the cosmos, but capricious in particular providential action. We begin, then, by taking up the question of the possibility of God's action in and through the world as it is at present (Section A). Section B will consider the 'history' of divine action since the Big Bang, and Section C questions of action in the future – eschatology and redemption.

SECTION A:
WHAT GOD IS DOING – PROVIDENCE AND MIRACLE (7.4–7.9)

7.4   How to think about providential agency

Is it possible to speak of God acting providentially in the life of a particular person or community? Is talk of miracle coherent? In an account based on the Christian tradition this means also considering the biblical accounts of God's particular action, and what is for Christians the most central of 'actions', the resurrection of Jesus.

The first precept to note is that particular divine action cannot be discernible as such by naturalistic analysis of the world. This is axiomatic from the point of view of *science*, because such descriptions are necessarily in terms of natural systems and regularities, related at some level to the experimentally testable. Supernatural agency is methodologically excluded as an explanation of such data. It is also axiomatic from the point of view of *theology* – divine disclosure always *invites* the response of faith, it does not *demand* the response of acceptance, since that would vitiate the importance of faith. The resurrection of Jesus is a prime example – the Risen Lord appeared only to believers.

A second point to note is that our experience of *personal* agency is of two types:

(a) we as mental beings influence our physical bodies;

(b) as mental-physical beings we act upon other beings and on the world around us.

However, it is important to stress that science can as yet give no clear account of what these two sorts of intentionality in humans involve. So human agency is a very imprecise basis for analogies to *God*'s action. Nevertheless it remains the best basis we have. As Clayton puts it: '*if* one is able to conceive of human intentional action in a way that is compatible with natural scientific accounts of the physical world, then one will have done the bulk of the work necessary for a theory of divine causation' (1997a:233). He goes on to assert that 'To the extent that she genuinely enters the disciplines in question, the theologian can make real contributions to this discussion' (of the mind–body problem) (1997a:239). In other words, because theologians seek to understand divine agency on the analogy of human intentionality, they can and should influence the debate about the mind–body problem in a direction which stresses the reality of intentionality.

7.4.1   Relation to the mind–body problem

Clayton recommends then that 'the question of how to construe divine action should be controlled by the best theories we have of the relationship of *our* minds to our bodies – and then corrected for by the ways in which God's relation to the universe must be *different* from the relation of our mental properties to our brains and bodies' (1997a:233). So our approach to a theology of divine action will depend on our choice of theory about the mind and the body and our choice of model of God's relation to the world.

Clayton then works through the different theories of mind–body relation (1997a:Ch. 9). He has no difficulty in inferring that *eliminative materialism*, which aims at the reduction of all mental phenomena to descriptions at the level of neurones, is unlikely to offer much understanding of free intentional agency – human or divine. He notes that *Cartesian dualism*, the postulate of some sort of soul-stuff in the head in addition to brain, is out of favour in psychology, philosophy and biblical exegesis alike.[5] *Functionalism* merely sees mental life as a series of functions or behaviours and declines to speculate on their metaphysical status, so it too is an unpromising candidate as a launch-pad for theological speculation on divine agency. Clayton then addresses *dual-aspect theory*, the same world being seen as having both mental and physical attributes, only to rule out its application to theology as smacking of Eastern pantheism, in the sense of God being thought of as a mere aspect of the world. He concludes that *a theory of mind as an emergent property of a particularly complex physical system* – a property which can then be regarded as *causative* within that system –

---

[5] Though dualism still dominates popular culture, and is particularly marked also in the 'strong' programme in artificial intelligence, and in contemporary science fiction with its tendency to 'software–wetware' dualism.

is the most helpful understanding of the mind–body problem in humans. A panentheist might speak of God's causative action on the-universe-as-a-whole in analogous terms.

Clayton has not genuinely allowed his account to be *controlled* by the debate about the mind–body problem. He has looked for the scientific theory with the most consonance to the God–world model he prefers. This has to be done – as was indicated in **1.10** – with great caution and provisionality. Moreover he has failed to see the possibilities offered by a dual-aspect theory of matter which sees appreciable mentality / spirit as only emerging within matter at the level of human beings (see **7.6 (iv)(a)** on Polkinghorne's treatment of dual-aspect theory).

7.5   Various views of God's action in the world: a classification

The ground of the discussion of providential action has been 'staked out' by various 'camps'. We begin by classifying these as follows:

(i) *sceptical naturalism*

   Willem Drees has surveyed the field with characteristic insight (1996:93–106), but is reluctant to speak of particular divine action because this might seem to undermine the adequacy of naturalistic explanations, to which he is committed. For different reasons Bultmann and his school also insisted on the adequacy of the scientific description of events (see **2.4**), as do non-realist theologians such as Don Cupitt.

(ii) *general providential action without particular gaps in the causal order*

   This view is espoused by Gordon Kaufman (1972) and even more radically by Maurice Wiles (1986).

(iii) *particular providential action without gaps in the causal order*

   In different ways this is proposed by

   (a) neo-Thomists, such as Austin Farrer;

   (b) those strongly committed to the image of the cosmos as the body of God; and

   (c) Arthur Peacocke with his concept of 'top-down' or 'whole-part' causation.

(iv) *particular providential action employing particular gaps in the causal order* Again there are three camps here:

(a) John Polkinghorne, locating the relevant 'gap' as being the one offered (supposedly) by non-linear systems such as give rise to the phenomenon of chaos,

(b) those such as George Ellis, Nancey Murphy, Robert Russell and Thomas Tracy who follow a suggestion of Pollard's that quantum theory offers the pertinent gaps, and

(c) process theologians who postulate that the course of development of every entity is particularly exposed to the divine persuasion in a way which is outside the descriptions of science (see **7.8**).

Again, Ward's *Divine Action* (1990) is a good starting-point. An invaluable overview of the debate as it stood in 1993 is provided by Russell *et al.*'s *Chaos and Complexity* (1995). The classification above is based on Tracy's essay in that volume (1995:289–324) – his relatively non-technical summary of the different positions is a good introduction to their intricacies. Clayton offers a careful analysis of the metaphysics of divine action (1997a:esp. Ch. 6). On Peacocke and Polkinghorne see **7.7**.

7.6   The causal joint

The different positions can be best distinguished by asking the question: what is the 'causal joint' at which God as a transcendent, immaterial cause interacts particularly with causative factors in the material world?

(i) Drees

His view would be that to search for an extra ingredient at a causal joint is to neglect the self-sufficiency of naturalistic accounts, one of the premises he sets out so clearly at the beginning of *Religion, Science and Naturalism* (1996:12–21).

(ii) Kaufman and Wiles

These both reject descriptions of divine action as particular to individual situations. God's relation is to the-world-as-a-whole, and history-as-a-whole, the relation of creating and sustaining the cosmos from moment to moment. As Tracy points out, this is essentially to subsume providence into creation, and pays a heavy theological price in so doing (1995:301–04).

(iii)(a) Neo-Thomists

Thinkers of this school speak of 'double agency', a concept developed by Aquinas and rearticulated in recent theology in particular by Austin Farrer (1966; 1967). God is the primary cause of all that is; in effecting the divine purposes God works always through secondary causes, through the laws of the universe and the activities of human agents. Our experience of God's activity is *always* mediated. God can work through these secondary causes to bring about particular results. But it is quite impossible to give an account of the causal joint, because (i) divine causation differs from any other kind – we should not expect to be able to characterise it within our own terms – and (ii) we have no 'pure-secondary causes' to look at – everything is informed by divine causation. We have no 'control experiment' by reference to which we might characterise the added causal ingredient of the divine.[6]

Anyone giving an account of divine action must respect these two points. But double agency has been much criticised, not least because of the difficulty in offering any satisfactory analogy which would illustrate it.[7] Polkinghorne, the most vocal representative of position (iv) above, has gone as far as to call Farrer's account 'theological doublespeak' (1994:82). Clayton suggests that if this model of divine agency claims any more than the mere sustaining of natural causes then 'it envisions a type of continuous divine intervention in the world that is no weaker than the classical accounts of miracles' (1997a:177). These criticisms are not altogether fair – what is clear from Kathryn Tanner's careful piecing-together of the 'rules' for this sort of discourse (1988:90–98) is that double agency cannot be abstracted from the intricate Thomistic reasoning from which it arose. It thus profits from the strengths of that system and suffers from its weaknesses. One of the latter relates to God and time (see our discussions at **3.5–3.9** and **6.6.1**). Any system based on the Augustinian–Thomist conception that God gave rise to the whole time-span of creation in the 'moment' of its divine

---

[6] See Stoeger's essay in *Chaos and Complexity* (Stoeger, 1995:239–61).

[7] Perhaps the most pleasing attempt, at least for double agency involving humans as secondary agents, is Tom Settle's of a ballroom dancer (a human agent) being 'led' by her partner (God) – though she also exercises her own technique and creativity (Settle, 1996).

inception runs into great difficulty in describing real freedom in other agents with whom God might enter into relation.

(iii)(b) The world-as-the-body-of-God

The use of this image is the one which makes strongest use of the analogy of human action, as mental beings 'on' physical bodies (see **7.4–7.4.1** above). But in the case of human action, descriptions in terms of the mental, the intentional, are *grounded in the physical*. The human 'intender' is not an autonomous entity existing independently of nerves and muscles; it is a body containing a brain. And as soon as we ground God in the physical world by making that world God's body we run into the problems touched on in **6.5.4**. Again Polkinghorne is a pithy critic, pointing out that pressing this analogy either places God too much in thrall to the world (unable to act autonomously because God is dependent on the inputs from a body, as human action is) or the world too much in thrall to God (humans could no more act freely than an organ of the body can).[8]

(iii)(c) Peacocke

Arthur Peacocke wants to use this same mind–body analogy, but with a very proper caution – 'in a human body, the "I" does not transcend the body ontologically in the way that God transcends the world' (1995:285). He is also very cautious about explicating the causal joint – such a description of the problem 'does not do justice to the many levels in which causality operates in a world of complex systems interlocking in many ways at many levels' (282). He does not find any theologically relevant gaps in the causal order, and is temperamentally most reluctant to contemplate anything smacking of divine *intervention* in the natural order (see **7.7 (iv)** on miracles).

So Peacocke follows Kaufman and Wiles in postulating that God's action is on the-world-as-a-whole, but he goes further than either in that:

(i) he offers a metaphor for divine action in terms of the way in which the properties of a whole system, such as a chemical

---

[8] Polkinghorne (1989:18–21). The difficulty is illustrated by the fact that Sallie McFague, one of the most eloquent exponents of the 'embodiment image', is able to give no account of divine action, beyond some vague talk of 'spirit'. She *describes* her model in *The Body of God* as being 'agential-organic' (1993:140f.), but the agential side is never given substance.

system far from equilibrium, or a biological ecosystem, affect the behaviour of individual parts. The nature of the whole, and of its environment, exerts constraints on the behaviour of the parts. This he originally called 'top-down causation' but now prefers to call 'whole-part influence' (Peacocke, 1999). Brain function may also be of this kind – our mental life being the highest emergent property (see **4.11**) of the brains in our bodies. The material world, on this model, has God as its boundary or environment; relationship with God is the highest emergent property of any physical system.

(ii) Peacocke allows the possibility that this general action of God's on the-world-as-whole might have particular effects – just as a boundary constraint in one of the systems described above might generate a particular, localised pattern.

Peacocke's God, then, is the environment of the cosmos.[9] His God's interaction with the world, by means of the input of information – is the highest-level emergent property of the cosmos as system, a system within which God is radically and totally immanent, as well as transcendent.

As Drees points out (1995:236), speaking of the environment of the whole universe can never be more than a metaphor, but it is the strength of panentheism that it can offer such a telling metaphor. Tracy also takes Peacocke to task for stretching a concept too far – he points out that the examples of 'top-down' causation we know about are all analysable in 'bottom-up' terms.[10] Top-down causation is a purely explanatory procedure, it is a bold strategy to invoke it for ontological

---

[9] A description which tallies with Moltmann's writing of the world as a system open to the creative energies of God (see **6.5.6**). In earlier writing Peacocke used the image of the cosmos as a developing child in the womb of its mother (1979:142). As he would be very well aware, this analogy is strictly limited – foetuses and mothers are, after all, composed of exactly the same material. Another favourite analogy of Peacocke's is that of God as an improvisatory composer, like J. S. Bach generating his fugues (1993:174–75).

[10] And the one system we don't at all understand is the human brain. Drees has elsewhere criticised thinkers for using top-down causation to explain the relation of the mind and the brain, and the mind–brain relation to explain top-down causation (1996:101–02).

purposes, and to suppose that a 'whole' can be invoked as an actual cause within a system (Tracy, 1995:note to 307).

(iv)(a) Polkinghorne

If Peacocke's carefully nuanced account can be seen as bold, then Polkinghorne's must be thought that much bolder. In *Science and Providence* (1989) Polkinghorne seemed not only to *locate* the causal joint of particular divine action but also to suggest a *means* by which God might effect such action. His account of providential action, moreover, included not only such classic instances in the Christian tradition as the virginal conception and empty-tomb-raising of Jesus, but even the validity of prayer for rain.

The key scientific observation for Polkinghorne is that non-linear systems of the sort that exhibit chaos are exquisitely sensitive to the conditions in which they develop (see **3.25–3.27**), and hence their development very rapidly becomes unpredictable.[11] That much is generally accepted. But Polkinghorne has gone further and proposed that these large-scale systems are ontologically indeterminate, not only unpredictable in terms of our knowledge but genuinely open to the future,[12] and that God can therefore influence each one of them by an input of 'active information' (without energy input, which could be detectable). God respects the regularities of the physical laws God has created and holds in being, but nevertheless has freedom to work through these indeterminacies.

Polkinghorne also embraces dual-aspect monism – the same world being seen as having both physical and mental or spiritual attributes (see **7.4.1**) – and he has written of a 'noetic world' (1988:Ch. 5), that aspect of existence to which complex mental organisation gives access. Though he derives the term 'noetic' from the Greek word for 'mind' he makes it clear that he thinks of this world in very broad terms – others would prefer the term 'spiritual', which we use in **5.4–5.7**. There may be non-material inhabitants of this world, not merely the truths of

---

[11] Real situations of human interest are full of such systems – it is not only the great red spot of Jupiter but the human heart itself which is thought to exhibit chaotic dynamics in its normal functioning.

[12] He is famous, or notorious, for possessing a sweatshirt bearing the slogan 'Epistemology models Ontology'. However, the ontological indeterminacy of chaotic systems is very much open to question, given that the equations that model these systems are entirely deterministic (see **3.27**).

mathematics, but also 'active intelligences . . . which traditionally we would call angels' (1988:76).

This thought-aspect of the cosmos might be the medium by which God's information enters physical systems. This would be consonant with the notion that it is to human minds, the material structure with the greatest noetic aspect, that God is able to make God's most sensitive and articulate self-communication.

(iv)(b) Tracy, Murphy and Ellis

Another approach to asserting particular providence through gaps in the causal order is to follow a suggestion first made by Pollard in 1958 and locate theologically productive indeterminacy at the quantum level, rather than at the macroscopic level. This is the approach of Tracy, Murphy and Ellis in *Chaos and Complexity* and has the advantage that there is more general (though not universal) agreement that these systems are genuinely non-deterministic (see **3.11–3.14**).

So Tracy gives the following five types of divine agency, in addition to the initial creation:

1. 'God acts directly in every event to sustain the existence of each entity that has a part in it.' (*Conservation*, see **7.3.1**)

2. 'God can act directly to determine various events which occur by chance on the finite level.' (*Quantum-level intervention*)

3. 'God acts indirectly through causal chains that extend from God's initiating direct actions.' (*Amplification of effects at quantum level*)

4. 'God acts indirectly in and through the free acts of persons whose choices have been shaped by the rest of God's activity in the world.' (*Persuasion* [presumably a function of 2. and 3.])

5. 'God can also act directly to bring about events that exceed the natural powers of creatures, events which not only are undetermined on the finite level, but which also fall outside the prevailing patterns and regular structures of the natural order' (*Miracles*, see **7.7 (iv)**)

   (The Tracy quotations and the basis of the titles are taken from Clayton 1997a:215)

EXERCISE 7.3

Compare the list above with the divine actions of Newton's God listed in **7.2**. After considering the material so far, decide which of these five modes of divine action you believe in. Note that Clayton comments: 'all but the last of these five can be accepted without affront to natural law' (1997a:215).

Both Peacocke and Polkinghorne reject quantum indeterminacy as a candidate for the causal joint. The link between the probabilistic world of quantum mechanics and the macroscopic world is still poorly understood (see **3.13**), nor is it known if there can be any equivalent to chaotic behaviour (where large effects are caused by small changes in initial conditions) within quantum systems. Except in devices designed to amplify them, the effects of quantum fluctuations tend to cancel out – the 'amplification' suggested by mode 3 above is therefore rather questionable.[13]

Among Peacocke's objections are:

(a) his sense that ontological indeterminacy has to be taken seriously – God could not logically have the knowledge to determine the precise result of a quantum event, and if God were to alter such an event, God would have to alter a great number of others simply in order to hide divine activity behind the observed statistics.

(b) a conviction that this picture of God continually determining the outcome of processes established in creation is at variance with the very fruitful emphasis in the scientist-theologians that God has created processes which *themselves* can, when sustained by God, give rise to the novelty, diversity and complexity we so celebrate (see Peacocke, 1998).

---

[13] Though it may be significant that two important candidates for loci of particular divine action – mutations in genetic material and neuronal events in the human brain – may both be instances where such amplification is possible. See Russell, R. J. (1998) on mutation – also **7.15.1**. On quantum events in the brain see Penrose, 1994:Ch. 7.

The case of quantum indeterminacy as a candidate for the causal joint is an important crux of interpretation in the area of scientifically informed theology. At first sight it is an enormously tempting line of argument:

> real freedom in agents, human and divine, requires an open future – genuine, ontological indeterminacy. The main (though not the only) interpretation of contemporary physics is that quantum systems possess such indeterminacy. Therefore, this is where divine agency can operate without detection, or interference in the autonomy of natural (particularly living) entities. There seems a real consonance, or at least compatibility, between quantum theory – the most imaginative, ingenious and counterintuitive element in natural science – on the one hand, and the demands of theology on the other.

However, as we have just seen, there are significant problems in making the argument cohere in detail. The science is not itself wholly coherent – the 'measurement problem' continues to bedevil quantum theory, and its metaphysical implications are still being argued out (**3.13**). Nor is the 'fit' the science offers, even judged at its most helpful, to the taste of every theologian.

Reluctantly, then, setting aside this quantum proposal we consider in more depth the differences between Peacocke and Polkinghorne. The relevant texts are: Peacocke, 1993:Chs. 9 and 11; 1995; 1998; 1999; Polkinghorne, 1989; 1995a:Ch. 6; 1995b; 1996a:Ch. 3; 1996b; and they merit careful study.

7.7   Peacocke and Polkinghorne compared

(i) Introduction

These two thinkers stem from different scientific traditions and, though both Anglicans, reflect two different theological instincts. This reinforces the point made in **1.5** that there is not one simple relation between science and Christian theology (let alone theologies derived from other faiths). Different sciences suggest different relations with theology, and different theological preconceptions lead to different approaches to the same data. Polkinghorne is a physicist, at heart one who analyses the mechanisms by which the material world operates, and theologically somewhat conservative, much influenced by Moltmann. Peacocke's science was the biology of macromolecules, the ideal vantage-point from which to consider different levels of description and the existence of irreducible levels of complexity. Theologically he belongs to a much more liberal Anglican school, much influenced by Geoffrey Lampe.

(ii) Approaches to panentheism and theodicy

This difference can be seen in their two approaches to *panentheism*. Polkinghorne remains suspicious of the concept. His theology holds the world at a distance from God, stressing divine transcendence. His God seems always in some sense an operator on the physics of the world. Panentheism, he thinks, *will be* the condition of the creation at its culmination at the eschaton (Polkinghorne, 1994:168). Peacocke wants to stress divine immanence. The creativity of the world, of which biology is so eloquent, is for him a sign of the divine omnipresence. And Peacocke is, as we have seen, willing to consider a range of metaphors for God in relation to the world. He finds panentheism a helpful member of this range.

They differ too in their approach to *theodicy*, Peacocke inclining to an 'Irenaean' approach which sees the world of suffering as a necessary context for the growth of free beings towards God, Polkinghorne to a 'free-will defence' – if beings are genuinely free they will be free to inflict suffering. (His extension of this to the problem of such 'natural evils' as earthquakes we treat in **7.15**.)

(iii) Models of divine action

However, though neither thinker would concede that he agreed with the other, their positions are not as dissimilar as has sometimes appeared. In particular, Polkinghorne's recent essays make clear that his conjectures about the causal joint are not so adventurously precise as they first appeared. In a paper originating in 1993 he writes:

> It is important to recognise that, in this scheme, the significance of the sensitivity of chaotic systems to the effects of small triggers is *diagnostic* of their requiring to be treated in holistic terms and of their being open to top-down causality through the input of active information. It is not proposed that this is the localized mechanism by which agency is exercised. *I do not suppose that either we or God interact with the world by the carefully calculated adjustment of the infinitesimal details of initial conditions so as to bring about a desired result. The whole thrust of the proposal is expressed in terms of the*

complete holistic situation, not in terms of the clever manipulation of bits and pieces [emphasis ours]. It is, therefore, a proposal for realizing a true kind of top-down causality. It may fittingly be called *contextualism*, for it supposes the behavior of parts to be influenced by their overall context. (1995b:154)

and in 1996:

It seems entirely conceivable that God also interacts with the creation through the input of active information into its open physical process. We glimpse, in a rudimentary way, what might lie behind theology's language of God's 'guiding' and 'drawing on' creation, language often associated with talk of the Spirit working immanently on the inside of creation. (1996b:248)

This is very close to Peacocke's emphases on divine immanence, whole–part influence, and God as the ultimate boundary condition. Granted, Polkinghorne still wants to speak of the ontological openness of non-linear systems, and has been rightly criticised for the logic by which he arrives at this.[14] However, a system-open-to-God-as-overall-context is very similar to Peacocke's whole–part-influence-on-the-world-as-a-whole, given that they both agree that (a) the future is not known to God – God is working with at least a genuine epistemic openness – and (b) divine action can have *particular* effects.

(iv) The question of miracle

Polkinghorne still sticks to his emphasis on the possibility of particular, revelatory divine acts in a way which Peacocke strives to avoid. So it is to their approach to 'miracle' that we now turn. The first point to make about miracle is that definition is all-important. The eighteenth-century philosopher David Hume's famous attack on miracle can be summarised as follows:

1. A miracle is a violation of the laws of nature.
2. We have uniform experience that the laws of nature are never violated.
3. Therefore, miracles cannot occur. (Purtill, 1997:67)

Hume's argument remains influential, particularly as taken up by Antony Flew (1997). But this approach is based on a premise which

---

[14] See for example Murphy (1995:327–29).

the new science no longer has on offer. As Flew says, (Christians) 'have to presuppose the existence of a strong natural order' (1997:54). But even granted a strong natural order, it is very clear from the science of unpredictability in non-linear dynamic systems (including the human brain) that it is inconceivable that the behaviour of a real-life system involving human beings could be the subject of a totally comprehensive scientific explanation. If we do not know – precisely – what the laws of nature prescribe in a particular situation we cannot be sure what would constitute a 'violation'. We have therefore to define miracle in theological terms rather than in terms of scientific regularities.

A possible definition would be: an extremely unusual event, un-familiar in terms of naturalistic explanation, which a worshipping community takes to be specially revelatory, by dint of the blessing or healing it conveys, of the divine grace.[15]

As Clayton emphasises, such a theological definition does *not* mean 'This event *could* not have occurred, that is without divine assistance, given what we know about the natural world' (1997a:178).

Polkinghorne has an extensive discussion of miracle in his *Science and Providence* (1989), and takes a very positive view of the possibility of such events. Again this is a reflection of his sense of the openness and flexibility of physical processes. God does not violate the regu-larities God has put into place (1996b:248f.), but God still has scope for working within the natural processes to generate remarkable results.

Peacocke takes a much more cautious view, questioning 'whether such direct "intervention" is compatible with and coherent with other well-founded affirmations concerning the nature of God and of God's relation to the world' (1993:183).

(v) The resurrection and virginal conception of Jesus

The normative Christian miracle of the resurrection of Jesus[16] finds our two theologians, again, close in many respects, but with differences of emphasis. Polkinghorne sees the New Testament accounts as, overall, offering a self-consistent account of a bodily resurrection which left a

---

[15] An alternative is simply to avoid the term altogether and speak as Murphy does of 'special' and 'extraordinary' divine acts (1995:330–32).

[16] See also **5.7** on resurrection and immortality.

tomb empty and which led to appearances of the risen Lord in a transformed type of body. 'The empty tomb is of great importance, "with its proclamation that the risen Lord's glorified body is the transmutation of his dead body; that in Christ there is a destiny not only for humanity but also for matter"' (1996a:55). Peacocke would agree that something happened which was no mere trick within the psyches of the disciples, but he is much more reluctant to accept either the emptiness of the tomb, or indeed the theological desirability of an empty tomb (1993: 279–88). Clearly other human tombs are not empty. The atoms that were 'us' become dispersed at our death. If we are resurrected with any sort of embodied status, it is because the pattern that was most distinctively ourselves has been held in God. Jesus' resurrection body was also of a different order, not easy to recognise, able to pass through walls. This must surely also reflect a pattern transmuted in God. So the atoms of Jesus' body are, for Peacocke's theological naturalism, much better left to disperse in the tomb.

Likewise Peacocke is very little disposed to accept the virginal conception of Jesus. In a careful analysis he points out how strange it would be if God's action in the world amounted in this particular case to supplying a complete set of chromosomes as from a human father. The old images of God's relation to living things: the pre-Darwinian specific designer of creatures, the pre-Humean cosmic tinkerer, would return with a vengeance in such a scenario. For Peacocke 'it is theologically imperative that the birth stories and the doctrine of the virginal conception of Jesus be separated from the doctrine of the incarnation' (1997:38). Whereas Polkinghorne, without concerning himself too much with the biological details, considers that 'the dual origin of the X and Y chromosomes ... seems a possible physical expression of the belief, in the words of the Nicene creed, that Jesus "by the power of the Holy Spirit became incarnate of the Virgin Mary and was made man". In other words, his conception was an act of divine-human co-operation' (1996a:79).

So two highly-trained scientist-theologians, both pursuing programmes of critical realism in science and theology, reveal how junctures arise when one has to accord one programme, the scientific or the theological, priority over the other. Both thinkers agree that the scientific data necessitate dispensing with an Edenic paradise from which humans 'fell' (see **4.16.2**), but they disagree over miracle, empty tomb and virginal conception.

7.8   Process schemes and double agency

It is hard to avoid concluding that efforts to derive a particular consonance between the new physics and accounts of divine action have met with very limited success. Theologians have been forced either into *pressing* quantum indeterminacy further than seems satisfactory (Tracy, Ellis and Murphy), or into *guessing* that epistemological indeterminacy in chaotic systems somehow models a real openness, to which scientific descriptions only approximate (Polkinghorne), or back to speaking of God as the 'context' of the physical universe, *asserting* that systems must be regarded as indeterminate because they unfold in the context of a personal God (Peacocke).

We conclude this section by considering briefly two other influential descriptions of divine action. It is not difficult to see that *process schemes* can accommodate divine activity in particular situations, since divine persuasion or lure is present in every interaction between entities. Close consideration, however, shows that process thought is in a similar position to that of the *neo-Thomists* – both introduce a type of influence which is at a remove at once both from our ordinary experience *and* from the scientific accounts:

- Neo-Thomists posit a divine influence which (a) knows the results of its actions already through the atemporal omniscience of God's action and (b) executes its purpose by being the particular primary cause behind secondary causes, and yet allegedly (c) still allows creatures their freedom.
- Process thinkers posit a sort of sentience which allows all entities, however inanimate, to be aware of the divine will and to respond to it (or not).

Indeed Settle considers a process metaphysic to be the natural result for a search for an appropriate account of double agency (Settle, 1996).

Those convinced for other reasons of the rightness of either of these positions will accept the version of divine providence that the account offers – but neither account offers any purchase on discussing a model of God in relation to the physical world as science describes it.

Where neo-Thomism and process thought differ so sharply is in terms of *theodicy*. The great problem with an account of providence in terms of primary and secondary agency is that the most evil of persons becomes a secondary agent of God.

The merits of process theodicy were pointed out in **6.3**, but we noted at **6.5.3** the question it raised – whether the process God is God enough to be the ground of hope. The neo-Thomist God, then, is so much God – omniscient, omnipotent – as to pose great problems for theodicy; the process God cannot be held to account for evils from which the divine fellow-sufferer has laboured to dissuade the entities concerned. Between these poles come the accounts of providence, general and/or particular, undertaken by a self-limiting God to whom the future remains not wholly known, that we have discussed in the rest of the chapter.

7.9 Conclusion

The discussion of the theology of divine action now seems to be resolving itself into a debate between quantum indeterminacy, contextualism (of which in their different ways Polkinghorne and Peacocke can be seen as representative) and some sort of metaphysical account of double agency – either along neo-Thomist or process lines. Perhaps the most interesting ways forward come from those who want to try and combine elements from the different camps. It is interesting that Nancey Murphy, in an essay of exemplary clarity, extends a quantum-indeterminacy-based account towards a new metaphysics of causation in which chaos theory and top-down causation both find a place (1995:338–57). Philip Clayton, working from Peacocke's panentheistic whole–part model of divine action, also makes room for special action at the quantum level (Clayton, 1997a:Chs. 7 and 8). Even Murphy, however, concedes that she does not know how much of a 'window' for special divine action quantum indeterminacy provides.

SECTION B:
WHAT GOD HAS DONE – THE HISTORY OF THE UNIVERSE (7.10–7.16)

7.10 The Big Bang and 'before'

We saw in **1.15** that contemporary speculations on the origin of the universe suggest that it may have begun in a quantum event of some kind, a chance fluctuation in a situation which contained no matter or energy, but only possibilities.

Just as Darwinian evolution pushed theological reflection on biology away from the notion of God designing individual creatures, so these quantum-cosmological speculations are, even before they are substantiated, tending to push theological reflection on physics further and further away from thought of the Big Bang as a precisely divinely controlled instant. That is not to say that God is not the ultimate cause of there being anything rather than nothing – as Ward says, the doctrine of *creatio ex nihilo,* while hardly mentioned by the Christian Scriptures, is nevertheless 'implicit in the Biblical doctrine that God is the creator and heaven and Earth, that he can do all things, that nothing is beyond his power' (1990:6). Nor is it to say that the laws and parameters governing the field of possibility were not set by God – again, the tradition has always presumed that whatever rationality governed the behaviour of the universe was a reflection of the rationality of God. Rather the presence of this ineradicable element of chance in the development of the universe calls forward images of God's creative action other than the merely mechanical.

For example, the biblical image of God as the potter (Isa. 64.8, Jer. 18.6, Rom. 9.21 – all with the stress on the absoluteness of God's power) bears further thought. Is not the activity of the potter at her or his wheel sometimes with a definite objective, but sometimes freer, more improvisatory? At those times the potter has set up the possibilities, and then allows shapes to appear, with which she or he then works. Or again (an image of which Arthur Peacocke is especially fond) God could be pictured as a composer of fugues who has set up the rules which circumscribe the form, but waits for the particular inspiration of the moment to dictate how the particular fugue will arise and grow.[17] The Hebrew Bible offers a haunting image of the primordial universe – however Genesis 1.1–2 are interpreted,[18] verse 2 does suggest two elements, a structureless primordium (*tohu-va-bohu* in the Hebrew) and a mighty or divine wind (*ruach elohim*). God, then, might be pictured as brooding on a sea of possibility, a contemplation which gave rise to the heavens and the earth. Again, as at **4.16.2**, we are not in any way attempting to project onto the biblical author any anachronistic cosmological awareness, merely to notice a mythic depiction which has some resonances with the newest physics. Peter Van Inwagen has

---

[17] See Peacocke, 1993:174–75.

[18] See Westermann, 1984:93–110 for a thorough examination of the exegetical options.

suggested that God, faced with an infinity of different but equally acceptable possible initial states of the universe, might simply decree 'Let one of this set be'. Van Inwagen considers that this form of creation, again consonant with the newest science, might be describable in a way which was free both of divine caprice and of divine dice-tossing carelessness.[19]

7.11   Anthropic considerations

In **3.19–3.23** we mentioned the apparent fine-tuning of the universe and identified different forms of the anthropic principle. What concerns us here is what Polkinghorne has called the 'moderate' and Drees the 'theistic' anthropic principle. Polkinghorne considers that the apparent fine-tuning of this universe so as to be precisely such as could produce life is 'a fact of interest calling for an explanation' (1991:78). Against this it is important to note Drees' objection that it is perfectly possible that these 'tunings' of the physical constants could disappear as our understanding grows (1996:271). It is fair to suppose, however, that it will still be worthy of comment that the origin of the universe was such an exceptionally-low-entropy-event, occupying such an infinitesimally tiny part of the apparent space of possibilities (Penrose, 1989:445).

Of the various explanations considered in **3.20–3.23** the most coherent seem to be either that this is the one universe – out of a huge number – which has the particular parameters that allow life to exist, or that this universe has been fine-tuned by a designer.

Although it is not possible to choose definitively between these possibilities 'the design hypothesis has a great deal to say for it' (Murphy, 1993:432). We agree that, to someone already committed to a theistic research programme, apparent anthropic fine-tuning provides previously unexpected confirmation. A programme which has as its core a conviction that God created a meaningful and life-producing universe would generate an auxiliary hypothesis to the effect that the conditions of the very early universe would be found to be those which

---

[19] Quoted in Tracy (1995:note to 321–22). Tracy's objection – that nothing can be actualised unless God actualises it, because 'there is no other agent on the scene' – seems to miss the point about quantum descriptions: that outcomes genuinely arise by chance (in sense (iii) in **7.3.1**) out of an array of possibilities.

would be likely to give rise to life at least within a portion of that universe. 'Anthropic' observations seem to confirm that hypothesis and to extend it by suggesting divine design by fine-tuning. *But this research programme continues to be in competition with others*, for instance the many-universe interpretation of quantum theory (**3.13 (iii)**), which makes this anthropic universe only one of an almost infinite number, and hence regards its properties as being of no special interest.

Divine 'tuning' of the Big Bang, if we were to accept it, might be envisaged as being as follows:

God creating the possibilities that have led to life, by setting the laws and parameters of the universe. We must accept that our knowledge here is very fragmentary – we can only guess at whether there could be matter based on other laws and physical constants. An astrophysicist could note that the stabilities of the elements hydrogen, helium, carbon and oxygen are such as to allow stars to develop and generate a whole range of other elements. A life scientist's sense would be that in this universe complex life could only have arisen roughly as it did – based on macromolecules made largely from carbon, hydrogen and oxygen. We have no means of knowing if other elemental systems are possible in other, 'differently tuned' universes. However, the universe we know has clearly been productive – of stars, of heavy elements and of second-generation stars around which planets containing those elements could cohere and, at least in one case, be a breeding ground for life.

The presence of laws and physical constants which look fine-tuned is in no sense a proof of God's existence or activity. As indicated above, however, it seems unlikely that all the anthropic coincidences will be accounted for scientifically, since they deal with the 'givens' of astrophysics, the laws and physical constants of the universe.

7.12   The early universe

Adherents of a theistic research programme, who see the coincidences as suggestive of a way in which God created the possibilities that have led to life, might press further and ask if the course of the very early universe might not also have involved a second type of divine tuning, that of:

God preserving a certain amount of structure during the very early universe's rapid expansion, its so-called 'inflation'. The theories of inflation developed in particular by Guth and by Linde[20] are in a sense hypothesis-savers; they came about to rescue a theory in difficulties. So they must be handled with more than usual theological care. It remains the case that the present universe is extraordinarily uniform – as though indeed it had been blown up like a balloon – but not *quite* uniform. Some structure survived and enabled galaxies to form – again, an essential prerequisite for a life-producing universe.[21]

However, as we move into the development of the universe it becomes very hazardous to assign particular events to the result of divine activity as one cause among others. A theistic-creation programme would predict that the Creator would have to preserve some structure in an inflating universe. We do observe such structure. Note that this prediction is not about the *creation* of possibilities, but about the actual chronology of development of this universe, and God selecting, or perhaps better protecting, certain possibilities so that life could occur. However there is every prospect that astrophysics will generate its own explanation of the persistence of structure during inflation. So a postulate of this sort of divine action can only be held very tentatively.

Those with a strong view of providence might go further and note how important the formation of the Moon may have been for the development of life on Earth – especially in slowing and stabilising the Earth's orbit and stimulating the mixing of nutrients through the action of the tides. They might suggest that, given that the very early Earth had become a place where the precious possibility of life had arisen, God might, again, have protected that possibility by allowing a massive collision to generate a satellite moon.[22] Such an action could no doubt have been effected through the input of 'active information' into a

---

[20] For an introduction to inflation see Smoot and Davidson (1993:174–91); for a more comprehensive account see Guth (1997).

[21] The detection of this non-uniformity in the microwave background, the radiation that is 'the echo of the Big Bang' (see **3.16.1**), by the COBE satellite is one of the most exciting *experimental* results in recent cosmology, and is recounted by Smoot and Davidson (1993).

[22] This idea first came to our attention in an unpublished talk by Professor Owen Gingerich. See also Comins (1993:1–49) for an account of the implications of there being no moon.

complex dynamical system, along the lines of Polkinghorne's proposals. But the suggestion advances the theistic research programme still less than the comment on inflation above, since present-day astrophysics could give an entirely adequate account of how the moon arose, as a chance event in the first two senses described in **7.3.1**.

7.13   The origin of life

The distinction between living and non-living things has, historically, been regarded as a very evident and profound one.[23] As was indicated in **4.7**, however, this distinction is not so easy to maintain as might have been thought. Moreover, recent consideration of the sorts of systems that may have given rise to life on Earth (such as the edges of hot mineral springs) suggests that in those sorts of conditions some sort of self-replicating system would be quite likely to develop (see Kauffman, 1995:60–69). There are a great many unanswered questions in this area. But the emphasis within the science has moved from supposing that there must have been a very extraordinary coincidence to generate life to thinking some sort of proto-life a likely consequence of certain conditions.

As was emphasised in looking at Big Bang cosmology in **1.15**, theology does well to track these developments in fundamental questions with caution. Even Darwin seems to have been uneasily aware that the very beginning of systems subject to evolution by natural selection was a possible 'gap' for God, a place in the unfolding of the natural world where the divine breath might have been specially breathed. With the development of our understanding of self-organising systems, that 'gap' has gone, surely for ever. Rather attention focuses once again on the remarkably promising system that the Earth was for the origin of life. Certain parameters seem to have been particularly favourable – the distance from the Sun, a chemically reducing environment, the presence of abundant water, high carbon dioxide levels which kept the early Earth warm enough to keep surface water liquid (and later provided the oxygen which higher organisms breathe) – and certain chance events seem to have been particularly propitious, such as the formation of the Moon (see above).

[23] One of the great developments in nineteenth-century chemistry was when Wöhler succeeded in producing a compound characteristic of living things, urea, from one which appeared characteristically *in*organic, ammonium isocyanate.

Can we then advance a fine-tuning argument as to God's action in respect of the early Earth? Not with nearly the force that it is advanced in respect of the universe as a whole. The notion that this planetary environment arose by 'chance' in our sense (ii) (**7.3.1**) – a purpose-free intersection of causal chains – is an eminently reasonable conjecture. Again, a 'many-planets' view – the notion that an Earth-type environment was quite probable given the number of stars in the universe – is much more convincing than the many-universes argument, since we are dealing with an observable and to some extent even testable proposition. What remains of the tuning proposal is no more than the argument above about the whole universe, that it seems remarkable that its laws and its matter should be just such as to engender life *somewhere* within it.

So any sense that God acted particularly to engender this planetary environment would have to lead to a proposal about the second type of providential action discussed above (**7.12**) – God acting to select or protect a particular set of possibilities.

7.14   The evolutionary development of life

As soon as organisms of any complexity arise, the universe acquires additional properties – the behaviour, experience (at however basic a level) and interaction of these organisms. If Polkinghorne's 'scientist-theologians' are right to insist that:

> God's act of creation involves a kenotic act of self-limitation, truly allowing the other to be. It is therefore necessarily a costly and vulnerable action in which divine almightiness is qualified by the loving gift of an appropriate degree of independence to the beloved creature. (1996a:45–46)

then it may be imagined that emergent properties related to the development of entities as delicate and complex as living organisms would impose further constraints on particular divine action to steer creation. The fugue, to go back to Peacocke's metaphor, acquires other motifs, which even the master improviser must respect. At the same time the range of possibilities for development is enormously increased. Eventually, according to the Gaia Hypothesis (see **6.8**), organisms caused a major alteration in the conditions of the Earth's surface. With the further growth of biological complexity came more intricate systems for responding to the environment. Peacocke has pointed out that this of itself must mean the development of pain and suffering, as well as the decay, death and indeed extinction which are necessary concomitants of the evolutionary process.

7.15   Questions of theodicy in respect of evolution

We mentioned in **4.4** that speaking of an evolutionary creation gives rise to severe problems for theodicy – the task of justifying God in the face of all the suffering caused to creatures of all kinds over more than a billion years. This implies the need to consider a category of evil outside those normally discussed in theodicy. Beyond 'moral evil' arising out of the activities of human beings, and 'natural evil', suffering caused to *humans* by the non-human creation (earthquakes, etc.), there is 'evolutionary evil', the suffering and seeming futility within the non-human creation as a result of natural selection.

The defences of God in respect of moral evil have been well summarised and analysed by Surin (1986). Among the best-known and most persuasive is the 'free-will defence' – humans' capacity for evil is a necessary corollary of their freedom to love and do good. Polkinghorne has advanced an extension of this in respect of natural evil, which he calls the 'free-process defence' (1989:66–67). Periodic destruction of human value by the natural order is a necessary corollary of God's allowing that order to be itself and to develop and change.

Beyond this, however, if elements of the non-human creation are judged to have any intrinsic value (**6.13 note 28**), then the evolutionary evil of their being created as part of a process which necessarily involves a great deal of suffering must be laid at God's door. A vast number of species, moreover, may have had a 'role' in creation at one time but are now extinct. Some extinction, admittedly, reflects moral evil, or at least questionable ethical choices. Indeed the rate of human-induced extinction is currently estimated at over 100,000 times the background rate (Leakey and Lewin, 1996:241). But there have been five great extinction events in the past (1996:44–56). The most recent and most famous is the one 65 million years ago which may have been triggered by an asteroid or comet 15km across colliding with the Yucatan Peninsula, and which eliminated an extraordinarily successful evolutionary 'project' called the dinosaur. But the previous event in the Permian era was much more extensive – it is thought that only 4 per cent of species survived. The cause is unknown.

Theologically this raises the question whether we have to envisage the God of this creation designing, or at least permitting, a process which has used millions of species merely as a means to an end, and then tossed them aside. Peacocke is content to say that God, while taking delight in every aspect of creation, suffers 'in, with and under the creative processes of the world' because 'God purposes *inter alia* to bring about a greater good thereby, namely, the kingdom of free-willing, loving persons in communion with God and each other' (Peacocke, 1998). The evolutionary costs are justified, for Peacocke, by the 'vale of soul-making' that the Earth ultimately becomes.

If so, our response might be analogous to the one famously given to the character Ivan Karamazov by Dostoevsky, that:

> Listen: if all have to suffer so as to buy . . . harmony by their suffering, what have the children to do with it – tell me, please? It is entirely incomprehensible why they should have to buy harmony by their sufferings. Why should they, too, be used as dung for someone's future harmony? . . . I don't want harmony . . . too high a price has been placed on harmony. We cannot afford to pay so much for admission. And therefore I hasten to return my ticket of admission . . . It's not God that I do not accept, Alyosha. I merely most respectfully return him the ticket. (Dostoevsky, 1958:286–87)

Might we not, on behalf of the millions of discarded species and the billions of creatures brutally predated upon or parasitised, want to substitute the word 'humanity' for 'harmony' and 'creatures' for 'children' and with Ivan return our tickets?

This is in effect the approach taken by Ruth Page in her *God and the Web of Creation* (1996). Not only does she mount a massive attack on anthropocentrism (see **6.4**) – she also protests against any significant notion of divine activity in creation at all. Her God is the creator of possibilities, a theme we have taken up in this chapter, but for Page God does not steer creation nor does creation's development serve some long-term divine purpose. To say either would in her view create unbearable problems of theodicy (Page, 1996:91–105). Rather God is a God of letting possibilities be (*Gelassenheit*, in the terminology of the philosopher Heidegger) and keeping company (*Mitsein*) with those possibilities as they unfold. There are some contradictions in Page's account,[24] and at times it smacks of an uneasy mixture of deism and process thought, but nevertheless she has marked out important ground. Creation of possibilities does as we have seen have interesting consonances with the newest theories of the origin of the universe (see **1.15**, **7.10**). Moreover, such a radically non-teleological account of God the 'creator' goes a long way towards solving the theodicy problems of evolutionary evil.

EXERCISE 7.4

Compare Page's view of God's relation to evolution with that of Keith Ward in his *God, Chance and Necessity*. Ward not only affirms that God has used evolution for the long-term purpose of giving rise to sentient life-forms, he also implies that this outcome did not have sufficient *a priori* probability for God to 'leave evolution to it', and that therefore part of the divine role was to adjust the course of evolution to steer it towards God's chosen goal (1996b:Chs. 4 and 7, also 1998:Ch. 6).

7.15.1   The probability of the early life on this planet evolving to give rise to freely choosing self-conscious beings

This is a vital issue, which we digress to examine, in order to formulate a theology of divine action in respect of evolution. The first thing to note is that – scientifically – we have no more sense of the size of this probability than we do of the probability of there being intelligent life elsewhere in the universe. In both cases estimates vary from close to zero to close to one (a probability of one reflects an outcome which is certain.) This has not however restricted either scientific or theological speculation!

One important guess is that of Pierre Teilhard de Chardin, the French theologian and anthropologist who remains the most ardent embracer of evolution as a working-out of God's purposes in the world (see especially his *The Phenomenon of Man*).[25] Teilhard regarded the progress

---

[24] As in her sudden acceptance of resurrection (1996:61), after she has gone so far to minimise the potency of divine action.

[25] For brief, if critical, summaries of Teilhard's work see Santmire (1985:155–71); also Lucas (1996:Chs. 5 and 6).

of evolution as leading by a near-inevitable sequence from the 'hylosphere', a world containing only inanimate matter, to the 'zoosphere', the world of living organisms. (Thus far Teilhard seems to foreshadow in a remarkable way recent thinking on the self-organising properties of matter.) He thought this process of 'intensification' had then led to the 'noosphere', the realm of consciousness and cultural information, which would spread throughout the world and become more and more dominant until mind became the central reality, and all creation would converge on the 'Omega Point', which he identified with the consummation of the cosmos in Christ (as in Col. 1.20). Again, one might say that part of Teilhard's vision has been fulfilled in the development of the Internet, a very rapidly growing web of information which is starting to cover the surface of the planet.

However, Teilhard has had very many critics – not merely in the Roman Catholic hierarchy which for many years proscribed his work. In a famously denunciatory review Peter Medawar rejected the scientific validity of any equation of evolution with inevitable progress (1996:1– 11). Teilhard's celebration of Western technology, even to the extent of praising the advent of nuclear weapons, rings hollow now. And passages like:

> Should the planet become uninhabitable before mankind has reached maturity; should there be a premature lack of bread or essential metals . . . should any of these conditions occur, then, there can be doubt that it would mean the failure of life on earth . . . So far as [these] conditions . . . are concerned, it does not seem that we have any particular need to fear the possibility of defeat. (Teilhard, 1966:118–19)

indicate a thinker whose perceptions were formed before it was evident just how endangered the 'human project' had become. Theologically, too, Teilhard seems to neglect the 'evolutionary evil' that we have been discussing, and the issue of theodicy that it raises. Hence the importance of Moltmann's conclusion, mentioned at **6.5.6**, that Christ's Cross must inaugurate the *redemption* of evolution.

For our purposes the other important guesses about the probability of the evolutionary process giving rise to organisms like ourselves are those of Ward himself and Stephen Jay Gould in *Wonderful Life* and also *Life's Grandeur*. Both put the probability as very low.

This leads Ward to suppose that:

> Taking natural selection alone, it seems to me highly unlikely that
> rational beings should ever come to exist in a universe like this . . .
> To make it likely that rational beings should emerge, there would
> have to be some weighting of the probabilities of events occurring
> which would make the emergence of rationality inevitable, sooner
> or later . . . I regard evolution by natural selection as a much more
> insecure and precarious process than seems compatible with the
> theistic idea of a goal-directed process . . . a continuing causal
> activity of God seems the best explanation of the progress towards
> greater consciousness and intentionality that one sees in the actual
> course of evolution of life on earth. (1996b:77–78)

This is both to overestimate our knowledge of the probability, and
to misunderstand the nature of probability itself. Evolution had to give
rise to some outcome or other, and the 'experiment' has only run once,
in this solar system at least. We simply cannot state that another
outcome would have been more likely, and that therefore God had to
tweak the system to make it run the right course. There is no parallel
with the possible anthropic 'tuning' of physical constants we noted
above. All we can do is note that the systems that have led to life do
exhibit a certain tendency to lead to greater complexity, environmental
factors permitting.

We have however to acknowledge the force of Gould's argument
(see **4.8.1**) that other outcomes to evolution, not involving freely
choosing self-conscious beings, were also perfectly possible, and that
particular historical circumstances, especially those of the great
extinctions, contributed enormously to the particular biosphere we have
today. For instance, Gould stresses that of all the different taxa of
creatures found in the fascinatingly diverse Burgess Shale none seemed
a much more probable survivor than another, but only the worm *Pikaia*
led to present-day vertebrates.

So once again those with a strong view of providence may want to
suppose that God, while respecting the freedom offered to the creation
in the interplay of chance and law, went so far as to protect the
possibility of freely choosing self-conscious beings at certain key
junctures.[26] Alternatively, at a time when scientific opinion seems so
divided (see **4.8.1** on the disagreement between Gould and Conway

---

[26] For a recent essay on the role quantum indeterminacy might have played in such
divine action see Russell, R. J. (1998).

Morris over the Burgess Shale) theologians may do well to suspend judgement.

7.16 Two possible theologies of divine action in respect of evolution

It is our view that Page is correct, to the extent that if God is described as imparting any direction to evolutionary creation with a long-term purpose, beyond the good of those creatures existing at that time, then the problems of theodicy *are* severe. The evolutionary theodicist's choices are two:

(a) to posit God merely as the passive, suffering companion of every creature, a view self-consistent but dubiously faithful to the Christian tradition, or

(b) to mount a defence of teleological creation using a *combination* of the theological resources we began to map out in Chapter 6:

   (i) if divine fellowship with creatures such as ourselves is in any sense the goal of evolutionary creation, then we must adopt *a very high doctrine of humanity* and suppose that indeed humans are of very particular concern to God (a doctrine which will be reinforced by reflection on the Incarnation of the Second Person of the Trinity in material form as a human). That does not in any way exclude a sense that God delights in every creature which emerges within evolution.

   (ii) as a consequence of (i) we must take very seriously *the Cross as costly to God,* as *part* of God's hugely costly way of taking responsibility for the creative process. (This aspect is missing from Ward's admittedly brief account of theism in *God, Chance and Necessity.*) Again this sense that a human death is a major part of the suffering of the Trinity does not exclude God's suffering with every creature who has ever suffered.

but also

   (iii) we must give *some account of the redemption of the non-human creation* such as the 'pelican heaven' of McDaniel (see **6.5.2**). A Trinity of loving relationship could never regard any creature as a mere evolutionary expedient.

Such considerations lead us naturally to consider the fate of the universe as a whole, which we do in Section C.

SECTION C:
WHAT GOD WILL DO (7.17)

7.17   Eschatology

A central element in the Christian tradition has always been the sense that God will ultimately effect the consummation of all creation (whatever that might mean). This eschatological category of divine action must therefore be included in any comprehensive account. (See however **3.22, 5.7** for our rejection of claims that physics itself can supply such a description via Frank Tipler's 'physical eschatology'.)

We have already noted (**6.2.1**) that process thought pictures the eternal co-development of God and the world. *One of the clearest conclusions of contemporary cosmology, however, is that this universe will not persist for ever – it will either collapse in on itself (the so-called 'Big Crunch'), or expand away to infinity (so-called 'heat death').*[27] *Any continuation of the matter or information in the present universe will have to be in a different form.*

Willem Drees, addressing eschatology in his *Beyond the Big Bang* (Drees, 1990:Ch. 4), chooses to rule consideration of the distant future out of court as more than a 'thought-experiment': 'It is not realistic to relate the future on a cosmological scale, counted at least in billions of years, to perspectives for humankind' (1990:117). His own interest in eschatology is oriented much less towards some conceivable long-term immortality than towards 'the call to conversion for the sake of a more just future' (1990:154). Indeed the yearning for justice, and a conviction that a greater sense of God's presence will be transformative in this direction, is a most important element in Christian eschatology.

It is no less reasonable, however, to do 'thought-experiments' about God's relation to the billions-of-years distant future than to speculate about the divine relation to the Big Bang. The scientific conclusion italicised above merits a theological response. In a sense the biblical accounts prefigure this conclusion in speaking of 'a new heaven and a

---

[27] At the time of writing (summer 1998) the latest calculations suggest that heat death is the more likely.

new earth', a 'new creation' (to which Christians already belong). Certain 'cosmic-Christological' texts speak of this reconciliation taking place in Christ (Col. 1.20, Eph. 1.10). This, then, is to be an order of creation which is in some way or other 'in God' and on which science can not therefore pronounce. Polkinghorne is the scientist-theologian who has developed this most (1994:Ch. 9, 1996a:53–55), writing that:

> It seems to me that it is of the essence of humanity to be embodied and that the soul is the immensely complex 'information-bearing pattern' in which the ever-changing atoms of our bodies are arranged. It is surely a coherent hope that the pattern that is me will be remembered and re-embodied by God in his eschatological act of resurrection. The 'matter' of that resurrected world will be the transformed matter of this dying universe, transmuted by God in his faithful action of cosmic resurrection. It will have new properties, consistent with the end of transience, death and suffering, because it will be part of a new creation, now no longer standing apart from it(s) Creator as the 'other', and so paying the necessary cost of an evolutionary world's making of itself, but fully integrated with the divine life through the universal reconciliation brought about by the Cosmic Christ. (1996a:54–55)

This however is not the only recourse in this highly speculative area. For instance, someone committed to speaking of an eternal co-development of God and the world might take refuge in a many-universes view (see **3.13 (iii)**, **3.21**). The heat death of this universe would leave all that was of value in the memory of God, where it would achieve at least an 'objective immortality' (Barbour, 1998:304),[28] but ongoing relationship with physical entities would take place in other universes.[29]

It will be observed that scientifically-informed eschatology tends to be more at home thinking of consummation over the very long timescales suggested by cosmology, the many billion years this universe

---

[28] Process thinkers are divided as to whether to postulate any 'subjective immortality', in which entities continue to experience themselves in this new state. McDaniel, as we have seen, postulates a 'pelican heaven' (**6.5.3**) – others follow Hartshorne in not seeing any need for this. On the latter view it is enough for entities to enrich the consequent nature of God.

[29] Some cosmologies imagine that there may be a process by which new universes frequently (on a cosmic timescale) bud off from existing ones. What remains clear, however, is that no new structure or information (still less a human being) could survive from one universe to the next.

has before it, than with the imminent end of things implied by apocalyptic elements of the New Testament.[30] But there is a consonance between cosmology and tradition to the effect that this universe will end, and anything which is to do with humans and their values would have to depend on God rather than presently existing physical processes for its continuation.

What 'the universal reconciliation brought about by the Cosmic Christ' might involve takes us beyond the scope of this book, certainly beyond the scope of ecological thinking as we presently understand it. But Gunton makes an important point when he writes:

> [T]here is in the Bible no redemption, no social and personal life, apart from the creation. It is therefore reasonable, especially in the light of Old Testament witness to the creation, to hold that the Bible as a whole is concerned with the future of creation . . . But the fact that it is Israel and Jesus who are at the centre of God's action in and towards the world means that it is the personal that is central, the non-personal peripheral. That does not rule out an ecological concern, but it cannot be of independent interest. (Gunton, 1992:33–34)

Human personhood, then, is of the first importance theologically (see **7.16**) but humanity will be redeemed, ultimately, as *part* of a new creation rather than *away* from contact with the rest of creation. It is worth noting too that many contemporary theologians have moved away from any sort of static picture of heaven to one which is dynamic, richly exploratory of relationships, an emphasis strong in Moltmann and also found in the passages just cited from Gunton and Polkinghorne. So in eschatology too we find the emphasis on a network of relationships, and on the inseparability of humans from their context in the cosmos, which has informed our search for models throughout the last seven chapters.

7.18   Conclusion

We have explored the vigorously debated territory of the compatibility of divine agency with the world described by contemporary science. Numerous possibilities lie between the trite materialist assertion that

---

[30] As to the possibility of an imminent apocalypse precipitated by a clash of spiritual powers, science can of course say nothing.

such action is impossible, and the over-optimistic assumption that the 'new physics' provides easy openings for models of the causal joint. Which possibility is adhered to will depend as much on the theological assumptions of the adherent as on the status of the science. Whatever position is adopted, construction of a coherent model of God's relation to the cosmos will rest on a coherent account of God's relation not only to the present world, but to the origin and development of the cosmos, and its final end.

FURTHER READING

CLAYTON, P. (1997) *God and Contemporary Science* (Edinburgh: Edinburgh Academic Press)

PAGE, R. (1996) *God and the Web of Creation* (London: SCM Press)

PEACOCKE, A. (1993) *Theology for a Scientific Age* (London: SCM Press, expanded edn.)

POLKINGHORNE, J. (1989) *Science and Providence* (London: SPCK)

RUSSELL, R. J. *et al.* (eds.) (1995) *Chaos and Complexity: Scientific Perspectives on Divine Action* (Vatican City: Vatican State Observatory)

—— (1998) *Evolution and Molecular Biology: Scientific Perspectives on Divine Action* (Vatican City and Berkeley, CA: Vatican State Observatory and CTNS)

WARD, K. (1990) *Divine Action* (London: Collins)

—— (1996) *God, Chance and Necessity* (Oxford: OneWorld)

BOOK FOUR

Chapter 8

Science and Education

8.1 Introduction to Book Four

The fourth part of this volume moves beyond our focus on the inter-action between scientific and theological developments to look at:

- science as it is considered in education, and the contribution science education can make to the debate (Chapter 8);
- science as it stands in relation to Islam, a monotheism at once similar to and very different from Christianity (Chapter 9);
- science's relation to the growth of technology and its effects on society (Chapter 10);
- the challenges posed by the technological possibilities raised by the new genetics (Chapter 11).

8.2 Science education and the science–religion debate: mapping the ground

Within society, the view that science and religion are at loggerheads is still a significant component of popular folklore. The view persists in spite of the scholarship developing in two major domains. Work over recent decades in *the history of science* has indicated the inadequacies of the idea of conflict as a generalisation about the ways in which science and religion have interacted in the past (Brooke, 1991; Cantor, 1991:289–95; Russell, C. A., 1985). Also, studies in *the philosophy of science* over the last half-century have highlighted the deficiencies of those views of science which put it on a pedestal as the final judge of truth in every sphere of human action.

287

Furthermore, the need to make judgements about the applications of science have underlined the role of values in principled decision-making. If research in these value-laden areas is taken seriously, there is a place for science education to make a major contribution to an understanding of the interplay between science and religion.

8.3   Meeting points

Four areas in which science education might make a contribution to understanding issues of science and religion lie in the ways it treats:

1. The content of science.
2. The nature of science (issues concerning the philosophy of science).
3. The applications of science.
4. How science operates as a social activity (issues concerning the history and sociology of science).

Each area will now be discussed in turn:

8.3.1   The content of science

The content of the science that is taught may raise issues of science and religion if:

(i) the scientific picture and specific religious texts are both *making apparent reference to the same subject.*

(ii) the content of the science prompts *wonder, and questions beyond the capabilities of science to answer.*

Taking these in order:

(i) Making apparent reference to the same subject

Examples where the scientific picture and religious texts may both *appear* to be referring to the same subject would be the astronomical issues of Galileo's time and the Darwinian controversies concerning the nature and origins of humankind (see **1.12–1.13**). A third example is the current debate, from both scientific and religious perspectives, concerning the origins of the universe (see **1.15** and Poole, 1995:81–97).

Some people attempt to read modern science into ancient religious texts, such as the Book of Genesis. But these texts were written long before modern science, for a very different purpose than to satisfy cosmological, biological or geological curiosity. Consequently such attempts have proved counterproductive. Certain attempts, in the time of Galileo, to drag astronomical theories out of Bible texts, prompted his famous quotation of 'an ecclesiastic of the most eminent degree: "That the intention of the Holy Ghost is to teach us how one goes to heaven, not how heaven goes"' (Seeger, 1966: 273).

At issue here is the hermeneutical[1] question about the meaning of particular religious texts when they include statements which might appear to be confirmed or denied by scientific discoveries. Many supposed puzzles disappear when the literary *genre*[2] of the ancient writing is taken into account. The problems generated by reading one's own ideas into a text (*eisegesis*), rather than understanding what the text is seeking to say (*exegesis*), sometimes arise from a mistaken view of what loyalty to the biblical text involves. To lose sight of the many types of literary *genre* which the Bible employs is to fail to treat the text seriously or carefully enough.

(ii) Wonder, and questions beyond the capabilities of science to answer

The remarkable world in which we live often prompts awe and wonder. Although awe and wonder do not necessarily have religious associations, it is not uncommon for religious factors to be involved. Christianity and Islam both emphasise wonder. This quote from the Psalmist is typical:

> When I consider your heavens . . . the moon and the stars, which you have set in place,
>
> what are we, God, that you care for us? (Ps. 8.3)

The apparent 'fine-tuning' of the universe for the existence of life as we know it is a current example of how the content of science prompts questions which lie beyond the capabilities of science to answer. Islam in particular places a strong emphasis on the possible religious

---

[1] *Hermeneutics* see **1.12 note 25**.

[2] Literary *genre* is the term used for an established category of composition which is characterised by distinctive language or subject matter. Poetry is an example of a particular literary *genre*.

implications of this 'fine-tuning' and Christians, too, see these 'cosmic coincidences' as entirely consistent with a purposeful Creator. The topic is explored in **3.19–3.23** and **7.11**. If the fundamental physical constants were even minutely different, even in some cases to as little as one part in 10^{60}, human life would not exist. Does this mean the universe was planned with us in mind or not? These questions go beyond what physics can cope with; they are *meta*physical in nature.

A realisation that there were questions which science was unable to answer went hand in hand with the beginnings of modern science some four centuries ago (Russell, C. A., 1987). The same is true today and numerous organisations exist to encourage debate about matters of science and religion.[3] However, alongside discussions about the interactions between science and traditional religions there has been a resurgence of mysticism in its various forms in what is loosely termed the New Age Movement. We touch on this in discussing *The Tao of Physics* in **6.9** – a more detailed examination of this heterogeneous collection of ideas is found in Lucas (1996).

Among others, cosmology, evolutionary biology and psychology are sciences whose content seems to relate in some way to religious beliefs. Some of the interactions are explored in Chapters 3, 4, 5 and 7. The educational importance of what has been said about the content of science is that issues of science and religion may arise naturally within science lessons and lectures when the topics referred to are encountered. This places a responsibility on the science teacher to be prepared to help their students to understand the issues in a non-trivial way, so as not to perpetuate the mistakes and excesses of the nineteenth-century conflict thesis.

8.3.2   The nature of science

Science education can make a contribution to understanding those issues of science and religion which relate to the nature of science itself, i.e. questions in *the philosophy of science*. It is most important that science education should address the nature and scope of the subject in which it seeks to educate (Woolnough, 1992). Two illustrations of how the

---

[3] E.g. in the UK Christians in Science, the Science and Religion Forum, and the Society of Ordained Scientists; in the USA the Templeton Foundation, Counterbalance and the American Scientific Affiliation; also the South African Science and Religion Forum and in Australia the Institute for the Study of Christianity in an Age of Science and Technology.

nature of science may impinge on matters of science and religion are raised by the following complex questions:

- Does science, in assuming the uniformity of nature, rule out the miraculous? (see **7.7 (iv)**)
- Does science indicate a deterministic world, perhaps thereby precluding religious teaching about freewill and human responsibility? (see **1.17, 3.11–3.14, 3.25–3.28, 7.3**)

But there are various questions in addition to these; questions about the status and the scope of science as a way of knowing about, and constructing a view of, the world. Extravagant claims about the status of Science with a capital 'S' have been made in which Science has been elevated to being the ultimate arbiter of meaning and truth. The scope of Science has been viewed as all-encompassing, particularly by the logical positivists (see **2.2**). This unjustifiable view of the omnicompetence of Science has resulted in attempts to get it to answer ultimate questions about moral 'oughts' as well as purpose and plan in the universe. The philosophy of science probes attempts like these. It also sets out demarcation criteria for (i) what distinguishes science from non-science and (ii) what kinds of questions science can hope to answer (e.g. Trigg, 1993).

An opposite strategy to that of almost deifying Science has been adopted by some of science's detractors. They treat the findings of science as simply the (empty) outcomes of the social conditioning of its practitioners. Such a view is in contrast to the general view of scientists, who see themselves as making provisional and corrigible attempts to describe and classify a real world, one which exists largely independently of its observers. We shall return to this point shortly.

One other aspect of science to note is its use of conceptual models. Science postulates theoretical models and tests them. Over recent years science education has emphasised the valuable role of models (see **1.9**) in helping to understand phenomena which may be invisible, new or conceptually difficult to grasp (cf. Association for Science Education, 1994). For instance there is the 'billiard-ball' model used in the kinetic theory of gases, the 'solar-system' model for atoms and the 'wave' and 'particle' models for light. But many models go far beyond pictorial representations. Religious thought also makes extensive use of models in referring to the invisible, the novel and the conceptually difficult. The topic of language in general, and of conceptual models in particular, forms an excellent way into teaching about the interplay between science and religion. Understanding the role of models can help to dispel the facile view, often encountered by RE teachers, that 'science deals with the hard facts, while religion is full of vague talk about shepherds, harvests and thrones in the sky'! Chapter 6 explores different models for God which have been developed in recent debates.

8.3.3   The applications of science

As will be seen in Chapter 10 there has been a growing concern in recent decades about the uses to which science and technology are being put and about their effects on our environment (Houghton, 1994; Russell, C. A., 1994). Although moral codes can be formulated without reference to religion, the world's religions have a great deal to say about how we *ought* to act. Their teachings inform and influence moral decision-making about how science, technology and medicine can benefit or mar society. Medicine in particular is a growth area with respect to ethical decisions, as issues like organ transplants, the use of transgenic materials, abortion, euthanasia, cloning and a host of other topics regularly make headlines. The applications of science feature extensively in science syllabuses.

8.3.4   How science operates as a social activity

Here we are concerned not with philosophical questions about how science and religion may or may not logically interact – including questions as to whether conflict or compatibility are the most appropriate descriptors – but of how science and religion *have been* and *are* perceived to have interacted in society. The relevant disciplines are *the history and sociology of science*. There are many ways in which science and religion have related over time, often with several different ways operating at the same time. It needs constantly to be borne in mind that there is no such thing as 'the' relationship between science and religion (Brooke, 1991:2ff.).

8.4   Some educational questions

As we consider the contribution science education can make to the debate about science and religion, a number of supplementary questions need to be asked and answered for particular educational situations. For example:

- What conceptual demands will be made in examining how science relates to religious beliefs? Will all pupils or students be able to cope with them and if so at what ages, bearing in mind what developmental psychology has to tell us?
- What contributions can/does science make to cross-curricular studies?
- What level of science education is to be considered, primary, secondary or tertiary? The remarks which follow will take particular account of science in the National Curriculum for England and Wales.

8.4.1   Primary education[4]

In starting to shape pupils' subsequent thinking about science and religion, the major factor at work at the primary level is the view of the scope and capability of science which pupils pick up from the teacher. Pupils need to be made aware of the limitations of science as well as its strengths. Since *Science in the National Curriculum* (1995) envisages no specific lessons on the nature of science at secondary, let alone primary level, ideas about science will be conveyed to primary pupils in an implicit rather than an explicit way. Thus it is crucial that the teacher of primary science should understand enough about the nature of the scientific enterprise not to purvey false notions about the scope of science. Science is *not* final truth; *nor* is it the ultimate test of meaning and truth in every other domain; *nor* is it competent to answer every kind of question which can be asked. Furthermore, teachers will need some knowledge of the history of science if they are to appreciate something of the ways in which scientific theories are overturned and be able to disabuse their pupils of entrenched ideas about the unbroken success and progress of science.

---

[4] Primary pupils' ages range from 5–11 years. First comes the reception year (R); at the end of this school year the majority of pupils will be five years old. The rest of primary education is divided up into two Key Stages (KS1 and KS2). The first year of KS1 is Year 1 (Y1) and at the end of this school year the majority of the children will be six years old. The rest of the years follow a corresponding pattern of ages and numbering. KS1 covers Y1 and Y2, KS2 includes Y3 – Y6.

8.4.2   Secondary education[5]

What has already been said about primary science education continues to apply, with additions, at secondary level. But here the *content* covered is likely to raise issues of science and religion in a way that would be much less likely at primary level.[6] For example, work in astronomy and biology may raise metaphysical questions about the origins of the universe, about life in general and human life in particular. When references are made to the Galileo Affair and the Darwinian controversies, it needs to be made clear that these were two great historical episodes which need to be treated carefully. This is because deeply entrenched folklore continues to perpetuate historically misleading popularisations of events. These two episodes have constantly been rewritten, adapted and edited to further the desire of certain pressure groups to present science and religion as in conflict (Russell, C. A., 1989). It seems probable that tendentious accounts of the Galileo Affair and the Darwinian controversies – together with extravagant claims about the nature of science – have been major factors in promoting and perpetuating the so-called *conflict thesis,*[7] that science and religion are constantly waging war (see **1.1**).

8.4.3   Tertiary education[8]

First degree science courses in the UK (with notable exceptions) are generally content based and many of them pay little attention to the

---

[5] Students' ages range from 11–16 years (16 being the statutory school leaving age). There are two Key Stages, KS3 (Y7 – Y9) and KS4 (Y10 – Y11). Y12 and Y13 are sometimes referred to as 'KS5', but this has no statutory basis. This covers the period of what was known as 'sixth-form studies'.

[6] Poole has surveyed *Science in the National Curriculum* (1995) for entries germane to science-and-religion issues with respect to both content and methodology in the Science Education section of the Church and Associated Colleges Project, *Engaging the Curriculum*. This project, involving the twenty-six Church and Associated Colleges, is based at Liverpool Hope University College, Liverpool L16 9JD and the Science Education materials are published as Poole (1998b).

[7] Also known as the *military metaphor* and the *warfare model*.

[8] For completeness it is worth pointing out that there are many taught postgraduate courses in science and religion. Many of these are listed in *Science and Religion: Course Program*, Radnor, PA: John Templeton Foundation. There are also substantial numbers of higher degree students and post-doctoral fellows working in particular areas of the interplay between science and religion. News of developments is given in *Science and Spirit*, 171 Rumford Street, Concord, NH, USA.

history and philosophy of science (HPS). One educational consequence of this pattern is that teachers of school science are initially unlikely to have encountered much about the history or philosophy of their subject to pass on to their pupils – implicitly or explicitly. Hence the *status quo* tends to be perpetuated and appropriate introductory ideas about HPS are under-represented within schools.

Science Studies at universities cover a huge range of topics, many of which have connections with science-and-religion issues in their content, historical development and philosophical underpinning. In addition to the subjects which have already been mentioned, geology, physics (relativity, quantum mechanics and chaos theory) and the behavioural sciences raise issues of this kind. For instance, geology relates to the age-of-the-Earth controversies; quantum mechanics features in debates about God's action in the world, while the behavioural sciences include psychological studies of religious belief and studies of the mind–brain problem.

The same points made earlier, about the presuppositions with which we approach our studies, apply at tertiary level as well as the others. As at primary and secondary levels, the implicit attitudes and world-views of teachers, lecturers and tutors influence their teaching. Science curricula, too, as we shall see in the next section, reflect particular world-views. It is useful to identify these world-views, particularly when they are not made explicit, and it is especially important to recognise our own!

What has already been said will have indicated the considerable range of educational aspects of issues in science and religion. The literature of studies in science and religion is already large and is growing rapidly, but space only permits a bird's eye view of some of the educational significance of this developing discipline.

8.5 Values and the curriculum: the way forward?

When *Science in the National Curriculum* appeared in 1989 it contained some imaginative thinking about the nature of science, the relationships of science to society and about historical perspectives on developments in science. A whole Attainment Target (AT17), covering Levels 4–10, was devoted to it, under the general rubric:

> Pupils should develop their knowledge and understanding of the
> ways in which scientific ideas change through time and how the
> nature of these ideas and the uses to which they are put are affected

by the social, moral, spiritual and cultural contexts in which they are developed; in doing so, they should begin to recognise that while science is an important way of thinking about experience, it is not the only way. (DES, 1989)

Examples of the practical outworking of the requirements of Levels 4–10 were given in Honey (1990). Included in AT17 were requirements which were germane to issues of science and religion, such as:

Pupils should:

- be able to give an historical account of a change in accepted theory or explanation, and demonstrate an understanding of its effects on people's lives – physically, socially, spiritually and morally, for example, *understanding the ecological balance and the greater concern for our environment; the observations of the motion of Jupiter's moons and Galileo's dispute with the Church.* [Level 7] [italics indicate non-statutory examples]

The second version of *Science in the National Curriculum* (DES, 1991) reduced the number of Attainment Targets from 17 to 4. The rubric from the head of AT17 became, with little change in the words, part of the General Introduction to the Key Stage 4 Programme of Study. The general result was a reduction in the treatment of topics relating to the four categories 'spiritual', 'moral', 'social' and 'cultural' (SMSC).

The third version of *Science in the National Curriculum* (DfE / WOED, 1995) resulted in these important SMSC aspects of science education being played down even more. Here the wording simply said:

Pupils should be given opportunities to:

2. **Application of science**
   (e) consider the power and limitations of science in addressing industrial, social and environmental issues and some of the ethical dilemmas involved. (KS4 Programme of Study [Double Science])

3. **The nature of scientific ideas**
   (c) relate social and historical contexts to scientific ideas by studying how at least one scientific idea has changed over time. (KS3 Programme of Study)

   (b) consider ways in which scientific ideas may be affected by the social and historical contexts in which they develop, and how these contexts may affect whether or not the ideas are accepted. (KS4 Programme of Study [Double Science])

Note how the limitations of science are dealt with differently from before. In an article in the *Times Educational Supplement* (Bausor, Black, Poole and Woolnough, 1995) the point was made that:

> the passage, 'pupils . . . should begin to recognise that, while science is an important way of thinking about experience, it is not the only way', has been removed. All that has been retained is a modified form of another passage from the General Introduction to the 1991 Key Stage 4 Programme of Study, which now reads, 'Pupils should be given opportunities to . . . consider the power and limitations of science in addressing industrial, social and environmental issues and some of the ethical dilemmas involved.' The new formulation is radically different from the old. The old focused on the inherent limitations of science in relation to issues of fundamental beliefs and commitments and in relation to other ways of knowing. The new could be interpreted as merely pointing out that science happens to be unable to deal with some aspects of particular problems.

Furthermore, the moral, spiritual and cultural contexts of science were all collapsed under the heading 'historical'. This shift of emphasis sat uneasily with the requirements of the Education Reform Act (1988) which stated that 'The curriculum for a maintained school' should be one which 'promotes the spiritual, moral, cultural, mental and physical development of pupils at the school and in society' (p. 1). It was also at variance with The Office for Standards in Education (OFSTED) (1993) requirement in *Framework for Inspection* which stressed that 'The promotion of pupils' spiritual, moral, social and cultural development is a "whole school" issue . . . other subjects [than religious education] can play no less significant a part in inviting pupils to reflect on the purpose and meaning of life' (OFSTED, 1993:17). Here lay a clear brief for attention to these issues to be strengthened, rather than attenuated, in science education as well as elsewhere in the curriculum.

A letter to the then Secretary of State for Education, to this effect, resulted in the following response from a spokesperson at the Department for Education:

> At the time of consultation the view taken was that cultural, spiritual and moral contexts were among the elements which comprised the 'historical context', and that there was no need to spell this out more fully. It was also felt that any study of the ways

in which scientific ideas may be affected by their social and
historical context would naturally raise the point that such ideas
are viewed in the context of other ways of looking at experience.
So, once again, it was not thought necessary to spell this out. For
these reasons I do not think that anything has actually been
removed or played down. There was certainly no such intention
. . . (DfE, 1995)

It was good to receive the assurance that there was no intention to
remove or play down the role of the social, moral, spiritual and cultural
contexts in science education. However, it is difficult to believe it could
seriously be imagined that teachers would unambiguously infer that
the term 'historical context' should include the cultural, spiritual and
moral contexts! It is not clear that there is any evidence to show that
the social, moral, spiritual and cultural contexts of science are well
taught on a wide scale in science lessons, but there is plenty of anecdotal
evidence which seems to point in the opposite direction. Another snag
about subsuming the moral, spiritual and cultural under the blanket
heading 'historical' is that it conveys the impression that they have
little or no place in the present-day life of pupils.

However, certain tragedies which attracted national attention in the
UK prompted a considerable ground swell of support for the promotion
of spiritual and moral values in society and for a greater emphasis to
be placed on them in schools. The *Schools Curriculum and Assessment
Authority* (SCAA) took initiatives in values education:

> The National Forum for Values in Education and the Community,
> set up by SCAA in early 1996, drew up a statement of values to
> which it was felt that all in society could agree. Extensive
> consultation in late 1996, including an omnibus survey of nearly
> 1,500 people by MORI, showed overwhelming agreement with the
> statement of values. SCAA has subsequently carried out the next
> phase of the work, which has involved gathering experts in the
> field of spiritual, moral, social and cultural education, to plan how
> best to translate the statement of values, and the preamble which
> sets it in context for schools, into practice. (SCAA, 1997a)

This initiative included the setting up of consultations and working
groups in subject areas such as science, in order to produce

> guidance for schools on their promotion of pupils' spiritual, moral,
> social and cultural development. This guidance will be supported
> by a directory of resources, booklets of case studies, guidelines for

community service and a glossary of the terms commonly used in this area . . . [in order to] inform the next review of the National Curriculum. (SCAA, 1997b)

The values themselves relate to the categories of The Self, Relationships, Society and The Environment and are set out in a number of places (e.g. SCAA, 1997c).

What has emerged from the valuable and encouraging work of SCAA is this: although the groups consulted represented a wide range of beliefs from multi-cultural, multi-faith Britain, there was widespread agreement over the values counted as worthwhile. However, imprecise terms like 'spiritual' and 'family' may be viewed in society in different ways while retaining the same words. As a result consensus may appear more general than in fact it is. Nevertheless, the outcome of the consultations is encouraging and provides a working platform, even though widespread agreement on values does not secure their widespread application and practice.

Furthermore, the National Forum for Values in Education and the Community made the point that their remit was only 'to decide whether there are any values that *are* commonly agreed upon across society, not whether there are any values that *should* be agreed upon across society. The only authority claimed for these values, accordingly, is the authority of consensus' (SCAA, 1997c).

The basis of the values expressed in this consensus is thus a pragmatic one. However, one could envisage a different consensus. If the opinions of certain bodies had been canvassed in, say, Germany in the late nineteen thirties and early nineteen forties, a very different set of values might have emerged, guided by and favourable to Hitler's National Socialism. Values are determined by beliefs and what is of the essence is the truth or falsity of the beliefs rather than, as is often assumed, the number of people who believe them (the fallacy of *argumentum ad numeram*).

Having made this point about the need for truth to inform the beliefs which give rise to the values, it should not be thought that the outworking is simple or automatic. It is not. Whereas different underlying beliefs can give rise to similar sets of values, as SCAA has found, similar underlying beliefs may spawn a variety of different courses of suggested action to deal with particular needs, such as managing the environment. Nevertheless, an important need has been identified nationally and the work of SCAA, now transferred to its successor, the *Qualifications and Curriculum Authority* (QCA, created in October 1997), has made progress in ensuring that teaching about spiritual, moral and other values is given a prominent place. It is to be hoped that this emphasis will also be made in the revision of *Science in the National Curriculum*, due to be implemented from the year 2000.

8.6   Resources

New journals, such as the *Journal of Values Education*, have appeared. Ever more public examination syllabuses are including the spiritual and moral dimensions of science. This creates further demands for classroom resources.

The *Association for Science Education* is actively engaged in work on values in science education – as are other associations of subject specific teachers – and the ASE has produced a *Summary of Policies* (January 1998) with a specific section entitled 'Values and Science Education' (p. 2). Here are a few excerpts from the section:

> ... the goals of science education should make explicit reference to values ... Within their own belief framework, teachers of science should uphold values of integrity, responsibility to learners and other teachers, and respect for the proper conduct of science ...
>
> Learners should be given opportunities to appreciate: ...
>
> • science's interrelationship with other disciplines in providing societal and cultural values
>
> • that the conduct of science is not value-free ...
>
> • that science has its limitations and cannot always provide clear-cut answers, particularly at the boundaries of scientific knowledge.
>
> ... Learners should be encouraged to evaluate the nature of evidence from science and elsewhere in making judgements about the use of science.

Unfortunately, the third bulletted statement cited above still merits a similar criticism to that made of *Science in the National Curriculum* (1995) cited earlier (Bausor, Black, Poole and Woolnough, 1995), namely that instead of being 'focused on the inherent limitations of science in relation to issues of fundamental beliefs and commitments and in relation to other ways of knowing ... [the statement can] be interpreted as merely pointing out that science happens to be unable to deal with some aspects of particular problems'.

The *Association for Science Education* was an early contributor to the demand for materials about the interplay between science and society, and issues of responsibility and value, with its Science and Technology in Society (SATIS) project, resulting in classroom materials at various levels. It also produced the *Science in Society* (1981) and the *Science In a Social CONtext (SISCON-in-Schools)* (1983) materials.

Recently, the *Charis Project,* from the Association of Christian Teachers, has begun to be published. Its starting point is the 1994 OFSTED discussion paper, *Spiritual, Moral, Social and Cultural Development.* The *Times Educational Supplement* (1996) comments on the first four books:

> Rarely can an idea have found its moment so precisely. With MPs shrieking from one television studio to another for education to be enriched with added morality, the Charis Project arrives on cue.[9]

Intended for 'the typical state school' and funded by the Jerusalem Trust, the materials are overtly Christian, but are expected to be 'acceptable to teachers of wide faith backgrounds or none'. *Charis Science* (Charis, 1997) consists of eleven units, each being intended to provide the basis for between an hour and a week's work at Key Stage 4. There are full teachers' notes and the students' sheets are photocopiable.

On the specifically science and religion issues, *God Talk: Science Talk – A Teacher's Guide to Science & Belief* (Brown, Hookway & Poole, 1997) has recently been published to help teachers who are using *A Guide to Science and Belief* (Poole, 1997) in classes. Based on five questions which young people frequently ask about science and religion, the *Teacher's Guide* contains photocopiable worksheets for class use.

Two videotapes on science and religion which serve as discussion starters in an educational context are *Whose World?* and *The Question Is. . .?*

Whose World?[10] contains six, 25-minute programmes, backed up by a booklet about the programmes and containing topics for follow-up discussion. The six programmes are entitled: 1. Does God Exist?; 2. The Big Bang; 3. The Grand Design; 4. Behold the Man; 5. Pain and Purpose; 6. Discovery Prone. Viewpoints of both atheists and believers are presented.

---

[9] *TES* (1996) p. 9.
[10] Available from CTVC, Beeson's Yard, Bury Lane, Rickmansworth WD3 1DS.

The Question Is. . .?,[11] sponsored by the Templeton Foundation, presents four 15-minute programmes, accompanied by a booklet about the programmes and containing suggestions for follow-up discussion. The four programmes are entitled: 1. Beginning at the beginning?; 2. The Origins of Life?; 3. Miracles?; 4. Science rules supreme? Once again, the viewpoints of both atheists and believers are presented.

8.7   Postscript

Finally, what about the future for the 'spiritual', 'moral', 'social' and 'cultural' (SMSC) in science education? Even now the post-2000 Science in the National Curriculum is being planned. In so doing, the following questions seem to be urgent ones to address:

- If the cited words about SMSC from the 1988 Education Reform Act are to be seen as more than ungrounded idealism, how can future versions of the National Curriculum promote 'the spiritual, moral, cultural, mental and physical development of pupils' more vigorously?

- In what ways will QCA's assessment programme seek to promote 'the spiritual, moral, cultural, mental and physical development of pupils', given that any curriculum requirements which are never assessed tend quickly to be forgotten?

- Into what model of overall curriculum planning will the spiritual and moral dimensions fit, since an examination of the current National Curriculum in all core and other foundation subjects shows that *none* has any general rubric saying that they should promote 'the spiritual, moral, cultural, mental and physical development of pupils'? In addition, no actual mention is made of the spiritual in *any* of these subjects and few references are made to moral issues.

Furthermore, the SCAA (1995) document, *Planning the Curriculum at Key Stages 1 and 2*, despite its reference to the phrase 'promote the spiritual, moral, cultural, mental and physical development of pupils at the school and of society' and its declared 'coverage of all subjects and aspects of the curriculum (including the National Curriculum and religious education) (pp. 8f.) makes no reference to cross-curricular links with religious education. Indeed, on p. 20 it presents an impoverished

[11] Available from the Christian Education Movement, Royal Buildings, Victoria Street, Derby DE1 1GW.

– even an objectionable – view of religious education in which the spiritual dimension appears to be almost entirely absent. Little more than a social study on what some people do appears to be intended.

Matters like these need to be, and in many cases are being, addressed. A pressing task is to synthesise the output from many different working groups in order to utilise the best ideas and materials for science education in the new millennium.

FURTHER READING

ASHRIF, S. (1998) 'Science teaching, culture and religious values', *School Science Review 79* (288) 51–54

ASSOCIATION FOR SCIENCE TEACHING (1998) *Values and Science Education,* policy statement (Hatfield: ASE)

CHARIS (1997) *Charis Science* (Nottingham: The Stapleford Centre)

FULLICK, P. and RATCLIFFE, M. (1996) *Teaching Ethical Aspects of Science* (Southampton: The Bassett Press)

McCLUNE, R. (1998) 'Science education for the year 2000 and beyond', *Education in Science 176,* 17–20

MILLAR, R. and OSBORNE J. (eds.) (1998) *Beyond 2000: Science Education for the Future – Report with Ten Recommendations* (London: Nuffield Curriculum Projects Centre)

Chapter 9

Islam and Science

9.1   Introduction

Sections **9.2** to **9.4** of this chapter provide a brief insight into the nature of Islam, in particular the concept of God, the role of the Prophet Muhammad and the origin and significance of the Qur'ān. In section **9.5** the past scientific developments of Islam are briefly examined. In section **9.6** we see how the doctrine of *tawhīd* (Oneness) is central to an understanding of a Muslim's concept of himself or herself, to God and to the created universe. Sections **9.7** to **9.9** briefly explain some of the many ways in which Muslims have tried to integrate modern science with Islam. Finally, in section **9.10** the particular difficulty of the interaction of Darwinism and Islam is examined.

9.2   The concept of God

Islam sees itself as the last of the three 'Abrahamic monotheisms'. It completes the sequence of revelation from Judaism through Christianity, then finally to Islam. It regards itself as the restorative revelation which seals the sequence. Islam also sees itself as a re-statement of the primordial, 'Adamic' monotheism, and moreover goes as far as stating that every human being is born a Muslim but may become something different as a result of the environment in which he or she is raised.

For Muslims God is Allāh; this is not a title, it cannot be translated as 'God'. Allāh is a personal name, often referred to as The Name of Majesty. Linguists suggest that it is derived from *al-llāh*, 'the divinity', although the word for 'god' in Arabic is *al-ilāh* and has a plural form.

305

There is clearly a common root but the word Allāh is a personal name; it is regarded as a revelation from God and has a sacramental value, both in its written and spoken forms.

Allāh acts with an absolute freedom of will, this being the ultimate reason why things are as they are, why things exist and why events happen as they do. He is the Creator of everything, of both good and evil, not just good alone. Allāh punishes those who involve themselves in evil, even though he is responsible for the existence of evil. He punishes those who disobey his command. The correct state of a human is to be a slave (*'abd*) to Allāh who is his or her Master (*Rabb*). This attitude, of servanthood or more correctly slavery, is manifest in the physical posture of the prayer rite, in which each Muslim touches his or her head on the ground before the majesty of God. Nothing escapes the will or the knowledge of Allāh – yet human beings seem to act with free will and are open to the punishment of hell if they attempt to turn against the will of God. The paradox between predetermination and freewill is a serious problem in most religions, but has an elevated importance in Islam. The main reason for this is the assertion that only God can act, hence the human will can only acquiesce to the act that God makes in the individual's mind. Thus the effective will of God precedes the human will. If God wills something evil in the mind then the mind cannot avoid it even though, as a result of God's command, he or she must not acquiesce to it.

There is no doctrine of original sin in Islam. Adam and Eve are regarded as being deceived by Satan, and because of that the guilt is upon Satan, not upon the first human pair. In fact Adam is regarded as the first Prophet in Islam, the last being Muhammad. In Islam the primary human faculty is the intelligence (*'aql*). Intelligence is required to see the truth, which is regarded as self-evident, that there is one Divinity, one Creator of the universe and of all living things. This truth is expressed in the principal confession of faith *Lā ilāha illā Llāh*, 'no divinity except Allāh'. The greatest sin in Islam is to deny this truth by 'associating' something with Allāh, indicating that it has divine or implicitly divine status. Thus a Muslim scientist would accept that Newton's laws are an expression or summary of the will of Allāh with regard to motion, but would reject the suggestion that Newton's laws determine motion.

The merciful nature of God in Islam is often misunderstood by non-Muslims. Each prayer, each act and each verse of the Qur'ān (Koran) starts with the words *Bismi Llāhi r-Rahmāni r-Rahīm*, 'in the name of Allāh, Absolutely Merciful-in-Himself, Infinitely Compassionate-to-His creatures'. The two 'Names of Mercy' *Rahmān* and *Rahīm* are derived from the root *rhm* which has the meaning 'matrix' or 'womb' and expresses maternal protection. The womb is taken as a prototype for the good mother who nourishes, protects and cares for her offspring. (It may be surprising that two of the greatest names of Allāh express maternal qualities, since the God of Islam is usually thought of, by Westerners, as being utterly masculine). Human beings are required to turn away from a state of *ghaflah*, 'heedlessness' towards Allāh. This act is called *tawbah* and is the spiritual act that redeems the individual. Then in a state of worship as a 'slave' of Allāh, the Muslim receives the fullness of Allāh's Mercy and total forgiveness.

The importance of intelligence as a gift from Allāh no doubt explains the development of knowledge in general and science and technology in particular in Islam. This is expressed in the often quoted *hadīth* (saying) of the Prophet Muhammad: 'The quest for knowledge is obligatory for every Muslim.'

Islam justifies natural science by regarding it as a process of studying the acts of the Creator. It therefore goes easily with an attitude of worship. The practising Muslim can, in principle, be a good scientist. This possibility and some of the difficulties involved are discussed in **9.5**, **9.7**, and **9.8** below. Technology is regarded as justified because it brings benefit and relief from toil for the community. The problems that arise from the application of science and technology in the modern world are only too well known both inside and outside of the Islamic world. Technology in a broader context will be discussed in the next chapter. To some extent the contemporary problems are caused by the energy sources that are used to drive modern industry, but other problems arise from biotechnology such as genetic engineering and, more recently, cloning (see Chapter 11). Such problems did not, of course, apply in the traditional Islamic world.

Islam has an ecological perspective which is based upon one of the functions that Allāh bestowed upon mankind. Adam and his seed were each given, by God, the role of *khalīfah*, 'vicegerent', and each individual was endowed with the duty and the power to care for and manage the Earth and its resources on behalf of the Creator. In principle this provides for the possibility of a full Islamic 'green' policy that includes the management and the conservation of ecological diversity. The role of vicegerent is obligatory upon every Muslim individual as well as upon government and organisations. Moreover there is a price to be paid for neglect or failure of this duty since each individual will have to give an account of his/her function as *khalīfah* on the day of judgement.

9.3   The religious dimensions of Islam: God, the Prophet and the Qur'ān

Islam resounds with the message of God's unity:

> Say: He, Allāh is One.
> Allāh the Infinitely Resplendent.
> He begetteth not, nor is He begotten. And there is none like unto
> Him
>
> (Qur'ān 112: 1–4, Sūra, *al-ikhlās* 'Purity of Faith')

The significance of the Islamic consciousness of the oneness and uniqueness of God cannot be underestimated. It is not simply a doctrine but an active organising principle which permeates religious thought and religious practice. It also provides the underlying axiom that explains Islam's scientific world-view.

The place of Prophet Muhammad in Islam is often misunderstood by Christians. Muhammad is human, not divine. He had both a human mother and a human father. He is a prophet, not an incarnation. He died and his grave is in Medina. Although human he is often said to be a 'jewel among men' and is always referred to with respect; thus after mention of his name a Muslim says 'upon him be blessing and peace'. The Prophet is the channel through whom the Qur'ān was revealed to the world. He listened to the Qur'ān being read by the angel Jibrā'īl (Gabriel) and then himself recited exactly what he had heard. The Qur'ān is therefore precisely the word of God, with nothing added and nothing taken away. This is why it is the absolute truth and this is why Muslim scientists treat it so seriously.

The Qur'ān, then, is regarded by Muslims as the literal, spoken words of God. It is in essence a 'recitation' rather than a book, and at its inception Muhammad was commanded by the angel to recite: 'Recite in the Name of thy Lord!' (Qur'ān 96:1, Sūrah *iqra'* 'Recite!'). The Qur'ān as written down consists of 114 sūras or chapters, ranked, more or less, in order of length, not in chronological order. The notable exception to the ordering is the first sūra *al-fātihah* ('The Opening'), which, because of its special ritual character and usage, is placed at the beginning and written or printed in a highly decorated form. The Qur'ān was the first Arabic text to employ vowel signs and other notations to ensure correct recitation. The Qur'ān has played a principal role in many respects: it is the key text for classical Arabic, it is the source of the legal system (*sharī'ah*) of Islam, it has been used as a source of mystical knowledge and it has a sacramental role during recitation. Since the Qur'ān is the spoken word of God, then to recite it is to be very close to God. The Qur'ān is therefore given great respect and reverence. The traditional exegesis of the Qur'ān is very different from the exegesis of the Gospels. Commentaries on the Qur'ān seek to explain the circumstances that provoked the 'descent' of the verses; there is also a methodology for employing one or more verses axiomatically in the development of Islamic Law. The verses are inviolable since they are taken to be the actual words of Allāh, transmitted unchanged to Muhammad by the Angel Gabriel, and then recited as speech by Muhammad. The Qur'ān is a written record of these occasional revelations.

By way of extension and because God spoke the Qur'ān in Arabic, it is also true that the Arabic language, both spoken and written, has a sacred nature. Thus the form of the Arabic Name of Allāh is sacred. The ability of the language to act as a vehicle in some sense for the 'presence' of its Author is so great that in June 1997 the sportswear manufacturing company Nike withdrew 38,000 pairs of trainers from its world-wide market because of an objection from Muslims that a new logo design, printed on the underside of the soles, resembled too much the Arabic Name of God.

9.4 The universe and its Creator

Numerous verses of the Qur'ān repeatedly affirm that God is the Creator of the universe.

> The Originator of the heavens and the earth;
> When He decreeth a matter He says unto it: 'Be', and it is.
>
> (Qur'ān 2:117, Sūra *al-baqarah* 'The Heifer')

In some respects the Qur'ān expresses itself in a way similar to the Book of Genesis. Thus the heavens and the Earth and all that is between them are said to have been completed in six days (Qur'ān 50:38). The Earth itself was completed in two days (Qur'ān 41:9). Having finished this creation God withdrew and took His place upon a throne.

Allāh it is Who created the heavens and the earth,
and all that is between them, in six days.
Then He mounted the Throne.
He directeth the ordinance from the heaven unto the earth,
then it ascendeth unto Him in a Day, whereof the measure
is a thousand years of your reckoning.
(from Qur'ān 32:4–5, Sūra *as-sajdah* 'The Prostration')

The above verses are typical of the way in which the Qur'ān often refers to a previous 'revelation' (in this case the 'days' of Genesis), adds a further previously unrevealed detail (the Throne of Ordinance), and reveals a mystery, the descent of ordinance and the ascent of confirming concordance (cf. Qur'ān 2:231), together with a comment on the difference between time as experienced by humanity and as experienced by God.

Some verses of the Qur'ān give details of processes involved in creation or of the intentions of the Creator. Six verses are listed below to give a sample of the sort of problems encountered by a Muslim scientist who wants to reconcile modern scientific knowledge with statements found in various parts the Qur'ān.

(a) Do not the unbelievers see that the heavens and the earth
were joined together [literally the two were one patch] before
we parted them.
We made from water every living thing.
(Qur'ān 21:30, Sūra *al-anbiyā'* 'The Prophets')

(b) Then He turned His will to the heavens,
and it was smoke.
He said to it and to the earth:
Come you two willingly or unwillingly.
They said: we come obediently.
(Qur'ān 41:11, Sūra *fussilat* 'They are Expounded')

(c) We created not the heavens and the earth
and all that is between them save with truth [*illā bil-haqq*],
and for a term appointed.
(Qur'ān 46:3, Sūra *al-ahqāf* 'Wind Curved Sandhills')

(d) And We created not the heavens and the earth and all that is
between them in play.
We created them not save with truth [*al-haqq*]
but most of them know not.
(Qur'ān 44:38–39, Sūra *ad-dukhān* 'The Smoke'; compare with 38:28)

(e) Allāh created the heavens and the earth with truth [*al-haqq*]
Lo! therein is indeed a sign [*āyāt*] for believers.
(Qur'ān 29:44, Sūra *al-'ankabūt* 'The Spider')

(f) And He it is Who created the heavens and the earth
. . . that He may try you, which of you is best in conduct.
(Qur'ān 11:7, Sūra *hūd*)

In many verses of the Qur'ān (see quotation (a) above) there is a challenge to 'the unbelievers' that they are unable to discern the obvious evidence of the Creator's work. Another assertion in the Qur'ān is that the creation was effected with and endowed with 'truth' (*haqq*) (see quotations (c), (d) and (e) above). Also in numerous verses (e.g. Qur'ān 6:97–99 and quotation (e) above) the Qur'ān describes the works of the Creator as 'signs' (*ayāt*) for 'those who understand' (*yufqahūn* – literally those who use *fiqh*, the deductive process of rational thought). Al Ghazzālī (1058–1111), the highly respected theologian and logician of Tūs, who is still revered by Muslims, encouraged the application of intelligence ('*aql*) to the texts of the Qur'ān as well as to all aspects of life. He wrote against *naql*, which is the process of simply 'copying' the thoughts of precedents. Bagley explains that

> for Al-Ghazzālī, as for others of his day, 'intelligence' meant deductive reasoning, from premises given by divine revelation; not inductive reasoning, through which new knowledge might be sought. He favoured the use of intelligence in support of religion, as well as for practical purposes, though he thought that religious discussion should not be excessive and that it should only be carried on by qualified persons. (Bagley, 1964: xxxiv)

Since the Qur'ān contains sections that have a quasi-scientific significance and because the verses are regarded as the direct words of Allāh and are therefore absolutely true, the Muslim can only apply deductive reasoning to them. Remember that the words are believed to be eternal truths, independent of the time or age in which they were first revealed. A Muslim scientist might, for example, attempt to link modern science and the Qur'ān with reference to quotation (a) in the following way:

- The Qur'ān says that the 'heavens and the earth', i.e. the whole of physical existence, were originally a single entity that was split apart. Thus, through science we would not be surprised to discover that the fundamental particles found in the 'heavens' (the 'out-there' universe), and in the matter from which the Earth is made, are identical.

- The Qur'ān says that Allāh made all living things from water. Hence the intimate and necessary relationship we observe between water and all plants and animals is readily understood in terms of their origin. It is reasonable to deduce, from the verse, that all living forms will be composed of a high proportion of water and this is what science has confirmed.

In addition to statements about the universe, animals and plants, the Qur'ān contains statements of epistemological significance. The Creator is said to have made all things 'with truth' (quotations (c), (d), and (e)). This explains, for a Muslim, why it is possible to understand creation by rational thought and intelligence, and why science aims at finding the elusive truth. Islamic metaphysics explains the intelligibility of creation as a dynamic interaction within the triad of the intelligent subject (*al-'āqil*), the intelligible object (*al-ma'qūl*) and intelligence (*al-'aql*), the latter being common to both subject and object (cf. Burckhardt, 1988:142). One of the differences between secular science and Islamic science is that the ability of science to gain knowledge through reason is taken as a presupposition without question or comment in the secular sphere (see Poole, 1990:26–29 and cf. Poole, 1995), whereas in Islam it is recognised and explained as existing because of the nature of God and of His creative act.

The status of scientific knowledge in Islamic thought is therefore very different from that in modern Western thought. Science is seen as providing only relative and provisional knowledge. It cannot be compared with the absolute truth spoken infallibly by God and recorded faultlessly in the Qur'ān. Thus, if there is a contradiction between science and the Qur'ān, then the science is likely to be assumed to be wrong. Science is also seen as a component of the social phenomenon of mankind; it arose in society and should therefore be regulated by the legal system (*sharī'ah*) that regulates society. Science in Islam does not have the autonomy, or the exclusive claim on truth, that it is often taken to possess in modern Western society.

9.5 The flourishing of science and technology in the Golden Age of Islam

The development of science in Islam is inseparably bound up with the expansion of the Islamic Empire. After the death of Muhammad, in 632, the four Caliphs established the *dār al-islām*, the 'Territory of Islam'. Very soon the territory ruled by Islam included Persia, Syria, Egypt and Mesopotamia. By the year 750 the territory had expanded to an empire stretching from Spain to India and including extensive parts of northern Africa. The Empire was held between the ninth and the twelfth centuries as a single vast unifying power. Its significance cannot be underestimated in constituting a foundation for the development of much of modern science. During the seventh to the ninth centuries Islamic scholars, working with the immense collection of Greek, Egyptian and Oriental documents in Alexandria (cf. Nasr, 1976:9), made a vast number of translations and compilations into Arabic. This effectively opened up the whole of the substantial knowledge of the ancient worlds and, very importantly, ensured its eventual survival for the West and for us today.

During the tenth and eleventh centuries of the Christian Era the developments that took place in the *dār al-islām* led to this period being named the 'Golden Age'. A group of *hukamā* (singular *hakīm*), 'natural philosophers', developed medicine, astronomy and mathematics. They refined algebra, improved and popularised arithmetic, founded plane and spherical trigonometry and developed the physics of optics. Their influence on the West was so great that many Arabic words are still used in these disciplines, words such as algebra, algorithm, zenith, azimuth, nadir; other words such as alcohol and alkali came into our language in the context of the chemical processes involved in alchemy, itself an Arabic word. During the course of the twelfth century scholars working in Sicily and Toledo translated the manuscripts that had been written during the Golden Age from Arabic into Latin. These included translations of philosophical works. Thus Thomas Aquinas (d. 1274) was able to read translations of the works of Plato and Aristotle as well as the thoughts of tenth-century Ash'arite theologians. Moreover Aquinas employed a secretary who could translate from Arabic into Latin.

An example of a *hakīm* working in the tenth and eleventh centuries is Ibn al-Haytham (965–1039). In the West, his name, like those of all the Islamic scholars, was transliterated as a single Latin word. In his case he became known in the West as Alhazen. He was outstanding in astronomy and in mathematics. His special success was in optical studies of lenses and mirrors. He compiled tables of the angles of incidence and refraction of light rays (published in his book *kitāb al-manādhir*) and so had the data required to discover Snell's Law. He extended his studies to determine the angle of refraction of the sun's light as it passed through the atmosphere (see Nasr, 1987), and thereby estimate the height of the atmosphere. He applied his studies of refraction to explain the optical properties of the eye. Another *hakīm*, named Abū Rayhān al-Bīrūnī (973–1051), in his astronomical studies, described the Earth as a sphere after observing the shadow of the Earth in lunar eclipses; by means of observations and trigonometric calculations he was able to calculate with some accuracy the circumference and radius of the Earth. These sophisticated observations were provoked because, for the *hukamā*, science was integral to Islam and equivalent to piety. Some of the best and most eloquent praises of science ever written come from the pens of Muslim scientists who considered their works to be acts of worship; an example is the great Andalusian scholar Abū Umar Yūsuf al-Qurtubī (d. 1071) whose book *The Comprehensive Account of the Enlightenment and Virtue of Science and the Prerequisites of Telling its Truths and of Carrying its Mission* 'has no contemporary parallel' (Sardar, 1980:88). The material presented in this chapter can only hint at the quality of science in Islam during the Golden Age; those wishing to read further are recommended the two excellent volumes by Nasr (1968; 1976) referenced in the Bibliography.

Given the links between science and technology it is not surprising that the Golden Age of Islam also gave rise to the invention of a great variety of machines and devices to make life easier. These range from simple tools such as scissors to complex automatic, water-powered machines which were used to lift water into aqueducts for distribution in cities. Machines were also developed for technical commercial purposes, for example weighing machines using Archimedes' Principle to determine automatically the density – and hence the purity – of metals.

The evidence that we gain from a study of the Golden Age of Islam is that human intelligence is regarded as a sacred gift from the Creator; its specific use to gain knowledge and to understand is positively encouraged in Islam. The main purpose of the study of the universe is to perceive the work of the Creator and thereby to enhance respect and an attitude of adoration.

The Qur'ān contains admonitions to provoke the acquisition of such knowledge and includes numerous axiomatic statements that Muslim scholars have employed to support deductive reasoning in their attempts to understand Nature. It is very important to note however that the work of the natural philosophers of the Golden Age included the use of inductive reasoning. The data on refraction gained by Ibn al-Haytham allowed him to look for a general law to describe the phenomenon, which he unfortunately failed to achieve because he used chords, rather than sine values, in an attempt to find what we now know as Snell's Law. Likewise al-Bīrūnī used a number of astronomical observations to infer a model of the Earth and the moon which then enabled him to calculate the size of the Earth. Such procedures, amongst several others carried out by the two scientists, show that inductive, empirical reasoning was quite natural to them, and apparently compatible with their concept of the relationship between the deductive reasoning that starts from the statements in the verses of the Qur'ān and their own observational investigations of nature. Traditional Islamic science at its best in the Golden Age was a blend of deductive and inductive reasoning, although the latter was much rarer than the former.

9.6   The Islamic paradigm of the universe

The doctrine of *tawhīd* is central to the Islamic understanding of the nature of the universe. *Tawhīd* means 'being one' or 'making one'. Manzoor (1984:155) defines the doctrine as the 'metaphysical and theological doctrine *par excellence* which gives the religion of Islam its unique profile and distinctive morphology'. Ayatullah Mutahhari (1985:74) comments on *tawhīd* as expressing the essential nature of the universe: 'the universe has for its essence 'from Him-ness' (*innā lillāh* [literally 'truly we belong to God']) and 'to Him-ness' (*innā ilayhi raji'ūn* [literally 'truly to Him we are returning', Qur'ān 2:156]). This relates to the idea referred to earlier in this chapter that the ordinance of God 'descends' to the Earth and, having accomplished its purpose, the knowledge of its effect returns back to God. The universe has its origin from God and to God it will return. The commands that govern the universe are given by God and the knowledge of their concordance sent back to Him. Mutahhari writes that the doctrine of *tawhīd* means that the universe is 'unipolar and uniaxial' (Mutahhari, 1985:74).

The doctrine of *tawhīd* is without doubt the principial axiom of the Islamic world-view. In a scientific context this doctrine seems to be intuitively true and inductively supported. Thus, for example, the fact that the Moon, the Earth and the Earth's oceans are moving in a gravitational system with a *single* centre of gravity is a confirmation of the axiom. Similar confirmations are seen in the *unifying* logic of the Periodic Table or the dynamic *integrity* of an ecosystem. The search for a theory of everything (GUT, the Grand Unifying Theory) and the proposal that the universe is derived from a singularity (see **1.15**) should also find easy acceptance as confirming the deductions that can be made from the doctrine of *tawhīd* (although many Muslims are uneasy with the apparent atheism and implied evolutionism of the Big Bang Theory). It is interesting to note the close match that exists between the deductive implications of *tawhīd* and the modern, inductive interpretation of the characteristics of the universe. Paul Davies writes that 'another highly relevant feature of the world's orderly contingency concerns the nature of that order, which is such as to bestow a rational unity on the cosmos. Moreover, this holistic orderliness is *intelligible* to us' (Davies, 1993:170). This conclusion, in the words of a respected modern scientist, is a succinct expression of what a Muslim could derive from a combination of the key doctrines of *tawhīd* and *al-'aql*, that is Unity and Intelligibility, by deduction from the Qur'ān and no other knowledge.

9.7   Islam and modern science

Science is apparently opposed to Islam if 'by science we understand a rational and empirical method of studying the phenomenon of nature' (for its own sake, without any control). 'The pursuit of knowledge is not an end in itself; it is only a means of acquiring an understanding of God and solving the problems of the Muslim community' (Sardar, 1984:22–23). Nasr adds to this the positive perspective that: 'the aim of all the Islamic Sciences . . . is to show the unity and interrelatedness of all that exists, so that, in contemplating the unity of the cosmos, man may be led to the unity of the Divine Principle, of which the unity of Nature is an image' (Nasr, 1987:22).

Kurt Wood has proposed that the interactions between the statements found in the Qur'ān and modern science fall into four categories or 'theses'. These are:

1. The Compatibility Thesis – the Qur'ān and modern science are not mutually contradictory in any respects, because the same God is the origin of both.
2. The Concordist Thesis – the Qur'ān contains scientific teaching.
3. The Veiled Reference Thesis – scientific statements are found in the Qur'ān that science does not yet understand.
4. The Verification Thesis – modern science proves that the Qur'ān has a divine origin.

   (Wood:1993:91–94)

These four theses are outcomes of a strong tension which exists between Islam and modern science. The tension exists because modern science never refers to God as creator, contains no explicitly God-based value system, and proposes, in the theory of evolution, that humanity is not a special creation. Abdullah Omar Nasseef, Professor of Geology at King Abdulaziz University writes that 'modern science does not want to speak of the Will of God or the attributes of God'. 'Religion teaches us that the universe, in fact the entire creation is for man and God wants man to behave as His representative on Earth. Nature is not a blind force evolving mindlessly on its own' (Nasseef and Black, 1984:6–8).

One of the bizarre, but actually tragic, consequences of the tension is the manifestation of a pseudoscience. Hoodbhoy comments that: 'fundamentalists often claim that every major discovery of modern science was long anticipated in the holy scriptures of their faith. Read the text carefully, they say, and you will find it there. But if you do not find it, either you have not done a good job at reading or the so-called scientific fact is a fake' (Hoodbhoy, 1991:65). This pseudoscience claims to show that the Qur'ān describes the chemical composition of milk, the effect of high altitude on humans, the nature of cumulo-nimbus clouds, that Adam and Eve 'fell' from another planet, predicts the incandescent light bulb, the atom bomb, the Sargasso Sea, the Hubble expansion of the universe, the structure of atoms, special relativity, airplanes, UFOs, and so forth. References to these will be found in Wood (1993) and Hoodbhoy (1991). The driving force for these bewildering ideas is explained by Wood's theses 2, 3 and 4 listed above.

They constitute a wonderful example of the misuse of deductive reasoning and of the fantasy that arises when a scholar loses genuine scholarship and seeks to prove what he or she *wants* to be true, rather than respecting truth as something refreshing, challenging and waiting to be discovered. Hoodbhoy rejects the notion of an 'Islamic science'. Other Muslims, such as Waghid (1996:90), propose a rationale for Islamic science that constitutes 'creative order, truth and justice'. Negus (1995:31) proposes that a better approach would be to 'define the Muslim scientist rather than Islamic science', using, as a role model, a great *hakīm* like al-Bīrūnī. Butt, after reviewing the opinions of several Muslim authors about the nature of the best expressions of Islamic Science, writes:

> the practice of Islamic science creates an atmosphere that encourages the remembrance of Allah, motivates behaviour according to the dictates of the sharia and promotes the conceptual values inherent in the Qur'ān. It is a living dynamic entity able to provide contemporary solutions to contemporary problems within the most humane and ethical framework in perfect harmony with man and nature. It is a science truly international in character. (Butt, 1991:64)

Wood has analysed the Compatibility Thesis. He suggests that the thesis 'seems to be an eminently reasonable operating principle for the believer'. He offers three possible approaches within the thesis:

> a *compartmental* approach that completely decouples 'spiritual' and 'scientific' kinds of knowledge, limiting scripture to the former; a *phenomenological* approach to the text which seeks to understand the Scriptural texts referring to natural phenomena in the context of the common knowledge bank of the original recipients of the word; and a *scientific exegesis* approach which seeks detailed scientific information in Scriptural texts. (Wood, 1993:92)

These three approaches present a range of possibilities. The most dangerous is undoubtedly the third, because it has a tendency to *force* a scientific interpretation upon verses of the Qur'ān.

Seyed Ali Ashraf reaffirms the traditional position that science should operate within 'basic limits set by the Qur'ānic revelations'. 'As the Muslim society is still dominated by the religious code of life, and as the acceptance of the religious code for all spheres of life is still a basic social assumption, it is possible for the Muslims to use scientific discoveries within the Islamic code of life and redirect technology for the benefit of mankind. The greatest problem is the theory of evolution' (Nasseef and Black, 1984:2–3). Seyed Ali Ashraf goes as far as stating four 'basic limits' with reference to evolution. These are, in a simplified form, that God is the only Cause, that the laws governing the universe are given by God, that Adam was a completely new species and did not evolve from a pre-existing species, and that Adam was the first Prophet.

There are about half a dozen Muslim writers who seem to support the theory of evolution and who have gone as far as trying to find evidence to support it in the verses of the Qur'ān. Shaikh Abdul Mabud, the Deputy Director-General of the Islamic Academy based at Cambridge, refers to this group (he lists the members of the group) as 'theistic evolutionists'. He writes: 'no matter what the theistic evolutionists think, the truth and authenticity of the Qur'ān does not lie in its being compatible with modern science' (Mabud, 1986:19).

Maurice Bucaille, a French surgeon and a convert to Islam, is a typical example of the 'theistic evolutionists'. His main book *The Bible, the Qur'ān and Science*, has been translated into ten different languages, including English. Another book, *What is the Origin of Man?*, supports human evolution. The final chapters of his book contain numerous quotations from the Qur'ān, which he claims refer to evolution. But Bucaille *bends the meaning* of the Arabic words to suit his own ideas. Wood comments that 'Bucaille proposes new meanings for Qur'ānic words to bring them into accord with modern scientific knowledge, without requiring any standard philological justification.' (Wood 1993:90).

The theory of evolution is without doubt the scientific theory most rejected by Muslims. The author (MRN) once advised a master's degree student, who was a practising teacher from Kuala Lumpur, on the teaching of science in primary schools. During the conversation she said 'we accept all science in Islam, there is no problem; but we reject completely Darwinism, because we believe what it says in the Qur'ān, that man was made by God'. Muslim students in Western countries are taught evolution in schools and colleges. They know the theory, will answer examination questions on it, but privately reject it totally.

9.8   Identifying problems and recognising points of agreement

There is, then, without doubt a tension between Islam and modern science. One thing which needs to be resolved is the conflict that appears to exist between the scientific-like statements in the Qur'ān and the discoveries and paradigms of modern science. There is the belief among Muslims that the Qur'ānic verses are absolutely true; it is also commonly held that the truth conveyed by the verses is independent of time and setting. There is an unwillingness to accept that some statements are true in a contextual rather than universal sense. This reluctance seems unnecessary. For example, when the Qur'ān refers to the universe it seems that a pre-Copernican or Ptolemaic model of the universe is assumed. Such a model, based upon Earth-centred appearances, does not impugn the integrity or truth of the Qur'ān as long as one remembers the cultural and historical context in which the revelation was received, recited and heard. The prime purpose of the Qur'ān is to provoke a response that leads to salvation. The Qur'ān is surely not a scientific treatise, and science is not indispensable for salvation. The two approaches identified by Wood within his Compatibility Thesis, namely the 'compartmental' and 'phenomenological' approaches, seem to offer a hopeful way forwards. It would make sense for Muslims to reflect upon the importance of the fact that the occasions of the 'piecemeal revelation' (*tanzīl*) of the Qur'ān were frequently context-specific and couched in a language that was for the immediate benefit of those hearing them. Such an approach would prevent the extravagant interpretations made by authors such as Bucaille, mentioned in section **9.7** above.

There are two very positive and constructive points of interaction between modern science and Islam, the first stemming from the definition of God as the One (*al-Ahad*) and the other from a definition of the human being, the vicegerent (*khalīfah*) of God.

The doctrine of *tawhīd* ('oneness'), which is so central to Islam, has a parallel that resonates through much of the thinking of modern science. This principle of unity-in-multiplicity is seen universally, in individual organisms, natural systems and in the mathematical formula used to describe their behaviour. Without doubt *tawhīd* is the strongest link between the essence of Islam and the discoveries of modern science.

In recent years, it has become more and more apparent that our planet is suffering from the damaging effects of some kinds of technology and that, unless corrective measures are taken, the future of the human species, and perhaps other forms of life, are threatened. In this context the concept of mankind as *khalīfah*, as being responsible for the stewardship of the world, is very apposite (see **9.2** above). In addition, as new developments take place in science, such as genetic engineering and cloning, many secular as well as religious people are asking for scientists to recognise a value-system and apply it, rather than naïvely believing that their work is neutral and that moral responsibility does not apply to them. The regulation of science by society is something natural to Islam, which has always seen science and technology as justifiable so long as they are for the service of the community and not a threat. Science cannot escape from the value context in which it exists, neither can it ignore the consequences of new discoveries.

9.9   Proposals for the regulation and Islamisation of science

In 1980 a comparative study of Islamic and Western science and technology was inaugurated within the International Federation of Institutes for Advanced Studies (IFIAS) in Solna, Sweden. This was also supported by Islam and the West International in Geneva. In September 1981 a seminar entitled Knowledge and Values took place in Stockholm, organised within IFIAS. Descriptions of the outcomes of the seminar are given by Butt (1991:43–64) and Sardar (1985). The Muslim scientists who gathered for the seminar identified ten 'Islamic concepts', which they put together in a hierarchic structure that would serve as a model of what is distinctive about Islamic science, and which might act as a guide for the development of policies for Islamic science throughout the Muslim world. The model is shown in Figure 9.1.

The pairs of contrasted social values at the bottom of the diagram are self-explanatory. The descending sequence of four concepts at the top of the diagram needs some explanation, especially for Christians. The highest concept in this paradigm of Islamic science is *tawhīd*, the Unity of the universe that we have already discussed above. It is important to remember that *tawhīd* also means 'making one'. It is thus a kind of constructive principle for the model. Ultimately, in practice,

FIGURE 9.1

Tawhīd (Oneness)

|

Khalīfah (Vicegerency)

|

'ibādah (Servanthood/worship)

|

'ilm (Knowledge)

POSITIVE VALUES	NEGATIVE VALUES
Halāl	Harām
(Praiseworthy/Wholesome)	(Blameworthy/Forbidden)
'adl	Zulm
(Socially Just)	(Tyrannical)
Istislāh	diyā'
(In the Public Interest)	(Wasteful)

Ten Islamic concepts for the development of Islamic policies on science.

it means a refusal to see any object, process or law existing as independent from God, the One. To do so is to commit the sin of *shirk* ('association' – i.e. ascribing to a created object a divine attribute, such as independent existence). *Khalīfah* is the divinely ordained function of humanity on Earth. Humans were given the trusteeship of the Earth, indeed of the universe, by God. They must not therefore exploit or pollute the planet. Each man and woman will be required to give an account of their trusteeship, to God at the Last Judgement. The concept of *'ibādah* indicates that a human is a 'slave' (*'abd*) before God, and so is required to worship Him. The same concept applies in fact to the whole creation, which according to the Qur'ān, praises its Creator and 'prostrates itself' (Qur'ān 55:6). After this comes knowledge (*'ilm*), where the application of science begins. The operation of science within society, its funding and the licensing of what it can or cannot do, is regulated by the three pairs of positive and negative principles. The model could, with some modification and development, be incorporated into the Islamic legal system or *Sharī'ah*. Whether or not this will ever happen is, however, another thing altogether.

An alternative approach to the Knowledge and Values IFIAS seminar is shown by the publications of the International Institute of Islamic

Thought (IIIT). This was founded in 1981 and is based in Herndon, Virginia. In 1987 a workshop on the Islamisation of Attitudes and Practices in Science and Technology was held at Herndon. A paper by the president of IIIT (al-'Alwānī, 1989:11), identified three major guidelines to effect Islamisation. Expressed in a simplified form these are:

1. Muslims should accept legitimately proven scientific facts.
2. All knowledge must be integrated into the Islamic (Qur'ānic) scheme of things.
3. Anything in modern science that is contrary to Islam must be rejected.

EXERCISE 9.1

Consider the following: if these precepts were adopted by Christian theologians, how would the debate with science look in terms of Ted Peters' classification in **1.4**?

Islam is a world-wide religion and the Muslim *Ummah* constitutes about one fifth of humankind. There have been a number of conferences in various parts of the *dār-al-Islām*, 'the house of Islam', which are intended to have global influences, affecting the Islamic expression of science and technology in all countries where the religion is found. These include the Organization of Islamic Conference Standing Committee on Scientific and Technological Co-operation (COMSTECH). This was established by the Islamic Summit in 1981 at Islamabad, Pakistan and it is composed of all the member states of the Organisation of Islamic Countries. 'COMSTECH aims at assessment of human and material resources, building on indigenous capabilities in the fields of science and technology, promotion and continuing co-operation and co-ordination in scientific and technological areas of its member states and creation of effective institutional structure for planning research, development and monitoring of scientific and technological activities at Ummah level' (ur-Rahman, 1995). Another example of pan-Islamic co-ordination of science is the conference held at Riyadh in Saudi Arabia in 1981. This conference led to the publication of a number of texts in English which focus on education as well as the 'Islamisation' of science. One of the texts, edited by Faruqi and Nasseef (1981) includes a chapter by al-Hashimi (1981) that deals with the problems of the 'Islamisation' of psychology. The author concludes that 'psychology can be studied in the light of Islamic Studies' (1981:67); he recommends that courses should be provided so that students and lecturers in psychology can gain 'a grounding in Islamic spiritual education, along with a detailed and scientific explanation of the Islamic concept of the human psyche'.

Islam recognises its strong heritage of science, developed during the Golden Age, and in modern times sees the importance of science and technology for economic benefit. Abdus Salam, the 1979 Nobel Prize winner in Physics, wrote:

> so far as the Sciences are concerned, the Muslim Ummah [world-wide Community] has a proud past. For 350 years, from 750 CE to 1100 CE, the Ummah had an absolute world ascendancy in Sciences. From 1100 CE for another 250 years, we shared this ascendancy with the emerging West. From the fifteenth century onwards – the period paradoxically coinciding with the great Empires of Islam (Osmnali in Turkey, Safvi in Iran, Mughal in India) – we progressively lost out. There is no question, but today, of all the civilizations on this planet, science is the weakest in the lands of Islam. The dangers of this weakness cannot be overemphasised since honourable survival of a society depends directly on strength in Science and Technology in the condition of the present age. (Salam, 1987)

Islam has, however, reacted against the way that Western science has developed. Western science, until relatively recently, has shown little if any concern for religion or the social consequences of its activity. The Islamic system, based on the *Sharī'ah*, described above, could perhaps control the more unruly developments of science, although there is no intention in Islamic countries to incorporate such changes into the *Sharī'ah* at the present time. The second reaction, to 'Islamise' Western science, which is perhaps the most popular option amongst many Muslim scientists, is more likely to be successful since it can operate freely in the academic world without the need for action by governments.

9.10   Islam and Darwinism

Finally there is the problem of the theory of evolution. In spite of those who write against it, and who argue that the theory is actually unscientific, because it cannot be falsified (see **4.8.4**), the theory is supported by overwhelming evidence. The theory of evolution may be generally true without the proposed mechanisms being complete descriptions of the way evolution has occurred. The main objection by Muslims is the apparent contradiction by evolutionists of the special creation of humanity. The Qur'ān, like the Book of Genesis, says that humans were created from clay or soil (see Qur'ān 15:26, 23:12, 55:14). The Qur'ān states that 'He created man from argillaceous clay, like pottery' and, more precisely, the creation was from: the 'quintessence of clay' (23:12) and the creative act was completed by a divine breath, thus 'when I have fashioned him and breathed into him of my Spirit, fall ye [the angels] down in obeisance unto him'. Given our modern knowledge, which was not available to the first recipients of the revelation during the seventh century in Mecca, we could interpret these mysterious words in a metaphorical way. However, the idea that humans came into being through the means proposed by Darwin is almost universally rejected by Muslims. The underlying reason for this is that evolutionary theory assumes continuity between the species, in this case between higher apes and humans, whereas special creation emphasises discontinuity and therefore the pre-eminence of humans. It would seem that with regard to organic evolution there is an irreconcilable difference between Islam and modern Western science. As a result of their rejection of Darwinism some Muslims find themselves allied to the special creationist movements, such as the Institute for Creation Research, an academic and research organisation based at Santee, California.

This section has dealt with an apparent stalemate in the interaction of Islam and the main paradigm of modern biology. Perhaps the way out of the dilemma is to re-examine the nature of each component, the nature and *raison d'être* of the Qur'ān and the nature of provisional 'truth' in empirical science. If the Qur'ān and modern science have different objectives then the conflict between them may be more apparent than real. The following quotation from al-Hashimi (1981:58) seems to be a very balanced and constructive point of view which gives respect to both Islam and science; its perceptive simplicity might provide a way forward: 'There can be no doubt that the Qur'ān is *not* [our emphasis] a book of psychological, scientific, geographical or cosmic theory. It is essentially a book of guidance.'

9.11   Conclusion

Muslims regard the Qur'ān as absolutely true. Moreover one of the most important names of Allāh is *al-Haqq*, 'the True'. Modern science attempts to discover the truth about the universe, but defines truth in a provisional sense. That which is 'true' is from a scientific point of view simply more complete and more universally applicable than some other, usually earlier, provisional scientific statement. *The meanings of truth in Islam and modern science are therefore quite different.* If the Qur'ān describes the rising of the Sun or the apparent movements of the planets around the Earth then these are certainly true statements because the Qur'ān is referring to the human perception of these events. al-Hashimi's remark (in section **9.10**) about the nature and purpose of the Qur'ān as a book of guidance is very apposite – since the Qur'ān uses the context of human understanding, in every respect and in every historical context, to make its points, which are always aimed at the destiny of humans who must one day come face to face with their Lord. Sufficient evidence has been presented in this chapter to show that it is possible for a Muslim to find a way through many of the difficulties in the encounter between modern science and Islam. Each needs to be treated with respect and understood in its own context. The flourishing of science in mediaeval Islam shows how supportive Islamic society can be to scientific developments. There is evidence that similar developments in the areas of science and technology continue today. It is also possible, at least in theory, for an Islamic society to control the destructive problems that may arise from some scientific discoveries and techniques by means of a system based upon the *Sharī'ah*. However, we note finally that in the interaction between modern science and Islam one striking contradiction remains: that is the question of the origin of humans.

BIBLIOGRAPHICAL NOTE

Two texts and translations of the Qur'ān are given below. The translations chosen are mostly from Pickthall's bilingual version, although this author (MRN) has also used the Yusuf 'Ali version. In some cases MRN offers his own translation of certain words using, for authority, J. G. Hava's *Al-Faraid: Arabic–English Dictionary* (Beirut: Catholic Press, 1964) and Hans Wehr's *Dictionary of Modern Written Arabic* (Ithaca, NY: Spoken Language Services Inc., 1976)

Qur'ān *The Holy Qur'ān. Text Translation and Commentary by 'Abdullah Yusuf 'Ali.* (Brentwood, MD: Amana Corporation)

Qur'ān *The Meaning of the Glorious Qur'ān translated by M. M. Pickthall* (Karachi: Taj Company) (undated bilingual edition)

FURTHER READING

Butt, N. (1991) *Science and Muslim Societies* (London: Grey Seal Books)

al-Ghazzali (1983) *Inner Dimensions of Islamic Worship*, transl. from the Ihya' by Muhtar Holland (Leicester: The Islamic Foundation)

Lings, M. (1985) *Muhammad: his life based on the earliest sources* (London: Islamic Texts Society and George Allen & Unwin)

Nasr, S. H. (1980) *Living Sufism* (London: Unwin Paperbacks)

Sardar, Z. (1989) *Explorations in Islamic Science* (London: Mansell)

Schuon, F. (1995) *Understanding Islam* (Bloomington, IL: World Wisdom Books)

Chapter 10

Technology and Christianity

10.1 Introduction

The relation between science and Christianity has been extensively explored by contemporary authors, particularly in relation to the physical sciences, astronomy, evolution and genetic engineering. The relation of technology to Christianity has been less well covered, and there are relatively few books in university libraries on the subject.

This apparent neglect of the subject cannot be defended in a technological age, where education, industry, government, health, agriculture and communication all affect and are affected by technology. An enormous proportion of UK government expenditure is on technological development, and an increasing number of UK university staff in science faculties are engaged in technological research. No discussion of the compelling issues of today – the environment and pollution, health, war and weapons, famine and poverty, leisure and creativity – can take place without reference to technology. And yet despite the formidable resources of technology, humans cannot agree about what is to be done about these problems. This chapter is an attempt at the difficult task of introducing the relation between technology and Christianity. It would take a whole book, rather than a single chapter, to do justice to the subject, and therefore only selected aspects can be presented. This chapter concentrates on some of the contemporary and controversial theological approaches to technology.

10.2 What is technology?

The general public, and many scientists, draw a distinction between so-called pure science and technology. Pure science is seen as the pursuit of truth for its own sake, whereas technology is thought of as the application of science to practical problems. Unfortunately, the history of science and technology shows that this is not what has actually been going on. For example, the steam engine was developed by trial and error prior to the Industrial Revolution in Britain, and was in widespread use before there was any satisfactory theory of thermodynamics to predict power output or other aspects of the machines' properties. (A good discussion of this area is given by Mathias, 1972.) Similarly, Marconi's development of the wireless telegraph anticipated the elaboration of a complete relevant physical theory (Basalla, 1988:102). In order to understand technology's relation to science and to religion, we must first define it. Basalla does so in terms of the devices or artefacts produced. He says:

> The artefact – not scientific knowledge, not the technical community, nor social and economic factors – is central to technology and technological change ... the final product of an innovative technological activity is typically an addition to the made world; a stone hammer, a clock, an electric motor. (Basalla, 1988:30)

However, modern technology often involves the novel use of existing devices, so that a more general definition is needed. Further, Basalla's approach does not consider the goal-directed nature of technology. A more satisfactory approach is that of Ravetz (1971), who defines a technological problem as an investigation directed at finding a way of making a specified practical change in the world. This may or may not require the assistance of new pieces of scientific theory, or result in a new physical device. However, the success of the technological project always depends on meeting the practical needs posed by the initial problem. A scientific project, on the other hand, is not tied to any particular outcome, as illustrated by, for instance, the discovery of penicillin.

However, when we speak of technology, we speak of more than a technical problem whose solution is some kind of means, or way of doing things. Technology in agriculture may call to mind, not a plough, but tractors and combine harvesters. The term technology implies an increase in power over the physical environment which humanity has experienced only in the last century and a half. It also implies improvement or progress of some kind. Western societies tend to consider that modern technologies provide the 'best' of a range of possible ways of doing things. It is important to notice that in fact the choice is not made in the laboratory or the factory. When domestic refrigeration was first developed, both gas and electric refrigerators were made. Gas refrigerators were cheaper to construct and run. They would have been the technology of choice, were it not for the economic factors that gave the electrical companies in the USA at the time the power to limit research and promotion of gas 'fridges, and to fund the development of electric 'fridges instead. The result is the world dominance of electric 'fridges.

Technology in modern society is, then, a phenomenon in which perceived practical problems are solved by increasingly powerful means, chosen by complex social processes. It is clear that values and goals must be implicated in those processes. Religions promote certain values and goals, and we may therefore expect to find relationships between the practice of religion and the use of technology in society.

10.3   Is technology good or bad?

Many historians and social scientists have examined the role of technology in modern society, and have come to differing conclusions about its value. The general public in Western Europe is ambivalent about technology. On the one hand, we applaud the technological contribution to modern healthcare; what we eat is dependent on food technology and what we wear is produced via textile technology. We welcome the progress brought by the electronic revolution. We recognise that technology benefits poorer parts of the world. Clean water, improved transportation and communication enable better education, healthcare and economic development. An optimistic view of technology stresses that such physical benefits lead to a reduction in human suffering and an increase in human happiness. They also bring an increase in human freedom and power which is seen as good in itself. Authors such as E. Mesthene (1967) are quite clear that technology is benign and makes the world a better place.

On the other hand, there is public concern that, for example, the global environment is being damaged by modern technology. Pollution by the enormous number of motor vehicles, by large scale industrial operations releasing dangerous chemicals, and by radioactivity from the nuclear industry, all contribute to environmental damage. There are many other anxieties about technology. The public is suspicious of medical technology applied to human reproduction. There has been a lot of controversy about test-tube babies and the new genetics (on the latter see Chapter 11). Authors such as Langdon Winner (1977) have claimed that technology is out of control and is threatening to be destructive for humanity.

The existence of these two kinds of view makes it plain that questions of value surround technology. Religions are sources of value in our society, both historically and in terms of present day interactions. We may therefore ask what kind of historical interactions there have been between technology and Christianity, before we look more closely at the question of technology today.

10.4   Technology and Christianity in the history of Western Europe

Two examples will be sufficient to show the breadth of the connections between technology and Christianity in Western Europe. The twelfth century was remarkable for a tremendous surge and development in one area of technology – that of building. The evidence for this still stands in the form of the great cathedrals of Europe. These building projects occupied much of the energy and effort of the cities and towns where they took place. Local craftsmen and labourers were employed directly, and artisans received commissions of various kinds, so that the church authorities acquired a degree of social control over the community via such projects. However, the cathedrals were more than monuments to church power. They were also vehicles for the extension of technical possibilities. Arnold Pacey has provided particularly acute analyses of social and religious aspects of technology, in both historical and contemporary contexts. In his book *The Maze of Ingenuity* (1992), Pacey refers to the pursuit of a *technical ideal*, and gives as an example some of the issues in the building of Durham Cathedral, begun in 1093. The practical problem at Durham was to construct a space that was both high and wide out of stone. Islamic builders of the period knew how to construct stone domes, but their techniques were not known to the builder of Durham. Previous buildings had often had wooden roofs, but stone was more fireproof and aesthetically more satisfying. The problem was solved by the construction of a network of stone ribs to support the curved stone vault that covered the space between the vertical piers of the nave. This provided the necessary additional strength to hold the vault in place, and made scaffolding easier since the vault could be filled in section by section. The networked ribs formed arches, which crossed the building diagonally and transversely. The diagonal ones were traditionally shaped, and semicircular. But the transverse ones had to be pointed to fit, and proved to be the precursor to the famous Gothic arch. However, the weight of the roof thus supported was too great to be held by the existing design of vertical piers, partly because the rib vault introduces a greater force thrusting outward, and the building was buttressed from the outside, with the first flying buttresses. The building of this cathedral, a project of religion, resulted in technological innovations which then spread rapidly through Europe.

The means by which such technology was disseminated were also connected closely to the religion of the period. Between 1112, when he came to the little-known abbey of Cîteaux, and 1153, when he died, St Bernard presided over a movement that founded 340 Cistercian abbeys in the period. Building methods were included in the information that was passed from the mother house to the new foundations, so that tunnel vaulting was built in Fountains Abbey only seven years after its appearance in 1140 at Clairvaux. The abbeys also used water mills, and harnessed water power for hammer forges and textile fulling mills. All of these technologies were passed on from place to place, spreading into local economies, by the agency of the monks. The reasons for their use of technology did not initially include a profit motive. They had a practical way of life, based on rules of conduct drawn up for spiritual reasons, which emphasised work as an activity valued by God. St Benedict's famous dictum was *Labore est Orare* – to work is to pray. Monastic technology served spiritual ideals. But there were others in society, merchants, farmers, craftsmen, for whom a profit was a significant requirement and who were under economic pressure to utilise technological improvements. In particular, the cloth trade of Northern Europe and Italy demonstrates such groups. Pacey asks whether the technological advances in Europe from the eleventh to the fourteenth centuries derive from the idealism of the Church or the needs of commerce. In the great push to build cathedrals following Durham, he sees the evidence as pointing to religious idealism as the major factor. As increasing wealth lead to the emergence of an educated class apart from the clerical and monastic leaders of society, so the number of cathedral-building initiatives grew. Between 1150 and 1280, eighty cathedrals were built or rebuilt in France, many in the wealthier cloth towns. If the *motive* was religious idealism, rather than profit, what were the *effects* on the technology employed? There were enormous advances in the capacities of the builders. Buildings were developed to be taller than ever before. The techniques of using the flying buttresses were refined and extended. The introduction of window tracery enabled bigger and bigger windows to be constructed. Pacey observes that the builders were never satisfied, always trying, for the glory of God, to better their handiwork. He suggests that this spirit of questing, and continuous innovation in pursuit of improvement, came to be infused into the technology to which we are heirs in the present age.

Interesting examples of other interactions between religion and technology can be seen later, in the sixteenth and seventeenth centuries. Pacey gives an illuminating account of mining and mineral technology after the Reformation. Martin Luther's father was a miner, and the region of Saxony where Luther lived was an important mining area. Attempts at giving mineral technology intellectual respectability had already been made, particularly by George Bauer, writing as Georgius Agricola (1494–1555). Bauer wrote, in scholarly Latin, the definitive account of his time of metal assaying and smelting techniques. He anticipated the emerging scientific approach of the seventeenth century with his emphasis on actual observations. But his work was not directly accessible to the miners of his time, since they did not read Latin. However, there is evidence that it was popularised, not by any obvious industrial or commercial interest, but by Lutheran pastors. Johann Mathesius included comments on mining and minerals in a book of sermons, and Pacey quotes a miner's hymn of the time. Pacey accounts for this by referring to the Reformation understanding of the 'priesthood of all believers', which consecrated the most humble human activity as a vocation of equal value to God, and which sought to remove religion from its association with abuses of wealth and privilege. Hence the need to value and improve mining technology, in order to recognise and enhance the contribution of the miners. Similar ideas for practical improvement in technologies generally were put forward by Francis Bacon (1561–1626), and Comenius (1592–1671) and Glauber (1604–70) in Eastern Europe and Germany. They represent a new tendency in Western intellectual life, which stemmed from the religious motive of benefitting the 'ordinary people'. Their lives would be bettered if they had improved technical education. Pacey observes that many of the subsequent attempts to bring this about were associated with Protestant groups opposed to excessive privilege in society. This motive of service to the community gives way to nationalist and mercantile ideals in the eighteenth century, only to reappear in some of the philanthropy of the nineteenth century.

Religion, then, can be shown to have provided motives for the development of technologies in Europe long before the industrial revolution, and to have influenced the kinds of developments taking place, as well as shaping attitudes to the practical transformation of the world.

10.5 The technical ideal: does technology have inherent values?

We normally think of technology as being, like science, about 'facts'. Since technology is concerned with producing defined practical changes in the material world, we suppose that it is about practical facts. However, on close examination, the situation is more complicated. For example, the technology involved in the construction of passenger aircraft cabins has been extended in recent years following a serious fire on an aircraft at Manchester airport. The discussion of this reveals two sets of assertions. The first set are uncontested and agreed by everyone. Plastic burns, producing toxic smoke. Smoke is dark and impairs visibility. Plastic is lightweight, reducing the load needed to be lifted for flight. And so on. The second set of assertions cause disagreements. Wool is a better upholstery fabric because it burns less easily – but it is heavier, more difficult to clean and more expensive. Smoke hoods would enable passengers to breathe during a fire – but they are bulky, difficult to put on and would slow people's movement. The first set of agreed assertions are 'facts'; the second set are not. It turns out to be the case that we have already gone through some process of evaluation and agreeing about a situation before we pronounce it to be a 'fact'. They include all kinds of things that we would normally take for granted, such as, in the example above, the concept that if smoke is 'toxic' then it is bad to expose people to it. Hidden in the 'facts' are assumptions that seem quite obvious in a simple example (the idea that humans are desirable, that it is not good to poison or kill them), but which are not mere observations about the world. These assumptions are related to values, the scales of desirability or worth by which we judge our activities.

Value can be understood as monetary worth, or as someone's ultimate reason for the actions of their life, or as a particular feature by which alternative courses of action can be chosen. Sociologists observe that what is valued is closely related to what is understood as good. Objects can also be valued, whether artistic, technological or religious, whether simple or complex. The process of realising values is difficult, since we may well want several good things at once. It may be necessary for practical reasons to put things in order of goodness or desirability, and only then begin the process of evaluation or judgement. Sociologists describe the way in which different groups of people organised in different societies can also have values that are shared within a group, but which may differ between groups. This feature of shared value is the basis of culture, and our values are culturally conditioned to the extent that we are exposed to values as practised and shared by the community we live in.[1]

The facts of modern technology are shaped by the values of culture just as those of the old cathedral builders were. The significant values we may note include most obviously the concept of efficiency. This is difficult to define, but implies increasing power; we can do more with less. Closely related is speed; a new technology is always faster in performing its task. A technology may embody negative values; every feature of a land mine is engineered in line with its purpose as an agent for maiming and killing humans. A 'better' land mine is one that kills more people more often. Other values are less obvious; the microwave and television are both devices that tend to reduce human interaction. It is not possible to cook a complete meal for a family faster in a micro-wave than by conventional means. The microwave is sold primarily as a quick means of cooking. Consequently, any group of people who rely on one for their meals develop the habit of eating sequentially, at separate times, rather than together. The conversation and interaction associated with a shared meal is reduced. Similarly, the use of a television in the main social space of a house may lead to a loss of conversation between people, because their visual attention and hearing are claimed by the television.

[1] See also **1.20, 11.8–11.10** on values.

10.6 The 'defining' role of technology

Many authors have pointed out that a particular technology may change human perceptions of possible behaviour. Lewis Mumford (1895–1990), in *Technics and Civilization* (1946) famously asserted that the invention of the mechanical clock, not the steam engine, was the key to the industrial age. Mumford argued that this was because the clock permitted human behavioural organisation that had not been possible before it, and this was because it redefined the human sense of time. Before the widespread use of reliable clocks, time was defined mostly in terms of the cycle of night and day, with its interaction with human biology, and the seasons. People experienced time in terms of time to eat, time to sleep, time to plough, time to make preserves, and so on. Time was structured by human activity – patterns of births, marriages and deaths. There was no feeling that each day or week should have the same quantity of activity arranged in it; people were variably active as the time and place demanded. The times of the seasons were perceived in terms of their interaction with human activity, so that spring, for a shepherd, was when the lambs appeared. This was not always on the same date, and so time was 'historical', about sequences of meaning which were both cyclical and cumulative. Periods of birth, growth, decay and death succeeded each other, and each passing layer of memory built upon the previous one. The clock disrupted this by introducing a regular, measured concept of time, not in step with the natural world, and independent of human activity. People no longer ate when they were hungry, but at the clock-determined 'meal-time'.

This new measured time allowed an enormous development in technology in terms of moving devices. The concept and means of regular measurement of time permits synchronisation of processes, reproducibility and standardisation of processes and regularity. A windmill provides numerous examples of this. For instance, mechanical synchronisation allows the hoppers to the stones to open as the sacks of grain are inverted at the top of the hoist, and timed grinding produces an equal particle size so that all sacks of flour are standardised and have similar cooking properties. Mumford claimed that the exploitation of these aspects of mechanically measured time was essential to the industrial revolution, and its inception had further effects on the human appreciation of time. With the advent of factory labour, time became something that could be bought or sold. The concept of free time, or leisure, appeared as the time that the labourer kept back for him or her self, and did not sell to the employer. Thus the new piece of technology, the clock, is associated with an alteration in human concepts which could not have taken place otherwise. This is referred to as the 'defining' role of a technology, which is to say, the way in which that technology causes human activity to be redefined.

The other particularly significant defining technology in Western Europe has been the invention of printing. Marshall McLuhan (1911– 80) characterised the stage of Western culture prior to printing as 'hearing humanity'. Words were immediately ephemeral, an instan- taneous experience, and there could be no developed sense of history. Printing changed this radically. Language became associated with writing, which, being permanent, could be analysed, pondered on, categorised and generally become the object of intellectual activity. McLuhan claimed that this caused a cultural explosion, in which the ear and eye were dissociated, and in parallel with this, there was a separation of the emotions and the intellect. In the twentieth century, the medium of the television and video screen call for a reintegration of the senses. The two-dimensional, indistinct image they project, smaller than the objects represented, require the viewer to participate in imagination, to fill up the gaps and make the shapes real in the mind. The input for this is both visual and aural, so that once again, the emotional impact of sights and sounds becomes significant. The act of intellectual analysis becomes harder and may be perceived as irrelevant. The controversy surrounding McLuhan's many contributions does not detract from the value of the observations he made on the defining roles of these everyday technologies.

If we look at the changes in human lives in Britain between the beginning of the nineteenth and the end of the twentieth centuries, we can see numerous examples of the defining effects of new technologies. The pedestrian-oriented street plan of the old city centres, with narrow closes and little market places interspersed, has been replaced with huge ring roads and out-of-town shopping centres, because the car has become a major defining technology. We shop, eat and socialise at a distance from our homes, in a manner that would have been un- recognisable to Jane Austen's characters, for instance. The advent of electricity, and lighting in the home and street, has changed the character of night completely. Our generation 'goes out' at night, when any sensible Victorian would have gone to bed. Our homes have changed, under the influence of the technologies of war and building. This is because the craftsman-built homes of the nineteenth century middle classes, which accommodated large families with grown-up children and servants, were mostly located in the cities and took the brunt of the extensive bombing in the Second World War. A large proportion of British housing stock was damaged or destroyed. In the post-war period, there was a concerted attempt to rehouse those affected by this, and modern building technology, with prefabricated and standardised components, was used. This gave rise to the small, two- or three-bedroom semis and the blocks of flats that are part of our urban landscape today. But the new houses have no room for an aging grand-parent, or an adult child. They have no large parlour to accommodate a Sunday gathering of the extended family, or even a piano. So many of the social patterns of the previous generation are now an impossibility, and society has to struggle to find new ways of providing social contact for old people, or housing for young single people. Later on we will look at some of the theological implications of the defining role of technology, and look at some other examples.

10.7   Does the origin of a technology have implications for its effects?

A major part of the definition of technology includes the solving of a given practical problem. Does the nature of the problem set control the particular values implicit in the means for its solution? Several authors have looked at this issue, and many have noted that the origin of a technology can be closely associated with particular defining effects. That is to say, the kind of problems to be solved are indeed associated with specific ways of revaluing aspects of humanity.

David Lyon has referred to the way in which modern electronics began in wartime (1988:26–27). The principles behind the silicon semiconductor emerged during work on radar. Later, the need to process information from radar became pressing. British radar stations were initially linked by voice and manual systems to military headquarters. In the USA in the Cold War, digital processing equipment was installed to speed up telephonic transfer. The needs of wartime code-breaking also contributed to the development of computation. The early valve-operated computers that were developed for these kinds of task were structured from the beginning with speed and security as prominent features. When the Bell Laboratories developed the transistor, they recognised its defence potential straightaway. Even today, the largest proportion of government funding for electronics research and development goes to the defence industry. The computers of the present still retain the initial capacities for speed and secrecy. However, this has proved to be at the expense of intelligence and intercommunication. It is still very difficult to get different computers to communicate, and fortunes have been made in the computer industry by those who have introduced simple 'networking' approaches. The great speed with which computers operate can now be either beneficial or detrimental, depending on the outcome. We may be glad that a police computer in the UK can pick out the alias of a confidence trickster in minutes, permitting his arrest and detention, but the same kinds of computer system allow police in countries under tyranny to pick out the names of political opponents or human rights activists. People then go quickly not to justified trial but to unjust detention or worse. Is such speed always a good thing? We may at least begin to question some of the values that seem to be associated with the adoption and promotion of new technologies in our society.

10.8 How do the values uncovered in contemporary technology relate to religious values? Mumford, Tillich and Reinhold Niebuhr

Lewis Mumford drew some explicitly religious conclusions from his work on the emergence of technology. He concluded that by the twentieth century, the accumulated effects of technology were re-defining previous religious ideals in new terms, in terms of the machine. He asserted:

> The machine was the substitute for . . . the Christian ideals of grace and redemption. The machine came forth as the new demi-urge that was to create a new heaven and a new earth: or at least, as a new Moses, that was to lead the barbarous humanity into the promised land. (1946:58)

Mumford claims that the religious reasons for human activity, such as had motivated the mediaeval monks and the cathedral builders of Europe, have been replaced by a belief in technology as a good in itself. This is often linked with a belief in 'progress' as an inevitable and beneficial consequence of the introduction of technology.

Certainly, these issues were controversial in the first part of the twentieth century, but relatively few theologians addressed the issues of theology and technology as such. Some were very positive about the benefits of technology, such as those associated with the Social Gospel movement, in line with the general religious optimism of the USA.

Paul Tillich (1886–1965) saw technology as an integral part of human culture. He gave culture and human experience a significant role in his theology, because it provided the questions and problems to which biblical revelation provided correlative answers. This does not mean that he endorsed all technological thinking in an unqualified way, but he did see it as constitutive of human experience. Nevertheless, he spoke of the open nature of technical possibility as being the root of conflict, because the possibility of doing something, the means, could be disconnected from the reasons for doing it, the ends. He wrote:

> This leads to tension from which many conflicts of our contemporary culture arise: the perversion of the relation of means and ends by the unlimited character of technical possibilities. Means become ends simply because they are possible ... Such distortion may affect a whole culture in which the production of means becomes the end beyond which there is no end. This problem, intrinsic in technical culture, does not deny the significance of technology but shows its ambiguity. (Tillich, 1978:61–62)

This concern for the proper relation of ends and means is also found in theological writers as different as William Temple and Jacques Ellul (see **10.9** below).[2]

The other significant American theologian to have commented on technology is Reinhold Niebuhr (1892–1971).[3] He is sometimes cited as having a positive assessment of technology. He was opposed to pacifism in the cold war, and argued for the moral legitimacy of nuclear weapons. But this information in itself does not tell us about the criteria Niebuhr used in his assessment of such technology, and his actual arguments were theological. He certainly took science and technology seriously, and in an essay on history and science, he remarked:

[2] See also **1.20** – 'can', the possible, does not imply 'ought', the imperative.
[3] For an assessment of Niebuhr see Tinsley (1973).

Christian culture was wrong in insinuating the specific insights and prejudices of a particular age into the 'credo', while modern science was wrong in assuming that its descriptions of detailed historical sequences in nature and history offered an adequate insight into the meaning of life. Thus we have been subjected for centuries to a conflict between a theology which had become a bad science, and a science which implied an unconscious theology . . . a theology of propositions about the ultimate meaning of life. (Quoted in Tinsley, 1973:89)

Niebuhr regarded science and technology as part of the contemporary culture which he believed should be subjected to theological critique. His attitude to technology was not therefore one of inevitable approval, and he was sometimes quite pessimistic about it.

10.9   Ends and means: Ellul and William Temple

However, the most extensive and important writer on theology and technology in the twentieth century is probably the French theologian, Jacques Ellul (1912–94). He was very much influenced by the theology of Karl Barth (see **2.6**). He has therefore a very clear view of the world and humanity as created by and dependent upon God. The purpose of all creation is to serve and glorify God, and to be redeemed by God. This redemption is effected by the life, death and resurrection of Jesus Christ, which manifests in human history the fulfilment which God promises for the universe at the end of time. Jesus Christ is both the mechanism, or 'means' of redemption, and the purpose or 'ends' of it. This is very important for Ellul's understanding of the difference between means (how things are done) and ends (why things are done). The shortest account of his theological views on this can be found in his book, *The Presence of the Kingdom* (first published in 1948). He says:

The first truth which must be remembered is that for Christians there is no dissociation between the end and the means. It is a Greek ethical idea which has caused this division. The point at which we ought to start is that in the work of God the ends and the means are identical. Thus when Jesus Christ is present the Kingdom has 'come upon us' . . . Jesus Christ in his incarnation appears as God's means, for the salvation of man and for the establishment of the Kingdom of God, but where Jesus Christ is, there also is this salvation and this Kingdom. (Ellul, 1989:64)

Ends and means, goals and the ways to them, are central concerns in theology. Christian theology supplies a framework within which Christians and their communities, the churches, can assess how well they are living out their traditions and witness. This involves discussing and defining the goals of the Christian community, as well as setting out criteria for their attainment.

Ellul argues that technology has provided a transformation of world-view, and has given modern society a new basis in terms of such ends and means. He says:

> The first great fact that emerges from our civilization is that today everything has become 'means'. There is no longer an 'end'; we do not know whither we are going. We have forgotten our collective ends, and we possess great means: we set huge machines in motion in order to arrive nowhere. (1989:51)

This new set of assumptions govern social, political and economic life, and he refers to it as 'La Technique'; I think the best translation would be 'Technological World-View'. These assumptions are in no sense identical with any technology itself; they are the sum of the conceptual changes resulting from the defining and formative effects of technology. Ellul has devoted several books to discussing this, the most important of which are *The Technological Society* (1964) and *The Technological Bluff* (1990). According to Ellul, the Technological World-View is the set of values initially ushered in by and associated with technology, but now detached from it, and providing an independent basis for value in the modern world. He describes several features characteristic of it. It includes assumptions that:

- normalisation or standardisation is desirable;
- increased speed is desirable;
- increased power is desirable;
- change is good in itself;
- growth or extension is good in itself;
- only rational or calculating logic is acceptable;
- all claims to value should be excluded – argument should be disinterested.

All of these assumptions are commonly linked to ideas of efficiency or effectiveness, and are recognisably part of public discussion about all aspects of society. Subjects such as government initiatives to bring certain kinds of technology into education, plans to reorganise aspects of the health service, or inquiries into road and rail transport services, are debated against a background of these assumed values.

These are all implicit values in technology that have been noted by other authors, such as those cited in the previous section. However, Ellul goes further than other authors in the claims he makes for the interaction between these values. Ellul argues that the grouping of these assumptions into this Technological World-View is not a random process, but can be described with significant aspects. He claims that it is:

- rational;
- artificial or constructed;
- autonomous with respect to value or authority;
- self-determining but not directed to an end.

In other words, the set of assumptions is not drawn from nature or given in any sense, but is a human creation. It does not allow for critique by any value system, such as religion, or for control by any authority, such as the state.

From a theological perspective, Ellul has serious objections to both the content of the Technological World-View and to its constitution and function in the modern world. These objections centre on this question of ends and means. The question asked is always 'Why?' 'Why do we do this – for what reason, or purpose, to what end?' The end can then be evaluated; we ask, is it good or bad, desirable or undesirable, because for Christianity, only the good is desirable. The effect of the Technological World-View is to replace such debate and evaluation of the ends with a discussion of the means. The question 'How?' replaces the question 'Why?' Evaluation – the weighing up of issues on a scale of good and bad – is specifically excluded from the Technological World-View. The search for power is unrestricted. Christianity restricts it by claiming that only God has ultimate power, and it is wrong for humans to seek it. We see terrible results whenever they do. The unqualified acceptance that greater speed, complexity and growth is always desirable in technology has obvious problems in relation to environmental concerns. Complex technologies consume energy and physical resources which could be better conserved if slower, simpler ways of doing things were used. The assumption that logical or calculation rationality is objective, scientific and 'better' than reasoning which includes value judgements is also a problematic one. Such rational arguments have been used, for instance, to argue for compulsory euthanasia for the mentally retarded, and indeed, this has been put into practice on such grounds. But society clearly cannot be organised on such amoral principles, because they quickly become immoral.

Ellul is easily misunderstood. It is essential to see the theological basis for his approach. He is not arguing for the abolition of technology, but for the reintroduction of the concepts of purpose, goal and value into the way we debate and use technology.[4]

It is worthy of note that William Temple (1881–1944), the Anglican Archbishop of Canterbury who had a great influence on the development of the British Labour Party during the Second World War, expressed some related ideas in his short book *Christianity and Social Order*, first published in 1942. He was dealing with the practical consequences of Christianity in terms of contemporary political, social and economic organisation. Nevertheless, the principles he invoked are still, if not even more, relevant in our present society, accustomed as we are to the technical fix as a solution for all ills. Temple asserted that all Christian claims or comments on society had to begin with an understanding of God as Creator, as having a divine purpose of love for all creation, and as having created humanity as part of that purpose. Consequently, humanity has a role to play and a destiny with God. All social organisation exists to empower humans in working towards that destiny. Consequently, he wrote:

> the means (industry, commerce) is to be judged by its success in promoting or facilitating the true ends of human life . . . above all, happy human relationships. (Temple, 1976:83)

He commented on the effect of the nineteenth-century expansion of technology:

> The immense possibilities opened up by the application of 'power'
> – water, steam and electricity – to industrial production so
> fascinated men that they ceased to ask what was the purpose of

[4] We take up this theme in our discussion of the use of biotechnology in Chapter 11.

this vast mass of production. It tended to be an end in itself. It was no longer subordinated to the general scheme of a complete human life in which it should be a part. (1976:85)

It is interesting that his remarks converge so much on the theological position of Ellul.

10.10   Current issues: technology and the information revolution

Technology has advanced even further since Temple's time, and the electronic revolution in computing and information technology has led to our age being described as the 'silicon society'. There may be quite specific theological implications associated with this. David Lyon has commented, from a Reformed perspective close to that of Ellul, about the possible redefinition of what it means to be human by the advent of electronic and computer technology, particularly in his book *The Information Society* (1988) . This may be happening in several ways. The widespread model of the computer has given rise to words which are now applied to humans – children particularly have been observed to do this. They speak of being 'programmed' to do something; of 'interfacing' with someone; they define themselves in terms of the similarities and differences between themselves and the computer. Computers also limit possibilities; even educational programmes will only display certain information, and only in a certain way; the Web pages of the Internet contain material that may or may not be true, but the use of the computer makes investigation of claims much more difficult. Computers may permit the previously unpermissable; the violent war games and interactive pornography now available separate the viewers' experience from the possible conse-quences of their actions.

David Lyon also sees important political consequences from the widespread use of the new technology, because it is not actually avail-able to every one. Poor underclasses are being created in the wealthier West, and developing countries are excluded more completely from participation in the electronic revolution. Computers distance those in powerful bureaucracies, looking at a screen in an office, from those whom they are meant to serve, enable or protect. There is the separation of the end, the recipient, whether a bank customer or a job seeker, from the means, the decision-making person, by the interposing of the machine. Lyon points to a reduction in human interaction as a significant consequence of this technology, and like Ellul, he sees this as negative in terms of the Gospel. He takes the work of bringing in the Kingdom very seriously. He argues that hope in God's future fulfilment and redemption of the world is a key feature of Christianity. Because of this, it follows that Christians cannot place their hope in technology itself, as he fears many societies are doing, but must hope in God. The consequence of this will be that Christians will be free to evaluate technology, to use it as a good servant, but not to allow it to become their master.

John Habgood, the former Archbishop of York, has also raised some concerns about the concept of information, particularly in the context of the Internet, in his Priestland Lecture for radio in 1994. Text and figures can be transmitted at speed and over distance; it can be edited or altered at will; it can be seen by anyone with sufficient economic power to gain access. However, such information is not subject to any process of critique and evaluation, such as takes place in conventional education. There is no guide present when such information is encountered. In a word, wisdom is absent, because mere possession of knowledge is not enough. Skills of assessment and judgement are required for wisdom, and they have to be learned through human interactions. Lord Habgood suggests that an increasing dependence on electronic means of communication may make us better informed, but we risk not being any wiser.[5]

10.11 Two contemporary theologians' responses to technology: Barbour and Susan White

There have been accounts of technology and theology which have been less critical than those cited so far; Ian Barbour provides one such view in *Ethics in an Age of Technology* (1992). Much of the book is devoted to a discussion of particular areas of technology such as agriculture, energy and electronics. He reviews a wide range of topics, and therefore does not have time to explore specific issues very deeply. The book attempts an objectivist stance; it begins with a survey of attitudes to technology as either favourable or unfavourable, but it does not address the difficulty of treating such a subject from a context-free position. Hence

[5] Again, we take up the theme of wisdom in Chapter 11, especially **11.9–11.10**.

it tends throughout to the social optimism that was a feature of earlier American thought. Barbour does consider biblical contributions to the critique of technology alongside philosophical and humanist perspectives, but does not offer any evaluation of these different perspectives. He commends process theology as particularly relevant to present crises, and this kind of theology is very different from any of the other Christian theological approaches mentioned in this article. In particular, process thought does not understand the role of Jesus Christ as pivotal in the ways that Tillich, Niebuhr, Ellul or Temple would. It has a much more positive view of human activity than other strands in Protestant theology. It sees more of a philosophical basis to religious truth than other theologies, and is usually associated with a universalist approach to other religions or value systems.

The difficulty with Barbour's use of this approach is that his overall optimism prevents engagement with the issues raised by other authors. He summarises his concerns in terms of the requirement for means by which technology can be directed to meet basic human need, research can be prioritised for the benefit of the majority, technology can be made environmentally friendly, work can be made satisfying and democratic control of technology ensured (1992:243–44). These ideals are assumed to be attainable without qualitative changes in technological thinking. But this very point is itself contested by the other authors I have cited. Further, Barbour is demonstrating a technical form of argument as he does this, since he concentrates on the means by which technology is to be controlled, shaped, directed, etc. He does not engage in any serious argument as to what the specific ends of technology are or should be, because his theological commitment to a basic common truth in all thought systems does not allow for actual critique. It is therefore very difficult to bring Barbour into relation with the contemporary discussion of value and technology.

A more recent contribution to the question of theology and technology comes from Susan White, who has written from the interesting perspective, not of systematic or philosophical theology, or political theology, but of the liturgy. Since this is of immense practical importance to Christianity, her book *Christian Worship and Technological Change* (1994) is significant. White asks what kind of challenges to Christian worship are being presented by the pervasive technology of our period. She argues that the conventional view of the liturgist is dominated by the problems of the historic transmission of text, and the role of ritual in liturgy. Both of these areas present obvious problems of cross-cultural understandings from the perspective of the technological society, and White notes:

> If the 'modern technological person' is discussed at all in the current climate, he or she tends to be discussed as a liturgical or ritual 'problem' . . . many theologians would subscribe, at least implicitly, to this idea that modern technology and technological ways of thinking are unalterably opposed to the nature of the religious quest. (1994:31)

White observes that while Christian mission has taken up the concept of inculturation, the expression of religious value in the symbols and practices of specific local cultures, this has not been extended to a recognition of the technological nature of present Western culture. Few hymns mention coal, steel or electricity; God's world is one of green hills with sheep on, and the factories are 'dark Satanic mills'. She proposes three issues through which this situation might be addressed. The first is the question of what technologies have actually affected or changed worship and liturgy. For example, the building of the great cathedrals and the invention of printing mark two obvious historical irruptions of technology into liturgy. Her second issue is the question of how these technological developments have shaped the subsequent forms of liturgy. Her third question is related to the concerns expressed by Lewis Mumford. She asks whether human technological self-understanding and social practice allows participation any more in a liturgy that developed with a pre-technological understanding of what it means to be human. Susan White gives details of some of the answers to these questions. She notes that the introduction of written script was associated with a decline in extempore community prayer. The introduction of the printing press has had an enormous effect on Western societies. White summarises its effects on worship:

> The press was an indispensable agent in the fracture of the Church's liturgical tradition. In the early years of the Reformation, print technology made possible . . . the dissemination of increasingly diverse and distinctive worship traditions . . . But print technology also made possible the strong conservative reaction to the Reformation . . . For the next four hundred years, the Tridentine rites remained virtually unaltered and were imposed almost universally, and the task of the Roman Catholic liturgist became almost entirely interpretative rather than creative. (1994:47)

She also looks at the effects of the computer revolution in the twentieth century. She notes three possible effects:

  (i) a great increase in source material for liturgy without appropriate selection;

 (ii) the encouragement of transient liturgical practice;

(iii) the covering-up of the origins of liturgical practice.

It is interesting that these effects depend on features of technology questioned by other authors I have already cited. Further, Susan White sees an effect of 'bureaucratisation' of liturgy as it becomes shaped by technologically-based management and distribution systems. Amongst other questions, she asks if a liturgy passed down by experts in church management structures can properly address itself to the needs of socio-economically diverse congregations. In the past, liturgy has certainly been reactive to technology. White uses Mumford's concept of the 'myth of the machine' to explore the question of how present-day Christian worship can intersect with a technological understanding of humanity. She focuses on the requirement for uniformity – the loss of play in both an engineering and a creative sense, the drive for progress to perfection or absolute control, and mechanistic logic as particular features of this model. How have these views, as transferred to humanity, affected worship?

Certainly the nineteenth century saw the emergence of religious revivalism which stressed the need to build a better world. Self-improvement became a moral imperative, and technology was an important part of that. This included the application of technique to religious practice – easy, rousing hymns, the 'mercy seat' for repentant sinners, short sermons directly appealing to the hearer's background. All these features were collected in manuals and circulated as necessary aids to the establishment of thriving churches. The more churches were managed on these ideal lines, the more they approached the perfect organisation on a mechanical model, the better they would be. Similarly mechanistic thinking caused a deference to expertise, argues Susan White, so that ministers were expected to have appropriate training in special areas – hospital chaplaincies, religious education, and so on. Such models also shaped the experience of the worshippers to some degree. Expectations of worship are now that it should be responsive to the needs of the congregation; ministers are required to evaluate their own work and form corporate links with others. Susan White quotes a recent book on parish work, and points out that in the text she cites, the word minister may be replaced by 'worker', the word worship by 'product' and the word parish by 'factory'. The text still makes perfect sense, and is identical with the kind of technological manual produced by nineteenth-century exponents of technical progress and efficiency in industry. This kind of rethinking of parish life needs to be recognised, and its implications examined theologically.

Susan White concludes with an assessment of the challenges of modern technology, both in itself and as a factor shaping society, to present day Christian worship. She notes the contribution of what she calls 'technolocical evil' in the shape of the Holocaust to the loss of credibility of public prayer. She notes the effect of the electronic media on human expectations of corporate worship – 'good' television attracts a large audience and leaves a warm glow; do modern Christians expect the same thing in worship? She concludes that attempts to exclude technology from worship are doomed to failure, and a purely negative condemnation of technology will be an ineffective measure. She argues:

> To the extent that worship can embody and sustain Christian love, hope and charity, then the dehumanizing, fragmenting, death-dealing elements of technology will be called into question. To the extent that technology can enhance the sense of human freedom, the unity of the global family, and the possibility of self-transcendence, then the irrelevant, individualist and repressive elements of worship will be called into question. In other words, if technology and worship can enter into a relationship of mutual critique, there is the possibility that both may undergo genuine renewal. (1994:122)

White does acknowledge that there are dangers in the present role of technology, but she seems to feel that there can be some mutual rapprochement of theology and technological thinking. Her difference with, for instance, Ellul, on this point may be more apparent than real. It may result from her making a less precise distinction between technology itself and the thought processes and ideologies that have come to accompany its use, than has been made by other authors. Nevertheless, White's contribution is novel and original.

EXERCISE 10.1

Examine a piece of modern liturgy from a major religious group. Consider in what cultural situation the liturgical imagery is grounded. Try to rewrite one prayer or passage in the light of White's insights, and the technological culture in which you live.

10.12   One technologist's reflection

Reflections on technology and religion or theology are not only originated by theological thinkers. Illustrative of contributions from practitioners of technology is that from the engineer Professor George Bugliarello in a useful collection edited by Matthews and Varghese (1995). President of the Polytechnic University of New York from 1973 to 1994, and a member of numerous national bodies in the USA, he is well known for promoting such discussion. His concerns are fairly typical. He notes a present day crisis of public confidence in technology, and argues that this relates to questions about several features of technology.

He is concerned first of all about the concept of technological progress. Early technology was accompanied by an optimism that power over the physical world could bring nothing but good for humanity; things would, as a result of the increasing use of technology, get better and better; humanity would progress. The destruction wrought by technological warfare, the environmental catastrophes of the second half of the twentieth century, and the increasing cultural questioning of the power of the electronic media, suggest that 'further good' is only a possible result of technology; it can also bring evils. Public confidence in technology cannot be restored, argues Bugliarello, until there has been some serious examination of how progress to good can be secured, and how evil as a technological consequence can be avoided.

Closely related to this is the question that he raises about the reason for science and technology. Why is it done? He argues that modern technology does not seem to have a clearly defined goal or end. Bugliarello thinks this also can and should be made clear. He feels that it cannot be done without a new accountability, a new sense in which science and technology can be seen to be answerable to society at large, with reciprocal responsibilities between the technologists and the communities that utilise their creations. He argues that all of these discussions about the goals and values of science must include a religious dimension, not least because science itself is global and therefore multicultural; the religious principles and ethics of the world religions must come into play in the working out of any new compact between technology and society.

10.13 Conclusion

Technology has been a feature of human life since its beginnings, from the first wood and stone spears to the silicon complexities of today. Humans have always felt the need to alter their physical environment, and from early on, religion has supplied explanations and motives for this. Theological evaluation of those motives has been less common. There might be good Christian theological grounds for distinguishing between the monastic applications of technology, which attempted to enact some practical good, and the building of the cathedrals. Some authors see no reason to attempt evaluation, and some see no theological difficulties with the situation. However it is clear that the introduction of technology has always been associated with changes in human behaviour, attitudes and values. Since the Industrial Revolution, there have been an increasing number of theological voices urging caution, and suggesting that the Church might not be faithful to its witness if it adopts the aspects of technological thinking that accompany the new technology. Such caution is supported by historians and sociologists, who point to common features of concern in technological thinking. Promotion of the value of speed, efficiency, increased power and growth, progress and the overt exclusion of value have all been repeatedly connected with the use of technology in modern societies. Even the practices of Christian worship can be shown to be affected by this. The problems do not seem to lie in particular technologies as such. Rather, the fundamental Christian understanding of the purpose, meaning and goal of humanity and the universe is seen to be at risk. These are the true 'ends', for which all human activity should be organised. From a theological perspective, the methods and mechanics, the means, of that activity, must not be allowed to replace its proper end, which is the calling of humanity to fellowship with God.

FURTHER READING

ELLUL, J. (1989) *The Presence of the Kingdom* (Colorado Springs, CO: Helmers Howard)

—— (1990) *The Technological Bluff* (*Grand* Rapids, MI; Eerdmans)

LYON, D. (1988) *The Information Society* (Oxford: Polity Press, Basil Blackwell)

MACKENZIE, D. and WAJCMAN, J. (1985) *The Social Shaping of Technology* (Milton Keynes: Open University Press)

PACEY, A. (1983) *The Culture of Technology* (Cambridge, MA: MIT Press)

TILES, M. and OBERDIECK, H. (1995) *Living in a Technological Culture* (London: Routledge)

WHITE, S. (1994) *Christian Worship and Technological Change* (Nashville, TN: Abingdon Press)

ZIMAN, J. (1995) *An Introduction to Science Studies* (Cambridge: Cambridge University Press)

Chapter 11

Biotechnology –
A New Challenge to Theology and Ethics

11.1 What is biotechnology?

The last chapter made it clear that technology, as the application of science, is not as cleanly separated from science as one might suppose. Biotechnology is no exception to this and can be defined as the general application of biology to commercial practice. Biotechnology encompasses the application of genetic engineering for particular commercial purposes. We will be focusing on genetic engineering in this chapter, as it presents a particularly sharp challenge to theology and ethics.

There is a vast literature on the medical use of genetic engineering. In general, genetic engineering is portrayed in a positive way in having particular medical advantages over other forms of chemical intervention. Most of the examples in the literature that stress the positive benefits of biotechnology focus on the medical advantages of human genetic engineering for the treatment and diagnosis of various genetically related diseases. Unfortunately, there is insufficient scope here to discuss these particular examples in any detail. We will mention it as a way of introducing the relevance of both theology and ethics to biotechnology. Peters has written a positive appraisal of biotechnology from a theological perspective, especially as applied to human genetic engineering (Peters, 1997b:157–78). We will be arguing in this chapter that the promise of biotechnology is, nonetheless, highly ambiguous. We shall be examining broader applications of biotechnology, especially in relation to agriculture, and we shall show that these applications of recent advances in genetics pose a number of problems from theological and ethical perspectives.

The increasing commercial availability of diagnostic kits for genetic screening of both mothers and their unborn children raises a number of issues which are of theological and ethical significance. In particular, when such kits are used to test the unborn child, we need to ask ourselves whether the information gained is really desirable (Hepburn, 1996). Some genes, such as that for Tay-Sachs disease, are always fatal. Other genetic diseases, such as phenyl-ketonuria deficiency, can be treated at birth. Other genes predispose offspring to developing disease, for example a gene called BRAC1 involved in breast cancer. However, there is always a margin of error and genetic tests work with *probabilities*, rather than show absolute certainties. The anxiety raised by the possibility of disease occurrence, especially those for which there is no known cure, seems unacceptable. Furthermore, we need to consider the special dignity of the unborn child. From a theological point of view we need to consider the assumptions about human nature which lie behind genetic screening. Are we stigmatising even further those with congenital variations? Are those mothers who refuse to have the tests going to be refused medical treatment of their children? Will insurance be denied those who refuse such tests or who are diagnosed as carriers of disease? Like other examples in biotechnology we need to ask who really is to benefit. Does the know-how automatically support its application? Is it the patient who will benefit or the producers of the diagnostic kits? What are the risks involved? For example, does the test itself carry a risk of induced abortion? Who is really in control? For example, do the patients have access to adequate counselling and how is this presented? Some of those on the forefront of new developments in biotechnology believe that the Church's role will primarily be to counsel patients who have gained knowledge from genetic screening methods.[1] But should the Church assume that such a development is either desirable or necessary? We will be looking at the question of different attitudes to genetic engineering further in relation to other examples in the section below.

---

[1] Paper given on 'What makes us what we are? Some recent developments in the biological sciences' by Professor Mark W. J. Ferguson at the John Templeton one-day conference 'Science and Religion: Where are the Frontiers Now?', Manchester University, 22 May 1998.

EXERCISE 11.1

What is your initial response to the idea of biotechnology for (a) medical purposes; (b) food production; (c) commercial purposes (as in, for example, manufacture of soap powder)? In each case consider the benefits, the risks and the political implications.

So far there are relatively few people affected by such genetic diagnostic testing programmes. By contrast, *all of us* are affected in some way by the application of biotechnology for agricultural purposes. Furthermore, such applications have *global* consequences in terms of the human community and the wider natural environment.

11.2 An appraisal of genetic engineering: what are the benefits?

(i) Background to the initiative in agriculture

In the late 1960s a 'green revolution' spawned an optimistic attitude to genetic engineering as applied to agriculture. Traditional plant breeding methods were used by scientists to develop high-yield varieties. When this was combined with more intensive use of fertiliser, there were vast increases in yield, especially in Third World countries. In India, for example, the wheat crop was doubled in six years. However, the dream that the green revolution could solve the world food crisis ran up against some unexpected difficulties. Small farmers and the rural communities were ousted by wealthier landowners who could afford the costly fertilisers.

(ii) Reduction in fertiliser use

More recently, there has been a drive for the development of crops that require *less* fertilisers. Much of the task of genetic engineering has been no more than to complement that of traditional breeding methods. However, instead of taking several years to develop a new crop, it now takes a matter of months. In this respect genetic engineering could be seen as *a liberation* from time constraints imposed by slow-growing crops. In a hungry world few would wish to legislate against the development of crops that could flourish in the poorer areas of the world hampered by dry, salty or nutritionally poor conditions.

(iii) Introduction of patents

While the green revolution was directed towards the needs of the Third World, at least in its original intention, contemporary genetic engineering is more often conducted in the West under industrial contracts requiring expensive *patents* for new varieties. The perceived novelty of genetic engineering techniques and the organisms they produce has allowed researchers to patent living organisms, and/or their parts or processes. Peters has shown that the fear of patenting in many cases is an emotional fear based on the misconception that life is controlled and determined entirely by genetic material (Peters, 1997b:115–41). While we would agree that the initial reaction to patenting in some quarters was highly exaggerated, Peters fails to consider adequately the wider social and environmental *consequences* of patenting, especially as applied to non-human species. In the case of crop plants, patenting has accelerated the trend towards monopolies in seed production by one or two large companies. Unfortunately, this has the overall effect of leading to the loss of genetic diversity (Barbour, 1992:191–92).

(iv) Maximisation of profits

In common with other commercial practices, the research aims at maximum profits. Projects such as the genetic engineering of bacteria to synthesise prescription drugs, or the modification of tomato, soybean and strawberry crops for the Western market all have a commercial aim. We only hear about a small fraction of these developments in the media. An engineered tomato known as FLAVR SAVR was the first genetically engineered whole food launched in the USA (King, 1994c).[2] This tomato has the gene that leads to softening 'scrambled', so that the tomatoes ripen without going squashy during transportation, which is to the commercial advantage of the producers. The worry that the tomato might not be 'safe' is largely illusory in this particular case.

(v) The particular case of animal cloning

The ability of scientists to clone sheep promises to allow unlimited production of sheep having identical genetic make-up. The breakthrough for *science* was that up until this time mammals could not be cloned. Ian Wilmut, working at the Roslin Institute in Edinburgh, led a

---

[2] Note that the journal *GenEthics News*, launched in 1994, gives up-to-date information on all the latest releases of genetically engineered organisms.

FIGURE 11.1

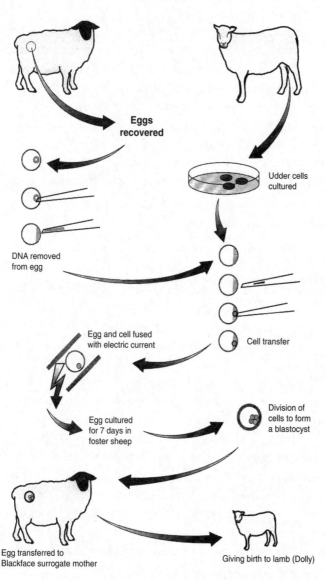

The production of 'Dolly': the first cloned sheep
(adapted from Bruce and Bruce, 1998:18, Fig. 1.5).

team which discovered it was possible to insert the genetic material of
a sheep's somatic cell into an egg cell that had its nucleus removed
(Wilmut *et al.*, 1997; King, 1997a, 1997b) [see Figure 11.1]. In most cases
hybrid cells failed to survive. However, in a small fraction of cases an

embryo developed which was then implanted into a surrogate mother. In one case a normal lamb developed.[3]

Polly, produced just six months later, was genetically engineered with some unnamed human genes. The announcement made in *The Independent* on 4 March 1998 stated that PPL Therapeutics were now able to produce the human blood clotting protein Factor IX in transgenic cloned sheep.[4] Movement of genes from one species to another is known as *transgenic* manipulation. Factor IX is necessary for the treatment of haemophiliacs. The level of production was sixty times that from human extracts. The benefit of such a technique is that it will solve the problem of obtaining sufficient quantities for medical needs.

11.3   What are the dangers?

(i) The threat to animal welfare

For the above example, what are the risks for animal welfare? What many do not realise is that it took many attempts to get just one cloned sheep. The unsuccessful attempts showed a range of abnormalities, especially enlarged size with concurrent risk to the mother. We might see this as a threat to animal welfare for the sake of human interests.

Transgenic manipulation raises further issues of importance to animal welfare. For example, pigs have been injected with human growth hormone genes, and sheep with genes from bacteria. How many genes can we introduce before it becomes a new species? Is it right to violate the 'pigness' of a pig? Those pigs that were engineered with a human growth hormone grew slightly faster than normal, but they were arthritic, had ulcers and were partially blind (King, 1994b). This was caused by excess production of growth hormone. In other words, although the gene could be introduced into the pig genome, *there was no regulation of the expression of this gene*. This example illustrates one of the risks of transgenic manipulation, that there is no way of knowing in advance how far such genes will be able to be regulated in the recipient organism.

---

[3] Note that strictly speaking this is *nuclear cloning*, rather than complete identity since the maternal egg is different. Egg cells contain mitochondria that *also* contain genetic material. But the idea that Dolly is a clone of her mother is a reasonable approximation to what happens.

[4] C. Arthur, Science Editor, 'What's White, Woolly, Says Baa and Earns £2 million a Year?'

(ii) Environmental risk assessment

Environmental risk factors associated with genetic engineering are related to the power of the technology to bring about irreversible change in the hereditary material of plants, animals and bacteria. For example, it is now possible to genetically engineer crop plants which are resistant to chemical herbicides. A Government advisory committee has given a Belgian company permission to release into the market a genetically engineered rapeseed which contains resistance to the herbicide 'Basta' (King, 1994a). This allows the farmers to control weeds in fields of rapeseed which would normally die on exposure to the herbicide. There were no public consultations prior to the decision by the committee. While the company denies any risk to the environment, it is not proven that the engineered rapeseed will have no harmful environmental effects. If anything, the *science* suggests the opposite, since rapeseed can cross-fertilise with wild mustard plants and even become a weed on roadside verges. Once these genetically engineered plants became established they would be difficult to control, as they would be herbicide-resistant.

(iii) The threats to human well-being

The long-term effects of herbicide-resistant crops to human health are unknown. Government regulations rarely consider indirect risks of this type. The increased dependence of the farmers on herbicides for weed control encourages an equal dependence on the *hybrid seed* sold by the same company as one package.

Hybrid seeds do not breed true to the next generation, which means that the next generation of plants is not uniform. Farmers rely on mechanized means of harvesting, which in turn makes them dependent on a crop which is uniform in height and time of ripening in order to achieve high yields. The traditional method of saving seed for the next year's crop is now impossible, or rather only possible with loss of yield. The farmers are forced to buy new seed and herbicide every year.

(iv) Loss of genetic diversity

Another indirect risk, which is also characteristic of conventional plant breeding, is the overall loss in genetic diversity.

Crops which grow from wild strains have a much greater variability that protects them naturally from pests and disease. When a crop is genetically engineered the resultant uniformity brings the desired increase in yield, but also carries a greater vulnerability to disease. This loss of variability within one species is irreversible. In order to find new sources of variation researchers have sought wild strains that have retained their genetic variability. These wild strains are on the whole confined to the poorer Southern continents.

(v) Potential allergic reactions to modified food

Another risk of transgenic manipulation is that new proteins in the transgenic food may cause potentially lethal reactions in humans. The US seed company Pioneer Hi Bred, for example, was forced to drop development of genetically engineered soybeans containing Brazil nut genes. Extracts of the genetically engineered soybeans reacted with human blood serum from individuals who suffered from nut allergy. While it might be possible to exclude certain plants that are known to cause allergic reactions, many foods are allergenic to a small number of people.

11.4   Some hidden agendas

In order to assess the impact of biotechnology we need to address the question of the overall direction of the research to date. This is a relatively young science, but as it is primarily a commercial enterprise, in the West at least, market forces drive it. We may like to ponder the fact that more money has been spent on the development of strawberries that can withstand frost conditions for the spring USA market than on improving the yield of basic subsistence crops, such as cassava, maize or bean plants in the Third World (Buttel, 1986).[5] Other rapidly expanding technologies include the development of tissue culture grown in laboratory conditions which have been engineered to produce 'synthetic' products. It may be only a matter of time before a biotechnological means is found to produce substitutes for substances such as vanilla or cocoa. If this were to take place we would witness a collapse in the economy of Madagascar, which relies on vanilla bean exports, and in the economy of West Africa, which relies on cocoa.

---

[5] Frost resistance in strawberries is achieved by genetic engineering of a bacterium which normally lives on the strawberries' surface and acts as a nucleation site for ice crystals. The modified bacterium loses this capacity.

We mentioned above the loss of genetic diversity is exacerbated through biotechnology. (See **11.3 (iv)**.) As a result it is only those parts of the world that are supposedly less 'developed' which have a reserve of 'wild' strains that still contain natural variability. The cash payment for the patent of these strains is far less than the potential benefit to its recipients. Vandana Shiva has called this and other similar practices 'biopiracy' (Shiva and Moser, 1995:214–25; Shiva, 1997). Biotechnology is becoming a means of oppressing Third World economies and seems to be driving a deepening wedge between rich and poor nations. While there is legislation in place, at least in principle, to protect us from possible health risks of genetic engineering, it becomes much harder to legislate towards research priorities.

There are other examples of where biotechnology is used in a way which seems completely unnecessary. For example, why is bovine growth hormone used to stimulate milk production, given the over-production of milk and excess of dairy products in the Western market? The idea that cows and other farm animals can be manipulated in this way for human benefit alone, encourages the human perception of animals as resources to be managed. Animals become simply 'bio-machines'. Where is the sense of the value of these creatures in and of themselves?

11.5   Public responses to genetic engineering

There has been a gradual awareness in recent years that the public's perception of risk has its own value and can contribute to the overall assessment of particular technologies. The acceptance or otherwise of a particular technology is thought to be dependent on public approval. Hence the public response to genetic engineering is a vital ingredient in its further development. In a recent survey, comparison of public attitudes to genetic engineering suggested that the manipulation of microbes and plants was acceptable, but that of animals and humans in particular was 'unnatural, harmful and dangerous' (Frewer *et al.*, 1997).

The Centre of the Study of Environmental Change based at Lancaster University is making a concerted effort to investigate public perceptions of risks associated with technologies such as the genetic modification of organisms. Unilever and a number of non-government organisations sponsored one of the more recent reports, *Uncertain World* (Grove-White *et al.*, 1997). The research is significant in and of itself as it demonstrates the way *some* large companies may be starting to show a more responsible attitude to the impact of new technologies. A research method known as *focus groups* involved guided discussions with nine small groups of people from different parts of the UK and with different social characteristics. The results overall showed very little public enthusiasm for biotechnology. Public perception identified commercial interest as lying behind many of the new proposed products, especially those related to food. Their concern seemed to be exacerbated by certain kinds of information, rather than reduced. This counters some of the arguments of the Ethics of Genetic Modification and Food Use (EGMFU) Committee that suggested public anxiety could be allayed by more information (EGMFU, 1994).

11.5.1   Religious dimensions to the public response

The *Uncertain World* report did not address the issue whether the public responses to genetic engineering had any religious dimension, whether implicit or explicit. However, close examination of the original data used to produce the document has revealed the following results.[6]

(i) The ordering of nature

Almost all respondents were anxious or worried about the idea that genetic engineering amounted to a 'messing about with nature'. Their sense of risk arising from such 'tampering' was related to possible effects on both their own health and damage to the environment. Furthermore, a strong sense of order in the natural world prevails; 'I don't think we should mess with nature. Nature was designed for specific reasons. We mess with it. We have no right'; 'it's actually broken the natural order'.

A deep sense of order in the natural world, with humanity having a special place, followed by animals and then plants, has its basis in the theological doctrine of creation. While the idea of the Creator as the divine Designer has gone out of fashion ever since the demise of natural theology (**1.3.1, 4.4**), a sense of design in the natural world does seem

[6] This research was funded by the Christendom Trust and conducted by the author (CD-D) in collaboration with Robin Grove-White and Bronislaw Szersynski – and by kind permission of Phil Mcnaghten, Sue Mayer and Brian Wynne who allowed open access to the original data collected from the focus group interviews.

to prevail in the public mind. In some cases a more explicit reference to theism surfaces. For example one respondent believed that interference with nature goes beyond permissible boundaries, for 'I'm not sure whether man should play God and change things for the better, for the lucre, at the end of the day'. For many, the idea of God *as such* is hidden, but the sense of ordering prevails.[7]

(ii) Natural is good

Another theme which surfaced is the idea that what is present in nature and untouched by human interference is good. Overall the *reason* for changing the natural to something else was questioned. While a form of biotechnology has been going on for centuries in cheese and beer-making etc., any attempt to try and persuade us that this is the same as genetic engineering was dismissed. The irreversible nature of genetic change is such that the original 'natural' form may be lost and this seems threatening. Most philosophers argue that equating the natural with value, that is what is natural is automatically good, is a weak philosophical argument. It has been dubbed the 'naturalistic fallacy'. Reiss and Straughan argue against the fear of genetic engineering as 'unnatural' for this reason (Reiss and Straughan, 1996:60–61).

However, it is more likely that the public insistence on the natural is less a philosophical premise than a theological one. By this we mean that there is an implicit *religious* concept that what is created is good. Again God's blessing of creation in Genesis and affirmation of the natural order in other Scriptural texts, especially the wisdom literature, affirms this as a core element of the Christian tradition. Matthew Fox and other radical eco-theologians have argued for creation-centred spirituality as a way of affirming the essential unity of all creatures with humanity (Fox, 1983:11). Other theologians believe that a romantic affiliation with the natural world is unnecessary and at times unhelpful in view of the realities of the harshness of the natural world (Page, 1991:7). Yet it is clear that diseases cannot be described as 'sinful' in any sense and overall there is in the public mind a 'yes' to creation as a gift from God. This sense of affirmation prevails as an implicit, rather than an explicit, theology.

[7] For further discussion of the idea of the order of creation, see Northcott (1996: 164–98).

(iii) The special place of humanity

In almost all cases there was a mixed reaction to the idea of transgenic experiments with human genes transferred to pigs or sheep. The reaction was particularly strong in cases where it was proposed that *human* genes enter the food chain. Common language such as 'it's disgusting', 'horrible', 'cannibalism', 'no, not that', and so on, all reflects an abhorrence at the idea that we might be consuming something of another human being. The report of the EGMFU Committee suggested that education might be the answer. For example, the Committee suggested that if the public was more aware that a *copy* of the human gene was used and this copy multiplied billions of times before entering the new species, then it would not necessarily cause a problem. However we are less sure. This is not a logical response to facts, but a deep-seated intuition towards the special place of humanity and our distinction from the rest of creation. When one respondent was reminded of the very tiny fraction of material that was of human origin, which might even share the same chemicals as bacteria, the reaction was the same.

Overall the theological notion that humans are made in the image of God prevails, albeit in a hidden form. Nonetheless, some were more prepared to object from explicitly religious grounds. Of fundamental concern was the source of the human gene; would it have come from a foetus? There was a sense that religious (in this case explicitly Roman Catholic) boundaries had been crossed by other medical research and that this may well happen again. Was this going to lead to an infringement of human dignity, especially in the case of an unborn child?

(iv) The place of animals

The response to experimentation with animals was cautious and in some cases caused concern as to whether the animals would be fairly treated. BSE was cited as an example of unnecessary slaughter of animals. Others were worried that experiments done on animals were the 'thin end of the wedge'. In general this was a weaker theme, but there was a greater sense of respect for animals compared with plants, for example. One group was concerned about introducing genes from animals that were not accepted as food on religious grounds. The EGMFU Report seemed to think that as long as an animal *looked* the same it could be considered to be this species and not another. Hence, it should not cause grave problems. However, would this work in practice? How many genes from a pig could be transferred to a sheep before it is no longer a sheep? Are looks alone an adequate guide? If there is repugnant distaste about eating even a gene of human origin, the same could be said for those who express distaste over eating pork or cows. The logic might suggest otherwise, but consumers do not necessarily respond to 'logical' analyses.

(v) Environmental value

What was somewhat surprising was a tendency in all groups to look at the wider environmental consequences of genetic modification. The long term and latent effects of BSE served as an example of how hidden dangers could surface much later. When soap powder was modified for example, the immediate thought in many minds was: what about the effect on the ecosystems? Furthermore, questions surfaced regularly about the Third World, and possible effects on poorer communities. Such global and broad ecological concerns perhaps reflect an implicit green theology which is holistic and integrates human need with the wider interests of the environment.

(vi) Recognition of human sin

While the notion of 'sin' was never mentioned, another clear theme was an underlying sense of mistrust of the motives of those involved. There were strong statements like 'it's all for human greed', 'it's for profit'. BSE again served as an example that reinforced the suspicion that the full story is never really made explicit. One participant commented: 'I think if I'd read that before BSE my thoughts might have been more positive . . . Sometimes we meddle too much . . . You can never be sure what the effects are going to be at the end of the day'. There was little belief in the underlying values of the organisations, especially supermarkets and the government. While the former was suspected to encourage such developments for pure self-interest and profit, the 'filthy lucre', the government was viewed with suspicion as those out of touch with the needs of ordinary people.

(vii) A liberation theology

Human weakness on an individual level has been recognised by Christian theologians throughout the centuries, drawing on the

Augustinian notion of 'original sin'. A more recent development has been the recognition, through the development of liberation theology, of sinfulness at a structural and organisational level. What is of particular interest is the overall sense of powerlessness expressed in the focus groups. There is a feeling of inevitability about the course of events and that such events will benefit a few. While 'oppression' is not a word which is used, at least some of the anxiety comes from this sense of being dominated by negative forces wielded by power-ful minority groups such as the Government and multinational companies.

Are there any signs of hope in this somewhat negative assessment? There are certainly signs that hope is still present, but sadly it does not seem to be the lot of the Church to be bearers of this hope. One group mentioned the idea that the Church *might* be able to become bearers of moral and ethical values, in other words, somehow act as a 'moral voice'. However, this was undermined by the perception that the Church was also a landowner, which would compromise its impartiality. Groups that did come over very strongly as bearers of an alternative vision were Greenpeace, Friends of the Earth and other non-government consumer organisations such as Watchdog. They were seen as those who could balance the discussion by presenting an alternative view that was unsullied by desire for profit. They are, possibly, bearers of an implicit liberation theology by challenging the *status quo* and speaking out for the people on their behalf. Just as liberation theologians owe a debt to Western theology, so too Greenpeace, for example, uses the tools of science to prove its points, as the recent document *Genetic Engineering: Too Good to go Wrong?* (Parr, 1997) suggests.

11.6   The possibility of human cloning

In the light of the overall public distaste for genetic modifications in-volving human genes, it is hardly surprising that there has been an overall negative public reaction to the possibility of human cloning. In January 1998 the Human Genetics Advisory Commission produced a Consultation document on Cloning Issues in Reproduction, Science and Medicine. They invited public responses to this document, but their further deliberations were not published until the end of 1998. Selections of this Consultation document are reproduced here, along with parts of this author (CD-D)'s own response taken from a letter sent to the Secretariat in April 1998. See also Exercise 11.2, following Box 11.1.

Box 11.1

EXTRACTS FROM CONSULTATION DOCUMENT ON CLONING

The UK has effectively banned cloning for the deliberate creation of whole human beings under the Human Fertilisation and Embryology Act 1990.

1.3 For the purposes of this consultation we draw the distinction between two types of cloning: on the one hand, human reproductive cloning, where the intention is to produce identical fetuses or babies; and on the other hand, what may be broadly called therapeutic cloning, which . . . includes other scientific and medical applications of nuclear replacement technology.

Response

My first concern is that although you, quite correctly, distinguish between reproductive and therapeutic cloning, the presentation is such that the link is not assessed or evaluated. I am concerned that giving the green light to all so-called 'therapeutic cloning' could open the door to reproductive cloning in a way that this document does not really consider adequately. For example in section 5.3 you note that one of the 'therapeutic' uses of cloning is in the treatment of infertility.

7.2 Nuclear replacement research can improve our knowledge about physiological processes and the genotype. For example, it is hoped that this work will offer a greater insight into the origins of cancer and other cellular development processes such as aging and cell commitment.

Response

What is the evidence that this research has additional benefits compared with other types of physiological research already taking place?

7.4 . . . The Committee went on to conclude that the special status of the embryo would permit some embryo research up to the fourteenth day of development provided the research was strictly controlled and monitored . . . Would the use of nuclear replacement techniques or embryo splitting to create embryos raise any new issues in relation to the special status of the human embryo?

Response

I would argue that the answer to this is yes, by permitting human embryonic nuclear replacement to take place the whole concept that the human embryo does have a special status starts to sound shallow and empty of meaning. . . . Even given the fourteen day-old restriction, what would prevent such modified embryos being taken and used elsewhere where restrictions are not enforced?

Section 8

**HUMAN REPRODUCTIVE CLONING:
THE ETHICAL IMPLICATIONS**

8.3 There are a number of situations where it has been suggested that cloning technology could be applied to make a 'copy' of another human being. . . . none of the activities suggested in these scenarios are permitted in the UK. . . . For example:

Parents might wish to replace an aborted fetus, dead baby or child killed in an accident. . .

An individual might seek to use cloning technology in an attempt . . . to cheat death.

Response

None of these supposed arguments in favour of reproductive cloning seems to have any real weight. From an ethical perspective it is abhorrent that those who have lost a child would be denied the grieving process on account of a 'replacement'. As noted throughout the text, the chances of such individuals having an identical personality and character is very slim, leading to further dis-appointment, false hopes and a waste of resources.

8.4 There are many general questions about intervention and reproductive technology, which are not unique to cloning. For example, what limits are there on the role of prior choice of characteristics of offspring, where this is scientifically made possible?

Response

The idea that parents can have designer babies implied by 8.4 seems highly objectionable and by no means reliable, leading to the marginalisation of all but so called 'perfect' individuals defined as such by the subjective opinion of the parents.

8.5 A potential application of human reproductive cloning by nuclear replacement might be used to assist human reproduction. A lesbian couple might wish to have a child . . . Another scenario might be where both individuals of a couple are infertile. . . . Would the use of nuclear replacement techniques be beyond the limit of what is ethically acceptable to resolve a couple's fertility problem?

Response

The possibility that children might be born to lesbian couples using this technique is objectionable. The ethical effects on the child seem to have been ignored in the overall quest for parental choice. Who would the child look to as his/her father? The short answer to the question raised is yes, it is beyond the limits of what is ethically acceptable. Infertility as such seems to have been raised to a reified status, so that any action is considered to be acceptable if only this problem is solved . . . it seems to ignore the potential disadvantages both to the individual born in this way, the community and the couple concerned.

NOTE: Professor Harris has argued in favour of cloning for infertile couples (Harris, 1997; Swain, 1998[8]). Other philosophers, such as Hilary Putnam from Harvard University, have put the case for an alternative view, insisting that cloning to gratify parent's needs is wrong (Putnam, 1998).

---

[8] Swain's report on John Harris's Amnesty lecture (given on 12 February 1998 in the Sheldonian Theatre at Oxford) was published in *The Times Higher Educational Supplement,* 23 January (Swain, 1998:17).

8.5 The nuclear replacement technology used to produce Dolly is still in its early stages. We do not know whether the work which created Dolly is repeatable in animals, nor is it known whether it can be replicated in humans. We should bear in mind that Dolly was the only normal lamb born from 276 similar attempts. Only 29 resulted in implantable embryos, all of which, except the one leading to Dolly, resulted in defective pregnancies or grossly malformed births . . . human cloned reproduction might be associated with similar 'wastage' rates and uncertainties about malformations.

How does this case differ from the experiments that first led to successful in vitro fertilisation (IVF) procedures?

Response

The possible malformations and failures, which are inevitable in developing human reproductive cloning, just add more weight to the argument against such technology being developed.

There are wide differences between human reproductive cloning and IVF. The first holds potential for abuse and manipulations, which would amount to eugenics. The second, (while tests are, in theory, possible to screen out 'abnormal' embryos) is reliant on the natural process, albeit taking place outside the human body. Philosophers have for a long time argued that 'natural' is not necessarily the good, but the opposite is not true either – this argument cannot be used to justify blatant artificial interference.

EXERCISE 11.2

Make your own response to the statements of the consultation paper before reading further. What issues do you find particularly significant?

11.7 Theological issues

(i) Biotechnology and models of God

Given the implicit theology emerging from public discussions of genetic engineering, it is relevant to ask: how far does the above pose a specific challenge to theology? Public religious intuitions need to be taken into account in developing an adequate theology. We could ask ourselves whether the different models of the God/world relationship are adequate in the light of the rapid changes taking place in our social fabric and our creaturely environment brought about by biotechnology. Some of the models suggested in Chapter 6 will be briefly assessed below.

The process theology model (**6.2–6.3, 6.5.1–6.5.3**) likens the world to an 'organism', rather than a 'machine'. At first sight, then, any idea of the natural world as a mechanism, which is presupposed in biotechnology, is rejected. Process theology would reject the reductionism at the heart of biotechnology (see **11.8 (i)**). Another concept in process thought is the notion that everything has a *telos* or goal, which is directed towards greater enrichment. Biotechnology suppresses this goal at the heart of all living things.

However, there are other strands in process thinking that might suggest a more positive appraisal. For example, the drive towards human enrichment and creativity is a strong element. A biotechnologist might suggest that the ability of humans to manipulate genes is just one more example of human creativity. Indeed, some leading exponents of biotechnology have suggested as much, that such a science is the flowering of our human potential. It can be used or abused, just like any other application of science (Reiss and Straughan, 1996:7). A similar view that stresses the power of human creativity is taken by Ted Peters, who insists that giving humans more freedom does not weaken the freedom of God (Peters, 1997b:159–62). The new genetics should be seen less as a threat than as an opportunity to exercise our freedom. Any moratorium on genetic engineering assumes that genetic determinism is in control, rather than humanity. However, we suggest that human freedom needs to include the *capacity* to reject, as well as affirm, latest developments in science. In general it is the positive appraisal of our human abilities that seems to win through in process thought. The increase in novelty possible through genetic engineering would also suggest that, in some contexts, process thinking would favour this approach (Palmer, 1998:157). We might ask ourselves how the God who lures all of creation into being could respond to the radical shifts in genetic make-up induced by transgenic transformations. In other words the positive assumption that seems to be behind process thinking does not seem to deal adequately with drastic genetic changes which are radically different from the 'natural' evolutionary process. The only response might be that God suffers with the creature, but it will lead to ultimate good. As was noted in **6.5.3** and **6.12**, McDaniel's modified process scheme is more Buddhist in flavour. From his perspective, biotechnology could not be supported in any form. The above confirms our conclusion that some strands of process theology tend to support biotechnology, while others oppose it.

Ecofeminist theology (see **6.4**, **6.5.4–6.5.5**) is clearer-cut. In general, it is more sceptical about the benefits of science. Theologians such as Rosemary Radford Ruether link the oppression of women by men with men's domination of the natural world (Ruether, 1992:173–201, 1996:1–8). Biotechnology becomes one more example of the oppressive abuse of the natural world. The same attitude would be characteristic of those who support creation spirituality, as the recent book by McFague indicates (McFague, 1997:5–25). If the world is the body of God and shot through with the spirit of God, then domination of any aspect of the creaturely world for human benefit would be totally unacceptable. Other feminist writers have a more specific *political* agenda and are particularly concerned with the global injustices incurred by biotechnology (Shiva, 1997).

Moltmann, in common with feminist theologians, has argued that our understanding of God influences the way we treat the Earth (Moltmann, 1985:1–7). God is no longer a God characterised primarily in terms of power, but in terms of love and response. His view shares some of the characteristics of process and feminist thinking, but he also takes into account perspectives from Eastern Orthodoxy. For Moltmann, technology has become a web into which we are caught up and trapped. This entrapment would apply equally to biotechnology. The liberation that Christ brings comes through his self-emptying kenosis for our sake. Moltmann's stronger sense of political justice in comparison with process thought allows his theology to be more directly sensitive to the social issues raised by biotechnology.

(ii) A theological future for creation

Moltmann's emphasis on the *future* is also of relevance to the problem we are discussing. Does his understanding of the future of creation encourage us to engage in genetic engineering? For Moltmann the new creation will be one where God will be 'all in all'. The world becomes transfigured by the presence of God through the participation of creation in God's infinite creativity (Moltmann, 1969:34; 1973:41). This echoes the Eastern Orthodox concept of participation of creation in the *energeia* of God (Zizioulas, 1990). Karl Rahner, similarly, insists that it is God's intention to give creation a supernatural end, which has an effect on the essence of being itself (Rahner, 1965:302–17). For Rahner, the natural knowledge of God as perceived in creation is not sharply distinguished from the revelation of God. However, the Christological dimension in Rahner's thought qualifies the themes of the future glory of creation. Moltmann, similarly, insists that the cross of Christ reminds us that the future of creation is not utopia on Earth. The promise of biotechnology is tempered by the realisation of human sinfulness.

(iii) Facing human sinfulness

The theological concept of sin is equally relevant to biotechnology as it faces squarely the possibility of human error of judgement. First, the cross of Christ reminds us both of the reality of the suffering of creation and the very real temptation of humans to sin in identifying their human enterprise with absolute value. Genetic engineering can never achieve utopia on Earth, especially when we are blind to its use as an instrument in suffering. Moreover, God's love for all creation demands a respect for the interests of all creatures, whether they are produced by genetic engineering or traditional breeding methods. The Creator's intention is towards future glorification. Hence the human motivation to develop new varieties and transgenic species needs to be carefully scrutinised.

It would be inappropriate to lay the blame for the abuse of genetic engineering on the scientists alone. We are all implicated in the social web of which scientists are a part. In seeking for a change in attitude amongst those more directly involved, a wider transformation of heart and mind, or *metanoia*, is needed which incorporates a sensitivity to creation in every aspect of our lives. This *metanoia* includes an attitude of humility and respect for all members of the human and non-human community. We cannot avoid sacrificial effort on our part. The words of the Ecumenical Patriarchate on the ecological crisis are relevant in this respect: 'This is a new situation, a new challenge. It calls for humanity to bear some of the pain of creation as well as to enjoy and celebrate it. It calls first and foremost for repentance, but of an order not previously understood by many' (1990:11).

(iv) Perspectives from liberation theology

A Christian theological perspective would insist on examining the long-term consequences to poorer nations, communities and the environment. It is this broader view which is essential to keep in mind when dealing with decisions about the validity of particular genetic engineering projects. In this way the wider human and cosmic contexts act as twin points of reference.

For some years questions to do with development were considered in a way which was detached from environmental issues. Development workers tended to despise environmentalists as those who seemed to pay more attention to the survival of animals, rather than people. More recently, there has been a greater appreciation of the interrelationship between environmental problems and development issues. This linkage is of special relevance to the particular questions surrounding genetic engineering, as highlighted in the case studies above. Boff has argued that technology does not exist in and for itself, but is adopted within a particular model of development, which is causative of the ecological crisis (Boff, 1997:65–70). The disruption of the basic connectedness with the universe is counter to the religious and spiritual traditions of humankind. He argues, further, that the relationship between ecology and poverty is a direct one, for the poor and oppressed belong to the natural world (Boff, 1997:107). What is striking in this most recent liberation theology is a shift towards a greater emphasis on mysticism as a way of generating the energy necessary for change. The theological outlines of this mysticism is unclear, but it seems to bear a resemblance to the radical cosmic eco-spirituality of Thomas Berry (Berry, 1987). Elsewhere Boff has suggested that 'the organ best fitted to comprehend this mystery is the heart and what Pascal called the esprit de finesse – intuition' (Boff, 1995:145). This bears some resemblance to the idea of wisdom that we will return to in the final section.

EXERCISE 11.3

Given the range of theological models available, which one(s) do you consider the best equipped to meet the problems posed by biotechnology? How might this theology influence ethics?

11.8   Ethical questions

Given the theological perspective we have been outlining, what are the implications for environmental ethics? The possibility of dishonesty in the use of environmental language to cover up materialist or power-craving instincts has to be exposed. The latter raises questions about human justice.

(i) *The ambiguous promise*

The extent to which we perceive genetic engineering as a threat or a promise reflects our own divided perceptions. On the one hand, we are anxious to solve the immediate problem; on the other hand, we search for the broader, more holistic 'visions'. The beneficial effects of genetic engineering in the development of new medicines, and the protection of animals and plants – and in some cases humans – against disease, are often cited by genetic engineers to justify their work and achievements. However, in some cases the root cause of the disease may be overlooked. For example, overcrowding and other unhealthy conditions foster many of the diseases in animal husbandry. To engineer the animals against disease does not get at the root of the problem. Genetic engineering is inevitably the fruit of a reductionist methodological approach (cf. **4.12**). The unashamedly anthropocentric (that is, human-centred) philosophy that is behind these developments is anthropocentrism at its worst: namely use of a particular technique purely for individual commercial benefit. On the other hand, the wider impact of genetic engineering leads to the anxiety that it is to the detriment of life and the planet as a whole.

(ii) *Is it 'natural'?*

It might be possible to argue against any genetic engineering on the basis that it is somehow unnatural, which we have already mentioned in the section on public issues. However, it is important here to distinguish between the use of genetic engineering to speed up what would be possible in normal breeding methods and its use in transgenic experiments. There are those who object to genetic engineering on the basis that it is an invasion of biological integrity. However, according to biologists' understanding of evolution, biological integrity *as such* does not exist. We share many of the same biological and physiological processes as other life-forms. It seems questionable whether natural selection is any more altruistic for the species than artificial breeding or genetic engineering. The philosophical basis for regulation and constraints in genetic engineering needs to be sought in avenues other than a vague notion of biological integrity.

In all breeding methods there is a tendency to treat animals and plants as commodities. Genetic engineering allows, then, an even greater detachment from the animal or plant in such a way that they can become highly vulnerable to exploitation. The philosopher Martin Heidegger rejects the idea that technology is neutral and is simply a means to an end (Heidegger, 1969:1–14). He suggests that modern technology has failed to 'bring forth' what was the original intention of the natural environment. Instead technology is confrontational and challenging. As such, *this is an unreasonable demand placed on the natural world*. He believes that the greatest illusion for human beings is to see everything as their own construction, since it drives out other forms of revealing from *within* the natural world. Heidegger did not exactly reject technology, but was acutely aware of its ambiguities for a genuinely human existence. The same attitude could be taken to the biotechnology revolution.

(iii) The need for respect

Paul Taylor has suggested that respect for the natural world is a key paradigm in the development of a theory of environmental ethics. We are all part of a single biotic community (Taylor, 1986:72–90). The question is whether recognition of mutual dependence constitutes a moral relationship as well. Robin Attfield argues against the idea that interdependence strengthens moral relationships, preferring the notion that all species that have interests have *moral standing* (Attfield, 1983:158). He believes that 'rights' are not the only basis of moral concern; something can lack 'rights' but still have moral standing. What does it mean for a species to have interests? This seems to be related to the idea of what constitutes respect. Immanuel Kant believed that if we treat people as a means to our own ends and do not recognise their ends, we are failing to show respect. Genetic engineering has to treat living things in a mechanistic way in order to achieve its goals. However, there is a distinction between treating a living thing purely as a means for our own ends, disregarding the creature's ends, and bringing our interests into line with that of the creature. This echoes the idea of Heidegger that we need to become sensitive to the 'revealing' within the natural world. However, it still requires *human* judgement and a form of empathy to decide exactly what the interests of the creature mean in practice.

There seems to be no need to reject all genetic engineering in principle, as long as we take into account the interests of the creatures concerned. It is clear that the extent of genetic manipulation that is acceptable must be qualified by the scientific knowledge of the evolutionary complexity of the organism.

The mixed reaction to *cloning* underlies a fear that this might be applied to humans, alongside a concern by scientists that public panic should not be allowed to stem research (Butler and Wadman, 1997). The hope is that the particular ethical problems raised by cloning can be clarified. The need to respect the dignity of humans has been used by some scientists to argue against human cloning (Kahn, 1997). As we have seen, Harris believes that cloning does not amount to an affront on human dignity (Harris, 1997). He compares cloning with IVF, arguing that those who support this cannot logically object to cloning, that cloning can do 'some good', so should be welcomed. However, the notion of respect *does* seem to be relevant in this context. As we have argued above, cloning raises issues as to the motives *behind* such a cloning process. Are we really giving due respect to an individual if she or he has no 'natural' father, unless we assume that he is the 'grandfather'? What are the consequences socially and in a religious sense? While the papal ban on all IVF and cloning is clear-cut, many would urge that a distinction can and should be made to differentiate the two processes. Furthermore, the concept of *human* dignity is founded as much on the theological principle of humanity as made in the image of God as on the philosophical Kantian notion of treating all creatures as worthy of respect (rather than simply as means to one's ends).

(iv) Environmental consequences

As well as the above concern for the interests of the creature, we need to take into account the long-term interests of the environment as a whole, as well as the interests of the whole human community. For example, if we take the example of herbicide resistance introduced by genetic engineering, there seems to be little evidence that this causes immediate harm to the species involved. If anything, the crop benefits as now it is resistant to herbicides. Nonetheless, as we showed above, the potential effects on the ecosystem and the farming community could be catastrophic.

Holmes Rolston III has argued for the idea of systemic value as a way of taking into account the worth of the whole ecosystem(s) (Rolston, 1989:188). This could possibly be a useful concept as applied to the above example. However, the idea needs some qualification, as it can lead to an over-romanticised view of the biological integrity of the system, which is a highly debatable topic amongst ecologists. Eco-systems emerge in a more random way than is implied by some 'deep green' philosophers. Having said this, there is no guarantee that the new ecosystem that would develop after human interference would be either desirable or controllable. It is ironical, perhaps, that genetic engineering, which seeks to assert human power over the natural environment, can lead to situations which could, potentially, become uncontrollable. The utopian dream of a custom-made world is supposed to lead to a fully controlled environment for human habitation. Charges of sentimentality abound, both against genetic engineers and in return, against the animal liberationists.

The philosopher A. A. Brennan suggests that one of the main problems in making decisions about the environment is our lack of honesty (Brennan, 1992:18). The first myth he highlights is that of 'restoring nature', after human interventions such as mining, indus-trialization, etc. There is a strong belief that, given the right technology, we could restore nature to the original condition. We could add here the myth of 'improving nature' as applied to genetic engineering. A good example would be the attempt by scientists, so far unsuccessful, to transfer nitrogen-fixing genes from legumes, such as clover and peas, to cereal plants, such as wheat. Such transgenic experiments promise to improve nature by giving wheat plants the potential to fix gaseous nitrogen so that they would become less dependent on artificial fertilisers. More often than not projects are given an environmental gloss as a way of appropriating funds.

(v) The concept of 'wild' nature

Another common myth is that of 'wild' nature. Rolston has used this idea as a paradigm for his philosophy of environmental ethics (Rolston, 1989:221). Attached to this myth is the concept that all 'wild' ecosystems are both *stable* and *diverse*. While the characteristic of biodiversity does apply to the tropical rainforest, this is not true for all other ecosystems. We are not saying that the preservation of biodiversity is mistaken, rather it cannot be supported by reference to 'wild' nature.

The myth that the ecosystem is in a perfect state of balance which inevitably leads to the preservation of biological diversity is important for 'deep green' philosophers, as it seems to provide a biological basis for non-interference. However, absolute non-interference is not really an option for humans, any more than any other species. It is the *form* of meddling that raises moral, aesthetic and policy issues. The biodiversity of *species* in this context needs to be carefully distinguished from the variability in a given species that we mentioned above (**11.3 (iv)**). Natural variability in one species is an in-built mechanism for protection against disease. But the loss of species *themselves* through loss of highly diverse ecosystems, as in the tropical rainforests, cannot be desirable either. There is a case for the careful cultivation of national parks and other 'artificial' natural systems as places with inherent value, in addition to a simple preservation of 'wilderness', which in Europe at least is virtually non-existent (Attfield, 1994). While we would argue the case against some of the extremes of genetic engineering practice as applied to agriculture, humanity still has a responsibility to work with the natural world in creative cultivation and 'sustainable' development.

11.9   A rediscovery of wisdom: some lessons from biotechnology

A theological critique requires a radical change of attitude in formulating the goals of biotechnology – from one based on consumerism and the individual pursuit of happiness to a more community-based view that includes respect for the whole environment.

There need to be much tighter controls on transgenic experiments, which are not possible by conventional breeding, but to ban all genetic engineering is unrealistic and most likely to be dismissed by those who are already in power. Peters has argued convincingly that we need to avoid shrinking back from genetic engineering through fear that genes *alone* control the destiny of life. However, his stress on human freedom is still highly anthropocentric and has a tendency towards the individualism of the Enlightenment. One of his main arguments for supporting genetic engineering is to reduce suffering of those humans with genetic disease (Peters, 1997b:58). No one would deny that some advances have positive benefits for humans. However, Peters also refuses to accept the idea of the natural world as in any way sacred

(Peters, 1997b:13). While Christian theology does not regard the natural world as divine in the pantheistic sense, we still need to place love and respect at the heart of our approach to the natural world. Awareness of the presence of God in creation can become the lens through which we seek out our responsibilities in caring for the Earth. The most common mind-set amongst genetic engineers is to fix on a particular problem or goal and then to find ways of achieving this goal. *A theological approach encourages those who are involved to see the wider social and religious consequences of these decisions.* There seems to be no real philo-sophical basis for complete abstinence from genetic engineering as applied to agriculture. Rather, following Heidegger, *we need to work towards the transformation of genetic engineering so that it comes to represent a more fully humane enterprise, in touch with the immediate and long-term effects.*

How can this shift come about? Few would reject the idea that the quality we need to foster and develop in formulating new directions for science is that of *wisdom.* Science can no longer afford to focus on short-term commercial interest at the expense of the wider interest of the community. The public face of science is damaged by the portrayal of biotechnology as a mindless machine, bent on its own discoveries regardless of the consequences. The insights of ordinary people carry their own wisdom, the wisdom of the non-specialist. Even here we see an implicit religious language emerging which is part of our own particular cultural heritage. Again, from the margins of the human community other voices are raised in protest against lop-sided practices and policies.

11.9.1   Wisdom in theology

However, wisdom in the *theological* sense can take us further into an understanding of an adequate relationship between God, humanity and the cosmos. It can become the basis for an eco-theology that takes into account the insights of contemporary feminist thinkers, but finds echoes back to the ancient writings of the early Church Fathers and Eastern Orthodox Christianity. (Deane-Drummond, 1997a). This marriage of East and West is important, as it serves to challenge the reductionist presuppositions of Western culture as expressed in science. It is, nonetheless, a marriage rather than a replacement. To reject *all* the technology we have developed thus far seems unrealistic and naïve.

Instead the goals and aims of this technology need to be redirected in the light of the whole picture.

Hardy has also suggested that wisdom is closely connected with our understanding of God and God's relationship with the world. (Hardy, 1998:136). Wisdom is the dynamic interwovenness of God, the whole cosmos and humanity. Wisdom is the means through which we discover how far our purposes are matched with those of God. It is the 'dynamic of human knowledge, understanding and practice on the one hand, and God and the fulfilment of God's purposes on the other' (Hardy, 1998:137). Theological wisdom is thus both within and beyond human understanding. It challenges all human arrogance and shows the proper ordering of things in their relationship to each other. We need to ask ourselves how far this sense of ordering has become distorted in the transgenic and cloning practices emerging in modern biotechnology. The ancients saw both the sciences and theology as having a place within an overarching wisdom. The temptation today is to follow Aquinas and identify wisdom with knowledge. Goodness is subordinated to what is known. This seems particularly relevant for modern biotechnology. The truncated view of wisdom as 'know-how' needs to be replaced by a fuller idea of wisdom as carrier of beauty and goodness. The Russian Orthodox theologian Bulgakov describes wisdom as truth and beauty, reflecting the divine glory. Luther and Calvin portrayed the Wisdom of God as the transcendental contradiction to all worldly wisdom, but said wisdom was now radically separated from its source. Those who practised science resisted this description of wisdom, so that wisdom instead became reduced to knowledge alone, detached from 'the dynamics of the truth and goodness of the multi-dimensional world from and to God . . . this in turn produced an inability to deal with the moral implications of the knowledge which was achieved, and a blindness to consequences' (Hardy, 1998:142).

Hardy suggests further that the re-opening of wisdom that we desperately need today comes through worship. Nonetheless, he does not spell out how this worship might find expression. Is this confined to the Christian community? We would prefer to advocate a shared search for the beauty and goodness of wisdom within the particular religious traditions of individuals and their communities. This would lead to the possibility of dialogue between different cultures and religious groups. The possibility of a global ethic, suggested by Hans

Küng, is attractive in this respect (Küng, 1990:56–62). The difficulty with this view and any which seek alliance across cultures is that we tend to end up with the lowest common denominator, which has no real impact in practice.

11.9.2   Wisdom in practice

The future of ethical practice through the lens of wisdom looks to the Ultimate Wisdom of God, which is both now, and 'not yet'. In this way wisdom can challenge those projects which assume that the future is one which just emerges from the present. If science is to have an ethic, a value that is truly rooted in knowledge of Being, then science must learn to listen to the voice of wisdom. One way where this could start would be in the design and implementation of science policy. Those responsible for making decisions for funding need to ask not just, 'Does this fit in with the logic of our current state of knowledge?' or, more insidiously 'Will this make a profit?', but 'Is this wise?', 'What are the long term as well as the short term benefits?', 'What effect will this have on the social and cultural context as well as the environmental context?' This would apply particularly to the whole issue of the possibility of human cloning which we discussed above. It is getting a grip on the complexity of each problem which can seem daunting; it is tempting to ignore the complexity in favour of one or other factor. The pressure just to look at one issue, to the exclusion of all others, is a legacy of scientific method which has conditioned us to think in this way in our ethical decisions as well.

One of the failures in biotechnology seems to be a failure to address the issue of who takes responsibility. Furthermore, we need to be clear about what these responsibilities are and who takes account of positive responsibilities, that is, duties that are specific to this profession. A clarification and demarcation of responsibilities, including protecting the environment, keeping a check on the advantage in the marketplace and consumer interests and concerns, all require proper use of wisdom. Busch *et al.* have suggested that we need adequate assessment of:

- future health risks associated with biotechnology;
- future environmental consequences;

- future burdens and benefits associated with the transformation of institutions;
- an assessment of decrease in quality of life associated with shift in nature and focus of science resulting from biotechnology research and development.

(Busch *et al.*, 1992:191–92)

We would like to add a fifth, namely *an assessment of the social and cultural impact arising directly out of the new technologies*. While it is linked to the last element on Busch's list, it puts emphasis on cultural and social impact, rather than 'quality of life', which could imply restriction to material good, or restriction to quality as defined from a Western perspective.

11.10 Conclusion

To conclude: overall we have shown that the promise of biotechnology is an ambiguous one and that the latest advances present new challenges for theology and ethics. On the one hand biotechnology promises, for example, to assist medical science in its search for the diagnosis and treatment of disease, while on the other hand it has the potential for profound negative environmental and social consequences. Issues such as patenting, transgenic experimentation, the loss of genetic diversity and particular threats to human and environmental well-being through direct and indirect influences all require careful consideration. The belief that all life is entirely defined by genetics needs to be challenged, but the consequences of the use of the technology have to be assessed carefully and with appropriate caution. The theological approach that may be best suited to assisting the struggle to find a future for biotechnology is that of *wisdom*. Wisdom incorporates the science of the Enlightenment, but looks to reshape it along different lines. It is a gathering up of what is positive in all our history, rather than ignoring what has taken place. Facing up to the difficulties of the present also means facing up to the negative, a *metanoia* from old attitudes that have been damaging and destructive. A theological approach to wisdom has no room for arrogance and a false utopia. Rather, it admits the reality of suffering and evil, but refuses to give them the last word. The God of Wisdom takes on the suffering and evil and challenges all human attempts to find wisdom as if it is a possession to be grasped and used for human aggrandisement. Wisdom can, furthermore, increase our capacity to wonder: to be full of awe at the beauty of the cosmos, in celebration of life as individuals and in community with the natural world.

FURTHER READING

BARBOUR, I. G. (1992) *Ethics in an Age of Technology* (London: SCM Press), pp. 85–115

BRUCE, D. and BRUCE, A. (eds) (1998) *Engineering Genesis: The Ethics of Genetic Engineering in Non-human Species* (London: Earthscan), pp. 77–109

DEANE-DRUMMOND, C. (1997) *Theology and Biotechnology: Implications for a New Science* (London: Geoffrey Chapman), pp. 79–101; 133–56

PETERS, T. (1997) *Playing God: Genetic Determinism and Human Freedom* (London: Routledge), pp. 1–26

REISS, M. and STRAUGHAN, R. (1996) *Improving Nature: the Science and Ethics of Genetic Engineering* (Cambridge: Cambridge University Press), pp. 43–89

SHIVA, V. (1995) 'Biotechnological Development and the Conservation of Diversity' in V. Shiva and I. Muser, eds (1995) *Biopolitics: A feminist and Ecological Reader on Biotechnology* (London: Zed Books), pp. 193–293

BOOK FIVE

Chapter 12

A Look to the Future

12.1 Introduction

We have shown that there is a conversation between different sciences and religion which need not be on the basis of conflict. We have stressed throughout the diversity of the relationships involved and their dynamic quality. Both scientific and theological models are frequently in a state of flux. Because of the complexity of the issues we do not offer a summary here – the ongoing exercise of the book has been that the reader make his or her own summaries. Instead this chapter will be given over to a consideration of how this 'special relationship' we have been studying might develop in the future.

12.2 One-way traffic

But before we do so we note one preconception which all our explorations has not overturned. We have rejected John Updike's caricature (**1.1**) that each science in turn has 'harried' theology out of a different sphere of influence. We have worked from the Bossey Circle (page 16) which calls on theology to learn from scientific insights and give rise to ethics and praxis, and we have encouraged readers to develop models to that effect. We have noted the possibility that the insights and images of different religions might feed the imagination of scientists. Both Drees and Clayton imply that theological preferences might influence a scientist in her/his choice of model (Drees, 1990:67– 68, see **1.15**; Clayton, 1997a:239, see **7.4**).

It is true that the innovative proposals of Copernicus and Kepler (**1.12**) were both informed by aesthetic, quasi-religious ideas from Greek thought. And Thomas Kuhn's work (see **2.10**) emphasised the limits that exist on what 'can be thought' in a particular scientific field – all sorts of factors influence this, including the symbolism of religion, and the metaphysics to which theology gives rise. But our wide-ranging survey of the sciences has turned up only two modern cases where a major scientist's choice of model was strongly influenced by theological inclination:

(a) Albert Einstein's vigorous opposition to the mainstream of quantum physics on the grounds that 'God does not play dice' (see **3.11 (iii)**). Reality could not, in Einstein's view, be probabilistic in its ultimate character. This provided quantum theory with its keenest critic, but the weight of opinion continues to be greatly against Einstein.

(b) Fred Hoyle's development of the steady-state theory of the universe in opposition to the Big Bang. As we indicated in **1.15** Hoyle's resistance to the idea of a 'Genesis-like' beginning led him to develop (with others) a very sophisticated counter-theory. But again, the weight of scientific evidence and opinion has run strongly against his view.

So these cases seem to be rare, and even in the case of the most distinguished of scientists religiously-informed insights need not necessarily be vindicated. We continue to grant the possibility that religion might have this sort of influence, but concede that overwhelmingly the traffic is in the other direction. Thus Watts: 'Theologians are more concerned with what scientists have to say than vice versa' (**5.1**). New scientific narratives inform and constrain what can be thought theologically, as we saw particularly with the doctrine of the Fall (**4.16.2**).

12.3   Looking to the future

It is relatively unusual for a book in either science or religious studies to spend time on guesswork about how the subject will develop beyond the date of publication. Such 'crystal-ball gazing' tends to be stimulated only by particular anniversaries or landmarks. Thus the conference celebrating the fiftieth anniversary of Schrödinger's *What is Life?* led to a book entitled *What is Life? The Next Fifty Years: Speculations on the Future of Biology* (Murphy and O'Neill, 1995).

Inevitably the end of the millennium comes to be seen as a point at which to take stock. Thus it has given rise to books with titles like *The End of History* (and, indeed, *The End of Science*!). It is also a time to try and look forward. However, it is enormously difficult to predict how interdisciplinary dialogues, such as those between sciences and religions, will unfold. Of necessity this unfolding will be a function of innovative developments in each particular science, and in theology in all its branches – from the scriptural to the systematic. Again, a very influential book on the *dialogue* can alter the whole way the relationships between subjects are viewed.

Holmes Rolston III has recently offered his gaze into the crystal ball (Rolston, 1996:61–82). He predicts, in effect, that cosmological physics is likely to continue to enjoy something of a 'special relationship' with monotheism, since so many physicists have seemed to discern a place for (at the least) a law-giving agent. He acknowledges that there is by no means the same link between evolutionary biology and monotheism and wonders if further understanding of the science underlying increases in biological complexity (see **4.8.2**) will bring a rapprochement between biology and theology. We are not clear that it will – a more comprehensive scientific explanation of complexification will not of itself promote a sense of divine immanence 'in, with and under' (to use Arthur Peacocke's much-copied phrase) biological processes. If anything it may serve to fuel a sense that the only sort of God that can function as an explanation is a God of initial conditions. A God who fine-tuned what we know as the anthropic coincidences (**3.19–3.23, 7.11**) is not *necessarily* more than a deist God. The God of the-tendency-of-complex-systems-to-move-to-the-edge-of-chaos could belong to the same stable.

The question we want to ask is slightly different – not, where will the different dialogues be in a few years' time? Rather, what will the matters of pressing concern be to those who teach and write and confer at the science–religion interface? Were this book to be rewritten in ten or twenty or thirty years, what would be its emphases? The besetting concern with divine action in the light of contemporary science, the main theme of five Vatican Observatory Conferences, seems to be running its course – at least in its initial form as a debate about determinacy, indeterminacy and the causal joint. We have reviewed the current impasse in Sections **7.6–7.9**. We expect the debate to revive in some years' time, fuelled by developments in cognitive science (see below).

12.3.1   Exploration across a range of religions

A marked development in the last couple of years has been *the general interest in exploring the relation of science to religions other than Christianity.* This is already of value (not least to the Christian) for a number of reasons:

(a) Looking at a range of religions challenges the constructs too easily put on Christianity as being the sole or necessary context for the development of knowledge about the natural world. We refer to the Golden Age of Islam at **9.5**. Chinese medicine provides a sophisticated system for describing health having only tangential contacts with the Western system for describing disease. And while Eastern religions have not given rise to a system as successful in interpreting physical regularities as Western science, it could be argued that they have been just as successful in promoting human wisdom (the need for which is so evident from our discussions in Chapters 10 and 11).

(b) The exploration of many-religions dialogue with scientific themes provides important common ground on which adherents of different religions can meet without some of the squabbling that inter-religious meetings have sometimes engendered. The self-confidence and general integrity of the scientific enterprise can provide a ground of mutual respect and hope from which inter-religious dialogue can take new steps towards understanding.

(c) Different religious views of the world provide, as was hinted at **6.9**, a new set of images and metaphors which may feed the imagination of scientists and hence broaden the range of models that can be generated.

We expect comparative studies involving different religions, and comparisons between the spiritualities of working scientists, to continue to be in the forefront of the debate.

12.3.2   The implications of the new genetics

There seems little doubt that the completion of the Human Genome Project, though it represents no major conceptual advance, will nevertheless be a landmark in the development of scientific knowledge of the human person. We mention the possibility of the growth of genetic reductionism at **4.12** and again in Chapter 11. At the very least the possibility of obtaining a one-dimensional string of letters which could be encoded on a 'smart card' or chip and which would describe the complete genetic inheritance of a human, including their propensities to contract certain diseases – not just the 'classic' genetic disorders present from birth such as haemophilia or cystic fibrosis but diseases typical of later life such as breast cancer – will challenge humans to attend closely to the nature of human being.

At the same time questions will continue to arise as to when human life can be considered to begin and end, and what procedures may be used to give rise to life, or to terminate it. These classic questions in medical ethics will require further intensive theological reflection on the person – also on the respective creative roles of God and humanity. What, for instance, constitutes *appropriate* co-creativity in the 'created co-creator' of Hefner's phrase? (Hefner, 1993) Does human cloning?

The possibilities offered by new genetics and new medicine will be a vastly important area in which theologians must understand the science, and question the values that prompt the directions in which it searches, in order to formulate ethical principles which are both relevant to the moment and faithful to the traditions from which the principles derive.

12.3.3   The status of animals

Allied to genetic progress will be developments in our understanding of the capacities and experiences of non-human animals and their abilities. These seem likely further to shade the distinctions between humans and the most intelligent and social of the other mammals (see **4.15.2–4.16.1**). Again the doctrine of humanity will be challenged by this, as will our understanding of the appropriate treatment of domesticated animals. Other figures will emerge alongside Andrew Linzey, who has been the pioneer in trying to provide ethical prescriptions in this area with a theological basis (see Linzey, 1994).

12.3.4   The science and theology of consciousness

We see the rise of consciousness studies – in the broadest sense – as the most important likely development in those areas of science in most active dialogue with theologians. We mentioned in **1.5** the rapid rise in neuroscience, and cognitive psychology will surely also develop apace, together with the understandings of intelligence provided by computer simulations of various sorts. But as Watts emphasises the study of *emotions* will be just as important as the study of computation-like problem-solving – possibly more so as leading to a more holistic picture of 'the brain minding the body' (cf. Damasio, 1995:159).

Not only will an increased understanding of consciousness, self-awareness and human agency affect our sense of our relation to other animals, it will also have a crucial effect on our understanding of human interaction, of sin, and ultimately of divine agency, to which human agency remains our principal analogy (**7.4–7.4.1**).

12.3.5   Physics

It may seem surprising that in this gaze into the future nothing has been said about physics. There may indeed be, in twenty years, a unified account of physical forces, a 'Theory of Everything'. But cosmological physics is a field already aware of its limits, aware that in considering such questions as to whether there is one universe or many, and whether this universe had a cause, the science presses up against metaphysical assumptions which it cannot itself dictate. That is why our guess is, like Rolston's, that there may be little change in the relationship between physics and theology.

An exception would be if a radically new understanding were to develop of the nature of quantum mechanics, or of its relation to the macroscopic world. We have shown how important quantum indeterminacy has been in the argument over the real, ontological openness of the world to the future – a change in our understanding of that would be of the greatest philosophical and theological significance. Equally, the implications of quantum non-locality, the continuing relations of quantised particles once they have interacted (see **3.11 (iii)**) have yet to be fully worked out. And a new consensus on 'the measurement problem' (see **3.13**) would have a great influence on our understanding of the macroscopic world. It is because these advances seem so elusive that we give them little prominence here.

12.4 The integration of science, technology, religion and ethics

Rolston ends his predictions with a consideration of the ethics of science and of the new technologies which grow around it. His plea is that science be applied more equitably to the question of how over five billion persons can live on this planet. That it be recognised that scientific knowledge confers power, that religious values are necessary if just and appropriate use is to be made of that power. Sustainability in human activity can arise only if science gives us the data by which we can know the resources we are wasting, and religion and ethics give us a new sense of justice and wisdom in their use. 'The dialogue between science and religion' Rolston concludes, 'is likely to continue. There will be a humane future only if we can integrate the two' (1996:78).

In ending on such a prophetic note we do not suppose that this integration can come easily, or be any freer of disputes and squabbles than any other 'special relationship'. But the momentum for increased dialogue *is* there, and the stakes, as the new millennium begins, could hardly be higher.

FURTHER READING

CHAPMAN, A. (1998) 'The Greening of Science, Theology and Ethics' in *Science and Theology. The New Consonance* ed. by Ted Peters (Oxford: Westview Press), pp. 211–27

HARDY, D. (1998) 'The God who is with the World' in *Science Meets Faith* ed. by Fraser Watts (London: SPCK), pp. 136–53

MURPHY, M. P. and O'NEILL, L. A. J. (1995) *What is Life? The Next Fifty Years* (Cambridge: Cambridge University Press)

ROLSTON III, H. (1996) 'Science, Religion and the Future' in *Religion and Science*, ed. by W. Mark Richardson and Wesley J. Wildman (London: Routledge), pp. 61–82

Appendix

A Note for Teachers

Quite a difference may be found between teaching the science–religion debate to science students and to those in the humanities with little or no science background.

Science students may have a strong grasp of the factual claims of contemporary science, and the mathematical and experimental basis on which those claims are arrived at. They are sometimes less strong at adopting a critical attitude to the sciences, or at seeing that science is one among a range of types of rational enquiry. So particular attention may be given to the philosophical material in Chapter 2. It may be helpful to point out that a highly sceptical empiricism, such as lay behind logical positivism, would make it next to impossible to advance science, as well as to contemplate any sort of theological scheme.

Students specialising in the humanities, in contrast, often lack confidence in addressing the conclusions of science. Indeed there are problems in expounding these conclusions without the use of mathematics. Much however can be done by means of diagrams and analogies.

One way in which it may be possible to catch the imagination of certain students (especially those who declare themselves 'allergic' to science) is through reference to literary works which raise scientific topics. It may be helpful to start a discussion of the Copernican revolution using *Paradise Lost* VIII, 117f., or of the anthropic principles using Dante's *Paradiso* X, 7–21. Tennyson's *In Memoriam* LV-LVI (interestingly published before *The Origin of Species*) provocatively raises issues about the relations between God and evolution.

To cite a few more recent sources: Tom Stoppard has a fascinating comedy *Hapgood* using the paradoxes of quantum mechanics as a metaphor for espionage. Graham Swift's novel *Ever After* turns in part on the struggles of a nineteenth-century thinker who realises he must accept the conclusions of Darwin. And the title poem of R. S. Thomas' *Mass for Hard Times* is one of many in which the poet uses the language and concepts of science to probe the question of humans' wisdom, or lack of it. Teachers will no doubt call their own favourite examples to mind.

Another useful stratagem is to bring into the class a practising scientist in the field being studied at the time. Not because that person is necessarily the best conveyer of the basic information the students need, but because it helps them to see the cast of mind of that particular type of researcher, and the ways they articulate their subject.

It is helpful to emphasise that students will know more than they think – if only from having heard reports of new scientific break-throughs in the media – and that they will already have preformed opinions, however little articulated, about the relation between sciences and the claims of religion. So although it may be that a certain amount of factual material has to be provided (as we have done in Chapters 3–5 in particular) a conversation needs to develop in which these pre-existing views are tested and honed.

We have provided a very extensive bibliography of printed sources, and referred from time to time to two journals important in the UK – *Science and Christian Belief* and *Zygon*. The former is the more 'evangelical' of the two. Other educational resources were mentioned in Chapter 8. More and more, however, fast-moving academic debates will draw on the World Wide Web as the primary means of communication. As a way in, we mention one developing resource which promises to be important in this connection: the Website of the Oregon-based organisation 'Counterbalance'. This can be found at http://www.counterbalance.org. At the time of writing Counterbalance are organising discussion lists, publishing articles on the Web, and producing a glossary of key terms in religion and science. They should be well worth consulting.

References and Bibliography

AL-'ALWANI, T. J. (1989) 'Islamization of attitudes and practices in science and technology' in *Islamization of Attitudes and Practices in Science and Technology*, ed. by M. A. K. Lodhi (Herndon, VA: Association of Muslim Scientists and Engineers)

AQUINAS, T. (1956) *On the Truth of the Catholic Faith: Summa Contra Gentiles, Book III: Providence*, transl. by V. J. Bourke (Garden City, NY: Doubleday & Co.)

—— (1964) *Summa Theologiæ, Volume I: Christian Theology (Ia.1)*, transl. by T. Gilby OP (London: Eyre & Spottiswoode)

—— (1967) *Summa Theologiæ, Volume 8: Creation, Variety and Evil (Ia.44–49)*, transl. by T. Gilby OP (London: Eyre & Spottiswoode)

—— (1975) *Summa Theologiae, Volume 14: Divine Government (Ia.105.5)*, transl. by T. C. O'Brien (London: Eyre & Spottiswoode)

ARMSTRONG-BUCK, S. (1986) 'Whitehead's metaphysical system as a foundation for environmental ethics' in *Environmental Ethics 8*, 241–59

ASHRIF, S. (1998) 'Science teaching, culture and religious values', *School Science Review 79* (288) 51–54

ASSOCIATION FOR SCIENCE EDUCATION (1981) *Science in Society* (London / Hatfield: Heinemann / ASE) [consisting of a Teacher's Guide and 12 Readers and suitable for a General Studies course for sixth forms]

—— (1983) *Science In a Social CONtext (SISCON)-in-Schools)* (Hatfield: ASE) [eight booklets providing for a General Studies course for sixth forms]

ASSOCIATION FOR SCIENCE EDUCATION (1986–) Science and Technology in Society (SATIS) [contains materials for 14–16 year olds, 16–19 year olds and 8–14 year olds] (Hatfield: ASE)

—— (1994) *Models and Modelling in Science Education* (Hatfield: ASE)

—— (1998) *Summary of Policies* (Hatfield: ASE)

—— (1998) *Values and Science Education,* policy statement (Hatfield: ASE)

ATKINS, P. W. (1981) *The Creation* (Oxford: Freeman)

ATTFIELD, R. (1983) *The Ethics of Environmental Concern* (Oxford: Blackwell)

—— (1994) 'Rehabilitating nature and making nature habitable' in *Philosophy and the Natural Environment,* ed. by R. Attfield and A. Belsey (Cambridge: Cambridge University Press), pp. 45–58

AYALA, F. (1985) 'Reduction in biology: a recent challenge' in *Evolution at a Crossroads,* ed. by D. J. Depew and B. H. Weber (Cambridge, MA: MIT Press), pp. 65–79

AYER, A. J. (1971) *Language, Truth and Logic* (Harmondsworth: Penguin, first pub. Victor Gollancz, 1936)

BAGLEY, F. R. C. (translator) (1964) *Ghazzali's Book of Counsel for Kings (Nasihat al-Muluk)* (Oxford: Oxford University Press)

BAK, P. (1997) *How Nature Works* (Oxford: Oxford University Press)

BALL, I. *et al.* (eds) (1992) *The Earth Beneath* (London: SPCK)

BANCROFT, A. (ed.) (1997) *The Dhammapada* (Shaftesbury: Element)

BANNER, M. C. (1990) *The Justification of Science and the Rationality of Religious Belief* (Oxford: Clarendon Press)

BARBOUR, I. G. (1968) *Issues in Science and Religion* (London: SCM Press)

—— (1974) *Myths, Models and Paradigms: A Comparative Study in Science and Religion* (San Francisco: Harper & Row)

—— (1990) *Religion in an Age of Science* (London: SCM Press)

—— (1992) *Ethics in an Age of Technology* (London: SCM Press)

—— (1998) *Religion and Science: Historical and Contemporary Issues* (London: SCM Press)

BARROW, J. D. and TIPLER, F. J. (1986) *The Anthropic Cosmological Principle* (Oxford: Clarendon Press)

BARTH, K. (1936) *Church Dogmatics, Volume I, Part 1*, transl. by G. T. Thomson (Edinburgh: T&T Clark)

—— (1957) *Church Dogmatics, Volume II, Part 1*, transl. by T. H. L. Parker, W. B. Johnston, H. Knight and J. L. M. Haire (Edinburgh: T&T Clark)

—— (1961) *Church Dogmatics, Volume IV, Part 3, I*, transl. by G. W. Bromiley (Edinburgh: T&T Clark)

—— (1968) *The Epistle to the Romans*, transl. by E. C. Hoskyns (Oxford: Oxford University Press)

BARTHOLOMEW, D. J. (1984) *God of Chance* (London: SCM Press)

BAR-YOSEF, O. and VAN-DERMEERSCH, B. (1993) 'Modern humans in the Levant', *Scientific American* 268 (4), 64–70

BASALLA, G. (1988) *The Evolution of Technology* (Cambridge: Cambridge University Press)

BAUSOR, J., BLACK, P., POOLE, M. and WOOLNOUGH, B. (1995) 'Keep your spirits up', *Times Educational Supplement*, EXTRA SCIENCE, p. XI, 29 Dec

BEIT-HALLAHMI, B. and ARGYLE, M. (1997) *The Psychology of Religious Belief, Behaviour and Experience* (London: Routledge)

BERG, P. and SINGER, M. (1992) *Dealing with Genes* (Mill Valley, CA: University Science Books)

BERNSTEIN, R. J. (1983) *Beyond Objectivism and Relativism: Science, Hermeneutics and Praxis* (Oxford: Blackwell)

BERRY, T. (1987) 'The Earth: a new context for religious unity' in A. Lonergan and C. Richards (eds), *Thomas Berry and The New Cosmology* (Connecticut: Twenty-Third Publications), pp. 27–39

BIRCH, C. *et al.* (1990), *Liberating Life* (Maryknoll, NY: Orbis Books)

BIRCH, C. and COBB, J. B. (1981) *The Liberation of Life* (Cambridge: Cambridge University Press)

BLACKBURN, S. (1994) *The Oxford Dictionary of Philosophy* (Oxford: Oxford University Press)

BOFF, L. (1995) *Ecology and Liberation: A New Paradigm*, transl. by J. Cumming (Maryknoll, NY: Orbis Books)

Boff, L. (1997) *Cry of the Earth: Cry of the Poor*, transl. by P. Berryman (Maryknoll, NY: Orbis Books)

Bohm, D. (1980) *Wholeness and the Implicato Order* (London: Routledge & Kegan Paul)

Bowker, J. (1995) *Is God A Virus? Genes, Culture and Religion* (London: SPCK)

Braithwaite, R. B. (1971) 'An empiricist's view of the nature of religious belief: the ninth Arthur Stanley Eddington Memorial Lecture', reprinted in *The Philosophy of Religion*, ed. by B. Mitchell (Oxford: Oxford University Press), pp. 72–91

Brandon, R. N. (1985) 'Adaptation explanations: are adaptations for the good of replicators or interactors?' in *Evolution at a Crossroads*, ed. by D. J. Depew and B. H. Weber (Cambridge, MA: MIT Press), pp. 81–95

Brennan, A. A. (1992) 'Environmental decision making' in *Environmental Dilemmas: Ethics and Decisions*, ed. by R. J. Berry (London: Chapman & Hall)

Broglie, L. de (1949) 'A general survey of the scientific work of Albert Einstein' in *Albert Einstein: Philosopher-Scientist*, ed. by P. A. Schilpp (La Salle, IL: Open Court), pp. 107–27

Brooke, J. H. (1991) *Science and Religion: Some Historical Perspectives* (Cambridge: Cambridge University Press)

—— (1996) 'Science and theology in the Enlightenment' in *Religion and Science: History, Method, Dialogue*, ed. by W. M. Richardson and W. J. Wildman (London: Routledge), pp. 7–27

Brooke, J. H. and Cantor, G. (1998) *Reconstructing Nature: The Engagement of Science and Religion* (Edinburgh: T&T Clark)

Brown, A., Hookway, S. and Poole, M. (1997) *God-talk: Science-talk – A Teachers' Guide to Science and Belief* (Oxford: Lion Publishing)

Brown, L. (1988) *The Psychology of Religion: An Introduction* (London: SPCK)

Brueggemann, W. (1984) *The Message of the Psalms: A Theological Commentary* (Minneapolis, MN: Fortress Press)

Bruce, D. and Bruce, A. (eds) (1998) *Engineering Genesis: The Ethics of Genetic Engineering in Non-human Species* (London: Earthscan), pp. 77–109

BRUNNER, E. (1953) *Eternal Hope* (London: Lutterworth Press)

BRYCE, D. (1984) *Wisdom of the Taoist Masters [a translation from the French of Leon Wieger's Les Pères du Système Taoiste]* (Lampeter: Llanerch Enterprises)

—— (1991) *Tao-Te-Ching*: Translated from the Chinese by L. Wieger – English language version by D. Bryce (Felinfach: Llanerch Publishers)

BUCAILLE, M. (1986) *What is the Origin of Man?* (Paris: Seghers, 4th edn).

—— (1989) *The Bible, the Quran and Science* (Paris: Seghers, 6th edn)

BUCKLEY, M. J. (1987) *At the Origins of Modern Atheism* (New Haven, CT: Yale University Press)

BUGLIARELLO, G. (1995) 'Science at the crossroads' in *Cosmic Beginnings and Human Ends*, ed. by C. N. Matthews and R. A. Varghese (La Salle, IL: Open Court), pp. 109–28

BULTMANN, R. (1985) 'New Testament and mythology: demythologizing the New Testament proclamation' in *New Testament and Mythology and Other Basic Writings*, ed. and transl. by S. M. Ogden (London: SCM Press), pp. 1–43

BURCKHARDT, T. (1988) *An Introduction to Sufi Doctrine*, transl. by D. M. Matheson (Lahore: Sh. Muhammad Ashraf)

BURKE, D. C. (1998) in *Science Meets Faith*, ed. by F. Watts (London: SPCK), pp. 42–58

BUSCH, L., LACY, W. B., BURKHARDT, J. and LACY, L. R. (1992) *Plants, Power and Profit: Social, Economic and Ethical Consequences of the New Biotechnologies* (Oxford: Blackwell)

BUTLER, D. and WADMAN, M. (1997), 'Calls for cloning ban sell science short', *Nature 386*, 8–9

BUTT, N. (1991) *Science and Muslim Societies* (London: Grey Seal)

BUTTEL, F. (1986) 'Biotechnology and agricultural research' in *New Directives for Agriculture and Agricultural Research*, ed. by K. Dahlberg (Totowa: Rowman & Allanheld)

CAIRNS-SMITH, A. G. (1990) *Seven Clues to the Origin of Life* (Cambridge: Cambridge University Press, rev. edn)

CAMPBELL, D. T. (1976) 'On the conflicts between biological and social evolution and between psychology and moral tradition', *Zygon 11*, 167–208

CANTOR, G. (1991) *Michael Faraday: Sandemanian and Scientist, A Study of Science and Religion in the Nineteenth Century* (Basingstoke: Macmillan)

CAPEK, M. (ed.) (1976) *The Concepts of Space and Time* (Dordrecht: Reidel)

CAPRA, F. (1976) *The Tao of Physics* (London: Fontana / Collins)

—— (1983) *The Turning Point* (London: Flamingo / Fontana)

—— (1996) *The Web of Life* (London: Flamingo / HarperCollins)

CASSIRER, H. (1989), *God's New Covenant – A New Testament Translation* (Grand Rapids, MI: Eerdmans)

Catechism of the Catholic Church (1994) [transl. of the *edition typical*] (London: Geoffrey Chapman)

CHARIS SCIENCE: Unit 1 The Value of Life (Sc2), Unit 2 Body Matters (Sc2), Unit 3 It's All in the Balance (Sc2), Unit 4 Watch Your Waste (Sc2), Unit 5 A Brief History of Atoms (Sc3), Unit 6 Metals (Sc3), Unit 7 Most Noble Nobel (Sc3), Unit 8 Continental Drift (Sc3), Unit 9 There's No Place Like Home (Sc4), Unit 10 The Big Bang (Sc4), Unit 11 Fuel Consumption (Sc4) (Nottingham: The Stapleford Centre)

CHURCHLAND, P. S. (1986) *Neurophilosophy: Towards a Unified Science of the Mind / Brain* (Cambridge, MA: MIT Press)

CLARK, S. R. L. (1993) *How to Think about the Earth* (London: Mowbrays)

CLAYTON, P. (1997a) *God and Contemporary Science* (Edinburgh: Edinburgh Academic Press)

—— (1997b) 'Inference to the best explanation', *Zygon* 32 (3), 377–91

COMINS, N. (1993) *What if the Moon didn't Exist?* (New York: HarperCollins)

CONWAY MORRIS, S. (1998) *The Crucible of Creation* (Oxford: Oxford University Press)

COPELAND, J. (1993) *Artificial Intelligence: A Philosophical Introduction* (Oxford: Blackwell)

COTTERILL, R. (1989) *No Ghost in the Machine* (London: Heinemann)

COULSON, C. A. (1958) *Science and Christian Belief* (London: Fontana)

CRAIG, W. L. and SMITH, Q. (1993) *Theism, Atheism and Big Bang Cosmology* (Oxford: Clarendon Press)

CRICK, F. (1994) *The Astonishing Hypothesis: The Scientific Search for the Soul* (London: Simon & Schuster)

CRUTCHFIELD, J. P. *et al.* (1995) 'Chaos' in *Chaos and Complexity: Scientific Perspectives on Divine Action*, ed. by R. J. Russell, N. Murphy and A. Peacocke (Vatican City: Vatican Observatory), pp. 35–48 [reprinted from *Scientific American* 225 (6), 46–57 (1986)]

DfE see Department for Education

DES see Department of Education and Science

DALAI LAMA (14th: Tenzin Gyatso) (1994) *A Flash of Lightning in the Dark of Night: a Guide to the Bodhisattva's Way of Life* (Boston: Shambala)

—— (1997) *The Buddha Nature: death and eternal soul in Buddhism* (Woodside, CA: Bluestar Pubns)

DAMASIO, A. (1995) *Descartes' Error* (London: Picador)

D'AQUILI, E. and NEWBERG, A. (1998) 'The neuropsychology of religion' in *Science Meets Faith*, ed. by F. Watts (London: SPCK)

DARWIN, C. (1859) *The Origin of Species by Means of Natural Selection or the Preservation of Favoured Races in the Struggle for Life* (London: John Murray). References refer to the 1985 Penguin edition, ed. by J. W. Burrows (Harmondsworth: Penguin), which contains the full text of Darwin's first edition.

DAVIES, P. (1974) *The Physics of Time Asymmetry* (Leighton Buzzard: Surrey University Press)

—— (1982) *The Accidental Universe* (Cambridge: Cambridge University Press)

—— (1990) *God and the New Physics* (Harmondsworth: Penguin)

—— (1993) *The Mind of God* (Harmondsworth: Penguin)

—— (1995) *About Time* (Harmondsworth: Penguin)

DAWKINS, R. (1978) *The Selfish Gene* (London: Paladin / Granada Publishing)

—— (1991) *The Blind Watchmaker* (Harmondsworth: Penguin, reprint with appendix)

—— (1998) *Unweaving the Rainbow: Science, Delusion and The Appetite for Wonder* (London: Allen Lane, The Penguin Press)

DEACON, T. (1997) *The Symbolic Species* (Harmondsworth: Penguin)

DEANE-DRUMMOND, C. (1996) *A Handbook on Theology and Ecology* (London: SCM Press)

—— (1997a) 'Sophia: The feminine face of God as a metaphor for an ecotheology', *Feminist Theology 16*, 11–31

—— (1997b) *Theology and Biotechnology: Implications for a New Science* (London: Geoffrey Chapman)

—— (1997c) *Ecology in Jürgen Moltmann's Theology* (Lewiston, NY: Edwin Mellen Press)

DENNETT, D. C. (1991) *Consciousness Explained* (Harmondsworth: Penguin)

—— (1995) *Darwin's Dangerous Idea* (Harmondsworth: Penguin)

DEPARTMENT FOR EDUCATION letter (21 March 1995)

DEPARTMENT FOR EDUCATION / WELSH OFFICE EDUCATION DEPARTMENT (1995) *Science in the National Curriculum* (London: HMSO)

DEPARTMENT OF EDUCATION AND SCIENCE AND THE WELSH OFFICE (1989) *Science in the National Curriculum* (London: HMSO)

—— (1991) *Science in the National Curriculum* (London: HMSO)

DEPEW, D. J. and WEBER B. H. (eds) (1985) *Evolution at a Crossroads* (Cambridge, MA: MIT Press)

—— (1995) *Darwinism Evolving* (Cambridge, MA: MIT Press)

DERKSE, W. (1993) *On Simplicity and Elegance: An Essay in Intellectual History* (Delft: Eburon)

DESMOND, A. and MOORE, J. (1992) *Darwin* (Harmondsworth: Penguin)

DEVALL, B. and SESSIONS, G. (1985) *Deep Ecology* (Salt Lake City, UT: Peregrine Smith)

DIAMOND, J. (1991) *The Rise and Fall of the Third Chimpanzee* (London: Hutchinson Radius)

—— (1995) 'The evolution of human inventiveness' in *What is Life? The Next Fifty Years: Speculations on the Future of Biology*, ed. by M. P. Murphy and L. A. J. O'Neill (Cambridge: Cambridge University Press), pp. 41–55

DOSTOEVSKY, F. (1958) *The Brothers Karamazov*, transl. by D. Magarshack (Harmondsworth: Penguin)

DOWDESWELL, W. H. (1984) *Evolution: a Modern Synthesis* (London, Heinemann Educational)

DREES, W. (1990) *Beyond the Big Bang: Quantum Cosmologies and God* (La Salle, IL: Open Court)

—— (1995) 'Gaps for God?' in *Chaos and Complexity: Scientific Perspectives on Divine Action*, ed. by R. J. Russell, N. Murphy and A. Peacocke (Vatican City: Vatican Observatory), pp. 223–37

—— (1996) *Religion, Science and Naturalism* (Cambridge: Cambridge University Press)

DUHEM, P. (1954) *The Aim and Structure of Physical Theory*, transl. by P. P. Weiner (Princeton, NJ: Princeton University Press, first French edn 1906)

DYSON, A. and HARRIS, J. (eds) (1994) *Ethics and Biotechnology* (London: Routledge)

ECUMENICAL PATRIARCHATE (1990) *Orthodoxy and the Ecological Crisis* (Gland: World Wide Fund for Nature)

EDELMAN, G. (1992) *Bright Air: Brilliant Fire: On the Matter of the Mind* (Harmondsworth: Penguin)

EDUCATION REFORM ACT (1988) (London: HMSO)

E.G.M.F.U. (1994) *Report of the Committee on the Ethics of Genetic Modification and Food Use* (London: HMSO)

EINSTEIN, A. (1923) 'On the electrodynamics of moving bodies' in *The Principle of Relativity: A collection of original papers on the special and general theory of relativity* by A. Einstein *et al.* (New York, NY: Dover), pp. 35–65

ELDREDGE, N. and GOULD, S. J. (1972) 'Punctuated equilibrium: an alternative to phyletic gradualism' in *Models in Paleobiology*, ed. by T. J. M. Schopf (New York, NY: Freeman Cooper & Co.)

ELLUL, J. (1964) *The Technological Society* (New York: Random House)

—— (1989) *The Presence of the Kingdom* (Colorado Springs, CO: Helmers Howard) (first published in French, 1948).

—— (1990) *The Technological Bluff* (Grand Rapids, MI: Eerdmans)

FARRER, A. (1966) *A Science of God?* (London: Geoffrey Bles)

—— (1967) *Faith and Speculation* (London: A. & C. Black)

FARUQI, I. R. and NASSEEF, A. O. (1981) *Social and Natural Sciences: the Islamic Perspective* (Sevenoaks: Hodder & Stoughton)

FEYERABEND, P. (1993) *Against Method: Outline of an Anarchistic Theory of Knowledge*, 3rd edn (London: Verso)

FIDDES, P. (1988) *The Creative Suffering of God* (Oxford: Clarendon Press)

FINOCCHIARO, M. P. (ed.) (1989) *The Galileo Affair* (Berkeley and San Francisco: University of California Press)

FLANAGAN, O. (1992) *Consciousness Reconsidered* (Cambridge, MA: MIT Press)

FLEW, A. (1955) 'Theology and falsification' in *New Essays in Philosophical Theology*, ed. by A. Flew and A. MacIntyre (London: SCM Press), pp. 96–99

—— (1997) 'Neo-Humean arguments about the miraculous' in *In Defence of Miracles: A Comprehensive Case for God's Action in History*, ed. by R. D. Geivett and G. R. Habermas (Leicester: Apollos), pp. 45–57

FLOOD, G. D. (1996) *An Introduction to Hinduism* (Cambridge: Cambridge University Press)

FOERST, A. (1996) 'Artificial intelligence', *Zygon* 31, 681–93

FORMAN, R. K. C. (ed.) (1990) *The Problem of Pure Consciousness* (New York, NY: Oxford University Press)

FOX, M. (1983) *Original Blessing: A Primer in Creation Spirituality* (Santa Fe, NM: Bear & Co.)

FREUD, S. (1928) *The Future of an Illusion*, transl. by W. D. Robson-Scott (London: Hogarth Press)

FREWER, L. J., HOWARD, C. and SHEPHERD, R. (1997) 'Public attitudes in the United Kingdom about general and specific applications of genetic engineering: risk, benefit and ethics', *Science, Technology and Human Values* 22 (1), 98–124

FULLICK, P. and RATCLIFFE, M. (1996) *Teaching Ethical Aspects of Science* (Southampton: Bassett Press)

GAZZANIGA, M. S. (1989) 'The organisation of the human brain' *Science* 245, 947–52

AL-GHAZZALI (1983) *Inner Dimensions of Islamic Worship*, transl. from the Ihya' by Muhtar Holland (Leicester: The Islamic Foundation)

GINGERICH, O. (1982) 'The Galileo affair' *Scientific American* 247 (2), 118–127

GLEICK, J. (1988) *Chaos: Making a New Science* (London: Cardinal)

GOODWIN, B. (1995) *How the Leopard Changed Its Spots* (London: Orion Books)

GOSLING, D. (1992) *A New Earth* (London: CCBI)

GOULD, S. J. (1991) *Wonderful Life: The Burgess Shale and the Nature of History* (Harmondsworth: Penguin)

—— (1996) *Life's Grandeur: The Spread of Excellence from Plato to Darwin* (London: Cape)

GRANBERG-MICHAELSON, W. (ed.) (1987) *Tending the Garden: Essays on the Gospel and the Earth* (Grand Rapids, MI: Eerdmans)

GREGERSEN, N. H., AND VAN HUYSSTEEN, W. (eds) (1998) *Rethinking Theology and Science: Six Models for the Current Dialogue* (Grand Rapids, MI: Eerdmans)

GREGORIOS, P. M. (1987) *The Human Presence* (Amity, NY: Amity House)

GREGORY, R. L. (ed.) (1987) *The Oxford Companion to the Mind* (Oxford: Oxford University Press)

GROVE-WHITE, R., MCNAGHTEN, P., MAYER, S. and WYNNE, B. (1997) *Uncertain World: Genetically Modified Organisms, Food and Public Attitudes in Britain* (Lancaster: Centre for the Study of Environmental Change)

GUÉNON, R. (1958a) *Man and his Becoming According to the Vedanta* (New York: The Noonday Press)

—— (1958b) *The Symbolism of the Cross* (London: Luzac & Co.)

GUNTON, C. (1992) *Christ and Creation* (Carlisle: Paternoster Press)

GUTH, A. H. (1997) *The Inflationary Universe: The Quest for a New Theory of Cosmic Origins* (Reading, MA: Addison-Wesley)

HABGOOD, J. (1998) *Being a Person: Where Faith and Science Meet* (London: Hodder & Stoughton)

HAMPSON, D. (1990) *Theology and Feminism* (Oxford: Blackwell)

HANSON, N. (1958) *Patterns of Discovery* (Cambridge: Cambridge University Press)

HARDY, D. (1998) 'The God who is with the world' in *Science Meets Faith*, ed. by F. Watts (London: SPCK), pp. 136–53

HARE, R. M. (1955) 'Theology and falsification B' reprinted in *New Essays in Philosophical Theology*, ed. by A. Flew and A. MacIntyre (London: SCM Press), pp. 99–103

HARRIS, J. (1997) 'Is cloning an attack on human dignity?', *Nature 387*, 754

AL-HASHIMI, A. H. (1981) 'Islamizing the discipline of psychology' in *Social and Natural Sciences: the Islamic Perspective* by I. R. Faruqi and A. O. Naseef (1981), pp. 49–70

HAUGHT, J. (1995) *Science and Religion: From Conflict to Conversation* (Mahwah, NJ: Paulist Press)

HAWKING, S. W. (1988) *A Brief History of Time* (London: Bantam)

HAY, D. (1987) *Exploring Inner Space* (Harmondsworth: Penguin, 2nd edn)

HEFNER, P. (1993) *The Human Factor* (Minneapolis, MN: Fortress Press)

—— (1996) 'Theological perspectives on morality and human evolution' in *Religion and Science*, ed. by W. M. Richardson and W. J. Wildman (London: Routledge), pp. 401–23

HEIDEGGER, M. (1969) *The Question Concerning Technology and Other Essays*, transl. by W. Lovitt (London: Harper Torchbooks), pp. 3–35

HEPBURN, E. R. (1996) 'Genetic testing and early diagnosis and intervention: boon or burden?', *Journal of Medical Ethics* 22 (2), 105–10

HESSE, M. (1980) 'In defence of objectivity' in *Revolutions and Reconstructions in the Philosophy of Science* (Brighton: Harvester Press), pp. 167–86

HICK, J. (1971) 'Theology and verification, reprinted in *The Philosophy of Religion*, ed. by B. Mitchell (Oxford: Oxford University Press), pp. 53–71

—— (1976) *Death and Eternal Life* (London: Macmillan)

HOLDER, R. (1993) *Nothing But Atoms and Molecules?* (Tunbridge Wells: Monarch)

HOLTON, G. and ROLLER, D. (1958) *Foundations of Modern Physical Science* (Reading, MA: Addison-Wesley)

HOMANS, P. (1970) *Theology After Freud: An Interpretative Inquiry* (Indianapolis, IA: Bobbs-Merrill)

HONEY, J. (ed.) (1990) *Investigating the Nature of Science* (Harlow: Longman / The Nuffield-Chelsea Curriculum Trust)

HOOD, R. W., SPILKA, B., HUNSBERGER, B. and GORSUCH, R. (1996) *The Psychology of Religion: An Empirical Approach* (New York, NY: Guildford)

HOODBHOY, P. (1991) *Islam and Science* (London: Zed Books Ltd)

HOPKINS, G. M. (1953) *Poems and Prose*, ed. by W. H. Gardner (Harmondsworth: Penguin)

HOUGHTON, J. (1994) *Global Warming* (Oxford: Lion Publishing)

HOWELL, K. J. (1996) 'Galileo and the history of hermeneutics' in *Facets of Faith Volume 4: Interpreting God's Action in the World*, ed. by J. van der Meer (Lanham, MD: University Press of America), pp. 245–60

HOYLE, F. (1982) *Facts and Dogmas in Cosmology and Elsewhere* (Cambridge: Cambridge University Press)

HUNSINGER, D. VAN D. (1995) *Theology and Pastoral Counselling: A New Interdisciplinary Approach* (Grand Rapids, MI: Eerdmans)

HUNSINGER, G. (1991) *How to Read Karl Barth: The Shape of His Theology* (Oxford: Oxford University Press)

IRONS, W. (1996) 'Morality, religion, and human evolution' in *Religion and Science*, ed. by W. M. Richardson and W. J. Wildman (London: Routledge), pp. 375–99

ISHAM, C. J. and POLKINGHORNE, J. C. (1993) 'The debate over the block universe' in *Quantum Cosmology and the Laws of Nature*, ed. by R. J. Russell, N. Murphy and C. J. Isham (Vatican City: Vatican Observatory), pp. 135–44

JEEVES, M. (1997) *Human Nature at the Millennium: Reflections on the Integration of Psychology and Christianity* (Grand Rapids, MI: Baker Books)

JOHN PAUL II (1988) 'A message to the Revd George V. Coyne SJ, Director of the Vatican Observatory' in *Physics, Philosophy and Theology*, ed. by R. J. Russell, W. R. Stoeger and G. V. Coyne (Vatican City: Vatican State Observatory)

JOHNSON-LAIRD, P. N. (1988) *The Computer and the Mind* (London: Fontana)

JONES, D. (1991) *Can Catholics Believe in Evolution?* (London: Catholic Truth Society)

JÜNGEL, E. (1983) *God as the Mystery of the World: On the Foundation of the Theology of the Crucified One in the Dispute Between Theism and Atheism*, transl. by D. L. Guder (Edinburgh: T&T Clark)

KAHN, A. (1997) 'Clone mammals: Clone man?', *Nature 386*, 119

KAISER, C. (1991) *Creation and the History of Science* (London: Marshall Pickering)

KAISER, C. (1996) 'The laws of nature and the nature of God' in *Facets of Faith Volume 4: Interpreting God's Action in the World*, ed. by J. van der Meer (Lanham, MD: University Press of America), pp. 185–97

KATZ, S. T. (ed.) (1978) *Mysticism and Philosophical Analysis* (New York, NY: Oxford University Press)

KAUFFMAN, S. (1995) *At Home in the Universe* (Harmondsworth: Penguin)

KAUFMAN, G. (1972) *God the Problem* (Cambridge, MA: Harvard University Press)

KEOWN, D. (1996) *Buddhism: A Very Short Introduction* (Oxford: Oxford University Press)

KING, D. (1994a) 'Government allows unlimited release of genetically engineered plant', *GenEthics News 1*, 2–3

—— (1994b) 'Animals, genes and ethics', *GenEthics News 2*, 8

—— (1994c) 'The FLAVR SAVR tomato – hard tomatoes, hard times', *GenEthics News 3*, 8

—— (1997a) 'Sheep cloning sparks world furore', *GenEthics News 16*, 1–10

—— (1997b) 'Animal cloning charges forward', *GenEthics News 19*, 1–2

KRINGS, M. *et al.* (1997) 'Neanderthal DNA sequences and the origin of modern humans' *Cell 90* (1), 19–29

KUHN, T. (1962) *The Structure of Scientific Revolutions* (Chicago, IL: University of Chicago Press)

—— (1970a) 'Logic of discovery or psychology of research?' in *Criticism and the Growth of Knowledge: Proceedings of the International Colloquium in the Philosophy of Science, London 1965, volume 4*, ed. by I. Lakatos and A. Musgrave (Cambridge: Cambridge University Press), pp. 1–23

—— (1970b) *The Structure of Scientific Revolutions* (Chicago, IL: University of Chicago Press, rev. edn with postscript)

—— (1970c) 'Reflections on my critics' in *Criticism and the Growth of Knowledge: Proceedings of the International Colloquium in the Philosophy of Science, London, 1965, volume 4*, ed. by I. Lakatos and A. Musgrave (Cambridge: Cambridge University Press), pp. 231–78

KUHN, T. (1971) 'Notes on Lakatos' in *Boston Studies in the Philosophy of Science, Volume 8, Proceedings of the 1970 Biennial Meeting of the Philosophy of Science Association: in Memory of Rudolph Carnap*, ed. by R. C. Buck and R. S. Cohen (Dordrecht, Holland: D. Reidel, 1971), pp. 137–46

KÜNG, H. (1990) *Global Responsibility* (London: SCM Press)

LAKATOS, I. (1970) 'Falsification and the methodology of scientific research programmes' in *Criticism and the Growth of Knowledge: Proceedings of the International Colloquium in the Philosophy of Science, London, 1965, volume 4*, ed. by I. Lakatos and A. Musgrave (Cambridge: Cambridge University Press), pp. 91–196

LAKE, F. (1966) *Clinical Theology: A Theological and Psychiatric Basis to Clinical Pastoral Care* (London: Darton, Longman & Todd)

LANCASTER, B. (1991) *Mind, Brain and Human Potential: The Quest for an Understanding of Self* (Shaftesbury: Element)

LASH, N. (1979) 'Can a theologian keep the faith?' in *Theology on Dover Beach* (London: Darton, Longman & Todd), pp. 45–59

—— (1986) 'Ideology, metaphor and analogy' in *Theology on the Way to Emmaus* (London: SCM Press), pp. 95–119

LAUDAN, L. (1977) *Progress and its Problems* (London: Routledge & Kegan Paul)

LAYTON, D. (1986) 'Revaluing science education' in *Values Across the Curriculum* ed. by Tomlinson, P. and Quinton, M. (London: Falmer Press)

LEAKEY, R. and LEWIN, R. (1996) *The Sixth Extinction: Biodiversity and its Survival* (London: Weidenfeld & Nicolson)

LEE, R. S. (1948) *Freud and Christianity* (Harmondsworth: Penguin)

LEOPOLD, A. (1949) *A Sand County Almanac* (Oxford: Oxford University Press)

LINGS, M. (1985) *Muhammad: his life based on the earliest sources* (London: Islamic Texts Society and George Allen & Unwin)

LINZEY, A. (1994) *Animal Theology* (London: SCM Press)

LLOYD, G. (1993) *Being in Time: Selves and Narrators in Philosophy and Literature* (London: Routledge)

LOCKE, J. (1960) *An Essay Concerning Human Understanding* (London: Collins; originally published 1690)

LODHI, M. A. K. (ed.) (1989) *Islamization of Attitudes and Practices in Science and Technology* (Herndon, VA: Association of Muslim Scientists and Engineers)

LOEWENTHAL, K. M. (1995) *Mental Health and Religion* (London: Chapman & Hall)

LOVELOCK, J. (1988) *The Ages of Gaia* (Oxford: Oxford University Press)

LUCAS, E. (1996) *Science and the New Age Challenge* (Leicester: Apollos)

LYON, D. (1988) *The Information Society* (Oxford: Polity Press / Blackwell)

MABUD, SHAIKH M. (1986) 'Theory of evolution: an assessment from the Islamic point of view', *Muslim Educational Quarterly* 4 (1), 9–56

McCLUNE, R. (1998) 'Science education for the year 2000 and beyond', *Education in Science 176*, 17–20

McCORMACK, B. (1995) *Karl Barth's Critically Realistic Dialectical Theology: Its Genesis and Development, 1909–1936* (Oxford: Clarendon Press)

McDANIEL, J. (1989) *Of God and Pelicans* (Louisville, KY: Westminster / John Knox Press)

—— (1990) 'Revisioning God and the self: lessons from Buddhism' in *Liberating Life*, ed. by C. Birch, W. Eakin and J. McDaniel (Maryknoll, NY: Orbis Books), pp. 228–58

McFAGUE, S. (1982) *Metaphorical Theology: Models of God in Religious Language* (Philadelphia: Fortress Press)

—— (1987) *Models of God* (London: SCM Press)

—— (1993) *The Body of God* (London: SCM Press)

—— (1997) *Super, Natural Christians* (London: SCM Press)

McGRATH, A. (1994) *Christian Theology: An Introduction* (Oxford: Blackwell)

—— (1998) *The Foundations of Dialogue in Science and Religion* (Oxford: Blackwell)

MacKAY, D. M. (1991) *Behind the Eye* (Oxford: Blackwell)

MACKENZIE, D. and WAJCMAN, J. (1985) *The Social Shaping of Technology* (Milton Keynes: Open University Press)

MACKEY, J. P. (1983) 'Trinity, Doctrine of the' in *A New Dictionary of Christian Theology*, ed. by A. Richardson and J. Bowden (London: SCM Press), pp. 581–89

MACKIE, J. L. (1971) 'Evil and omnipotence', reprinted in *The Philosophy of Religion*, ed. by B. Mitchell (Oxford: Oxford University Press), pp. 92–104

—— (1982) *The Miracle of Theism: Arguments For and Against the Existence of God* (Oxford: Clarendon Press)

MacKINNON, D. (1968) 'Philosophy and Christology' in *Borderlands of Theology and Other Essays* (London: Lutterworth Press), pp. 55–81

MACQUARRIE, J. (1977) *Principles of Christian Theology* (London: SCM Press, 2nd [revd] edn)

MALONY, H. N. and LOVEKIN, A. A. (1985) *Glossolalia: Behavioural Science Perspectives on Speaking in Tongues* (New York, NY: Oxford University Press)

MANZOOR, S. P. (1984) 'Environment and Values' in *A Touch of Midas: Values and Environment in Islam and the West* ed. by Z. Sardar (Manchester: Manchester University Press)

MARGENAU, H. and VARGHESE, R. A. (eds) (1992) *Cosmos, Bios, Theos* (La Salle, IL: Open Court)

MARSONET, M. (1996) *The Primacy of Practical Reason: An Essay on Nicholas Rescher's Philosophy* (Lanham, MD: University Press of America)

MATHIAS, P. (1972) *Science and Society, 1600–1900* (Cambridge: Cambridge University Press)

MATTHEWS, C. N. and VARGHESE, R. A. (eds) (1995) *Cosmic Beginnings and Human Ends* (La Salle, IL: Open Court)

MATURANA, H. and VARELA, F. (1980) *Autopoiesis and Cognition* (Dordrecht: D. Reidel)

MAYR, E. (1964) Introduction to Charles Darwin's *On the Origin of Species: A Facsimile of the First Edition* (Cambridge, MA: Harvard University Press)

MEDAWAR, P. (1996) *The Strange Case of the Spotted Mice* (Oxford: Oxford University Press)

MEISSNER, W. W. (1984) *Psychoanalysis and Religious Experience* (New Haven, CT: Yale University Press)

—— (1987) *Life and Faith* (Washington DC: Georgetown University Press)

—— (1992) *Ignatius of Loyola: The Psychology of a Saint* (New Haven, CT: Yale University Press)

MENG, H. and FREUD, E. L. (eds) (1963) *Psychoanalysis and Faith: The Letters of Sigmund Freud and Oskar Pfister* (New York, NY: Basic Books)

MERCHANT, C. (1992) *Radical Ecology* (London: Routledge)

MERTON, T. (1968) *Zen and the Birds of Appetite* (New York, NY: New Directions)

MESTHENE, E. (1967) *Technology and Social Change* (Indianapolis, IN: Bobbs-Merrill)

MEYERSON, E. (1985): *The Relativist Deduction: Epistemological Implications of the Theory of Relativity* (Dordrecht: D. Reidel)

MIDGLEY, M. (1996a) 'One world, but a big one', *Journal of Consciousness Studies 3*, 5–6, 500–14

—— (1996b) 'Science in the world', *Science Studies 9* (2), 49–58

MILLAR, R., and OSBORNE J. (eds) (1998) *Beyond 2000: Science Education for the Future – Report with Ten Recommendations* (London: Nuffield Curriculum Projects Centre)

MITCHELL, B. (1973) *The Justification of Religious Belief* (London: Macmillan)

MOLTMANN, J. (1969) *Religion, Revolution and the Future*, transl. by M. D. Meeks (New York, NY: Charles Scribner's Sons)

—— (1973) *Theology and Joy*, transl. by R. Ulrich (London: SCM Press)

—— (1974) *The Crucified God*, transl. by R. A. Wilson and J. Bowden (London: SCM Press)

—— (1981) *The Trinity and the Kingdom of God*, transl. by M. Kohl (London: SCM Press)

—— (1985) *God in Creation*, transl. by M. Kohl (London: SCM Press)

—— (1990) *The Way of Jesus Christ*, transl. by M. Kohl (London: SCM Press)

MONOD, J. (1972) *Chance and Necessity*, transl. by A. Wainhouse (London: Collins)

MORAVEC, H. (1988) *Mind Children: The Future of Robot and Human Intelligence* (Cambridge, MA: Harvard University Press)

MUMFORD, L. (1946) *Technics and Civilization* (London: Routledge)

MURPHY, M. P. and O'NEILL, L. A. J. (1995) *What is Life? The Next Fifty Years* (Cambridge: Cambridge University Press)

MURPHY, N. (1990) *Theology in the Age of Scientific Reasoning* (Ithaca, NY: Cornell University Press)

—— (1993) 'Evidence of design in the fine-tuning of the universe' in *Quantum Cosmology and the Laws of Nature: Scientific Perspectives on Divine Action*, ed. R. J. Russell, N. Murphy and C. J. Isham (Vatican City: Vatican Observatory), pp. 407–35

—— (1994) 'What has theology to learn from scientific methodology?' in *Science and Theology: Questions at the Interface*, ed. by M. Rae, H. Regan and J. Stenhouse (Edinburgh: T&T Clark), pp. 101–26

—— (1995) 'Divine action in the natural order: Buridan's ass and Schrödinger's cat' in *Chaos and Complexity: Scientific Perspectives on Divine Action*, ed. by R. J. Russell, N. Murphy and A. Peacocke (Vatican City: Vatican Observatory), pp. 325–57

—— (1996) 'On the nature of theology' in *Religion and Science: History, Method, Dialogue*, ed. by W. M. Richardson and W. J. Wildman (New York, NY: Routledge), pp. 151–59

MURPHY, N. and ELLIS, G. F. R. (1996) *On the Moral Nature of the Universe: Theology, Cosmology, and Ethics* (Minneapolis, MN: Fortress Press)

MURRAY, P. D. (1998a) 'Theology after the demise of foundationalism', *The Way 38*, 160–69

—— (1998b) 'Theology in the borderlands: Donald MacKinnon and contemporary theology', *Modern Theology 14*, 355–76

MUTAHHARI, M. (1985) *Fundamentals of Islamic Thought* (Berkeley, CA: Mizan Press)

NAGEL, T. (1974) 'What is it like to be a bat?' *Philosophical Review 83*, 435–50. Reprinted in T. Nagel, 1979, *Mortal Questions* (Cambridge: Cambridge University Press)

—— (1986) *The View From Nowhere* (Oxford: Oxford University Press)

NAIRNE, R. (1997) *Tranquil Mind: An Introduction to Buddhism and Meditation* (Kalk Bay, SA: Kairon Press)

NASR, S. H. (1968) *Science and Civilization in Islam* (Cambridge, MA: Harvard University Press)

NASR, S. H. (1976) *Islamic Science: An Illustrated Study* (London: World of Islam Publishing Co. Ltd.)

—— (1980) *Living Sufism* (London: Unwin Paperbacks)

—— (1987) *Science and Civilization in Islam* (Cambridge, MA: Islamic Text Society, 2nd rev. edn)

NASSEEF, A. O. and BLACK, P. J. (1984) *Science Education and Religious Values* (Cambridge: The Islamic Academy)

NEGUS, M. R. (1995) 'The concept of Islamic Science and the thought patterns of a Muslim scientist', *Muslim Education Quarterly 12 (4)*, 30–36

NORTHCOTT, M. (1996) *The Environment and Christian Ethics* (Cambridge: Cambridge University Press)

OFFICE FOR STANDARDS IN EDUCATION: HANDBOOK FOR THE INSPECTION OF SCHOOLS (1993) Part 4, Guidance on the Inspection Schedule (London: HMSO)

OSBORN, L. (1992) 'The machine and the mother goddess: The Gaia hypothesis in contemporary scientific and religious thought', *Science and Christian Belief 4*, 27–41

PACEY, A. (1983) *The Culture of Technology* (Cambridge, MA: MIT Press)

—— (1992) *The Maze of Ingenuity* (Cambridge, MA: MIT Press, second edn)

PAGE, R. (1991) 'The Animal Kingdom and the Kingdom of God' in *Occasional Paper No. 26, The Animal Kingdom and the Kingdom of God* (Edinburgh: The Church and Nation Committee of the Church of Scotland and the Centre for Theology and Public Issues), pp. 1–9

—— (1996) *God and the Web of Creation* (London: SCM Press)

PAILIN, D. (1989) *God and the Processes of Reality* (London: Routledge)

PALEY, W. (1802) *Natural Theology: Or, Evidence of the Existence and Attributes of the Deity Collected from the Appearance of Nature* (Oxford: J. Vincent, 2nd edn)

PALMER, C. (1992) 'Stewardship: A Case Study in Environmental Ethics' in *The Earth Beneath* ed. by I. Ball *et al.* (London: SPCK), pp. 67–86.

PALMER, C. (1998) *Environmental Ethics and Process Thinking* (Oxford: Clarendon Press)

PALMER, M. (1997) *Freud and Jung on Religion* (London: Routledge)

PANNENBERG, W. (1976) *Theology and the Philosophy of Science,* transl. by F. McDonagh (London: Darton, Longman & Todd)

PARR, D. (1997) *Genetic Engineering: Too Good to Go Wrong?* (London: Greenpeace)

PASCAL, B. (1966) *Pensées,* transl. by A. J. Krailsheimer (Harmondsworth: Penguin)

PEACOCKE, A. (1979) *Creation and the World of Science* (Oxford: Oxford University Press)

—— (1986) *God and the New Biology* (London: Dent)

—— (1993) *Theology for a Scientific Age* (London: SCM Press, expanded edn)

—— (1995) 'God's interaction with the world: the implications of deterministic "Chaos" and of interconnected and interdepen-dent complexity' in *Chaos and Complexity: Scientific Perspectives on Divine Action,* ed. by R. J. Russell, N. Murphy and A. Peacocke (Vatican City: Vatican Observatory), pp. 263–87

—— (1997) *The Idreos Lectures* (Oxford: Harris Manchester College)

—— (1998) 'A positive theological appraisal of biological evolution' in *Evolution and Molecular Biology: Scientific Perspectives on Divine Action,* ed. by R. J. Russell, W. R. Stoeger and F. J. Ayala (Vatican City and Berkeley, CA: Vatican Observatory and CTNS)

—— (1999, in preparation) 'The Sound of Sheer Silence: How Does God Communicate with Humanity?' in *Neuroscience and the Person: Scientific Perspectives on Divine Action,* ed. by R. J. Russell, N. Murphy, T. Meyering and M. Arbib (Vatican City and Berkeley, CA: Vatican State Observatory and CTNS)

PENROSE, R. (1989) *The Emperor's New Mind: Concerning Computers, Minds and the Laws of Physics* (Oxford: Oxford University Press)

—— (1994) *Shadows of the Mind: A Search for the Missing Science of Consciousness* (Oxford: Oxford University Press)

—— (1997) *The Large, the Small and the Human Mind* (Cambridge: Cambridge University Press)

PETERS, T. (1997a) 'Theology and natural science' in *The Modern Theologians*, ed. by D. Ford (Oxford: Blackwell), pp. 649–68

—— (1997b) *Playing God: Genetic Determinism and Human Freedom* (London: Routledge)

—— (1998) 'Science and theology: toward consonance' in *Science and Theology: The New Consonance*, ed. by T. Peters (Oxford: Westview Press), pp. 11–39

POLKINGHORNE, J. (1988) *Science and Creation* (London: SPCK)

—— (1989) *Science and Providence* (London: SPCK)

—— (1990) *The Quantum World* (Harmondsworth: Penguin)

—— (1991) *Reason and Reality* (London: SPCK)

—— (1994) *Science and Christian Belief: Reflections of a Bottom-up Thinker* (London: SPCK)

—— (1995a) *Serious Talk* (London: SCM Press)

—— (1995b) 'The metaphysics of divine action' in *Chaos and Complexity: Scientific Perspectives on Divine Action*, ed. by R. J. Russell, N. Murphy and A. Peacocke (Vatican City: Vatican Observatory), pp. 147–56

—— (1996a) *Scientists as Theologians* (London: SPCK)

—— (1996b) 'Chaos theory and divine action' in *Religion and Science: History, Method and Dialogue*, ed. by W. M. Richardson and W. J. Wildman (London: Routledge), pp. 243–52

—— (1998) 'Beyond the Big Bang' in *Science Meets Faith*, ed. by F. Watts (London: SPCK), pp. 17–24

POOLE, M. W. (1990) 'Beliefs and values in science education: a Christian perspective (Part 1)' *School Science Review*, March 1990, 71 (256), 26–29

—— (1994) 'A Critique of aspects of the philosophy and theology of Richard Dawkins', *Science and Christian Belief* 6 (1), 41–59

—— (1995) *Beliefs and Values in Science Education* (Buckingham: Open University Press)

—— (1997) *A Guide to Science and Belief* (2nd edn) (Oxford: Lion Publishing) [illustrated in colour, aimed at a general readership]

POOLE, M. W. (1998a) 'Science and science education: a Judeo-Christian per-spective' in *Socio-Cultural Perspectives on Science Education: an International Dialogue*, ed. by W. W. Cobern (Dordrecht: Kluwer Academic Publishers)

—— (1998b) *Teaching about Science and Religion: Opportunities within Science in the National Curriculum* (Abingdon: Culham College Institute)

POPPER, K. (1959) *The Logic of Scientific Discovery* (London: Hutchinson)

—— (1963) *Conjectures and Refutations: The Growth of Scientific Knowledge* (London: Routledge & Kegan Paul)

—— (1972) *Objective Knowledge: An Evolutionary Approach* (Oxford: Oxford University Press)

PRANCE, G. (1996) *The Earth Under Threat: A Christian Perspective* (Glasgow: Wild Goose Publications)

PRIGOGINE, I. and STENGERS, I. (1984) *Order Out of Chaos: Man's New Dialogue With Nature* (London: Heinemann)

PUDDEFOOT, J. C. (1996) *God and the Mind Machine* (London: SPCK)

PURTILL, R. L. (1997) 'Defining miracles' in *In Defence of Miracles: A Comprehensive Case for God's Action in History*, ed. by R. D. Geivett and G. R. Habermas (Leicester: Apollos), pp. 61–72

PUTNAM, H. (1981) *Reason, Truth and History* (Cambridge: Cambridge University Press)

—— (1998) 'Why fraternity cannot be cloned', *The Times Higher Educational Supplement*, 30 January, pp. 18–19

QUINE, W. V. (1953) 'Two dogmas of empiricism' in *From a Logical Point of View: Nine Logico-Philosophical Essays*, 2nd edn (Cambridge, MA: Harvard University Press), pp. 20–46

RADHAKRISHNAN, S. (1958) *The Bhagavadgita: with an Introductory Essay, Sanskrit Text, English Translation and Note* (London: Allen & Unwin)

UR-RAHMAN, A. (1995) Standing Committee on Scientific and Techno-logical Cooperation (COMSTECH). Conference Papers of the International Conference on Science in Islamic Policy in the Twenty-first Century, March 26–30, 1995. 3 Constitution Avenue, G-5 / 2 Islamabad-44000, Pakistan

RAHNER, K. (1965) *Theological Investigation:* vol. 1, transl. by C. Ernst (London: Darton, Longman and Todd)

—— (1989) *Foundations of the Christian Faith*, transl. by W. Y. Dych (New York: Crossroad)

RAHULA, W. (1998) *What the Buddha Taught* (Oxford: OneWorld)

RASMUSSEN D. T. (ed.) (1993) *The Origin and Evolution of Humans and Humanness* (Boston, MA: Jones & Bartlett)

RAVETZ, J. R. (1971) *Scientific Knowledge and its Social Problems* (Oxford: Oxford University Press)

REGAN, T. (1990) 'Christianity and animal rights: the challenge and promise' in *Liberating Life*, ed. by C. Birch, W. Eakin and J. McDaniel (Maryknoll, NY: Orbis Books), pp. 73–87

REISS, M. and STRAUGHAN, R. (1996) *Improving Nature: the Science and Ethics of Genetic Engineering* (Cambridge: Cambridge University Press)

RESCHER, N. (1973) *The Coherence Theory of Truth* (Oxford: Clarendon Press)

—— (1992a) 'Idealism' in *A Companion to Epistemology*, ed. by J. Dancy and E. Sosa (Oxford: Blackwell), pp. 187–91

—— (1992b) *A System of Pragmatic Idealism, Volume I: Human Knowledge in Idealistic Perspective* (Princeton, NJ: Princeton University Press)

—— (1993a) *A System of Pragmatic Idealism, Volume II: The Validity of Values* (Princeton, NJ: Princeton University Press)

—— (1993b) 'In matters of religion' in *Philosophers Who Believe: The Spiritual Journeys of 11 Leading Thinkers*, ed. by K. J. Clark (Downers Grove, IL: InterVarsity Press)

—— (1994) *A System of Pragmatic Idealism, Volume III: Metaphilosophical Inquiries* (Princeton, NJ: Princeton University Press).

—— (1995) 'Pragmatism' in *The Oxford Companion to Philosophy*, ed. by T. Honderich (Oxford: Oxford University Press), pp. 710–13

RICHARDSON, W. M. and WILDMAN, W. J. (1996) *Religion and Science: History, Method, Dialogue* (London and New York: Routledge)

RIDLEY, M. (1993) *Evolution* (Oxford: Blackwell Scientific Publications)

RING, K. (1980) *Life After Death: A Scientific Investigation of Near-Death Experience* (New York, NY: Coward McCann & Geoghegan)

ROLSTON III, H. (1989) *Philosophy Gone Wild: Environmental Ethics* (Buffalo, NY: Prometheus Books)

—— (1994) *Conserving Natural Value* (New York, NY: Columbia University Press)

—— (1996) 'Science, religion and the future' in *Religion and Science*, ed. by W. M. Richardson and W. J. Wildman (London: Routledge), pp. 61–82

RORTY, R. (1979) *Philosophy and the Mirror of Nature* (Princeton, NJ: Princeton University Press)

ROSE, S. (1997) *Lifelines: Biology, Freedom, Determinism* (Harmondsworth: Penguin)

RUETHER, R. R. (1992) *Gaia and God* (London: SCM Press)

—— (ed.) (1996) *Women Healing Earth* (London: SPCK)

RUSSELL, C. A. (1985) *Cross-currents: Interactions between Science and Faith* (Leicester: InterVarsity Press)

—— (1987) 'Some founding fathers of physics', *Physics Education* 22 (1), 27–33

—— (1989) 'The conflict metaphor and its social origins', *Science and Christian Belief* 1 (1), 3–26

—— (1994) *The Earth, Humanity and God* (London: UCL Press)

RUSSELL, R. J. (1996) 'T = 0: Is it theologically significant?' in *Religion and Science: History, Method, Dialogue*, ed. by W. M. Richardson and W. J. Wildman (London: Routledge), pp. 201–24

—— (1998) 'Theistic evolution and special providence: does God really act in nature?' in *Evolution and Molecular Biology: Scientific Perspectives on Divine Action*, ed. by R. J. Russell, W. R. Stoeger and F. J. Ayala (Vatican City and Berkeley, CA: Vatican Observatory and CTNS)

—— *et al.* (eds) (1988) *Physics, Philosophy and Theology* (Vatican City: Vatican Observatory)

—— (1993) *Quantum Cosmology and the Laws of Nature: Scientific Perspectives on Divine Action* (Vatican City: Vatican State Observatory)

—— (1995) *Chaos and Complexity: Scientific Perspectives on Divine Action* (Vatican City: Vatican State Observatory)

Russell, R. J. (1998) *Evolution and Molecular Biology: Scientific Perspectives on Divine Action* (Vatican City and Berkeley, CA: Vatican State Observatory and CTNS)

—— (1999, in preparation) *Neuroscience and the Person: Scientific Perspectives on Divine Action* (Vatican City and Berkeley, CA: Vatican State Observatory and CTNS)

Sadakata, A. (1997) *Buddhist Cosmology: Philosophy and Origins* (Tokyo: Kosei Publ. Co.)

Salam, A. (1987) 'The future of science in Islamic countries' *A paper given at the Islamic Summit held in Kuwait in January 1987*

Santmire, H. P. (1985) *The Travail of Nature: The Ambiguous Ecological Promise of Christian Theology* (Philadelphia: Fortress Press)

Sardar, Z. (1980) 'Can science come back to Islam?' *New Scientist* 88 (No. 1224): 212–16.

—— (1985) *Islamic Futures: the Shape of Things to Come* (London: Mansell)

—— (1989) *Explorations in Islamic Science* (London: Mansell)

—— (ed.) (1984) *A Touch of Midas: Science, Values and Environment in Islam and the West* (Manchester: Manchester University Press)

Savage-Rumbaugh, E. S. (1993) *Language Comprehension in Ape and Child* (Chicago, IL: University of Chicago Press)

Scheffler, I. (1967) *Science and Subjectivity* (Indianapolis, IA: Bobbs-Merrill)

Schilpp, P. A. (ed.) (1949) *Albert Einstein: Philosopher-Scientist* (La Salle, IL: Open Court)

Schools Curriculum and Assessment Authority (1997a) 3\5229\1, 19 May (London: SCAA)

—— (1997b) *Initial briefing notes for meetings of subject-teachers* (London: SCAA)

—— (1997c) 3\4292\1 (London: SCAA)

Schrödinger, E. (1969) *What is Life?* (Cambridge: Cambridge University Press; first published 1944)

Schuon, F. (1968) *In the Tracks of Buddhism,* trans. M. Pallis (London: Allen and Unwin)

—— (1995) *Understanding Islam* (Bloomington, IL: World Wisdom Books)

SEEGER, R. J. (1966) *Galileo Galilei, his Life and Works* (Oxford: Pergamon)

SELLARS, W. (1963) *Science, Perception and Reality* (London: Routledge & Kegan Paul).

SESSIONS, G. (ed.) (1995) *Deep Ecology for the 21st Century* (Boston, MA: Shambhala)

SETTLE, T. (1996) 'The dressage ring and the ballroom: loci of double agency' in *Facets of Faith and Science, Volume IV: Interpreting God's Action in the World*, ed. by J. M. van der Meer (Lanham, NY: University Press of America), pp. 17–40

SHIVA, V. (1997) *Biopiracy: The Plunder of Nature and Knowledge* (USA: South End Press)

—— and I. MUSER (eds) (1995) *Biopolitics: A Feminist and Ecological Reader on Biotechnology* (London: Zed Books)

SHREEVE, J. (1996) *The Neandertal Enigma* (London: Viking)

SINGER, P. (1990) *Animal Liberation* (London: Cape, rev. edn)

SMART, N. (1995) *Worldviews: Cross-Cultural Explorations of Human Beliefs* (Englewood Cliffs, NJ: Prentice-Hall, 2nd edn)

SMOOT, G. and DAVIDSON, K. (1993) *Wrinkles in Time* (London: Little, Brown)

SORABJI, R. (1983): *Time, Creation and the Continuum: Theories in Antiquity and the Early Middle Ages* (London: Duckworth)

SOSKICE, J. M. (1985) *Metaphor and Religious Language* (Oxford: Clarendon Press)

—— (1993a) 'Bad language in science and religion' in *Explorations in Science & Theology: The Templeton London Lectures at the RSA* (London: RSA), pp. 69–78

—— (1993b) 'The truth looks different from here, or: on seeking the unity of truth from a diversity of perspectives' in *Christ in Context: The Confrontation Between Gospel and Culture*, ed. by H. D. Regan and A. J. Torrance (Edinburgh: T&T Clark), pp. 43–59

—— (1998) 'The gift of the name: Moses and the burning bush', *Gregorianum 79* (in press)

STANESBY, D. (1985) *Science, Reason and Religion* (London: Croom Helm)

STANNARD, R. (1991) *Black Holes and Uncle Albert* (London: Faber & Faber)

STANNARD, R. (1996) *Science and Wonders: Conversations about Science and Belief* (London: Faber & Faber)

STOEGER, W. R. (1995) 'Describing God's action in the light of scientific knowledge of reality' in *Chaos and Complexity: Scientific Perspectives on Divine Action*, ed. by R. J. Russell, N. Murphy and A. Peacocke (Vatican City: Vatican Observatory), pp. 239–61

STRINGER, C. B. (1992) 'The evolution of early humans' in *The Cambridge Encyclopedia of Human Evolution*, ed. by S. Jones, R. Martin and D. Pilbeam (Cambridge: Cambridge University Press), pp. 241–51

STRINGER, C. B. and McKIE, R. (1996) *African Exodus: the Origins of Modern Humanity* (London: Cape)

SURIN, K. (1986) *Theology and the Problem of Evil* (Oxford: Blackwell)

SUZUKI, D. T. (1970) *Mysticism: Christian and Buddhist* (London: Allen & Unwin)

SWAIN, H. (1998) 'Yes it's OK to clone', *The Times Higher Educational Supplement*, 23 January, p. 17

SWINBURNE, R. (1979) *The Existence of God* (Oxford: Clarendon Press)

—— (1993) 'The vocation of a natural theologian' in *Philosophers Who Believe: The Spiritual Journeys of 11 Leading Thinkers*, ed. by K. J. Clark (Downers Grove, IL: InterVarsity Press), pp. 179–202

TANNER, K. (1988) *God and Creation in Christian Theology: Tyranny or Empowerment?* (Oxford: Blackwell)

TAYLOR, J. G. (1991) Chapter 7 of *The Ghost in the Atom*, ed. by P. C. W. Davies and J. R. Brown (Cambridge: Cambridge University Press), pp. 106–17

TAYLOR, P. (1986) *Respect for Nature: A Theory of Environmental Ethics* (Princeton, NJ: Princeton University Press)

TEILHARD DE CHARDIN, P. (1959) *The Phenomenon of Man*, transl. by B. Wall (London: Collins)

—— (1966) *Man's Place in Nature*, transl. by R. Hague (London: Collins)

TEMPLE, W. (1976) *Christianity and Social Order* (London: SPCK; originally published 1942)

THEISSEN, G. (1984) *Biblical Faith: An Evolutionary Approach,* transl. by J. Bowden (London: SCM Press)

TILES, M. and OBERDIECK, H. (1995) *Living in a Technological Culture* (London: Routledge)

TILLICH, P. (1952) *The Courage to Be* (London: Fontana)

—— (1978) *Systematic Theology, Vol. 3* (London: SCM Press)

Times Educational Supplement 2 (1996) 'True to the spirit', 6 December, p. 9

TINSLEY, E. J. (ed.) (1973) *Reinhold Niebuhr* (Peterborough: Epworth Press)

TIPLER, F. J. (1995) *The Physics of Immortality: Modern Cosmology, God and the Resurrection of the Dead* (London: Macmillan)

TORRANCE, T. F. (1969) *Theological Science* (Oxford: Oxford University Press, reissued 1996, Edinburgh: T&T Clark)

—— (1976) *Space, Time, and Resurrection* (Edinburgh: Handsel, reissued 1998, Edinburgh: T&T Clark)

—— (1985) *Reality and Scientific Theology* (Edinburgh: Scottish Academic Press)

TOULMIN, S. (1990) *Cosmopolis: The Hidden Agenda of Modernity* (Chicago: University of Chicago Press)

TRACY, T. F. (1995) 'Particular providence and the God of the Gaps' in *Chaos and Complexity: Scientific Perspectives on Divine Action*, ed. by R. J. Russell, N. Murphy and A. Peacocke (Vatican City: Vatican Observatory), pp. 289–324

TRIGG, R. (1993) *Rationality and Science: Can Science Explain Everything?* (Oxford: Blackwell)

—— (1998) *Rationality and Religion* (Oxford: Blackwell)

UPDIKE, J. (1986) *Roger's Version* (New York, NY: Ballantine)

VAN HUYSSTEEN, J. W. (1989) *Theology and the Justification of Faith: Constructing Theories in Systematic Theology*, transl. by H. F. Snijders (Grand Rapids, MI: Eerdmans)

—— (1997) *Essays in Postfoundationalist Theology* (Grand Rapids, MI: Eerdmans)

—— (1998) *Duet or Duel? Theology and Science in a Postmodern World* (London: SCM Press)

VANSTONE, W. H. (1977) *Love's Endeavour, Love's Expense* (London: Darton, Longman & Todd)

WAGHID, Y. (1996) 'Creative order, truth and justice: the rationale of Islamic science', *Journal of Islamic Science* 12 (1), 87–101

WARD, K. (1982) *Holding Fast to God: a Response to Don Cupitt* (London: SPCK)

—— (1987) *Images of Eternity: Concepts of God in Five Religious Traditions* (London: Darton, Longman & Todd)

—— (1990) *Divine Action* (London: Collins)

—— (1991) *A Vision to Pursue* (London: SCM Press)

—— (1992) *Defending the Soul* (Oxford: OneWorld)

—— (1996a) *Religion and Creation* (Oxford: Oxford University Press)

—— (1996b) *God, Chance and Necessity* (Oxford: OneWorld)

—— (1998) *Religion and Human Nature* (Oxford: Clarendon Press)

WATTS, F. (1994) 'Are we really nothing more than our neurones?' *Journal of Consciousness Studies* 1, 275–79

—— (1998a) 'Brain, mind and soul' in *Science Meets Faith*, ed. by F. Watts (London: SPCK)

—— (1998b) 'Science and theology as complementary perspectives' in *Rethinking Theology and Science: Six Models for the Current Dialogue*, ed. by N. Gregersen and W. van Huyssteen (eds) (Grand Rapids, MI: Eerdmans)

—— (ed.) (1998c) *Science Meets Faith* (London: SPCK)

—— and WILLIAMS, M (1988) *The Psychology of Religious Knowing* (Cambridge: Cambridge University Press; reissued 1994, London: Geoffrey Chapman)

WEBSTER, J. B. (1986) *Eberhard Jüngel: An Introduction to his Theology* (Cambridge: Cambridge University Press)

WEBSTER, R. (1996) *Why Freud Was Wrong: Sin, Science and Psychoanalysis* (London: Fontana)

WEINER, J. (1994) *The Beak of the Finch* (London: Cape)

WELCH, C. (1996) 'Dispelling some myths about the split between theology and science in the nineteenth century' in *Religion and Science*, ed. by W. M. Richardson and W. J. Wildman (London: Routledge), pp. 29–40

WERTHEIM, M. (1995) *Pythagoras' Trousers: God, Physics and the Gender Wars* (New York, NY: Times Books)

WESTERMANN, C. (1984) *Genesis 1–11*, transl. by J. J. Scullion (London: SPCK)

WEYL, H. (1949) *Philosophy of Mathematics and Natural Science* (Princeton, NJ: Princeton University Press)

WHITE, L. JR. (1967) 'The historic roots of the ecologic crisis', *Science 155*, 1203–7

WHITE, S. (1994) *Christian Worship and Technological Change* (Nashville, TN: Abingdon Press)

WHITEHEAD, A. N. (1967) *Process & Reality: An Essay in Cosmology* (New York: Macmillan, first published 1929)

WHITROW, G. J. (1980) *The Natural Philosophy of Time* (Oxford: Clarendon Press)

WILES, M. (1986) *God's Action in the World* (London: SCM Press)

WILLIAMS, B. (1978) *Descartes, the Project of Pure Enquiry* (Harmondsworth: Penguin)

WILMUT, I., SCHNIEKE, A. E., McWHIR, J., KIND, A. J. and CAMPBELL, K. H. S. (1997) 'Viable offspring derived from fetal and adult mammalian cells', *Nature 385*, 810–13

WILSON, E. O. (1975) *Sociobiology: the New Synthesis* (Cambridge MA: Harvard University Press)

—— (1995) *On Human Nature* (Harmondsworth: Penguin; originally published by Harvard University Press in 1978)

WINNER, L. (1977) *Autonomous Technology* (Cambridge, MA: MIT Press)

WITTGENSTEIN, L. (1967) *Philosophical Investigations*, 3rd edn, transl. by G. E. M. Anscombe (Oxford: Blackwell)

WITTGENSTEIN, L. (1969) *The Blue and Brown Books: Preliminary Studies for the Philosophical Investigations*, 2nd edn (Oxford: Blackwell)

WOOD, K. A. (1993) 'The scientific exegesis of the Qur'an', *Perspectives on Science and Christian Faith (Journal of the American Scientific Affiliation) 45* (2), 90–94

WOOLNOUGH, B. (1992) *Science & Religion: Friends or Foes?* SATIS 16–19, No. 125 (Hatfield: Association for Science Education)

WORTHING, M. W. (1996) *God, Creation and Contemporary Physics* (Minneapolis, MN: Fortress Press)

WULFF, D. M. (1991) *Psychology of Religion: Classic and Contemporary Views* (New York: John Wiley)

ZIMAN, J. (1978) *Reliable Knowledge* (Cambridge: Cambridge University Press)

—— (1995) *An Introduction to Science Studies* (Cambridge: Cambridge University Press)

ZIZIOULAS, J. D. (1990) 'Preserving God's creation', *Kings Theological Review 13* (1), 1–5

Index

Individuals and organisations cited in the References and Bibliography appear in bold.